Psychodrama with Trauma Survivors

Psychodrama with Trauma Survivors

Acting Out Your Pain

*Edited by Peter Felix Kellermann
and M.K. Hudgins*

Foreword by Zerka T. Moreno

Jessica Kingsley Publishers
London and Philadelphia

First published in the United Kingdom in 2000 by
Jessica Kingsley Publishers Ltd,
116 Pentonville Road,
London N1 9JB, England
and
325 Chestnut Street,
Philadelphia PA 19106, USA.

www.jkp.com

© Copyright 2000 Jessica Kingsley Publishers

Second impression 2001

Library of Congress Cataloging in Publication Data
A CIP catalog record for this book is available from the Library of Congress

British Library Cataloguing in Publication Data
A CIP catalogue record for this book is available from the British Library

ISBN 1 85302 893 2 pb

Printed and Bound in Great Britain by
Athenaeum Press, Gateshead, Tyne and Wear

Contents

Foreword

At the dawn of psychotherapy, Sigmund Freud explored trauma as expressed in an individual's life history and brought to light in psychoanalysis. Trauma usually occurred within the setting of the family and represented one or more emotionally shocking events.

Contrasting this model, Moreno viewed trauma in a larger context, not only intrapersonally, but also interpersonally. He noted that during World War I, for example, entire populations were being subjected to traumas from a large number of sources. At this point in history, the treatment of trauma on a larger, more public scale became his focus. Psychodrama began as a method of group therapy, education, a theatre that was designed not only to change the life of individuals, but to heal the traumas of the world. Psychodrama contains elements of action, interaction and experiential therapy involving body and mind.

The opening sentence in Moreno's *Who Shall Survive?*[1] is: 'A truly therapeutic procedure cannot have less an objective than the whole of mankind' (p.3). Such a Utopian dream may be hard to realize but it became a leitmotif for Moreno and his students – that is, to take as daring and inclusive a step as was necessary to eliminate suffering.

For example, in the early phases of World War II, a psychotic patient who believed he was the true Adolf Hitler presented himself at Moreno's clinic, where there were a number of German Jewish refugees also in the hospital. During his treatment, it was somehow possible for the refugees to get in touch with their own little Hitlers. After his discharge, these refugees dealt with their own traumas. Their psychodramas enabled them to become the judges of the Nazis in an early projection of the Nuremberg trials, but with

[1]   Moreno, J.L. (1953) *Who Shall Survive?* New York: Beacon House.

the actual victims doing the judging. The appeal of this form of therapy and its healing and cathartic effects were clear to all.

Before the fall of the Iron Curtain, we worked in Russia with survivors of World War II, during which the Russian people suffered unimaginable traumas, with death becoming a constant companion. In Finland, we dealt with the people's experience of both Russian and German oppression. In recent years, a number of psychodrama specialists have worked with the children of the Third Reich, bringing them together with Jews, Holocaust survivors and their descendants.

I worked with grandchildren of the Nazi period in what had once been a synagogue in Fruedenthal, Germany, and which is now a cultural centre dedicated to educating German children about what happened in Germany before their birth. There these young participants used psychodrama to encounter and confront their own forebears in an unforgettable session. At the psychodrama conference in Jerusalem in 1996, we witnessed an encounter between an Arab and a Jew, which led to a group therapeutic process of healing.

How pleased Moreno would be to know that after the Falklands war, psychodramatists on both sides of the Atlantic – Dalmiro Bustos in Argentina and Marcia Karp in England – worked with the soldiers of the war and their families to help heal the miseries they had all endured. Having lived through two world wars himself, he would wish such events never to occur again, but given the realities, working on both sides to reduce suffering was certainly what he would most heartily support.

In the 1953 edition of *Who Shall Survive?* Moreno wrote the following statement:

> This edition is a call for integration of the behavioral and therapeutic sciences.
>
> It starts from the premise that it is both desirable and necessary to develop systematic theory which embodies in it the best elements of speculation, research and therapy, and which does so in a truly universal manner.
>
> Secondly, we believe that sociometric and sociatric approaches to common human and scientific problems hold one of the major keys toward such an integration. Among the sociatric approaches, particular attention will be given to group psychotherapy, psychodrama, socio-drama, and ethnodrama (Moreno 1953, p.ix).

This book is an example of Moreno's dream: the integration of the behavioural and therapeutic sciences. It covers an extensive arena of trauma and presents treatment that covers a vast field of interventions that are group-centred and experiential, and action models of healing today's global traumas. This collaboration details the work of international experts who practise psychodrama in many different countries. These authors have come a long way from the beginnings of looking at traumatized populations as well as individuals, and this book shows the rich applications and range of work possible.

Kate Hudgins and Peter Felix Kellermann are to be congratulated on having brought together a very skilled contingent of authors – themselves among them – whose work is truly universal. One can only hope that trauma victims will meet with the heartwarming skills and commitment that these authors have revealed.

To paraphrase Moreno's *Who Shall Survive?* once more, '[They] are [psychodramatists] dedicated to the internationalism of science – not only in word but also in action'.

Zerka T Moreno, February 2000,
President, Zerka T Moreno Workshop, USA.
Beacon, NY,

Introduction

In today's world, the horror-stricken faces of people can be seen everywhere: around earthquakes, floods, accidents, violence, addiction, physical and sexual abuse, wars, genocide and political torture, to name just a few traumas. Both natural and social traumas create unbearable stress and disruption for individuals, families, groups, and entire societies, at times threatening the very survival of the human race. People are wounded, abused and neglected and respond with characteristic panic, rage and despair. In addition, trauma patterns of survival are unconsciously transmitted from one generation to another.

In order to prevent the long-term sequelae of natural and social catastrophes, we are increasingly called upon to find rapid and effective methods of treating post-traumatic stress reactions. As Zerka Moreno notes in her foreword, psychodrama has been known as one of the most powerful approaches to the treatment of traumatized people for more than half a century. The reason for this is very simple. Psychodrama reaches to the hearts of people who cope with the everyday difficulties, misfortunes, crises and disasters of life. But it also does much more.

As every good drama does, each psychodrama conveys the hidden, horrific realities of such victims and survivors through enactment. In many cases these clients show parts of themselves that they have always tried to conceal from others and from themselves. As a result, their shame, terror, hatred, rage, and images of unimaginable pain are finally shared. Old wounds are carefully reopened and healing may commence again.

Psychodrama can provide a safe place to consciously re-experience unprocessed trauma and bring hope of new possibilities to people whose lives and families have been impacted by overwhelming catastrophe. As a healing art, psychodrama is a flexible form of brief experiential treatment in which the therapist draws upon a range of different principles and procedures to tailor treatment to each individual and his or her situation.

Post-traumatic stress

In this book, trauma is defined as any life-threatening, emotionally overwhelming catastrophe that breaks through a person's ordinary coping mechanisms, whether in childhood or as an adult, whether from a single episode or from a lifetime of abuse. Clinically, most of the contributors use some version of the diagnosis of post-traumatic stress disorder (PTSD), which includes symptoms cycling from defensive protections such as psychic numbing and dissociation to intrusive sensations and fragmented images from sensorimotor memories of the past.

Accurate diagnosing of PTSD following World War II gave hope for many symptoms long thought untreatable, and recent neurobiological study of sexual trauma and war trauma has added much to the understanding and healing of PTSD. The last ten years of research show that traumatic experiences result in a variety of symptoms. Trauma survivors manifest deficits in neurotransmitters, disrupted brain pathways, unprocessed sensorimotor memory, primary process thinking, distorted object relations, dissociated intense affects, primitive defences, transferential relationships and uncontrolled re-experiencing behaviours. As the impact of trauma is documented, effective treatment can also be developed.

Experiential treatment of trauma

While the field searches for faster and more effective treatment, experiential psychotherapy is being increasingly recommended as a viable treatment alternative for trauma survivors. What becomes obvious with the accurate diagnosing of PTSD is that many of the symptoms are unconscious, non-verbal, right-brained experiences that cannot in fact be accessed through talk therapy. Unconscious acting out and re-experiencing of unprocessed trauma happens all the time for victims of trauma. Experiential methods provide safe, structured, therapeutic ways consciously to re-enact past traumatic experience so that new healing endings can guide the future.

Classical psychodrama

Psychodrama is the seminal action method of experiential therapy as noted by Zerka Moreno, as she anchored its development into earlier times of trauma. Although in this book classical psychodrama has long been a group therapy method, the contributors also note the use of psychodrama in individual therapy. A therapeutic session usually includes warm-up, action, working through, closure and sharing. A variety of standard interventions such as doubling, mirroring, role reversal, soliloquy, concretization and maximization are used.

However, it is also true that psychodrama has been less used within the field of traumatic stress than other therapeutic approaches. One reason for this might be that psychodrama is an extremely complex endeavour that may not be suitable to all clients and therapists. For example, the dramatization required by the client and the directive action demanded of the therapist may not be the choice for everybody.

A more important reason for the meagre use of psychodrama within many treatment settings is that it has been insufficiently investigated and documented. Although experiential psychotherapy is beginning to be shown to be as effective as psychodynamic and cognitive behavioural approaches, psychodramatists have as yet little to offer to show that what they do is more effective or at least as effective as other action approaches.

The present action

This book is an attempt to correct this situation. An international group of psychodramatists describe their experiential practice and present some of their therapeutic results. These are experienced clinicians, and in many cases trainers, who attempt to integrate theory with practice to create safe paths of change for even the most severe traumatization. Together their chapters provide a forceful documentation of how psychodrama may be successfully utilized with a great variety of traumatized populations, including survivors of physical, sexual and emotional abuse, traffic accidents, traumatic war experiences and the loss of significant others. Several well-integrated models of experiential treatment are offered for all clinicians to use. Final chapters describe how psychodrama is used to alleviate the suffering of secondary survivors, the spouses, descendants and caregivers to whom a hidden trauma may be transmitted.

Unifying themes

There are several themes that unify the chapters in this book. Foremost is the belief, stated above, that experiential treatment, and specifically psychodrama, is a treatment of choice for people who have experienced trauma. The very symptoms that are documented as caused by traumatic experience can be directly treated with action methods. Haunting scenes of past traumas, transfixed in memory, may be put in motion through conscious re-enactment. Internal reality is concretized and becomes more tangibly seen and worked with by both client and therapist. As a result, new endings of empowerment may be introduced to replace guilt, helplessness and terror.

The possibility of developmental repair though experiential healing is another theme that runs through the chapters of this book. Contributor after contributor documents scenes of surplus reality that can be enacted to stop the obsessive symptoms of the past. Thus, a war refugee may get another chance to say goodbye to a lost comrade. A mother may find the courage to protect her children from sexual abuse, and an adolescent sexual offender may learn how to feel some empathy for his victim. Developmental repair provides true integrative healing of core traumas, not just symptom management as often happens in talk therapy.

In addition, a number of the contributors provide structures for safe re-enactment of the horror of core trauma scenes. As most clinicians and researchers believe these days, for full healing to occur the core trauma must often be revisited to release dissociated emotions and change trauma-based cognitions. Conscious re-experiencing of such scenes helps to break the cycle of trauma and violence that so often becomes the lifelong path of trauma survivors. Psychodrama creates a place for the client to *act out* pain within the containment of therapy rather than repeating the trauma on oneself or towards others.

However, when using psychodrama with trauma survivors, there is the potential for uncontrolled regression and retraumatization if experiential methods are not grounded in solid theory and competent practice. Eclectic in technique and integrative in theory, these contributors anchor their practice in classical psychodrama as well as in psychodynamic formulations, theories of behavioural learning, and/or recent trauma theory. Most contributors support the possible transmission of trauma across generations.

The contributors subscribe to the holistic notion of looking at the possible integration of body, mind, emotion, and spirit when treating traumatized people. One of the most important common denominators of these chapters is that they recommend safe and conscious re-experiencing when using psychodrama with trauma survivors. The reader will repeatedly be reminded about the importance of using action methods to promote control, containment, and stability. Thus psychodrama is used not just as a method of expression and catharsis, but also as a powerful method of restraint and re-integration.

Overview of structure

The book is divided into five parts. In the first chapter, Peter Felix Kellermann, from Sweden and Israel, introduces the impact of trauma and presents the basic therapeutic aspects of psychodrama with traumatized people. Illustrated with short case vignettes, these principles include re-enactment, cognitive reprocessing and discharge of surplus energy, surplus reality, interpersonal support and the use of healing rituals.

Part 2 of the book explores the use of psychodrama for the treatment of grief and mourning, emphasizing that loss is the core emotion of trauma. In Chapter 2, Adam Blatner from the USA describes the use of psychodramatic methods for facilitating bereavement and grief work. Techniques such as the 'final encounter' and the use of surplus reality and sharing to facilitate the process of helping a person coping with significant loss are discussed and illustrated in a case vignette.

Similarly, Marisol Filgueira Bouza and José Antonio Espina Barrio from Spain present their work on brief psychodrama and bereavement in Chapter 3. As the loss of rituals often lengthens the bereavement process, they propose a kind of brief, problem-centred or 'anthropological' psychodrama that includes a specific structure to facilitate the mourning process. With the aim of unblocking fixations in the natural mourning process, they work in a goal-directed fashion to prevent repression (and denial), provide emotional support and reconstruct new interpersonal bonds.

Part 3 describes the diverse psychodramatic treatments of a variety of different traumatized populations, showing how people move from being victims to becoming survivors. As the reader will see, psychodrama can be a primary treatment with people of different ages and from different countries. It can also be used as an adjunctive method to complement traditional talk therapies.

In Chapter 4, Marcia Karp from the UK presents a 16-year follow-up case study of her psychodrama treatment with victims of rape and torture. She also emphasizes the importance of restoring a sense of personal control, of reducing guilt and shame, and of using techniques of empowerment. As an answer to the question of why psychodrama helped, she suggests that psychodrama provided new visualizations and new verbalizations to substitute for trauma-associated states.

Chapter 5 begins with a personal account by the protagonist of a psychodrama session that dealt with sexual abuse. Eva Røine describes the setting and overall principles of how she and her team work with traumatized people in Norway. With examples from experiences in a psychiatric ward, she then goes on to describe three more people who experienced severe traumatization. Basing her work both on theories of somatic re-experiencing and on learned helplessness, she emphasizes the importance of hope as a therapeutic agent.

In Chapter 6, Anne Bannister from the UK gives a short account of prevalent theories of childhood sexual abuse and describes a very careful and sensitive approach to treat eight- to nine-year-old children who were severely abused. This combination of creative play therapy, dramatherapy and psychodrama provides an opportunity for these children to repair some of the developmental damage they have experienced and to increase confidence in themselves and in others.

In Chapter 7, Tian Dayton from the USA describes how psychodrama can effectively work through the complex web of trauma and addiction. She presents clear techniques such as the 'trauma line', 'the living genogram', and 'social atoms for recovery' to help clients identify the traumatic events and family relationships that are connected to their addictions. She offers hope for people many thought could not use psychodrama.

In Chapter 8, Marlyn Robson describes how psychodrama and cognitive behavioural therapy are integrated in a community programme for adolescent sexual offenders in New Zealand. This programme attempts to make it safe for the adolescents to re-experience both their role as perpetrators and as former victims. With the help of various games and warm-up exercises, they address their shame, develop victim empathy, enhance responsibility, restructure cognition and attempt to repair their inner social network.

In Chapter 9, Clark Baim from the UK gives an account of how to use psychodrama with adult men who have committed acts of sexual abuse, including adult rape, child sexual abuse and predatory sexual murder. The effects of early abuse, traumatic sexualization, maladaptive learning and poor attachment history are discussed. Giving the role of offender and the role of victim equal credence, it is suggested that the ideal is to focus both on offence done and the post-trauma remembered. Confronting both these roles within psychodrama may help to modify the offender's victim stance, external locus of control and affect dysregulation.

In Chapter 10, Kerry Paul Altman from the USA presents a general introduction to the psychodramatic treatment of multiple personality disorder. Some broad theoretical and methodological principles provide a framework for understanding two case examples. These examples illustrate how to use this approach to encourage internal communication and development of a co-operative internal system. He demonstrates the safe expression of powerful emotions within a controlled setting with clear boundaries for an agreed-upon action therapy experience.

In Chapter 11, Grete Leutz from Germany describes how dissociative states of consciousness may arise as an adaptive response to Holocaust memories. Through two elaborate case examples, she illustrates how such states may appear suddenly and unexpectedly and how they may be treated within psychodramatic crisis intervention.

Jörg Burmeister from Switzerland introduces an integrative therapeutic approach to working with survivors of traffic accidents in Chapter 12. Psychodrama is used in homogeneous survivor groups in combination with individual and family therapy. The chapter includes a review of core concepts, specific strategies and a description of the setting and different stages of the treatment process. Emphasis is put on understanding the special characteristics of this population in terms of pathological grief, somatic injuries, pain control, loss of body functions, guilt, concerns of juridical claims and memory disturbances. He concludes that rehabilitation may become a lifelong project that also includes existential and spiritual components.

Part 4 presents two models of experiential healing that integrate classical psychodrama with additional frameworks for comprehensive models of treatment for trauma. Having seen many uses of psychodrama with different populations, these models attempt to provide an organized framework for its use with all natural and social traumas.

In Chapter 13, Kate Hudgins, from the USA, presents her therapeutic spiral model for treating PTSD. With the use of client-friendly graphics such as the 'spiral image' and 'trauma bubbles', she provides a clinical framework that aims to guide the therapeutic process and prevent uncontrolled regression and re-traumatization when using experiential methods with trauma. Types of re-experiencing dramas and principles of conscious re-experiencing are detailed to guide the concretization and transformation of the trauma-based roles of victim and perpetrator safely. For this purpose, a modified intervention module of the 'containing' double is also introduced.

In Chapter 14, John Raven Mosher and Brigid Yukman, also from the USA, explore the parallel evolution of the cycles of life and the cycles of the seasons. These contributors show how they converge into universal cycles of healing that can be used with trauma survivors. They provide a model for the treatment of trauma, integrating classical psychodrama and shamanistic medicine. Case examples demonstrate the power of these methods.

Finally, Part 5 emphasizes various concepts and treatment principles of secondary traumatization and the transmission of trauma across generations. In Chapter 15, Anne Ancelin Schützenberger, from France, gives a short summary of her theories of the anniversary syndrome, in which a symptom such as illness or separation manifests itself in the descendant when he or she is at the age when a trauma occurred in an ancestor's life. With the use of genosociograms and psychodramatic enactments she provides many examples of how life scripts may be seen in the light of a person's family heritage.

Michael Burge from Australia describes how war trauma affects the entire family through primary and secondary transmission in Chapter 16. Two case studies are presented in which psychodrama and art therapy within a role theoretical framework are employed to provide relief from traumatic pain in both the first and second generation of survivors. The symbolic representation of the resolution process is emphasized as well as the importance of helping the client to differentiate between past and present and to develop a broad perspective of the influences on their reactive aggressive and self-defeating emotions and behaviour.

In the final chapter, Rory Remer from the USA addresses the complexities of secondary survivors, the people in the social support network of a trauma victim who are affected in one way or another by the trauma of the primary survivor. He suggests chaos theory and sociatry as a conceptual framework for secondary victims in helping them cope with the complexity of the healing process involved.

Future projection

This book presents clear evidence that psychodrama, when done competently and safely, is a treatment of choice for trauma survivors. Yet the use of psychodrama with traumatized people still poses many questions with no clear answers. For example, should clients who have experienced similar traumas be treated in homogeneous groups? Is psychodrama as effective with people who suffer from 'chronic PTSD' (such as combat fatigue disorder and Holocaust survivor syndrome) as it is with people who suffer from more recent traumatization and crises of life with relatively milder stress responses? What is the optimal duration of psychodrama therapy with various traumatized clients? Are a few protracted re-enactments of the traumatic event sufficient in brief psychotherapy or is a longer exposure to the individual and group process called for? What is required in terms of ego strength and psychological-mindedness in order to be able to benefit from psychodrama? Taking into consideration that traumatized people will forever be changed by their experiences, which therapeutic objectives can be reasonably set as goals for the treatment?

All these questions highlight the need for further and more specific process and outcome research to substantiate the descriptive case studies reported in this book with more objective means. Until the findings of such research come out, this book will have to suffice as a preliminary document.

But this document should not be underestimated. It tells the healing stories of Adrian, Alec, Andrew, Barbara, Caroline, Greta, Fintan, Harrison, Jill, Mary, Sandy, Sue and Warren and thus touches all trauma survivors who speak their pain. Having learned to 'act out their pain' safely in the therapeutic setting, these clients share their healing through psychodrama. Our contributors detail the gift of walking side by side with people who have experienced trauma. We invite you to share this journey with us.

Kate Hudgins and Peter Felix Kellermann
Virginia, USA and Israel. March 2000.

PART 1

Treating Trauma in Action

CHAPTER 1

The Therapeutic Aspects of Psychodrama with Traumatized People

Peter Felix Kellermann

Even if the trees seem to be growing exactly as they did before, and the rivers seem to follow the same course, and the lives of men appear to be exactly as they were, still nothing is the same. (Boyle 1961)

After a traumatic event, life is no longer the same as it was before. People who have experienced trauma feel that they have changed substantially. Their identities, their affects and physiological responses, their outlook on life and their interactions with others have somehow undergone a total transformation. There is no more safety, predictability and trust. 'All survivors recognise that bad things can now happen to them, that invulnerability is an illusion' (Janoff-Bulman 1992, p.81). Their ordinary adjustment strategies had proven inadequate and they were unable to cope. As a result, the overwhelming fear, powerlessness and loss of control became a permanent learning experience that they are unable to forget.

Post-traumatic stress disorder (PTSD) is a diagnostic term used for describing such states of body-mind. This condition characteristically consists of anxiety and depression following a known traumatic event. The person is continuing to re-experience the trauma (in vivid recollections and nightmares), has reduced interest in the external world and suffers from various more or less physical symptoms such as hyper-alertness and sleep disturbances (American Psychiatric Association 1994). Frequently, there is a contradictory (and largely paradoxical) effort both to remember and to forget, both to approach and to avoid the traumatic event in a compulsive, repeated fashion. Like a broken record that is spinning around and around, intrusive experienced images and painful memories keep coming back while there is a conscious effort to avoid them and not to think about them. Desperate and often futile efforts are attempted to regain some kind of inner balance and emotional equilibrium in order to 'get on' with life.

The phenomenology and aetiology of PTSD has been well known for more than a century and various psychotherapeutic approaches have been applied in its treatment. One of the classical approaches, developed by Jacob Levy and Zerka Moreno, is psychodrama. Based on the time-honoured therapeutic principles of re-enactment and catharsis, as well as on the novel elements of ritual and narrative, psychodrama has been successfully employed with numerous traumatized clients for over 50 years. In fact, much of classical psychodrama has focused on re-experiencing stressful life events ever since its inception because such re-enactments easily lend themselves to dramatization and therapeutic exploration. Lately, the effectiveness of psychodrama and other experiential methods of psychotherapy in alleviating some of the deleterious effects of PTSD have been more widely acknowledged. However, while psychodrama is a brief, cost-effective and very powerful treatment modality, it has been insufficiently investigated in the literature. It is therefore the purpose of the present chapter to describe the use of psychodrama with PTSD and to discuss some of its therapeutic principles. After a brief review of the relevant theoretical foundations, the basic therapeutic aspects of psychodrama with traumatized people will be illustrated with some brief case vignettes. Finally, a cautionary note will be added about the needs of traumatized people for safety and the risk of retraumatization if these needs are not respected.

Theoretical foundation

The theoretical foundation of psychodrama treatment of PTSD can be described simply. A person who has been exposed to a very stressful event is overwhelmed and in a state of emotional and cognitive turmoil. For example, a person who was involved in a car accident in which people were injured or killed, a girl who was told that her former boyfriend had committed suicide after she had terminated the relationship, a man who attended his wife in a hospice until she died, a soldier who was nearly killed in an explosion, a girl who was rescued from drowning and a man who was physically abused by his father all through childhood may be expected to experience some or all of the symptoms of PTSD described above. Traumatic life-events include the impact of war, natural disasters and abuse. The misfortunes and miseries of human life are endless, leaving people horror-stricken, heart-broken and in grief. Whether a person has experienced the death of a close relative or friend, severe illness, rape, physical assault, burglary, crippling accidents, hospitalization, imprisonment, torture, failure in pregnancy and birth, divorce, unfaithfulness of spouse, unrequited love, acute social failures, bankruptcy or other financial loss, there is a normative state of emotional crisis. Obviously, the amount of stress experienced by the individual is highly subjective. For example, a seemingly moderate event, such as minor medical surgery, may be very traumatic for a frightened child, while the same event for a fearless adult may be experienced as less painful.

The immediate response to a stressful situation is often described as a state of shock: a kind of physical and mental short-circuiting. In this acute state, people experience either numbness and disbelief or hysteria and a breakdown of mental energy. It usually takes some time cognitively to grasp the new reality and let its consequences 'sink in'. However, when the painful truth is finally comprehended and 'the iron has entered into the soul' ('*haeret lateri lethalis aroundo*'), a reactive phase follows which involves a physical yearning and protest, fear and rage, as well as a sense of profound emptiness and loss. Images, emotions and recollections that are too painful are pushed out of awareness, but remain hidden within the body like foreign substances with psychosomatic manifestations (van der Kolk, McFarlane and Weisaeth 1996). From here on, the experiential journey of readjustment to the new reality is often unpredictable and may take many different paths. Some people are able to work through their loss and readjust to the new reality. Others remain stuck in a state of disorganization and despair as a result of their inability adequately to integrate the painful experiences and may develop various signs of mental distress, including PTSD (Wilson, Smith and Johnson 1985).

In particular, people who develop PTSD have somehow lost their capacity of resilience. This may be likened to a violin, which cannot be used unless its strings are strained; but if we put too much pressure on the strings, they will snap. So will people who have endured too much emotional stress. Moreno described such a state of breakdown or paralysis in finding an adequate response to a sudden, unexpected and potentially life-threatening event as a loss of spontaneity:

> 'The sense for spontaneity, as a cerebral function, shows a more rudimen-
> tary development than any other important, fundamental function of the

central nervous system ... Taken by surprise, people act frightened or stunned. They produce false responses or none at all. It seems that there is nothing for which human beings are more ill prepared and the human brain more ill-equipped than for surprise. The normal brain responds confusedly, but psychological tests of surprise have found that fatigued, nerve-racked and machine-ridden people are still more inadequate – they have no response ready nor any organised intelligent reaction to offer to sudden blows which seem to come from nowhere' (1923/1972, p.47).

Thus, people who are inadequately 'warmed-up' for change, from a somatic, psychological and social point of view, will be less likely adequately to cope with a stressful event. Spontaneity as a self-regulating process mediates between the outer and inner world and is responsible for the emotional equilibrium of the person. This description of spontaneity as an inner adjustment mechanism to outer stress is important not only for understanding the processes involved in psychological trauma but also as a description of the processes involved in recovery and in the basic goals of psychodrama with PTSD. As such, the recovery of spontaneity may be regarded as the 'leitmotif' (the essential goal) for psychodrama with people who suffer from PTSD.

On the basis of this theoretical foundation, psychodrama aims to provide the protagonist who has become fixated in the trauma resolution process with an opportunity to remember, repeat and work through the painful events from the past. Such a process of re-enactment is assumed to be therapeutic insofar as it may help the protagonist to re-integrate emotionally and to process cognitively (re-cognize) his or her overwhelming loss and thus to enable the growth of spontaneity that may alleviate the psychological impact of trauma.

Therapeutic aspects of psychodrama with PTSD

Which are the major principles of working with traumatized people in psychodrama? The therapeutic aspects of psychodrama with post-traumatic stress disorder are very similar to those of psychodrama in general, as described by Kellermann (1992). First, repressed experiences of the traumatic event are re-enacted within a safe environment. Second, there is a cognitive re-processing of the event to provide a new understanding of what happened and work through unconscious conflicts that may be connected to the event. Third, emotional catharsis is allowed to emerge to drain the emotional residue from the trauma. Fourth, an imaginary element of 'surplus reality' is introduced to expand the protagonist's world-view. Fifth, there is a focus on how trauma affects interpersonal relations and on means to prevent isolation. Sixth, therapeutic rituals are performed to transform the event into a meaningful experience of life. Finally, if the trauma was a collective group experience, there is a communal act of crisis sociodrama to help readjust to a new state of social balance. These aspects, as depicted in Table 1.1, represent universal elements of traumatic experiences as well as therapeutic factors of psychodrama in general. However, it is important to point out that they should be regarded more as overall therapeutic ingredients than stages of a complete therapeutic process. They rarely occur in the described order, nor are they necessarily put into motion all together during the same session. They will be here illustrated with case vignettes from actual sessions.

Table 1.1	
Therapeutic aspects of psychodrama with traumatized people	
1. Re-enactment	Acting out
2. Cognitive re-processing	Action insight
3. Discharge of surplus energy	Emotional catharsis
4. Surplus reality	As-if
5. Interpersonal support	Tele
6. Therapeutic ritual	Magic

1. Re-enactment

The girl had lost her mother in a tragic accident. She said: 'You left me and never came back. I got so sad and lost.' The woman playing her mother told her that she was sorry for leaving her and that she missed her very much. Each detail of their final leave-taking was re-enacted. The protagonist wanted to replay that scene again and again, telling us how she had felt, what she had done that day and how scared she had been when they had told her that mother would never return. The saga was repeated over and over until the group thought that they would never hear the end of it. It seemed to hold some secret significance for the protagonist that we did not fully understand.

But the repetitive re-enactments seemed to reassure her. Only after having shared with us her feelings of guilt and later having confronted and reprimanded her mother for leaving her, was she able to move on and embark on a long process of mourning.

Repetitive re-enactments of traumatic events are both characteristic signs of traumatization and an essential part of most trauma treatment approaches. While repetition compulsion may be understood as a habitual and mostly unsuccessful attempt to master intolerable stress, the intentional process of remembering, repeating and working through provides the platform for most trauma treatment approaches, including psychodrama. Such therapeutic re-enactment and re-experiencing involves going over the traumatic event again and again, to verbalize memories and sensations in every detail and to present in action whatever is impossible to put into words. Getting the traumatic experiences out into the open is in itself a liberation from the earlier tendency to repress the emotional impact of the event. This functions according to the homeopathic principle of cure by taking a medicine that produces the same symptoms as the disease, so that 'poison and counter-poison neutralize one another'. As the therapeutic agent in an anti-toxic serum, psychodrama thus provided 'more-of-the-same' traumatic material to produce an involuntary reaction that heals the system.

The behavioural acting out of past events provides a means to return to the origin of fixed positions and to search for ways to open up new paths of development. More than desensitization, such a re-experiencing provides a framework in which a person can *be* where he or she *is*. This includes remaining in the hurricane experience of trauma despite the fact that it is just spinning around without direction. Moreno's (1923/1972) dictum that a true second time is a healing from the first sometimes involves also a third, fourth and twentieth reproduction that strives towards act-completion of an unfinished event. In between such sessions, protagonists continue to rehash the event in their imagination, in their dreams and in various symbolic forms, until they have found some inner resolution. However, as apparent in the example above, re-enactment in itself is often insufficient to provide such resolution and often needs to be accompanied by other elements, such as the working through of unconscious conflicts and some cognitive reprocessing of the event.

2. Cognitive reprocessing

A man complained of recurrent flashbacks from the terrible scene of terrorist bomb attacks: the sight of mutilated corpses, the smell of burned flesh and sounds of pain and cries for help from the wounded. He himself had escaped without physical harm but had been severely shaken emotionally by the event. He had tried for some time to remain calm and to stop thinking of the bomb attack but the images and sensations kept intruding on him and filled him with anxiety. In a warm-up before the psychodrama, he had chosen to depict a tortoise as an object of identification because, 'That is the way I feel. I move as if in slow motion. I want to close up within my shell. Everything seems to be so unreal as if I was in a dream, or in a movie'. Apparently, he acted as if he was still in the middle of the inferno and had to shield himself from the horror surrounding him. He was moaning and wailing, 'This is too much for me'. In order to get some distance from the scene, the director suggested that he looked at himself from outside, as if in a mirror. This was in fact what he had done in reality at the moment of crisis. The mirror technique, however, had a paradoxical effect on him that enabled him in a strange manner to *see* what had actually happened. This detached perspective enabled him for the first time to re-cognize horrific details without becoming overwhelmed by them and to start to process the perceived information cognitively. Through this process of detachment and involvement he became gradually more able to replace the frightening pictures in his mind that produced the uncontrollable flashbacks with concrete representations of the event on the psychodrama stage that were tangible and, as such, less frightening.

Most trauma theories view PTSD as a response to the inability of traumatized people to process the new information and to store it in memory. The aim of therapy is therefore to help them integrate the conflicting information and to construct new meanings of the old and the new (Horowitz 1976; McCann and Pearlman 1990). Such cognitive re-processing of traumatic events, sometimes leading to 'action-insight,' enables traumatized people to make sense of a world that has momentarily lost structure and meaning. Because of their tendency to dissociate ('I knew what happened, but had no feelings about it'), there is usually a great need to integrate perception in consciousness through verbalization. Thus there is an active effort to help them to transform pure sensory recall into a more integrated experience with a narrative, or a 'personal history' of what happened. In traumatized people, however, such a gradual increase in self-awareness is often accompanied by a powerful discharge of surplus energy.

3. Discharge of surplus energy

The man had overheard his alcoholic father fight with his mother during the night as a child. He had asked his parents to be quiet but had been hit and reprimanded in a humiliating manner. He had then been sent to bed. Still smelling the bad breath of his father, the boy was left alone in his bed and slowly started to sob hard. The crying became more and more heavy and he cried as if there was no end to his tears. The director urged him to 'let go' and let his body do what it needed to do. Ultimately, the tears stopped but his body went into spasms, convulsing with the hiccupy gasps and shudders that are the aftermath of heavy crying. 'I'm going to throw up,' he whispered. Someone brought a bucket to let him cleanse his stomach of the disgust that he had kept within him for so long. He lay still for a while and then expressed his feelings towards his parents also in words. As a closure, a different father held him until he calmed down sufficiently to return to the group.

Emotional catharsis is the experience of release that occurs when a long-standing state of inner mobilization finds its outlet in affective expression. For traumatized people with a lot of pent-up emotion that has built up like steam in a pressure cooker, such an opportunity to 'blow off steam' is usually very healing. According to Levine (1997), the symptoms of trauma are the result of a highly activated incomplete biological response to threat, frozen in time. By enabling this frozen response to thaw, then complete itself, trauma can be healed. Thus, residual energy from the event is discharged. However, as Kellermann pointed out, a release should not be provoked for its own sake but should include resistance-analysis, working through, and integration: 'Catharsis is neither induced, nor inhibited, but allowed to emerge in its own time and in its own form' (1992, p.83).

Traumatized people are often more fragile and vulnerable than others and have adopted more or less primitive defences in order to shield themselves from their overwhelming feelings of pain. It is therefore essential that they are first supported in their personal state of emotional equilibrium and that a suitable mixture of arousal and relaxation is achieved in the warm-up phase of the session. The problem is often to find a suitable combination of support and confrontation, of detachment and involvement, and of flight and fight with people who have so much dammed-up emotions within themselves. Clearly, only when sufficient internal control has been developed should emotional catharsis be encouraged and it should then be followed by some kind of corrective emotional learning experience, frequently enacted in imagination.

4. Surplus reality

The guilt had overpowered him ever since he had been a soldier in war. He re-enacted the night of the combat when his battalion was suddenly over-powered and he watched, from a hiding place, as his wounded friend was captured and later shot. He could not see much but remembered that he almost fainted out of pure fear. He wanted to shout his lungs out but he had to keep his breath. He felt that he had let his friend down and that he was a murderer now: 'I killed him, I killed my friend,' he exclaimed, and added that he wished that he had the courage to do to himself what he had done to his friend. The group responded with dreadful silence to this confession of suicidal predilection.

Following this re-enactment of what had actually happened in the past, the director suggested that the protagonist enact what had never happened, but what he would have liked to happen. The man had so much wanted to rescue his friend and willingly took this opportunity. In a very moving scene, he picked up the auxiliary playing his wounded friend and put him in a safe place. When holding his friend, something seemed to break loose within him and he started to cry for his friend as if for the first time. Tears literally burst from his eyes, splattering his shirt and for a while, he was totally blinded. The auxiliary was also very moved and said to the protagonist: 'It was not your fault that I died. You were my friend. I know that you did the right thing. If you had tried to rescue me, we both would have died. You will have to live for both of us. Stop punishing yourself for my death!' The protagonist listened carefully as if these words had an almost mystical power to relieve him of his terrible guilt.

Surplus reality scenes such as these may be introduced in psychodrama with traumatized people to undo what was done and to do what needs to be undone. The psychodrama may thus symbolically transform tragic life scenarios both in terms of changing a traumatic event and in terms of allowing for a different emotional response. Naturally, any such use of imagination does not have the goal of encouraging reality distortion. 'As-if' is rather used to come to terms with an impossible outer reality through strengthening the inner subjective world of the traumatized person.

Such existential validation, or affirmation of personal truth, acknowledges the tendency of traumatized people to dissociate in order to maintain their sanity. People who doubt that what they went through was what actually happened get an opportunity to show their subjective perception(s) of the events without being questioned by the director and the group. Thus, a gradual and largely paradoxical process of perceptive (de-)sensitization is put into motion in which 'bits and pieces' of outer reality are digested. This emphasis on personal, subjective or poetic truth, at the expense of historic or objective truth, may perhaps be considered as one of Moreno's main contributions to trauma treatment. Clearly, however, such existential validation of a person's inner reality is dependent on a supportive environment and on interpersonal support.

5. Interpersonal support

An obese and very unhappy woman who had been abused and neglected as a child of various foster parents presented herself to the group. She said that she felt ugly, unlovable and that she hated herself. For years, she had built up layers and layers of shields to cover up her inner being as much as she could. After having re-enacted some characteristic and highly abusive scenes from her childhood, she was standing defenceless like a lost child in the middle of a chaotic universe. At that moment, she suddenly became very likeable and attractive. The group watched her amazing transformation. Then, by some strange architectural and meteorological coincidence, the sun came out behind the clouds through a far-away window in the ceiling, illuminating the now blinded woman. It was that late afternoon sun with its dark red colours, warming the heart directly. It surely warmed all our hearts. It was like a fairy tale with love radiating all over the place. Megavolts of ego strength were melting her muscular armour and building her self-image. The group was also taken by the moment, full of admiration for their 'beauty-queen'. The director urged her fully to open herself up to all the positive energy from the sun, to allow her to be filled with its love.

Taking the cue from the sun, and reinforcing its effect with ego-building hypnotic suggestions, a double whispered: 'I am a loveable person! ... A beautiful woman!' The woman was shining with pure joy. Such rituals of direct attention were celebrated by millions of children at their birthdays and many other occasions but she had never before experienced them. Here, she absorbed it all and it seemed to give her strength and hope and self-esteem.

This somewhat unusual example may illustrate the need of some traumatized people to 'shine' in their lives and to receive interpersonal support and appreciation. Adults who have survived abuse as children are especially amenable to some kind of corrective interpersonal learning experience to counteract their impaired sense of trust, security and 'belonging-to-the-human-race'. As pointed out by Allen and Bloom (1994), the group can help in the social re-integration of traumatized individuals by providing a new sense of safety, self-esteem and intimacy. Furthermore, the group helps traumatized people to brake their isolation (Figley 1993) and to find that their emotional responses are shared with many others who have experienced similar traumatic events. As a result, some of them move on from being helpless victims to becoming coping survivors. Such transformations may be celebrated in communal forms of therapeutic rituals.

6. Therapeutic ritual

About six months after a multiple murder in an institution, 16 of the surviving staff members invited a psychodramatist to help them deal with some of the emotional residues of the event. Naturally, many were traumatized and in deep mourning. In order to contain these strong emotions, but still provide a suitable outlet for them, the director was guided by the principles of containment and safety provided by the use of therapeutic rituals. After some initial presentations and some sociometric exploration of the group, participants were asked to choose a plant that would most accurately depict themselves. Various kinds of flowers and trees were presented, including an almond tree with deep roots but without blossoms, a lilac tree with leaves hanging and an orange tree with thick skin, but 'they are squeezing me to produce more juice ...' the young woman exclaimed. A heavy feeling of repressed grief overshadowed the group.

The director then introduced the 'Talking Stick' to the group. This is an old native American ritual in which an object (usually a branch, but here an empty cup was used) is passed around the group, allowing each one who holds the object to say whatever he or she wants. Other group members will be quiet but may say 'Hau!' if they agree with what has been said. Participants thus talked about their sense of sadness, fear and powerlessness in the wake of the terrible events that had killed their colleagues. Someone asked: 'Would the group be able to support all the feelings of despair?' As the cup had been passed around the group twice, now warm from being held by so many hands, it was put in the middle of the room as a tangible symbol of the group theme. The young woman who had earlier depicted the orange tree suddenly exclaimed: 'I want to throw the cup out the window in order to get rid of the pain!' Someone else responded that the pain would still remain and that we needed to face it together rather than avoiding it. The director urged the group to form a physical ring of support and cohesion that was also intended to break the taboo of touching that is sometimes prevalent in groups of colleagues working together. There was a break and then an individual psychodrama session with the young woman mentioned above.

In the individual psychodrama session, the woman revealed that she had thoughts about leaving her position, feeling that she had no more strength to cope, because constant nightmares made her unable to sleep. In the first scene, she refused to accept more work from her boss. She also refused to accept help from anybody other than Paula, but Paula had been brutally killed and 'nobody can take her place'. An empty chair was put on stage to represent the absence of Paula and the woman expressed her feelings of grief and yearning for Paula. When she was done, the director asked a group member to volunteer to take the role of Paula. A senior colleague consented and sat in the chair. Seeing her, the protagonist embraced her and cried heavily, asking her several questions: 'Are you cold? How do you feel? Do you also miss me? Do you know what happened? Are you also lonely?' The director urged the protagonist to reverse roles with her dead friend and, after some initial apprehension, she agreed. In the role of Paula, she revealed to the group that Paula had been pregnant at the time of her death and that she could not stand the thought of the baby being killed. 'Everything is meaningless,' she exclaimed angrily. The protagonist then returned to her own role and the auxiliary playing Paula said: 'Go on living your own life. My life is over. I love you and I want you to remember me. Farewell! Goodbye!' The woman playing Paula left the scene and returned to the group. After a final scene in which she talked to her boss, group members embraced her and thanked her for expressing so much of what they had also felt. As a group closure, the cup, now symbolically filled with memories, tears, anger and flowers, was again put in the middle of the group as a kind of memorial commemorating the people who had died.

This kind of crisis sociodrama (Kellermann 1998) may illustrate some of the healing principles of therapeutic rituals. Obviously, such traditional ceremonials have been commonly used since time immemorial by communities who have been hit by detrimental 'acts of God', as described by anthropologists and others (Johnson *et al.* 1995). In psychodrama, rituals help people to make transitions in life and to adjust to their new circumstances within a structured framework. In the aftermath of traumatic experiences, rituals are especially important in giving people a sense of safety and security and helping them express their feelings in a symbolic manner.

Thus, groups who have experienced terrorist attacks, being taken hostage, surviving earthquakes, train accidents, sinking ships, fires and other disasters may profit from such a collective act of mourning and a working through of their common misfortunes. Socio- and psychodrama with traumatized people, based on the universal principles of 'Mother Nature', lend themselves excellently to the utilization of such rituals through the use of mythology, symbols and narratives.

Discussion

The phases of re-enactment, cognitive re-processing, discharge of surplus energy, surplus reality, interpersonal support and therapeutic ritual in psycho-drama surely constitute a holistic framework for the treatment of traumatized people. From a theoretical point of view it puts emphasis on the multi-dimensional emotional-organic-intra- and interpersonal-social systems involved in any traumatic experience. From a practical point of view, it relies on a broad framework of technical eclecticism as a powerful approach for re-enacting and re-experiencing traumatic events of life (Kellermann 1995).

This power, however, should be viewed as a two-edged sword with the ability both to heal and to harm. In the hands of unskilled practitioners, there is always the risk of retraumatization and/or revictimization. Because of their earlier experiences of losing control (over themselves, their bodies and their environment) and of being manipulated into doing things that they did not want to do, the need of traumatized people for a 'gentle touch' is critical. Such an approach must recognize their basic needs: safety, holding and closure. For example, the director should make every effort to prepare for the session in terms of explaining what is going to happen at each stage of the process and to get the protagonist's consent to participate in each part of the work. Furthermore, the protagonist should be given as much control as possible over the amount of emotion that is expressed in each scene. Obviously, the golden rule of client-centred therapy, manifested in the attempt of the director to 'follow' the protagonist, rather than to be manipu-lative, is crucial.

Such empowerment of the protagonist is in itself an essential part of trauma therapy as forcefully emphasized by Herman in her book *Trauma and Recovery*:

> In addition to hypnosis, many other techniques can be used to produce an altered state of consciousness in which dissociated traumatic memories are more readily accessible. These range from social methods, such as intensive group psychotherapy or psychodrama, to biological methods, such as the use of sodium amytal. In skilled hands, any of these methods can be effective. Whatever the technique, the same basic rules apply: the locus of control remains with the patient, and the timing, pacing, and design of the sessions must be carefully planned so that the uncovering technique is integrated into the architecture of the psychotherapy (1992, pp.186–187)

Furthermore, as we have seen in the above examples and as we will see in this book, all the major techniques of psychodrama should be adapted to the special needs of traumatized people and to their varying degrees of 'learned helplessness', the feeling that their destiny is shaped by external forces over which they have no control. For example, the double technique may be used for 'containing' emotions (Hudgins and Drucker 1998), rather than for unrestrained abreaction. The mirror technique may be used to get some detachment from oneself and some distance from the frightening event when things become too painful. In fact, involvement and distance seem to be the two main forces that evolve around the central axis of balance within each single psychodrama session. In order to maintain such control, the protagonist should be sensitively guided through 'tolerable doses of awareness, preventing the extremes of denial on the one hand and intrusive-repetitiousness on the other' (Scurfield 1985, p.245).

In summary, there should be a continual effort to keep the two forces of tension and relaxation appropriately balanced within the protagonist and in group members during the traumatic re-enactment. While the role playing method in itself may stimulate further emotional arousal and a loss of control, the basic techniques of psychodrama, if properly used, help to increase control. Thus, in the midst of emotional upheaval, the traumatized clients are helped again to find a sense of safety, to reconnect to themselves and to others, and to process cognitively their overwhelming experiences. In dramatic terminology, the principle of involvement promoted by Stanislavky is combined with the principle of distancing promoted by Brecht.

Another adaptation of technique concerns the use of role reversal with traumatized people. As pointed out by Ochberg (1988), victims of violence are very sensitive to being blamed for wrongdoings that were done to them. It is therefore suggested, as a general rule, that protagonists who have been hurt by other people should not be asked to reverse roles with these people. They first need to become more in touch with their own feelings, which are so often confused and chaotic. Most importantly, their pent-up aggression needs to be asserted and channelled to the outside source. Any request for premature role reversal at this stage runs the risk of being interpreted by the protagonist as a subtle message to understand the motives of the other and perhaps to accept them. As a result, protagonists might turn their aggression against themselves and further increase their sense of guilt. Representational (and sometimes reciprocal) role reversal may be suggested only in those cases in which the victims themselves, often after a long process of trauma resolution, express a need to take the role of the other.

Psychodrama should attempt to provide an environment in which traumatized people are no longer seen as objects that are being pushed and pulled and shaped by forces that are outside themselves. They should rather be encouraged to view themselves as active and responsible in constructing their lives and as co-therapists in their very personal journeys of trauma resolution.

References

Allen, S.N. and Bloom, S.L. (1994) 'Group and family treatment of post-traumatic stress disorder.' *Psychiatric Clinics of North America 17*, 2, 425–437.

American Psychiatric Association (1994) *Diagnostic and Statistical Manual of Mental Disorders: DSM-IV.* Washington DC: AMA.

Boyle, K. (1961) *Breaking the Silence: Why a Mother tells her Son about the Nazi era.* New York: Institute of Human Relations Press.

Figley, C.R. (1993) 'Introduction.' In J.P. Wilson and B. Raphael (eds) *International Handbook of Traumatic Stress Syndromes.* New York: Plenum Press.

Herman, J. (1992) *Trauma and Recovery.* New York: Basic Books.

Horowitz, M.J. (1976) *Stress Response Syndromes.* New York: Jason Aronson.

Hudgins, M.K. and Drucker, K. (1998) 'The containing double as part of the therapeutic spiral model for treating trauma survivors.' *The International Journal of Action Methods 51*, 2, 63–74.

Janoff-Bulman, R. (1992) *Shattered Assumptions: Towards a New Psychology of Trauma.* New York: The Free Press.

Johnson, D.R., Feldman, S.C., Lubin, H. and Soutwick, S.M. (1995) 'The therapeutic use of ritual and ceremony in the treatment of post-traumatic stress disorder.' *Journal of Traumatic Stress 8*, 2, 283–291.

Kellermann, P.F. (1992) *Focus on Psychodrama.* London: Jessica Kingsley Publishers.

Kellermann, P.F. (1995) 'Towards an integrative approach to group psychotherapy: an attempt to integrate psychodrama and psychoanalytic group psychotherapy.' *The International Forum of Group Psychotherapy 3*, 4, 6–10.

Kellermann, P.F. (1998) 'Sociodrama.' *Group Analysis 31*, 179–195.

Levine, P.A. (1997) *Waking the Tiger: Healing Trauma: The Innate Capacity to Transform Overwhelming Experiences.* Berkeley, California: North Atlantic Books.

Moreno, J.L. (1923/1972) 'The theater for spontaneity' (translated and revised as 'The philosophy of the moment'). *Sociometry 4*, 2, 1941. Reprinted in *Psychodrama 1* (1972).

McCann, I.L. and Pearlman, L.A. (1990) *Psychological Trauma and the Adult Survivor.* New York: Brunner/Mazel.

Ochberg, F.M. (1988) *Post-traumatic Therapy and Victims of Violence.* New York: Brunner/Mazel.

Scurfield, R.M. (1985) 'Post-trauma stress assessment and treatment: overview and formulations.' In C.R. Figley (ed) *Trauma and its Wake* (Vol. 1). New York: Brunner/Mazel.

van der Kolk, B.A., McFarlane, A.C. and Weisaeth, L. (1996) *Traumatic Stress: the Effects of Overwhelming Experience on Mind, Body and Society.* New York: Guilford Press.

Wilson, J.P., Smith, K. and Johnson, S.K. (1985) 'A comparative analysis of PTSD among various survivor groups.' In C.R. Figley (ed) *Trauma and its Wake* (Vol. 1). New York: Brunner/Mazel.

PART 2

Loss

The Core Emotion of Trauma

CHAPTER 2

Psychodramatic Methods for Facilitating Bereavement

Adam Blatner

Trauma is a most complex phenomenon, involving elements of de-centering, disempowerment, the instillation of strongly negative images and experiences, the evocation of symmetrically negative feelings of revenge and self-loathing, and guilt and shame for all these and other processes. Among these also are profound losses – of innocence, a positive matrix for memory, trusted relationships, archetypal connections, and valued parts of one's self, such as a belief in one's own power.

Treatment for trauma is correspondingly multifaceted, requiring a host of varied interventions. Grief work is the process of healing the psychosocial dislocation caused by loss of intrapsychic and social relationships. This chapter will address the theoretical and practical approach to grief work, emphasizing the utility of a psychodramatic technique I've called 'the final encounter'.

Bereavement, or grief work, is the process of coping with a significant loss. In terms of role theory, it involves the substitution of an internalized role or other social role relationships for the lost relationships. In addition, grief work involves a number of other components, such as identifying irrational or residual areas of guilt or countering tendencies towards social isolation or pathological denial.

Grief work is needed not only for losses by death. People can also suffer meaningful losses of pets, locations (such as a home, contact with neighbourhood and old friends), the dream of a marriage, contact with children through divorce and so on. People who have had a heart attack or the loss of a limb also go through grief, because functional roles are part of the living intrapsychic social network. Furthermore, what must be grieved for is not only the other person (or situation), but also the *function* one played in relation to that lost other, one's own role, which may have been more of a part of an identity than any feelings of closeness towards the other. Thus, some people suffer profound grief after losing someone for whom they played a role of caregiver over many years.

Grief work is a type of psychological healing and, like the healing of a physical wound, it cannot be imposed by will. However, this natural process may be facilitated by various psychotherapeutic methods, just as there are medical techniques for cleansing or binding a wound. Because psychodrama integrates elements of intuition, imagination, emotion, and the power of feeling oneself 'doing,' that kinaesthetic source that anchors experience in the body, it adds a depth of feeling to verbal and cognitive modes of therapy.

'The final encounter' is a technique I've developed for promoting the emergence of internalized role elements (Blatner 1985). This approach is a variation of the auxiliary chair technique, and similar to its derivative, 'two chair work', popularized by Fritz Perls in Gestalt therapy. The technique involves establishing a scene in which the bereaved person has a conversation with the lost other, represented by the auxiliary (empty) chair. Since in fact the other has died, moved away, or become unavailable in other ways, such a scene utilizes the principle Moreno called 'surplus reality' (Blatner 2000).

This is a relatively simple technique that can be used by non-psycho-dramatists – physicians, lay counsellors, hospice workers and so forth. Although I use the term 'director' and 'protagonist,' it must be recognised that the process is not being applied as part of a classical psychodrama. One of the advantages of this rich approach is that its component methods can be applied beyond formal group therapy contexts. The final encounter may be conducted as a process with the client or bereaved person alone, or within a family or supportive group setting.

Surplus reality

Psychodrama, related as it is to the artistic power of drama, utilizes the power of imagination in constructing more multi-levelled, psychologically 'real' experiences. For example, in the movies, an interaction may be accompanied by a 'voice-over,' or in ordinary theatre, a character may offer an 'aside' to the audience. Such dramatic devices recognize the dual levels of mind in por-traying not only what happens, but also what *doesn't* happen, what might be 'said' mentally but not physically (Blatner 1996).

The idea of constructing something psychologically valid but realistically impossible, then, is a natural part of human experience. Psychotherapists should not feel so committed to the promotion of the ideal of 'being realistic' and 'cutting through denial' that they fall into the error of themselves being in denial of the depth of psychological experience. Psychodrama generates a context in which, instead of having to take sides, both levels of experience can be contained. There's a realistic assessment of 'what happens' and also the 'surplus reality' of what does not happen and perhaps never could happen, but in another sense, it does indeed unfold in the realm of imagination.

Applied to grief work, the scene is a kind of seance, the psychodramatist daring to propose that, 'For psychotherapeutic purposes, let's imagine that you [the bereaved] could have that conversation after all. Let's imagine that he [the lost other] could come back, in spirit, and encounter you'. It is surprising that most clients will accept this suspension of disbelief, just as they do when watching an absorbing movie.

Focusing on specific experiences

Healing requires a degree of acceptance of the loss, because the replacement of the actual role relationship with psychological representations, which is what internalization does, involves some degree of conscious engagement with the loss. As long as the mind is avoiding that reality, the healing cannot proceed.

Unfortunately, the mind operates along two channels, one part seeking to engage reality and another that regresses into childish illusion, sustaining the belief that the loss hasn't occurred, or in other ways subtly avoiding the full impact of that reality. Many different defence mechanisms are brought to bear in this process.

It's unwise to force or confront the bereaved, demanding full engagement in accepting the loss. This will only disrupt the more natural transition that is needed. Instead, gentle experiences can be suggested which allow for a balancing of engagement and yet hold on to the illusion of restoration.

One of the more common and insufficiently appreciated defences is that of speaking in generalities. This supports the defences called intellectualization, de-realization, isolation of affect and denial. Speaking in terms such as 'I really loved Grandpa' is a compromise, seeming to communicate, but not bringing the bereaved into direct experience of what was most lovable about Grandpa, or whoever the lost other might be.

To counter this tendency towards vagueness, psychodrama offers the idea of picturing a scene, and requires some specificity of time, locale, objects in the scene and actual words or gestures. These are concrete elements which give texture and serve as powerful agents for evoking a more vivid engagement with the lost other and experience of the relationship. By heightening this experience, the compromise is hinted at: one can 'have' the other mentally while also beginning to accept that the other is not present in actuality.

By inquiring about specific elements in memories and moving away from vagueness of language or abstract ideas, the director can significantly intensify the healing without throwing the bereaved into overload.

Active neutrality

The natural process of grief work involves a fluctuation of ego states, a process of gradually accustoming the mind to the loss by going back and forth between two roles. One part seeks to cope, identifies with being mature and realistic, and accepting of the actuality of the loss. (This would resemble what Eric Berne termed the 'adult' Ego State [Berne 1964].) However, significant loss brings forth what Berne called the 'child' Ego State, and this process is also called regression. Part of the self begins to operate along the lines of a child's way of thinking, that if one desires something fiercely enough, talks about it, and protests, then this exercise of will may magically succeed. In terms of loss, the mental mechanism is 'undoing.' This role, then, says, in effect, 'I don't care about any mean old reality. I only know I want Grandpa back alive!'

An interesting example of this regressive tendency is the way bereaved people often become caught up in asking 'why?' questions, which mask the underlying belief that 'If I could only know why, I could fix it, undo what has been done'. During grief work, if counsellors can gently double for these beliefs, it begins to neutralize their seductive power: 'Sometimes I wish I could go back and somehow do the right thing'.

That 'sometimes' is important, because if the counsellor, in trying to be empathic, reflects only the more regressive role as if it were the whole of the protagonist's experience, then the adaptation-seeking role will feel demeaned, as if the counsellor cannot recognize the degree to which there is also an effort to be 'grown up.' On the other hand, if the counsellor allies with this adult role, then the inner child will feel 'you don't understand! This is too painful to accept!' The solution is to interpose the realistic ideas of 'sometimes,' and 'parts of you.' These two elements allow for the opening of the bereaved person's mind to not having to take a stand, to allowing for the inclusion of both roles, and their natural need to weave back and forth.

What is being countered is also the widespread subtle cultural norm that people should feel unified in their being – but in fact, as role theory notes, people can feel various ways about things and this ambivalence need not be experienced as intolerable inner conflict. Thus, the counsellor can reinforce the appropriateness of permitting a vivid experience of regression without shame, and of subtly affirming a belief in the long-term capacity for healing.

From the psychodramatic viewpoint, this approach is a variant of the 'multiple ego' technique, making explicit the way the personality can contain sometimes opposing roles, and from the psychoanalytic perspective, this technique amplifies the deeper meaning of therapeutic neutrality.

Thus, it is important for the counsellor not to seem to take sides; not to ally either with the part that seeks restitution nor with the part that seeks adjustment to reality. The bereaved is partially aware of the regressive quality of the part that seeks restitution, and would feel shamed if this were how the comforter sees him. On the other hand, there's also resentment towards the seeming coldness of the subtle message, 'Get real. He's dead. Deal with it'. Since both voices are operating in grief work, the counsellor can acknowledge both empathically, acknowledging that either stance makes sense, going with the natural pendulum swing until the bereaved person comes to some point of balance. This involves an implicit validation and internalization of both stances: 'While the inner child part of me doesn't care about the reality and wants him back, the mature part of me wants to cope and go on with life'.

The final encounter

The aforementioned considerations may be used throughout the grief counselling or support, but at a certain point in grief work, usually some time after the first phase of shock and denial, it may be useful to help the bereaved 'finish' the ongoing implicit dialogue which is part of any relationship (Abell 1978; Buckman 1989; Kaminski 1981; Volkan 1975; Weiner 1975). Indeed, part of the stress of grief is this 'unfinished business', which involves three issues, framed as three questions: 'What have we shared?' 'What have you meant to me?' and 'What did I mean to you?'

For some clients actually talking to a chair or getting up and changing seats is too much of a stretch, too dramatic. Others will find this device helpful in making the process more vivid. For the former group, a fair amount of the benefit may still be attained simply by inviting the images to flow, by addressing those key questions. To repeat, being very specific about the answers is crucial, lest the tendency to vagueness in the service of avoiding the sharpness of the loss end up undermining the actual grief work.

There is no rational way to accommodate to this tension, but through the power of surplus reality, at the level of psychological and emotional truth, it is possible to hold on to that which is (at the material level of existence) actually lost. Through song, poetry, drama, mementoes, rituals, or simply claiming certain images, qualities, or memories, the presence of the other is internalized and retained.

What if the other has many negative qualities? In psychological reality, people construct also the relationship with the idealized other, as well as the actual and imperfect, perhaps even malignant other. So, for example, the bereaved might say, 'You never spent much time playing with me and really seeing me, but I will imagine that you can really see me and know me now'.

Case study

The protagonist, a woman in her early forties (with the assumed name of Sue) is grieving the suicide about two decades ago of a cousin who was like a brother to her (we'll call him Larry). Various issues relating to this lost other's place in the family and its implications for the bereaved person's own experience of her extended family had been addressed. But there remained that sense of 'unfinished business'. To foster a greater degree of internalization, we set up a 'final encounter', the cousin imagined to be manifested in a facing empty chair.

First, the director, standing to one side, poses the question: 'What have we shared?' The bereaved is encouraged to come up with a couple of specific anecdotes of memories. 'We were buddies,' Sue began. 'We got into mischief together.' The director prompted, 'Give me an example'. The client offered a slight clarification: 'Oh, we were always running around and things'. Director: 'I still can't picture it – where would you be, what were you doing?' The point here is to bring the memory to a level so that it can indeed be pictured vividly enough to be staged.

Then the lost other was asked what 'he' remembered, and the bereaved left her role, changed parts, and sat in the facing seat, 'becoming' cousin Larry. Director to Larry: 'What do you remember doing with your cousin Sue?' And again a specific vignette is evoked, imagined from the cousin's viewpoint. The generation of alternative perspectives thickens the associative mental network and 'anchors' the memories deeper in the psyche.

After a few of these exchanges, the therapist as psychodrama director moves to the second question. 'What have you meant to me?' he prompts, and Sue repeats the question and begins to describe some qualities evoked by the memories of that relationship. 'Whenever I find myself taking things too seriously, if I think of you, I begin to think of fooling around, joking, finding some outrageous possibility.'

The general form of the response that is most constructive is the 'whenever I experience/do [so and so] I am reminded of the way you ... and that also reminds me to ...'. Again, the point here is to find some behavioural response that symbolizes the best quality of the other.

In cases where there is a negative element in the relationship, that reminding, that life lesson, is simply reversed. 'I remember that you were afraid of affection, and instead I'll be more affectionate with my son, so he won't be afraid of this wonderful part of life.'

The last question can be one of the most powerful in the healing of grief. Our culture tends to overdo its suppression of 'selfishness' to the point where many people are afraid of consciously entertaining the idea that they are deeply meaningful to others in their close social network. And yet, people do carry implicit questions such as, 'What do I mean to you?' and 'Do you know I'm here?' If we would stop and think about it, it would become clear that there's a high probability that we matter to others about as much as they matter to us. (This is an indirect implication of Moreno's concept of 'tele' [Blatner 2000, pp.191–194]). But there are tendencies to retain more childish complexes that fail to recognize the complexity of others, and also their capacity to be affected by us.

In healing grief, unspoken questions such as this need to be answered, because the process of internalization of the best qualities of the lost other operate more effectively when it is sensed that the relationship was mutual. Thus, the final question in the grief work was to explore with Sue in the role of Larry: 'Sue, I want to tell you, too, what you meant to me'. At a deep level, people have fantasies about what others think and these include more realistic and more desire-filled components. In other words, if you and I are in a relationship, I imagine both what I would like you to think of me and, if pushed, I can think about what you probably think of me. There's also the category of what I might fear you think of me. The point here is that people can be encouraged to risk imagining what they might have meant to others, and in most cases this is positive.

What if, on the other hand, a person knows they've been a burden, a trial, and a source of pain to the lost other? The director can encourage the bereaved then to imagine what the other might have hoped for and desired, pointing towards the positive image that others wish for us. There's no guarantee of a happy resolution to all encounters, but a fair amount of leeway exists for some creative negotiations.

Some further technical refinements

If the bereaved is able to enter into a more dramatic enactment (rather than the scene simply being imagined), there is extra power in having the bereaved as protagonist speak directly to the 'other' in the empty chair. Clients have a tendency to slip out of role and re-engage the director as a therapist to whom they are narrating a story, talking *about* the other rather than *to* him. The therapist as director must remind the protagonist, sometimes repeatedly, to 'Say that to him directly'. Or the director might double – reframing what has been said as an 'I-Thou' statement directed at the imagined other in the facing chair.

Closing the encounter can occur when there is a slight drop-off of tension, when the main impetus of act hunger has been fulfilled. The main things that needed to be said seem to have been stated explicitly, even if in the sphere of surplus reality. It may have been better for some of these things to have been stated while the lost other was still alive or present; but for the purposes of healing, replaying an encounter that didn't have a chance to occur in reality still offers a surprising degree of psychological healing.

The director asks, 'Can you let him go now?' or 'If he had to go now, how would you finish the scene?' The bereaved often says something like, 'We would hug'. Director: 'Go ahead'.

The protagonist gets up and imagines embracing the lost other. The tension dissolves. The protagonist indicates a finishing of the scene, and the director makes this more explicit.

Sharing

If the process is done in a family setting or a group setting, it can be even more powerful. The specific imagery expressed by the bereaved tends to evoke other memories, some relating to the same lost other (if this involves family) or to other people entirely. Still, when the three questions are finished and the encounter is brought to a close, others often will want to share their own losses.

The director or therapist should interrupt tendencies by others to psychologically 'analyse' the protagonist, and redirect the response to sharing how what was witnessed might have evoked responses in the others' own lives.

It is interesting that, as others share their images, the process in turn evokes yet other memories and insights in the protagonist who did the final encounter exercise. Without having to be spoken about openly at that time, the grief work continues to expand psychologically and become more deeply rooted.

Thus, it can be healing for all concerned if this process can happen in an extended family group, or the social network of those who were most associated with the lost other. The final encounter can be part of memorial services, for example, for those who have died of AIDS, suicide, or other situations in which there have also been helpers working with the psychosocial aspects of the loss.

Further processing can be encouraged through working with a journal, or writing letters to the bereaved, and also writing a letter from the lost other to the bereaved (Rynearson 1987).

Applications

This process can be varied in order to adapt to the loss of parts of the body, a special status or position, a hoped-for dream, and many other types of loss. Whether the lost entity is an inanimate object or complex abstraction, it can nevertheless be personified, treated as if 'it' could speak, as if it were a living spirit. Thus, an unborn or even unconceived baby can engage in an encounter with a parent who is suffering from childlessness or a miscarriage. A woman can encounter the career she gave up to have a family. People can even re-engage the sense of loss attached to a concept of God that has failed to sustain their courage, and in so doing, perhaps broaden and renew that concept.

In addition, the final encounter technique may be adapted for using in addressing the following situations:

- helping a friend or client cope with the loss of someone important, whether that loss is in the past or future

- preparing for one's own death or leaving a social network

- reviewing your and your family's experience with bereavement, even months or years after the initial loss

- dealing with the loss of a favourite pet, a part of one's body, a meaningful job, an important belief system, a country or home town, or other significant role relationship.

Admittedly, a full psychodramatic exploration of this process would require a trained therapist; nevertheless, the basic considerations may be carried in the minds of everyone dealing with a loss. The issues noted above might give some sense of what needs to be communicated directly in order to finish the business of the relationship.

In summary, psychodramatic techniques offer an approach that may be woven into a setting of ongoing therapy or as part of a professionally facilitated professional training, self-help, or personal growth group. Unfinished business, dealing with all kinds of losses, is an important theme in most people's lives. Knowing that there is a method for working through these feelings is itself a form of reassurance and direction.

References

Abell, R.G. (1978) 'Saying goodbye to parents.' In H.H. Grayson and C. Loew (eds) *Changing Approaches to the Psychotherapies.* New York: Spectrum.

Berne, E. (1961) *Transactional Analysis in Psychotherapy.* New York: Grove Press.

Blatner, A. (1985) 'The principles of grief work.' In *Creating your Living: Applications of Psychodramatic Methods in Everyday Life,* 8. San Marcos: TX (A privately produced monograph)

Blatner, A. (1996) *Acting-in: Practical Applications of Psychodramatic Methods* (3rd edition). New York: Springer.

Blatner, A. (2000) *Foundations of Psychodrama: History, Theory, and Practice* (4th edition). New York: Springer.

Buckman, R. (1989) *'I Don't Know What to Say...' How to Help and Support Someone Who is Dying.* Boston: Little, Brown & Co.

Cohen, D.R. (1978) 'Psychodrama: Coming to terms with death.' *Psychology Today 12,* 2, 104.

Kaminski, R.C. (1981) 'Saying good-by – An example of using a "good-by" technique and concomitant psychodrama in the resolving of family grief.' *Journal of Group Psychotherapy, Psychodrama, and Sociometry 34,* 100–111.

Parkes, C.M. (1985) 'Bereavement.' *British Journal of Psychiatry 146,* 11–17.

Rynearson, E.K. (1987) 'Psychotherapy of pathologic grief.' *Psychiatric Clinics of North America 10,* 3, 487–499.

Volkan, V.D. (1975) 'More on "re-grief" therapy.' *Journal of Thanatology 3,* 2, 77–91.

Weiner, H.B. (1975) 'Living experiences with death: A journeyman's view through psychodrama.' *Omega 6,* 3, 251–274, 1975.

CHAPTER 3

Brief Psychodrama and Bereavement

Marisol Filgueira Bouza
and José Antonio Espina Barrio

Western culture is imbued with the idea of immortality. Sick people are sent to hospitals where all their non-working organs are restored, and they are only sent home when they have 'magically' recovered. Death occurs at home with increasingly less frequency. Hospitals and mortuaries replace this rite of passage in a cold and aseptic way. Frequently the dying person is not told that the end is near, and the surviving relatives are not allowed to show their feelings of loneliness and loss.

Rites of passage signal the changes in the continuum of our lives, and are an important stage in personality development (Espina Barrio 1992; Feinstein and Mayo 1993). For Eliade, the rites of passage go through two steps: in the first one, the 'death' of the previous stage is recognized and, in the second, the bereaved person is 'reborn' to the new stage. Leach follows Gennep's stages (separation, growing apart and incorporation), asserting that each stage needs a series of rituals which make up the whole rite of passage.

Nevertheless the dead person is not watched over any more at home, there is no 'funeral wake'. His virtues or defects are not proclaimed and the expression of feelings allowing for the bereavement process is not fostered, except in some isolated villages. It is not surprising that such a repression of feelings works from the depth of our organism, appearing afterwards as a psychosomatic ulcer, stress or depression.

Anthropological psychodrama tries to recover the ancient rites that give greater meaning to our lives and also lead to an improvement in our skills and resources. It is not just a rehearsal out of time and place, but a new recreation.

The Spanish Psychodrama Association (AEP) has worked widely with this type of psychodrama (Filgueira, Varea and Gonzalez 1996; Lamas and Filgueira 1992 and 1993).

Anthropological psychodrama tries to unblock the normal process of bereavement. After the verbal comment on feelings, the protagonist is asked to choose the scene he wants to start with. It usually includes the dead person. If he chooses this encounter, our first goal will be to make him recognize the separation between him and the loved one. Psychodrama makes an encounter with the dead person possible, in order to tell him how much we miss him, and deal with outstanding issues. One can reverse roles with the person who died, embody his feelings, and understand from there the separation of their beings.

The mirroring technique enables everyone to look at their existential situation from a distance, as if they were on a balcony.

Role reversal with the relatives (dead person and family) facilitates recovery of one's social environment and offers a chance to experience the different ways to solve bereavement. The stage of relatives' incorporation requires recognition of the irreversible loss and the expression of feelings of loneliness, and finally the chance to say goodbye to the dead person. Even though the word farewell can be used, it is better for the protagonist to say to his loved one which qualities he is going to keep inside. In this way the protagonist is keeping his memory alive and enriching himself with new skills. When the qualities of the one who died are incorporated, he is then accepting the death and fostering a process of personal development.

The psychodramatic process is always the same but the therapist's attitude differs depending on the context. In psychodrama for bereavement workshops, the first goal is help and not to harm the protagonist, prior to the dramatic result. There is no continuity and it is necessary to look after all participants, so that they do not feel left out. During group psychotherapy, with ongoing sessions, the goal is to help the protagonist get to the point he wants to reach, but never any further. If the psychodramatic programme has not been completed, we will have further sessions. We allow a margin for the bereavement to work itself out and then take on new objectives. We have also worked in different contexts, such as the individual and the family (Espina Barrio 1993; Filgueira Bouza 1995 and 1996).

Brief psychodrama focusing on bereavement

The process of psychodrama applied to brief, problem-centred psycho-therapy goes through the following steps:

1. A situation of emotional blockage is detected in the clinical evolution or the patient's life.

2. It is decided that intervention with psychodrama is necessary.

3. The psychodramatist and the therapeutic team work under the same direction. It is not compulsory that the team should have been trained in psychodrama, but it is useful.

4. The first exploratory session is fixed, either with the patient alone or with his relatives. Information which is already known about the patient makes specific goals possible. These are the warm-up phases of the treatment session.

5. The scene may be suggested by the patient or worked out by the therapeutic team. The latter usually occurs when the patient does not collaborate or if there is a specific interest in working through a specific situation. The psychodramatist directs the scene. The members of the therapeutic team and/or the relatives of the patient, when they are present, take part as auxiliary egos, if necessary. The auxiliary egos should always follow the psychodramatist's indications and help him. Once the scene is worked through, the patient and/or the relatives comment on the work done, its effects and prognosis for closure and sharing. After the discussion, the team may prescribe tasks for future sessions and follow-up for the patient and family.

6. Afterwards, the team alone reviews the diagnosis, discusses the intervention, checks the results and poses hypotheses on the expected evolution. The session's contents are compiled and recorded.

7. In the next session after the intervention, the results and hypotheses are checked. If the evolution was good (that is, if the expected effects are obtained and maintained), no more treatment sessions are held, but the patient would return to his usual therapist for the traditional follow-up. If the evolution was not successful, the option of holding more psychodramatic sessions is considered, or new intervention strategies with different orientations are designed.

In the beginning, any case can be admitted for treatment, but this is only continued if there is at least a minimum guarantee of improvement for the patient.

Bereavement and melancholy show similar symptoms: a deeply painful mood, lack of interest in the outside world, loss of ability to love and inhibition of all functions. Melancholics suffer a loss of self-esteem with a wide range of self-blame. Normal bereavement is a state of deep suffering due to the loss of a loved one that time progressively alleviates. Pathological bereavement is a reaction to a known but not accepted loss. Melancholy is a reply to an unconscious loss, unknown by the individual. Every bereavement process needs time; reality usually wins, but it takes considerable time and energy.

The bereavement process has several stages:

1. Shock and numbness: a reaction of bewilderment, a feeling of emptiness and emotional outbursts or calmness when receiving the news. This lasts between several hours and a week.

2. Denial and isolation: the individual cannot believe what happened ('It is not possible, it is not true!'). He becomes isolated from his environment.

3. Anger: aggressive outbursts and reproaches against the people around. This starts two or three weeks after the loss. The bereaved person finds reasons everywhere for complaint and irritation, expressing an attempt to regain the lost object ('Why is this happening to me?' 'Why did he/she leave me?'), and, sometimes, self-reproach ('Why didn't I do more for him/her?').

4. Pact or haggling: the disappearance starts to be acknowledged, but the individual searches for a way of palliating or compensating for the situation by means of an exchange, promises or postponement ('Only a few months more'; 'Take me with him/her'; 'If he/she comes back, I promise to ...').

5. Depression, disorganization, and hopelessness: the moment of the most intense suffering. Once the irreversibility of the situation has been acknowledged, disconsolate weeping starts, as well as restless memories and a feeling of proximity to the dead person, which may sometimes turn into hallucinations. This period may last from a month to several months after the loss.

6. Acceptance: acknowledgement of the obvious with more serenity.

7. Fading of cathexis, separation and resolution: saying farewell and breaking the ties with the lost person. The individual may still hope to regain that person but realizes that this is impossible.

8. Recovery: progressive return to functionality.

9. Reconnection with the environment and establishment of new bonds with people.

All these stages may be summarised into three:

1. 'No! It's not true, it didn't happen.'

2. 'Yes, but no. It happened, but I can't accept or deal with it.'

3. 'Yes, it happened and I must accept it and deal with it.'

The normal working out of the loss requires going through all the stages, which takes about a year on average. In order for the process to take place without major problems, the stage of anger and its venting are absolutely necessary, as well as re-linking with reality.

The symptoms of pathological bereavement include becoming stuck at any stage, usually in denial of the loss, and/or an exaggeration of the expected symptoms of grief, and/or the appearance of altered forms of behaviour which may be dangerous for the physical health of the patient (carelessness, attempted suicide and so forth). The lack of a conscious and foreseen farewell leaves a large number of matters unresolved: everything one would have liked to do but never did with the deceased while he was alive. The loss denial and the repression of feelings are the main symptoms of bereavement pathology.

The treatment of pathological bereavement has four main goals:

1. Preventing repression: forcing the patient to remember and relive the events.

2. Emotional support: compensating for helplessness.

3. Social assistance: giving an apprenticeship in coping with life events and problem-solving skills.

4. Reconstruction: helping with the establishment of new bonds.

Psychodrama brings the deceased person and all the key figures of the affected person to the scene. The auxiliary egos play these roles. The presence of meaningful objects relating to the deceased (clothes and personal objects, photographs, letters and so forth) allows for emotional venting. The farewell and dealing with outstanding issues work out the relationship with the dead person and facilitate the re-linking with the environment.

The therapeutic process also goes through several stages. Looking to the past, there is first an insight and acknowledgement of the death (imminent or past). Second, there is a mental cancellation of outstanding issues. In the present, there is a leave-taking ritual with the expression of contained feelings. Looking to the future, there is finally a search for some support in the outside environment, which may partially and potentially replace the lost person. Thus, there can be a return to the 'real' world and a new link to people who are still alive.

Here, we only present the most relevant data of the cases of bereavement. All cases of bereavement treated with psychodrama produced satisfactory outcomes, even the most severe ones. The risk of suicide or the presence of pseudo-psychotic symptomatology is usually misdiagnosed as major depression or psychosis (Filgueira Bouza 1989, 1990 and 1995).

Case studies

Female, 57 years old

She was hospitalized in a catatonic and stuporous state. Later on this appeared as 'paradoxical calmness' due to the 'shock' caused by her mother's death. The patient was confronted with her dead mother in an imaginary scene. The mother invites her to say goodbye two minutes before dying (the limit time technique to provoke a new reaction in an extreme situation). This allowed the patient to express the rancour she felt for having been abandoned. The venting itself implied the acknowledgement of loss. Once the denial of death disappeared, the normal process of bereavement could take place, followed by recovery.

Male, 60 years old

He was hospitalized after a severe suicide attempt, suffering from stress and uneasiness, which developed into a manic state with headaches, a creeping sensation and a feeling of fainting. This was diagnosed as major depression. He had made several suicide attempts after his son's recent death in a car accident. When he went into hospital he was in a state of 'hopelessness', with an intense loss of functionality. He had visual Lilliput hallucinations (he could see his son's friends as little men appearing in the grass while he was harvesting, and he needed to put them on one side, in order not to harm them). He suffered hypnagogic hallucinations (he could see the priest who buried his son, coming to pick him up) and auditory hallucinations (the voices of his other sons, who had emigrated to a far country, saying they were coming back home). He was then diagnosed as suffering from acute hallucinatory psychosis. A role reversal between the patient and his dead son led to the unblocking. In the role reversal the patient, playing his son, asked himself (the patient) to stop trying to regain him (the son) and to go on living and to turn his affection to his other sons and the rest of the family. As this request came from his 'favourite son', whom he (the patient) could refuse nothing, he found the necessary energy to make the effort, and start the re-link.

Female, 18 years old

She was treated as an outpatient for self-injuring emotional outbreaks, dizziness, fainting fits and loss of functionality after her sister's death in an accident, during a trip she (the patient) should have made instead of her sister. She wanted to kill herself to join her sister and was in a state of 'shock and denial'. We forced her to accept the death by organizing visits to the cemetery, the engraving of the headstone, candles in her sister's memory. We proposed an imaginary role reversal with her parents, the other brothers and sisters and friends, to make her feel the effects of her possible absence (if she killed herself). There, she found the reason to keep on living. She re-linked and recovered functionality.

Male, 59 years old

He was treated as an outpatient for bereavement. His wife had disappeared and he suspected she had committed suicide by throwing herself into the river, because she had a long history of depression and attempted suicide. He was undergoing the bereavement process in advance of acknowledgement of death, as his wife's body had not yet been found. We worked with his feelings of blame (he thought he should have controlled her more). Also he played out outstanding issues (what they were about he didn't say – he didn't do this with the deceased). Finally he could say farewell to a desired grandson, not yet born, and re-link with his daughter, in a future projection. There was an intense venting of emotion, with consequent full recovery of health and functionality. He did not have a relapse, as we had expected, when the corpse of his wife was found in the river a month later.

Conclusions

- Psychodrama is a useful means of recovering lost rites.
- It helps to unblock fixated situations of bereavement.
- It complements other therapies, such as psychopharmacology and individual psychotherapy.
- It can be implemented in moments of crisis, for instance, during psychiatric hospitalization.
- It can be applied within the family or in group settings with the same results.

From our experience, we have worked out a simple programme to help the primary care teams to unblock fixated bereavement situations. Rather than an actual therapeutic intervention, it is a preventive programme. If its application doesn't work, then one may proceed with psychodrama.

Programme for coping with bereavement

1. Comments on how much one misses the loved person may help with the acknowledgement of death and aid the patient to express contained emotions.

2. Informing the deceased what happened after he or she left may further acknowledge the loss and may improve acceptance and help connect the relative with his social environment.

3. Collecting the belongings of the dead person, or doing some of the things that the dead person would have done, may further help to internalize the loss (Espina Barrio 1995).

References

Espina Barrio, A.B. (1992) *Manual de Antropologia Cultural.* Salamanca: Amari.
Espina Barrio, J.A. (1993) 'El Cuerpo Muerto – Psicoterapia del Duelo: Individual, de Pareja, Familiar y Grupal.' *Informaciones Psiquiatricas 2 Trimestre,* 132, 275–285.
Espina Barrio, J.A. (1997) 'Psicodrama del Duelo.' *Journal of A.E.N. 64,* 275–285. Valladolid.

Feinstein, D. and Mayo, P.E. (1993) *Sobre el Vivir y el Morir – Un Programa de Afirmacion de la Vida para Enfrentarse a la Muerte.* Madrid: Edaf. (V.O., Mortal Acts)

Filgueira Bouza, M.S. (1989) 'Psicodrama: Intervenciones Focalizadas.' *Siso Saude 14*, 7–29.

Filgueira Bouza, M.S. (1990) 'Psicodrama: Intervenciones Focalizadas II.' *Siso Saude 15*, 36–54.

Filgueira Bouza, M.S. (1995) 'Psicodrama: Focal del Duelo Patologico.' *Informaciones Psiquiatricas 140*, 237–251.

Filgueira Bouza, M.S. (1996) *El Psicodrama Focal en la Practica Clinica.* (Unpublished.)

Filgueira M.S., Varea, L. and Gonzalez, A.I. (1996) *La Noche de San Juan: Una Perspectiva Psicodramatica.* La Coruna: Diputacion Provincial.

Lamas, S. and Filgueira, M.S. (1992) 'Pranto: Psicodrama Popular contra el Duelo Patologico.' *Vinculos 4*, 81–127.

Lamas, S. and Filgueira, M.S. (1998) 'El Carnaval de Laza: Psicodrama y Antropologia.' *Folklore 206*, 39–62.

PART 3

Traumatized People

From Victims to Survivors

CHAPTER 4

Psychodrama of Rape and Torture
A Sixteen-year Follow-up Case Study

Marcia Karp

The house of a woman and man living in Africa was violently broken into one night. Their seventeen-year-old daughter was visiting them. The man was shot in the leg; the woman and her daughter were raped and tortured. The two women escaped by courageously running into the night when the eight perpetrators were trying to repair their car. At that moment they thought the man, their husband and father, was dead. Miraculously, they were all reunited at a neighbour's house where they eventually ran for cover. The couple and their daughter went back to where they had been living before moving to Africa. The mother, aged 48, was treated with psychodrama two years after the event.

Sixteen years have now gone by. We have kept in touch since the treatment. With this chapter in mind, I interviewed the protagonist about what worked and what differences have occurred as a result of the psychodramas. The interviews are with the patient, Jill, her husband, with whom she lives, and their daughter. I shall discuss this event from four perspectives: an overview of what happened; an interview with the protagonist and her husband 16 years after the psychodrama; the psychodramatic interventions from the therapist's and protagonist's perspectives; and the theoretical considerations and applied techniques. The chapter concludes with the protagonist's summary.

What happened?

It is early in the 1980s when eight black African men shoot the lock off the security gate, then kill the dogs and enter a house belonging to a white couple and their 17-year old daughter who is visiting them. The couple had just returned from abroad. While they were away the government elected to oust from the country all those who were residing illegally in that part of Africa. Because of this government decision, their house guards were made illegal and had disappeared, leaving no protection on this particular night. The intention of the eight, who entered after midnight, was robbery. Some of the men had guns, some had machetes, and some had broken coke bottles as weapons. The law of the land at that time specified that robbery was punishable by death. 'You Rob, You Die', exclaimed police posters. Burglars, more often than not, used deadly violence to assure no witnesses survived to provide evidence. If caught, the thieves would be tied to poles, machine gunned, and their bodily remains thrown into the water. The eight were about to commit violence in a violent nation.

The following are the words of Jim, the husband, who had worked for three years in Africa.

Jim: When they finally broke through the doors and came upstairs we were still together. There was no way of putting up a defence against eight people who had guns and knives and everything you can imagine. We tried to throw mattresses down the stairs to block them coming up. We asked if we gave them money, would they go away? I gave them the grocery money from that week, but they just took it and climbed over the mattresses. I had a bow and arrow that I fired and it hit one of the guys in the chest. This infuriated them and they started shooting. I was shot in the leg. They bundled us down the stairs and the two girls were pushed away from me. I was shoved into the kitchen with two fellows, and that is where our stories split. I was unaware of anything that went on for a long time; your sense of time goes out the window. But I was fighting one chap who had a curved switchblade, the other one had pistols. I'd already been shot and was fighting these two guys. I kept close to them on the ground thinking that if I stayed close to them they wouldn't fire for fear of hitting the other one.

The gun went off, they hit me on the head with it and I lost consciousness. When I woke up I think they assumed I was dead and left me on the ground. They must have thought the bullet had killed me, but it hadn't, though my leg was spurting blood. I left through the door that led to the back yard. I could see and hear nothing. It was totally silent. I went to get help.

During this time, Jill was taken to another room and raped. They held broken bottles to her neck so she couldn't move, and then they rammed cane poles up her backside after the rape. She heard the gun go off where her husband was being held. They had dragged her 17-year-old daughter away. As they did so, her daughter said, 'Mummy I can handle this'. The daughter was raped in another room. The whole scenario took three hours.

Jill: The only reason I'm alive is that they couldn't start the car. They had Ruth and me on the floor. A fellow with a gun said, 'I'm going to kill you,' and somebody else yelled, 'You no move, I go, I come back and kill you.' They had done the damage and wanted to get rid of the evidence. We were the evidence. It was only when they loaded up the car they had stolen and tried to start it that we escaped.

I grabbed Ruth's hand and ran. Ruth wears contact lenses; without them she has poor eyesight so I kept hold of her hand. We started heading for our neighbour's house. I saw their fluorescent lights were on and I was afraid we'd be seen so we crawled under the fence, through the sewerage drain and crawled on our hands and knees under another fence to the house next door. Some men came running out with machetes. I thought they'd found us, but it turned out to be the guards at a house two doors away. When I looked up at the back door through the grill, I saw somebody at that door. I couldn't believe it. It was Jim. He thought we were dead, and we thought he was dead.

After the rape it was two days before we saw a doctor. He gave us a perfunctory examination after which we were supposed to fly straight back home. I had promised Ruth a holiday in the Ivory Coast, which was also my favourite, so we went. While there, Jim's arms and legs started swelling, and I thought, if this gets to his throat what is going to happen? I called the hotel's front desk for medical help. A tall black nurse came in response to my call. There was a knock at the door and a woman, about six foot three tall, was standing holding a needle about a foot long with anti-histamine. 'It is probably some allergy he has to the bullet,' she said, and injected him. A colleague of Jim's came in. We were standing on the balcony. This is two or three days after the rape, and we're looking down at somebody walking around the pool. He has a broken leg and walks with crutches. The colleague says, 'See Jill, you got off easy, that person's got a broken leg.' I nearly threw him over the balcony. I thought, 'What does he mean, he's got a broken leg. I'm not damaged?' Rape is not recognized by many to be as damaging as physical injury.

We didn't get psychiatric help until we were referred by our family doctor, and that was only because I was getting so depressed and going under. He said, 'Maybe we should send you to a psychiatrist.' 'Maybe we should send you' – it was an afterthought. We had been invited to business dinners and everybody would just act like, 'Oh, hi, you're back from Africa'. I couldn't handle it; I would just walk right out again. People don't want to hear about it. How can you talk about rape at a dinner party?

How the patient got to psychodrama

About two years after the event, after many medical consultations and conventional psychiatry and psychopharmacology, Jill's psychiatrist recommended psychodrama.

Jill: My depression was so bad I couldn't leave the house. I was taking 19 pills a day. They wanted to give me electric shock treatment. I went to the hospital and took a tour round and said, 'I want to go home, I don't like it here. I don't like the feeling of it and I don't want to be here.' The doctor said, 'I don't know what else to do, Jill. There's only one other thing I can think of and that's psychodrama. I can't really explain it; you have to do it. I'll give the therapist a call this evening and see what we can arrange.' I remember, Marcia, that you then called me that night and you told me you could see us for an individual session preliminary to group work.

The presenting problem

Jill: I had gone from a woman in control to a submissive nothing. I felt broken, like the padlock they shot off our gate. The padlock didn't work any more and neither did I. I lost part of my life. I was depressed and my physical condition was getting worse. It was a combination of that, and feeling such anger at Jim's business. They hadn't done anything to help or contacted us to see how we were doing. I just needed someone to care. His company never acknowledged what happened. They were the ones I hated. It's not just the rape; it's what was done to my mind. My mind was all screwed up. I didn't want to see anyone or go anywhere.
Ruth: Mom was afraid of everything. She couldn't shop for food, answer the telephone, talk to anyone, go to other people's houses; she was housebound. I was so worried about her. She just wanted to sit in the corner.

The psychodrama warm-up

Jill: We drove down to Devon and stayed overnight in a hotel. Marcia told me I'd have to stay two or three nights but Jim couldn't stay with me, and that upset me. Marcia met me at the train station, and then I came to Holwell. I was very scared, I couldn't sleep. The next morning we went to the theatre. There was this old room with pillows on the floor, lots of chairs and a little balcony like a pulpit. I wondered what I was walking into. There were around 10 or 12 other people there. I'm trying to recall what the problems were. There was a lady who hadn't said goodbye to her dead father, a man with marital problems, some nuns and someone from a prison, a psychiatrist from Argentina and my roommate, a psychologist from South Africa.

Marcia started talking to the group. There was interplay between her and the others and then they acted out some of the situations. I thought, I'll just sit here and watch this, I can always go home tonight. Then something happened. Marcia, who is always acutely aware of everything that is going on, looked at me and asked me to get up. I didn't want to. So Marcia told everyone to turn the other way so that they wouldn't look at me. I was very fearful of being looked at. I believe that was because when I was being raped, all the men were looking at me.

I don't know how it began, but we started going through what had happened and then people were making noises like the dogs, other people were making noises like the generator, it was as if I was back at the night of the rape. There were lights to make it seem real because when the armed robbers came in, there were fluorescent lights on at our house so it was lit up like Disneyworld. I was back there and it was happening again.

Marcia: How was that for you? To be in it again?

Jill: I was shaking and crying and I was so scared. The whole thing was very traumatic.

The therapist's perspective

From the first interview, I saw that Jill was numb and frightened. My responsibility as her guide through this unfortunate material was not to re-traumatize her. I remember thinking, after meeting Jill and Jim, 'What could possibly be helpful after the power of what has happened to them?'

Green (1994) found that in general, only a quarter of us will develop full-blown PTSD after exposure to trauma, and half of those people will improve over time, even without treatment. Green stated, however, that rape caused higher rates of PTSD and that it was harder to recover from human-caused trauma. The type of traumatic event influences the number of people who will develop PTSD and rape has consistently been found to pose the greatest risk for its development. In fact, Resnick *et al.* (1993) found that when rape caused physical injury and was life threatening, almost 80 per cent of victims developed PTSD.

I felt extremely protective of Jill from the outset. She was like a fragile flower whose petals mustn't be bent, but I sensed that a strong fertilizer was needed to help her grow. Would a group be too much for her? Would leaving Jim, on whom she depended for her life force, be possible? What would she be like after nights and days in a strange setting away from what was familiar and safe?

In fact, my experience, confirmed by colleagues, is that torture victims, who make a decision never to reveal what happened to them, only get better when the power of secrecy is broken. They need to permit themselves to contravene their own vow by sharing the totality of the experience with others in a safe setting. In Jill's case, she had the courage to try to find safe places, but members of society had severely and repeatedly disappointed her. This added insult to injury, and to her was additional abuse. People were so shocked that they either didn't want to hear about it or couldn't deal with it, thus creating further isolation and depression.

My first sense was to tackle the many video tapes playing in her head about what she wished she would and could have done to prevent her daughter from being raped, her husband from being shot and the dogs from being killed. I somehow imagined that Jill's need would be to ventilate unexpressed thoughts and emotions to the perpetrators. She seemed uninterested, as if that was not her task. A more primary task was to show us a sequential account of what happened, while she narrated. It felt as if the whole event had not been unravelled in such a complete way, with herself safely distanced from it. The 'what-if' scenarios were a constant and major preoccupation, so we dealt with them one at a time.

The 'surplus reality,' the 'what-ifs' in Jill's mind, filled her nights and meaningless days. This obsession with what Jill had been unable to prevent because of her powerlessness, and subsequent self-accusation, justifies a basic psychodramatic concept that the deepest catharsis is often achieved by completing those actions or relationships which life may never permit. Taking the protagonist into this reality potentially leads to three steps in psychodrama: doing, un-doing and re-doing. As Jill narrated the re-doing, she allowed the group members who had listened to her with their backs turned to face her. This was an important moment in the development of Jill's trust. Then the group enacted each scene, taking them seriously as an option to survival.

Psychodramatic enactment – the 'what-ifs'

Scene I: Hiding Ruth

Jill wished she had hidden her daughter Ruth under the bed. She picked two auxiliaries to play herself and Ruth and then proceeded to hide Ruth under the bed. Jill picked this particular bed because it had slats and holes in it. When Ruth was put under a series of chairs to represent that bed, I asked Jill: 'How long would she have been under the bed?' Jill answered 'Three hours,' and realized at once, out loud, 'Ruth may not have had enough air to survive'.

Scene II: Protecting her husband

Jill picked someone to play her husband and seven men and one woman to be the perpetrators. As they dragged Jim away, she instructed the auxiliary portraying herself to hold on to him. She saw how impossible it was to prevent the perpetrators from dragging him away. She was helpless against eight armed men.

Scene III: Protecting the dogs

Jill picked two members of the group to be the family dogs, and the same group members as before maintained the perpetrator roles. The auxiliary ego Jill went out to bring the dogs in as she first entered the house. Minutes later the perpetrators broke in, found the barking dogs, and killed them.

Summary of 'what-ifs'

Exploring, in action, her options of control was managed well by the group, respectfully and with that quiet honouring that individuals can achieve when the frailty of the other is plainly seen.

It is interesting to note that in Scene I, a partial representation of the real bed was all that was needed for the protagonist to release her guilt. In Scene II her replayed attempt to overcome her helplessness proved to be in vain. In Scene III she realized the dogs would have been killed only minutes later, whatever she had done.

Implicit but not verbalized, it became clear that if Jill had resisted in any scene, she would have been killed on the spot.

The enactment of actual events

Scene IV

Having relieved herself of the 'what-ifs' the protagonist was now motivated to show us sequentially what actually happened. The same auxiliary egos were used.

Scene IV opened with the beginning of the night, as it occurred, moment by moment. The big step forward was not only that Jill was able to look at the reality of her trauma, but also that she became ready to become an actor in her own psychodrama. She never took her own role; however, when she showed us where in the room her daughter was held as she was dragged away to be raped, I asked Jill if she was willing to take the role of her daughter. She agreed and stepped into the action, relieving the auxiliary from Ruth's role. Then I asked her, 'Ruth, what do you mean when you say "Mummy, I can handle this"?' She looked at me and said, 'I mean, the one thing I want is for my Mum to stay alive. I can look after myself and I want her to look after herself.' Jill in that role reversal learned that she successfully did the one thing her daughter wanted her to do. She stayed alive. Not only did she do that, but she also picked the one possible moment that she could have escaped with her daughter and ran, successfully, and kept them both alive.

The enactment of farewell and closure in surplus reality

Scene V

Jill and Jim came to see me one month later for a follow-up group. By then, Jim had developed confidence in the process as well.

Because of their precipitate departure, there was no opportunity in life to establish proper closure with their much-loved house servants, the ones that stayed and the guards who had to leave. This farewell was part of a closure process that was missing. The couple was worried about the welfare of their staff members and wished to acknowledge their gratitude for the good care these people had given them over the time of their stay in Africa. They had literally been ripped apart from each other and the couple wished to repair that.

The scene began with Jill and Jim taking all the roles of the staff members, expressing how sorry they were, as staff, that this trauma had occurred. The scene took place standing outside their home in Africa.

The couple then selected group members to take the roles presented. Jill and Jim were now in their own roles, and faced the auxiliary egos as their staff.

This was the first time that Jill played herself in a scene that returned to the African setting. What was striking was that she did not blame anyone but expressed her distress at the anguish these events may have caused. It is essential to note that this had been her social 'atom', as she was actively involved with the black community, assisting in mother-and-child care.

Therapist's observations and review of the therapeutic process

Marcia: To sum up our therapeutic interaction from the beginning: First we had a phone call, then an individual session with you and Jim in preparation for your work in the group. Next, a residential weekend in which you had a three-hour psychodrama, and one month later, you and Jim, during a residential weekend, established closure on the events in Africa in psychodrama. Can we begin by reviewing your first session and your physical response to it.

Jill: After the first three-hour session, I remember going back to my room. The Argentine psychiatrist came in and said, 'Jill, don't worry about the shaking, that's good for you, just keep shaking'.

Marcia: You could not bear anyone behind you. We had to readjust the stage so that absolutely nobody touched you unexpectedly, and nobody came from behind. That was very frightening for you. At the beginning of the session you were paralysed with fear, then slowly you began to shake and then you really shook.

The shaking can be understood as the exact opposite of the frozen state that you were in since the event took place. You contained all the fear, guilt and horrors in your body, which were both impossible and dangerous to reveal during the original trauma. As you returned to the scene of the trauma, psychodramatically, and were protected by the safe environment, you could thoroughly experience that shaking. Catharsis is a purging of blocked and frozen emotions. This occurred quite naturally, without any prompting on my part. I recognized it, and did not disturb the process. It happened throughout this three-hour psychodrama, lasted for about an hour afterwards and then stopped. The trembling, emotional and physical release led to the second part of the catharsis, which was prolonged, and peaceful sleep. Shaking and trembling was a psychosomatic role you had not allowed yourself. It was made appropriate which led to your relaxed state.

Jill: Yes, even when I went to my room, the shaking happened again, just thinking about reliving it. While I was going through the psychodrama, I couldn't see any point in it. I thought, 'Why am I putting myself through this? It would have been a lot easier just to sit at home and not leave the house.' At the time I did not understand what it was doing. When I went home, Jim picked me up at the train station; I was somewhat of a zombie. I said I was too tired to talk about anything and went straight to bed. Jim knew nothing about psychodrama either so he was very anxious to know what had happened. The most amazing thing was that I slept for 30 hours. Jim was so concerned, he couldn't believe that I could just keep on sleeping. Finally he woke me and said, 'Do you know how long you've been asleep? Since you came back on Sunday and this is Tuesday morning.' I just couldn't believe it.

Marcia: What do you remember, Jim, of her coming back?

Jim: She had some elements of being a zombie, like in a partial trance state. She wasn't reacting to normal stimuli, visual or anything else. We went home and whereas one would return from a more normal experience wanting to talk about it, she didn't want to say anything. All she could do was climb between the sheets.

She hadn't slept well since Africa. She used to wake up at 2.45 every morning; that was the time of the attack. Whatever she had experienced at Holwell was emotionally draining. She was totally exhausted. It was 30 hours of deep sleep.

Why did psychodrama help?

Psychodrama provided new visualizations and new verbalizations to substitute for trauma associated states. In the book entitled *Traumatic Stress: The Effects of Overwhelming Experience on Mind, Body and Society*, van der Kolk states:

> Post-Traumatic Stress Disorder occurs because of a person's inability to process a traumatic experience adequately. Treatment for the pathological elements associated with the fear structures of anxiety-disordered people should modify these elements and two conditions would be required after the reduction of fear: activation of the fear memory and provision of new information including elements that are incompatible with existing pathological elements in the structure so that a new memory can be formed (van der Kolk, McFarlane and Weisath 1996).

The treatment recommendations in the book are based on empirical research and recent neurophysiological results from PET scans. 'Psychodrama can activate the fear memory but should not re-traumatise. It can empower the person by contracting new states of mind during the trauma scenes and can encourage new visualisations and new verbalisations to substitute the trauma associated states' (Hug 1998, personal communication).

Marcia: We, as humans, tend to look at our failures more than we look at our successes in life. What happened that changed you from a woman who stayed in the house, was petrified to go out, to be with people, to one who is able to go out alone in the dark, drives everywhere, meets people, has parties, is very sociable and lives a relatively normal life?

Jill: I think reliving it and being in control was the key, because before I was not in control, they were. One of the things that bothered me so much was my daughter. When they put the gun to my head, and she said, 'Mummy, I can handle this,' that bothered me dreadfully. They took her away from me and I couldn't do anything to help her. Then in psychodrama we enacted that, turned it around the other way. It wasn't that I'd let my daughter down. It was that my daughter had wanted us both to survive. I did stay alive. By re-enacting it, I could see a different way of looking at it. I saw it from Ruth's point of view and that made me feel stronger. I still do feel some guilt but up to that point I felt I had let her down and that was very difficult to live with.

Marcia: What else did you see or feel differently when you were in the role of your daughter and said, 'Mummy, I can handle this'?

Jill: Ruth didn't want a dead mother and she was reassuring me that she could handle herself. If I had been dead, Ruth would have been devastated and I hadn't thought of it that way.

Marcia: So as a mother, you thought, 'I would be devastated if something happened to her,' but what you hadn't perceived was that she would be devastated if something happened to you?

Jill: That was it. At the time I believed that Jim was dead as well. When we enacted it, Jim was not dead. Prior to the psychodrama, the only time I went out of the house was with him to make sure he would come back.

Marcia: Are you saying that when we re-enacted the scene you realized that Jim was shot in the leg and, in actual fact, he was still alive, not dead as you had imagined?

Jill: Yes, he was shot in the leg. They fought with him in the kitchen with a knife and a gun. The gun went off while one of the men was raping me. Jim had been concussed and, I guess, fell to the ground. One of the men said to me, 'He's dead. They've killed your husband. You're next.' I just expected to be next and I ... I had to relive it again and realize that he wasn't dead and that Ruth wasn't dead and that we were alive.

I found it very interesting that a friend I had known for many years, a reporter, used to call me up after Africa and ask, 'Jill why don't you go out?' I said, 'I can't, I don't want to go anywhere.' He called back about a week after I'd been to psychodrama and said, 'What's happened to you?' I asked him what he meant. He said, 'Your voice, it's changed; you're different.'

Marcia: Do you remember, Jim, the time when Jill became more mobile after sleeping 30 hours?

Jim: It happened within a reasonable space of time; in other words, it happened closely enough to psychodrama to put a cause and effect to it. Maybe it was a couple of weeks, more or less. It was an array of things. Slightly less dependence on me, a greater ability to act on her own when we went out, in other words, to move into situations which she had avoided in the previous couple of years.

Marcia: Jill, I want to ask you a point blank question because the readers may be asking this question too. Did you say to yourself, 'What is this psychodrama? Something has worked here,' or did you think, 'Ah, they've got the medication correct finally,' or did you think the combination of the medication with psychodrama and your psychiatric visits – you were being seen one to one at that point, and taking anti-depressants – that together it all worked?'

Jill: It changed because I stopped taking some of the medication. I went down to three pills, two of those were sleeping pills and one was an anti-depressant. In the week afterwards, I said to my psychiatrist, 'I'm fed up with all these pills ... Now I feel different.' I had a big grey blanket over me and it was soaking wet; somebody removed it. That was the feeling that I got after the psychodramas. Well, maybe a big grey cloud, but it was just as if I was walking around with my own little personal cloud, which would not leave me. But then all of a sudden, the sun shone and it felt better and better.

Marcia: Analyst Malcolm Pines [1989, personal communication] did some research when he was a young registrar working for an insurance company. He made a study of people who had automobile accidents. Some retain their symptoms and some move on quite quickly from the experience. The question in the study was 'Why?' The study showed that people who are used to having control over their own life do worse when a trauma occurs. People who are followers, people who don't create their own lives, are used to changing direction, and do better. Other people and circumstances already control them. Those used to being their own master, controlling their own destiny when this trauma comes out of the blue, have much more difficulty recovering from it. Would you say that you fit into that category, Jill?

Jill: Yes, the category of having to be in charge, because of the independent nature of my work, is definitely me. The morning after it happened I was in charge. I called the Embassy and got hold of the doctor while someone was trying to stem the flow of blood from Jim's leg. I gave them hell, I told them what I thought about them when they wouldn't come to the house. Two of the doctors wouldn't come without police escorts and I told them they were both hypocrites. I refused to see a doctor at the Embassy because he would not come, even with guards. Jim finally saw a doctor, a friend of ours, who took care of his leg.

He wouldn't examine Ruth and me because he felt that, as a black doctor and personal friend, it was too traumatic for him to touch me. It wasn't until we got back home about four days later that we were sent to the Venereal Disease Hospital located in a major London teaching hospital.

Jill was horrified and embarrassed to find herself and her daughter publicly classified as belonging to a group of people who, to coin a Victorian phrase, were no better than they should be. It was a significant after-shock, and should have been handled privately to avoid further trauma to an already traumatic situation.

Jill: It was at that time I started feeling that I was going down. It steadily got worse and worse.

Marcia: Do you think you dealt with the situation as a person in control, but after that life stem of emotional strength was cut off, somehow you dwindled in your psychological vitality, your ability to have confidence in yourself, your ability to cope and be in control? Does that make sense?

Jill: Yes, I was so much in control after it had happened. One of our neighbours had come over. She had heard the noise. All the generators were on but she had heard this yelling for help. She said she really didn't feel she could do anything. I was so mad I picked up a yam pounder, a stick about three feet long they used for pounding yams, and I started chasing her. Our next door neighbour just caught me before I would have hit her on the head with it. I went from being like that to being completely submissive, a nothing. I was like a sponge; you could do anything with me. Immediately afterwards it was all still there – but then it just went, it all drained out of me.

Marcia: After the first psychodrama with Jill, you, Jim, returned with her one month later for a follow-up residential group. Do you remember your impressions?

Jim: Well, I was immensely interested in just what had happened, what had caused Jill to react the way she did. My reaction was that there were extremely powerful emotional forces let loose which, unless the person running the psychodrama remained totally in control, could be almost dangerous. It's like lighting a fire, but you were the buckets of water standing by, to put it out if it got out of control. I was very impressed by the strength of the various emotions that people let loose and I felt then that the reason Jill has come to this turn-around situation was in allowing some of this stuff to come out.

I've thought a lot about this since. Psychodrama provides what blood-letting used to in the 19th century in a controlled situation, whereas I found that the release of emotions, just in a general sense, could be quite destructive for family or society, if it's just allowed to come randomly. This is a con-trolled, guided situation.

Recurrence of post-traumatic stress

After the psychodramatic treatment, psychotherapy was maintained between Jill and a new psychiatrist. There were occasional telephone and individual face-to-face contacts with me during that time.

Marcia: When you had a recurrence of post-traumatic stress disorder years later, what were your symptoms? Did you get frightened and anxious again? I remember you phoned me in Britain, but let's remind ourselves of those symptoms at that time.

Jill: I couldn't do anything. I was just completely numb again. I was a zombie. I was crying and all I wanted to do was pull the covers over me and sleep. I didn't want to see anyone, I didn't want to go anywhere, and I couldn't react to anything. I had no feeling and Jim took me to the doctor. He said, 'I want to put you in hospital.' I said, 'No, I can't go, I can't leave my cats, my husband.' But in two hours I was in the hospital. I was completely numb. I don't remember any part of it.

Marcia: Jim, you are a witness to how she was prior to this hospitalization and a witness to after the incident in Africa. Were there similarities? Was this an anniversary reaction? Or what?

Jim: There were certain similarities as Jill has described, but what she has left out is that shortly before this outbreak we worried how all this treatment would be paid, and that seemed to lead into this disorder.

Jill: There is another thing that is so important. Before this, Ruth called up and asked for help. She'd never had any psychiatric counselling. She rather pooh-poohed the idea of anything being wrong with her and her not being able to handle it. I was very concerned about her. The doctors talked about 'the resilience of youth', but it concerned me. I felt that Ruth was not emotionally maturing, she was physically maturing but not emotionally. She was stunted, I thought. When she telephoned and said, 'Mummy, I need help,' I just broke down because we were not in a financial position to help her.

Marcia: But that was also what you were dreading all those years?

Jill: I feared this was going to happen one day. I didn't believe in the resilience of youth. It just doesn't get put away and forgotten about. It's there all the time. She wanted help, she was crying out for help, and I had to help her, but financially how were we to do this? I don't know whether it was the emotional strain of having to go through this, or having to explain again to everybody what happened, or having to tell them that my daughter was in a very bad situation. I just couldn't cope any more.

I wish when I'd had the post-traumatic stress disorder, that I had been able to go to psychodrama. I really felt that going into hospital and them giving me medication and turning me into a zombie didn't help me, it didn't get it out of me, it didn't solve anything. We had some verbal therapy but it wasn't dramatic. It didn't dig into me, it didn't get the things out of me and when I came out of hospital – I think it was about three weeks later – I didn't feel the relief I felt after psychodrama. Medication is not the answer for me. It's psychodrama. It was able to get everything out without medication. But to be put into hospital ... That didn't do it. I don't think it helped me. My doctor would probably disagree with me, but I don't think it did.

Marcia: So what you're saying is that the hospitalization submerged or suppressed the passion, the fear, the anger, and whatever, so you could get by day by day with medication. What psychodrama did was to say: 'Let's actually attenuate, or turn up the dial on all those feelings, thoughts and memories,' and what medication did was turn the dial down on them. Maybe that's the difference.

Jill: In hospital I had two sessions per week, but it was one on one, it wasn't re-enactment, it was a recitation with more pills. The reality was not there. It was like telling a story, whereas in psychodrama you relive it. The difference is between telling a story and re-living it. In reliving it you go through the emotions; otherwise it's just like reading out of a book, it doesn't have the same impact. When you're talking about it, you are just a submissive person discussing it. But when you're re-enacting it, you have to be in control because you have to say: 'All right, if I had my choice this is what I would have done'. Psychodrama gives you the feedback in the action that you don't get talking about it. It gets it out of you.

Marcia: I wonder if seeing yourself from a distance whilst you narrated the scenes for others to enact in the drama enabled you to regain control and somehow retain your sanity in the situation. The observer/spectator role was given back to you to balance out the role of the actor; before you had only been in the heat of the action. Distancing enabled you to become the director of the action as well as the observer of the action. Up until that point, you couldn't get yourself out of the role of actor.

In the exclusive role of the actor, one can get stuck. The distinction between verbal therapy and action therapy is that verbal therapy activates the spectator/observer where action therapy, such as psychodrama, activates all three components of the personality: the director, actor, observer. In his paper on psychodrama and trauma, Kipper writes:

> Exposure to a terrifying experience freezes the formal biochemical, physical, perceptual, cognitive, emotional, psychological and behavioural processes. That results in an adverse effect on the neuro-transmitters and a disruption of brain pathways and leaves sensorimotor memory unprocessed. Simultaneously, it encourages primary thinking process, distorted object relations, disassociated intense affect, primitive defences, and uncontrolled re-experiencing behaviours. In other words, such experiences were registered primarily on the sensorimotor level. With their research, van der Kolk and his collaborators demonstrated that such (emotionally) overwhelming experiences have never been properly coded and, therefore, could not have been removed from intellectually coded memory. Rather than being repressed, they are stuck on the sensorimotor level. To retrieve such painful memories, one needs to use methods of treatment that address sensorimotor memories by invoking the experiences on the level on which they would have been stored (1998, p.116).

Restating van der Kolk, Jill re-visualized, using new verbalizations and thought processes to substitute the old state of mind, thereby contracting a new state of mind about the very same situation. If the brain can restructure traumatic experience and memory, we have hope for the future in treating severe cases like Jill's.

Summary: theoretical considerations and applied techniques

In addition to the principles of psychodrama with sexually abused adults that were first described in Karp (1991), I shall here emphasise three theoretical considerations and their applied techniques: restoration of control and safety; reducing guilt and shame; and empowerment.

Restoring control and safety

Dr Judith Herman in *Trauma and Recovery* states:

> Trauma robs the victim of a sense of power and control: the guiding prin- ciple of recovery is to restore power and control to the survivor. The first task of recovery is to establish the survivor's safety. This task takes prece- dence over all others, for no other therapeutic work should even be attempted until a reasonable degree of safety has been achieved (1992, p.159).

TECHNIQUES USED FOR SAFETY FIRST AND THEN CONTROL

Immediate attention was paid to Jill's needs, making sure they were heard and met. A quick response was made to her doctor's call for help and I made myself accessible. She was first allowed to watch others participate in action before she entered the stage space. Because of her fear the group was asked to turn their backs on her at first until she was ready to be seen. In order not to relive the trauma, the protagonist was invited to tell the story and co-direct the subsequent enactment. The distance provided safety. She instructed and watched group members play out her scenes, occasionally entering the scene to correct the action. For example, Jill entered the scene because a broken bottle held to her neck, represented by someone's shoe, was held in the wrong place. She corrected it and exited the scene. For the event to see the light of day, it had to be represented exactly as it happened and with her in control of the information.

The 'what-if' scenarios gave the protagonist opportunities to make the changes and to manage uncontrollable events, expanding the zones of safety and control. Even though she learned that these changes would not have protected her loved ones, Jill was enabled to experience control. Thus she was prepared to co-direct the psychodrama of the actual events without her safety and control being shattered.

Reducing guilt and shame

'Victims of rape and torture should have therapeutic debriefing as standard procedure whenever there is a crisis or traumatic incident' (Parkinson 1993, p.7). Reviewing the rape scenario after the fact, many women reported ignoring their own initial perceptions of danger, thereby losing the opportunity for escape. Fear of conflict or social embarrassment may prevent victims from taking action in time. Later, survivors who have disregarded their own 'inner voice' may be furiously critical of their own 'stupidity or naivety'. Transforming this harsh self-blame into a realistic judgement may in fact enhance recovery. According to Herman, 'The essential element of rape is physical, psychological and moral violation of the person. Violation is a synonym for rape. The purpose of the rapist is to terrorise, dominate and humiliate his victim to render her utterly helpless. Thus rape, by its very nature, is intentionally designed to produce psychological trauma' (1992, p.57).

TECHNIQUES TO REDUCE GUILT AND SHAME

Role-reversal with Ruth was the main tool used to reduce the mother's guilt about her daughter being raped. In life itself she could only be herself. In psychodrama she could take the role of the significant other that most concerned her. The role reversal gave her a perspective that she had not had before. By trying to protect her daughter she was endangering her own life. Her daughter did not want protection at that price. Jill stayed alive and protected Ruth against the ultimate guilt of being responsible for her mother's death.

The enactment of the escape scene in which Jill managed to maintain enough control to escape and save her daughter and herself, and the realization that she was in fact in control, reduced shame and guilt. Reviewing and re-experiencing survival helped Jill own her pride in saving her life and that of her daughter. A concomitant result of this was a later resolution and commitment to help her daughter recover with psychological guidance.

THE RESTORATION OF THE PROTAGONIST'S CENTRAL ROLE STRUCTURE

A number of central roles were threatened and obliterated during the rape and torture. The role of protector, mother, wife and woman were eradicated and replaced by the role of victim. The loss and guilt had to be faced first, then the actual role of victim, and released by restoring Jill's control in the situation. After the guilt and failure in these roles was expiated through the psychodrama, she was able to reclaim the dignity and value of the central roles of mother, wife and so forth.

Empowerment

For some, the process of re-empowerment is a re-kindling of hope. Trauma imbalances the entire human organism. The mind and body tremble with fear and horror. Despair erases the present and the potential for the future, as emphasised by Herman: 'Empowerment and reconnection are the core experiences of recovery. She begins to take concrete steps to increase her sense of power and control to protect herself against future danger and to deepen her alliances with those whom she has learned to trust' (1992, p.197).

Techniques of empowerment

The protagonist's story was believed, not denied or swept aside. The group appreciated the true impact of these events. The protagonist was able to determine her own time and space. She decided where she stood in the room, and with whom. She entered, moved about and exited the stage at her own discretion. She became the central figure in the psychodrama where before she had been used as an object.

In the actual event she was alone; within the psychodramatic format she had co-actors who went through a common experience with her and could then share the impact of these horrible events. Removing the roles from the auxiliary egos that played the perpetrators helped her distance herself from the total involvement of the traumatic events. Group members resumed their own identities as members of the therapeutic group. They were acknowledged and thanked for their help in restoring her power.

The protagonist's summing up

When I asked Jill how psychodrama helped her recovery from rape and torture, her response was: 'I had to relive it again to fully realize that Jim, Ruth and I were not dead, that we remained alive. The reliving of that night and being in control was the key, because when it happened I was not in control of anything. If I had died, Ruth would have been devastated. I had not thought of it that way. I stayed alive, which is the only thing she wanted. The difference is in telling a story and re-living it. With the one to one psychiatrist, I was a narrator. In psychodrama I was actively participating and I had the control to change the events.'

Jill, her husband and married daughter are still close, growing and enjoying this journey we call life.

References

Green, B.L. (1994) 'Psychosocial research in traumatic stress: an update.' *Journal of Traumatic Stress 7*, 24.

Herman, J. (1992) *Trauma and Recovery*. New York: Basic Books.

Karp, M. (1991) 'Psychodrama and piccalilli: residential treatment of a sexually abused adult.' In P. Holmes and M. Karp (eds) *Psychodrama: Inspiration and Technique*. London: Tavistock/Routledge.

Kipper, D. (1998) 'Psychodrama and trauma: implications for future interventions of psychodramatic role-playing modalities.' *The International Journal of Action Methods, Psychodrama, Skill Training and Role Playing 51*, 3, 113–121.

Parkinson, F. (1993) *Posttraumatic Stress*. Arizona: Fisher Books.

Resnick, H.S., Kilpatrick, D.G., Dansky, B.S., Saunders, B.E. and Best, C.L. (1993) 'Prevalence of civilian trauma and posttraumatic stress disorder in a representative national sample of women.' *Journal of Consulting and Clinical Psychology 61*, 984–991.

van der Kolk, B.A., McFarlane, A.C. and Weisath, L. (eds) (1996) *Traumatic Stress: The Effects of Overwhelming Experience on Mind, Body and Society*. New York: Guilford Press.

CHAPTER 5

The Use of Psychodrama with Trauma Victims

Eva Røine

Maria's psychodrama, in her own words[1]

I have tried to describe a psychodrama with Eva Røine. It is about my early childhood when my uncle abused me sexually. It may seem that the drama moves forward very quickly, but there is more between these lines than meets the eye of the reader. I am afraid of my inner secrets but I also want to reveal them.

The first protagonist of the day is about to be chosen. I close my eyes and silently pray: 'Do not let it be me today!' The truth is, however, that if I really had not wanted to be chosen, I would not have been sitting with the group in the circle. But I was.

A warm hand is placed on my shoulder. I close my eyes again. More hands are put on both shoulders. I open my eyes, look around, and count; one, two, three, four choices. Once more, I close my eyes with the knowledge that my drama will be staged today. I have clenched teeth, shallow breath, and clammy hands. I feel cold. My body is obviously resisting. It seems to know that I am going to uncover secrets that I have been hiding for so long. I take a deep breath and stand up. I leave the circle and walk across the floor. The group shifts into a circle around the stage. The lights are turned on, and I find myself on a little stage. I have a leader who will lead me through the drama and I have Eva who will supervise the leader. I also have the circle of people who will stay and help enact my drama with me. I feel that I am in safe hands,

---

1   Maria's narrative is translated by Ann Zwick

but I am also very frightened because it will now be difficult to continue to hide much longer.

'What is your theme today?' I am asked. 'I want to be free. I want to have the courage to live fully. I want to show who I am,' I reply. 'Can you recall a scene about this and show us?'

I remember a scene that is not so painful. I am about 10 years old. The teacher is telling me that I am stupid and that I will never amount to anything. We set up a classroom to enact the scene.

'No,' says Eva, 'we have to find a different scene.'

I again escape to a scene in which my father brings me to the orphanage. We try to play out a little of this scene. I cry about my longing for love that was not there and about the desire to be seen. Eva looks at me and says, 'I think we should look for another picture'.

I know which one. I knew it before I walked over to the stage. It is painful. My body fights against it and sobbing takes over as soon as I realize what I am about to enter. I want to run away, but I also want to be here. I know that this has to be done and that I have to let it out.

I feel naked, looking at the others for a clue about what they are thinking. Their faces and eyes seem to convey understanding. They see my pain. I feel warmth, love and certainty that this will help carry me through this drama. I feel reassured and safe.

I describe my parents' bedroom, showing where the door was, the window, the bureau, the bedside tables, the closet and the bed, crying the whole time. I am being torn apart and strongly resisting all that is coming to life around me and within me.

'Can you sit on the bed?' 'Yes,' I respond. Eva says, 'Just cry and let it out. When you are ready, I want you to lie down on the bed.'

Once again, I want to run out of the room. It is so realistic, as if I am back there. All the old feelings well up inside me and I am afraid that I'll make myself disappear, shut myself off, the way I always have. I can't really believe that this will loosen the barriers.

I heard a voice saying: 'This time you will not flee inside of yourself. You will react!' I lie down and cry. I am still afraid, feeling humiliation, desperation and shame.

The person I have chosen to play the part of my uncle enters the room. In a way, I seem to be travelling through time. I am in the here and now but at the same time, all of this sends me back to a different situation in the past. I know what I want to do. I know very well why I am here.

'When your uncle walks towards you and when he begins to talk to you and to touch you, I want you to protest, and say "no"'' Saying no? Maybe I can do it, I think. My body resists but I attempt a silent 'no'. 'Say it louder!' I am instructed. 'No,' I say a little louder; and convulsive sobs well up from my stomach. Then something happens that I thought would never happen. From the depth of my innermost being, I suddenly feel rage and I start to scream: 'NO! ... NO! ... NO!'

Then comes a violent flood of tears that I had held back for more than 30 years.

A woman from the group whom I had chosen to represent my mother approaches the bed and puts her arms around me. She cries with me and gives me the love that I never had. It feels very good. While in her arms, I encounter the little child within me. I sob heavily and intensely. I can feel the warmth from mother and hear her comforting words. She is embracing me with compassion and she is crying her own tears of desperation over all that had happened. We stay that way together on the bed until I breathe more easily and the crying has eased. I sit up, utterly exhausted. It feels like I have moved a mountain.

'Could I ask you to join me for one more scene?' Eva says. 'Yes,' I answer automatically despite my fear. I am less resistant now. I might just be too tired to resist. I have felt rage, sorrow, humiliation, shame, desperation and bitterness and the loneliness of a child. I have carried a heavy burden by myself, believing that there is nobody in this enormous world that can help. In a sense, the child in me thought that this is the way the world is.

These thoughts go through my head as I stand in front of the group. Now I have revealed it all. But then I realize that there is nothing to fear any more. Nobody will judge me and I can be safe here.

I know that this will be an intense scene. My director and I are asked to leave the room. Eva comes out to tell us that she has set up a scene in which my daughter is lying in bed and that my uncle is there and will attempt to abuse her.

'Now I want you to go in there and react to what you see!' I tell her that I don't think I can do it because I fear that it will be a dreadful sight. 'Go in when you are ready,' Eva says.

I take a deep breath and try to collect my strength. Despite my fears, I stand up and enter the room cautiously. As I enter the room, something strange happens. It is as if someone has released a magical spell within me. The sense of time and the sense of location lose their grip on reality and I start to perceive the same disgusting filth as I had before. Then I react. I remember my thoughts as I rapidly approach the bed: 'He must see that I am furious. He must get up and run away.' Then I see that he has recognized me and that he is afraid of my anger.

I cannot recall everything I said. I know that I drove him from the bed, that I shouted at him, chasing him around the room while cursing him vehemently. I told him what a swine he was. How could he? Then I threw him out of the room, slamming the door behind him with all my strength. Still holding the handle, I stayed by the door for a while crying in despair over this man.

My daughter comes towards me and I embrace her. I understand that I am now giving her the love and warmth that I myself would have wished to receive back then and there. With a sense of completion, the past and the present seem to fuse together.

My drama ends here. Exhausted and drained, but also happy and relieved, I slowly return to the group. I have disclosed my secret and I have been able to say 'No!' My thoughts and feelings were received with a great deal of love and respect.

As a child, I had been both in individual and in family counselling. At that time, I was not aware of the events surrounding my uncle's abuse. The first time in my life when I could bring this to the surface, although my parents learned about it when I was around 12, was when I was 17 or 18 years old. Much later, as an adult, I started to deal with these experiences more seriously and went to a psychologist for many years. I talked and talked but never got behind the words and into my feelings, not because I didn't want to, but because as a child I had learned well how to escape from my feelings and how to disappear inside myself in order to avoid facing reality. I had also learned, when I was far too young, that the world was evil. As a result, I had to carry my shame by myself and try my best to cope with things alone.

Working together in a group increased the effect of the healing process. The group encouraged me and provoked me to disclose what I had kept within for so many years. I doubt that the emotional impact would have been as powerful in individual therapy. The public display of pain and vulnerability was in itself rewarding, since the group received my presentation with acceptance and love. In two psychodrama sessions, I feel as if I have released more feelings and more of myself than I have done during the past 20 years of therapy.

Three weeks have passed since my last drama. I have been tired but am very optimistic about the future. I have found faith in the fact that I will live more fully and that I have the courage to show others who I am. A few days after my last drama, when I was fetching my two youngest children from kindergarten, I became aware of a new sense of inner freedom. As the three of us were having fun together, I suddenly felt a bubbling laughter emerge from the very depths of my being — a light, warm and heartfelt laughter I had never known before. Right then and there, I knew why.

The setting

Maria's story of her psychodrama illustrates how we work with deep traumas at the Norwegian Psychodrama Institute. She described how she experienced the drama, from the first reluctant steps and avoidance strategies to the point where she entered the painful events. Maria said afterwards that she knew that she was ready at this time to disclose the most vulnerable part of her life's drama. She still participates in such groups to work through other problems but we both know that she will not have to come back and work on the 'old story' again. It is amazing how she has changed. She speaks confidently and allows herself to show more of her feminine side. In fact, she has become a real beauty.

Maria had attended the so-called 'on-site' supervision and therapy groups that the Institute offers to the public. Groups such as this have been an integral part of the Institute for the past ten years and have created a widespread psychodrama network throughout Norway. The groups run from Friday evening until Sunday evening and encompass some 20 hours of therapy and training. Participants come from all parts of Norway. Professionals refer some people while members who have benefited from this group experience in the past refer others. The circumstances of people coming to these groups are somewhat special and may lead to surprises on the first evening when new and old members meet and group cohesion is established. In order for the group to become a safe haven for people with deep emotional pain, unconditional acceptance of each participant is essential. An oath of confidentiality is therefore introduced at the beginning of every weekend along with a small ceremony to establish tele and encourage trust.

This experimental setting with a mixture of therapy and training has proved to be very helpful for both group members and students alike. It lets group members see first hand how powerful psychodrama can be while providing excellent training for three students from the Institute who get a chance to work together with a senior trainer/therapist under direct 'in-vivo' supervision. The students direct the sessions with the senior director intervening when necessary to deepen the process. A process analysis is done after each session with the three students and senior trainer taking part, but without the presence of the other group members.

Retraumatization

When working with traumatized populations, the question of retraumatization is frequently discussed both in Norway and elsewhere. Such a discussion invariably raises the question of whether psychodrama treatment of trauma is contraindicated. While there seem to be some professionals that warn against conducting psychodrama with traumatized populations, others suggest that this approach is one of the most effective for alleviating the pain patients endure from such experiences. This latter view is also our own position and we disagree with the allegations that psychodrama leads to retraumatization and revictimization. Ildri Ginn, the director of the Boston Psychodrama Institute and a primary trainer at our yearly summer seminars, says:

> The trauma sits as a character pattern in the body. It has to be worked out. We must find the language of the body and follow it without pressing. But if the therapists have not understood and experienced the traumas of their own lives, they will not dare to descend into the depths of the patients' pain either. When treating such patients, it is more dangerous to stop half way than to go the whole way. Thus, revictimization and retraumatization may happen when the therapist is too afraid of encountering his or her own anxiety (Ginn 1999, personal communication).

Having worked with Ildri and her combination of psychodrama and bioenergetics for more than ten years, I have experienced many sessions in which powerful traumatic episodes were re-enacted, but which had satisfactory, safe and often joyous endings. I would like to emphasize, however, that this approach is not suitable for all traumatized people. Beyond motivation and ego strength, suitability depends to a large extent on the stage a person has reached in his or her individual process of growth.

Two approaches to psychodrama and trauma in America

I was introduced to psychodrama when I came to America in 1971 to study psychodrama therapy with drug addicts at the Daytop Village in New York City (Røine 1997). I immediately knew that this would become my own method of working. I attended several training groups and soon had the privilege of meeting Hannah Weiner and becoming her assistant. Hannah had been a close student of J.L. Moreno and was considered to be one of the most talented. Together with Hannah, I visited different state mental hospitals where I experienced difficult sessions, was cast in strange roles and lived through turbulent group processes. Her approach to treatment was to meet the problem head on and slowly work through the traumatic experiences that evolved. Hannah Weiner was one of the most creative, warm and courageous therapists I have ever seen work and I learned much through my association with her. She showed me classical psychodrama and group psychotherapy at its best. Unfortunately Hannah died much too early and could not teach us more.

In contrast to this approach, I also had the opportunity to observe psychodrama as it was practised at the Veteran Hospital in Manhattan. The focus here was on social learning and rehabilitation and the attitude seemed to be to avoid dealing with the traumatic experiences directly. While the sessions were very interesting and the use of psychodrama as behavioural training was rather clever, I found their methods hard to adopt mainly because of their avoidance of deep pain and their fear of revictimization. When the staff members cooperated with the patients to repress painful memories, the suffering came out in so many other ways, such as in nightmares or in psychosomatic illnesses, which were then often treated with medication. We have seen with our own sailor veterans in Norway similar symptoms and approaches. Perhaps one need not exclude one or the other approach completely but attempt to work with a combination of them. In such a treatment strategy, the working through of deep trauma may be followed by a phase of rehabilitation and behavioural rehearsal.

Psychodrama in a psychiatric ward

The most challenging experience and training I received during my first years of practice was when I worked as a psychologist for eight years at the Ulleval Psychiatric Hospital in Oslo. There I was allowed to use psychodrama and a small theatre was built for that purpose in the basement. Stage lights were installed according to the model used by Jim Enneis in the psycho-drama theatre at St Elizabeth's Hospital in Washington DC. The patients admitted to our ward were mainly suffering acute crises of life but some were inmates who came via the prison hospital after having attempted suicide. The idea was that if patients were sufficiently motivated and were evaluated as being able to benefit from this method, they were taken to the theatre as soon as possible after being admitted. The first session would normally be a monodrama to map out the patients' inner resources and outer social network. A doctor, a nurse and myself conducted these first evaluative sessions. Later, patients were asked if they would like to join a psychodrama group to further explore their problems. We were rather open as to who could join the psychodrama groups but felt that people who were acutely psychotic would not be able to participate in the group in a constructive manner. These patients would sometimes work by themselves in mono-drama with a small therapeutic team from the clinic.

As an illustration of this work in a psychiatric ward, I would like to give three examples of the psychodramatic treatment of traumatized patients from the crisis unit with varying backgrounds.

Ola, a victim of rape

Ola was a huge man who had to be treated with extreme care because he was suspicious, erratic and very moody. Until now, very little progress had been made to establish contact with him and I was allowed to enter Ola's intense dream world. Ola was encouraged to talk and draw pictures and play around with words and sounds. He soon began to laugh when we studied the various pictures coming from his dreams. But one day he presented a dream about a black and a white sheep. He immediately became anxious and wanted to withdraw from our session. Eventually we could continue and he presented the two sheep in the pasture next to his childhood home. The black sheep wanted to approach the white sheep but someone had constructed what seemed like a barbed wire fence to stop military tanks, which separated the two sheep. By this time, Ola was used to reverse roles and identified his brother as the white sheep while identifying himself as the black sheep. Ola's father was a priest and the family was strict fundamentalist. This made me think of the fable of the lost son who is eventually welcomed home by his father. I tried to encourage him to enact this on stage, but it was not the right key. The father, or God, was vengeful and punitive. Ola started to get agitated and in this state revealed that he was jealous of his brother who was 'spotless' like the white sheep.

We continued along this line until a wolf appeared in his dream. I first thought it was the father or God, but it turned out to be Ola himself who plunged at the white sheep (represented by a cushion). Ola was now sitting between the two sheep cushions, one white and one black, and he became confused. He then realized that the wolf was not himself but his uncle, the brother of his father, who had raped him when he was ten years old. This was the breakthrough I was looking for. In the following sessions, Ola slowly remembered and worked through what had happened in his childhood. He remembered the barn where the rape had taken place and he was able in the imaginary setting of psychodramatic surplus reality to take revenge on the terrible 'wolf' who had hurt him before.

We continued working with the animal symbols rather than directly attacking the uncle. Because of his strict upbringing, a direct confrontation with the abusive uncle would have been too difficult. Ola had made the connection and we continued to recognize the real villain while working with the symbolization. In this manner, we were able to release his rage by trapping the beast and killing it with a magic weapon. In retrospect, I think hospitalization provided a safe setting for the gradual process of rebuilding confidence in him and in the outside world. When Ola realized that the wolf was much bigger and stronger than the sheep, he understood that he was not to blame. To end our sessions together we had a ceremony and changed the black sheep into a white sheep so that he could now meet his brother and father in a new light.

Ivar, a suicidal paedophile

Ivar was nearly 60 years old when he arrived at the hospital from the prison unit. He had tried to commit suicide after being arrested for child abuse. After the initial monodrama, he was to become a member of our psychodrama group for several months. A sweet, 16-year-old girl who was addicted to drugs also participated in the group. She became an excellent auxiliary ego for Ivar, taking the role of a girl Ivar had known when he was eight years old. After his parents were killed in a car accident, Ivar had been placed in an orphanage. From there, he used to visit this girl and enjoy the warm atmosphere of her home and the food that her mother prepared for them. The two children remained friends for a long time and experimented with innocent sexual games in a hidden room.

One day while being engaged in such sexual playing, the mother called the little girl home. As Ivar watched the little girl cross the street on her way home, he saw a big truck and heard loud screeching brakes and he learned that she had been hit and that she had died. Later in Ivar's adult life he had been arrested several times for approaching young girls and fondling them. After a re-enactment of this earlier situation, we used a combination of psychodramatic and behavioural therapy in the treatment of Ivar. With the help of the fellow patient as auxiliary ego we played out the scene of Ivar approaching a young girl. Immediately when he contacted her, we shone a thick heavy red light on him. This was enacted over the course of many weeks, during which time Ivar became more aware and ashamed of his actions.

Ivar gradually improved and was released from hospital. At a follow-up meeting, Ivar said that he had had the inclination to contact young girls, but would see the red light and then decide to abstain. Because of his criminal record and the difficult task of working through his traumatic experiences, Ivar later returned to our group and we continued to uncover the deeper layers of his traumatic life story when his parents had been killed. Ivar became gradually more able to grieve the terrible loss of his parents and his childhood playmate. Having worked through these two major traumatic experiences from his past, Ivar again seemed to be able to control his terrible sexual urges and was finally released from hospital and returned to his wife and his previous job.

Juan, a victim of torture

We have not had many victims of torture in therapy in Norway. Before coming to Norway, Juan had been a citizen of Argentina where he and his brother had been captured and treated as the enemies of the state. The brother was tortured to death in the room next to the one in which Juan was being kept. As a political refugee in Norway four years later, Juan was still severely traumatized from this experience and was admitted to the clinic in a state of paralysed fear and helplessness. His terrible experiences were re-enacted in psychodrama. For this purpose, the two rooms were set up again; one with Juan and the other with his brother. Juan's catharsis came when he was put in the role of his brother and could, for the first time, give voice to the screams that he had heard in the Argentinean prison and that had followed him ever since that time. After this intense release of pent-up pain,

Juan became more able to mourn the death of his brother. His condition improved rapidly after this session.

Theories of trauma resolution

The combination of theories and research from two different sources makes a valid statement for the use of psychodrama on traumatized people. Taken together, Levine's (1997) work on 'somatic experiencing' and Seligman's (1992) theories of 'learned helplessness' make a strong case for the use of psychodrama with such people. Both authors utilize animal imagery to explain various strategies of survival.

For example, Levine uses the image of an impala. The impala is a very fast animal in Africa and when being attacked by a stronger animal it becomes absolutely still, in order to make the aggressor believe that the prey is dead and make later escape possible. Research has shown however that this must happen in a very short time because the enormous energy spent on the chase can become 'frozen' and the impala would then die. Such frozen energy would mean being in a state of paralysis and helplessness and giving up hope of survival. Levine once saw this in a comatose patient. Thinking very quickly and in despair he shouted, 'Here comes a tiger, quickly climb up that tree!' The patient immediately started to scream and in her fantasy saw the tiger, which made her instantly move. This experience gave Levine the idea for the title of his 1997 book *Waking the Tiger.* This type of involvement from a therapist towards a client is very like a psychodrama. Psychodrama is a therapeutic method that does more than 'talk' about doing. In psychodrama, imagery and action is encouraged to evolve spontaneously and immediately, as demonstrated by Levine. Furthermore, rather than viewing traumatization as an illness, Levine views it as a state of excitement, as a kind of frozen energy that is disconnected from past experience. The healing of trauma has a direct effect on the living and feeling organism. Unsuccessful attempts to release the trauma can fixate them. This may then lead to compulsion and overstimulation. That is why it is so very important to follow through completely when opening up such wounds.

Seligman's theories also fit very well with psychodrama and with the ones presented above. In his 1992 book *Helplessness: On Development, Depression and Death,* Seligman described the role of 'learned helplessness' in traumatized people. Such a state is largely due to an inability to control a situation of extreme anxiety: 'When an animal or person is faced with an outcome that is independent of his responses, he learns that the outcome is independent of his responses' (p.46). This means that it is best to stop trying, because every effort is futile and will have no effect. The result will be loss of self-esteem and self-image. By reconstructing the traumatic events in psychodrama, the protagonist is encouraged to control the situation in a new manner. Thus, while it is naturally impossible to undo a traumatic event, the protagonist will be urged to re-experience it as an 'active participant' rather than as a 'helpless observer'.

Hope as a therapeutic agent

Psychodrama is an optimistic form of therapy. It looks for resources within people instead of focusing on pathology and introduces the dimension of hope in the process of psychotherapy. Moreno's (1953) philosophy of spontaneity and creativity emphasizes the importance of living in the 'here and now' and his concept of the 'I-God' suggests that we are co-creators and therefore have the power and magic within ourselves to change. How strange and powerful this dimension of hope can be is illustrated by Leonard Shengold in his book *Soul Murder: The Effects of Childhood Abuse and Deprivation.*(1989). Here he cites a very moving story, taken from a chapter of Primo Levi's book *The Drowned and the Saved* (1987). A survivor of Auschwitz, Levi describes how the 'soul' murderers' guilt was passed on to the victims. In Auschwitz, death squads consisting of Jews were forced to take other Jews to the gas chambers. The members of these squads were provoked, even angered, when they realized that the new inmates at the camp harboured hope of being released and that they did not realize they were going to die. One day as they were cleaning out the gas chambers they came across a young girl still alive. Miraculously she had survived. The Jewish squad hid and fed her. As a result of her survival, something inside them had changed. They had received proof of some kind of hope. Shengold then goes on to write: 'The anecdote shows the temporary and almost miraculous reversal of the defensive dehumanisation (ridding themselves of the capacity to care about others) that those being mistreated and tormented impose on their victims, pushing them towards taking on the guilt of their tormentors and also towards becoming like them.' (1999, p.101) Shengold also points out how degradation and contempt take away hope. He again cites Primo Levi: 'A single Anne Frank excites more emotion than myriads who suffered as she did, but whose image has remained in the shadow. A recognisable "person" is part of the human family and therefore hard to "kill"' (Levi 1987, p.100). In psychodrama after psychodrama we have learned that when the recognizable protagonist bears witness to hope for the future, it has a great impact on the entire group. Thus, the protagonist rises to the collective "family" and fights on behalf of all of them.'

Techniques

Working with traumatized people requires a sensitive touch, the right timing and the use of a variety of effective techniques. The director must ensure a safe atmosphere between the protagonist and the group. Naturally, the building of trust is an essential part of the process of therapy with traumatized people. The length of time given for the session is another important issue. A session that deals with trauma should not be abruptly ended because of rigid rules of time, such as the exact 'therapist hour'.

In the hospital setting we were often frustrated because staff members sometimes had to leave the sessions in order to attend meetings. Naturally, this should be avoided if possible because protagonists who are traumatized will easily feel abandoned and imagine that they are again ridiculed and/or stigmatized. However, while we are concerned with time, we have also found that sessions must not be too long, which sometimes happens because of the protagonist's seemingly inexhaustible needs and because the protagonist was afraid to approach the subject and is now so relieved and overjoyed about finally being able to work that he or she will never find an end.

Another possible reason for not wanting to end the session is that the protagonist has become so accustomed to being a victim that he or she wants to stay in that role for ever. This situation is not uncommon and must be dealt with when it arises. I once led a long session that lasted five hours and ten minutes. Although I still believe it was a necessary duration for the protagonist, it was very exhausting for everyone else involved. It is therefore important for the director to attempt to focus succinctly and to keep clear boundaries of trust, time and physical touch. Above all, the director must have courage to touch at the very emotional depth of the subject.

Role reversal with the perpetrator

An aspect of Moreno's (1953) role theory that is of vital importance when working with traumatized people is the ability to role-differentiate. Some protagonists have a very limited role repertoire. By reversing roles with the other and exploring a wider reality they may be better able to recapture their own authentic selves. This is also why we sometimes encourage the protagonist to reverse roles with the abuser. Though one should not recommend such role reversal too fast, the director may sense at one time or another that the protagonist is ready to 'experience the other', and then be secure enough quickly to suggest the role reversal. Depending on the timing, the fears and humiliation of the trauma can thus be changed and the inner transformation achieved. It is through role reversal that protagonists will become able to differentiate between themselves and the other, thereby separating themselves from the guilt and shame of being too closely associated with the terrible act itself.

We have seen this to be true with all kinds of trauma cases from rape to lengthy sexual abuse as children or other kinds of systematized torture. With a clear contract between the protagonist, the director and the group, the enactments can be done very realistically so that the group can bear witness to protagonist ordeals and show the world in action what really happened.

Supportive therapy is not enough to heal traumatized people. Simple understanding and unconditional acceptance are insufficient ingredients to alleviate the emotional pain caused by war, incest, rape and other acts of violence. As Schützenberger pointed out, 'the unconscious has a good memory' (1999, p.66) and it tends to find various channels of expression when prevented from being uncovered. Medard Boss said something similar: 'Traumatic experiences are imprisoned life melodies. They must come out and play in the whole orchestra of human life. And from each individual will come music to be played with the orchestra of the world' (1980). Imprisoned melodies of life? Their release is perhaps what all therapies, including psychodrama, are all about.

References

Boss, M. (1980) Lecture given at *Modum Hospital for Neuroses*, September.

Levi, P. (1987) *The Drowned and the Saved*. London: Sphere Books.

Levine, P. (1997) *Waking the Tiger: Healing Trauma: The Innate Capacity to Transform Overwhelming Experiences*. Berkeley, California: North Atlantic Books.

Moreno, J.L. (1953) *Who Shall Survive?* New York: Beacon House.

Røine, E. (1997) *Psychodrama: Group Psychotherapy as Experimental Theatre*. London: Jessica Kingsley Publishers.

Schützenberger, A.A. (1999) *The Ancestor Syndrome*. London: Routledge.

Seligman, M.E.P. (1992) *Helplessness: On Development, Depression and Death*. New York: W.H.Freeman & Co.

Shengold, L. (1989) *Soul Murder: The Effects of Childhood Abuse and Deprivation*. New Haven: Yale University Press.

CHAPTER 6

Prisoners of the Family
Psychodrama with Abused Children

Anne Bannister

Fintan was eight when he managed to tell his teacher about 'the white van that took him and his sisters to the bad place'. The teacher had been worried for some time because Fintan was dissociating in class and was unable to learn, although he was very creative in art classes. She contacted the authorities and Fintan and his sisters (aged six and four) were able to make statements about the horrific physical and sexual abuse regularly inflicted on them, and on several other related children, by their parents, grandparents and other relatives. A number of people were prosecuted and received prison sentences. Some of the subsequent therapeutic work with Fintan is described in *The Healing Drama* (Bannister 1997). His sisters and cousins also received therapy, which included psychodrama and dramatherapy.

Fintan and his sisters each reacted differently to their experiences but all of them showed multiple symptoms, including problems with anger (either inhibition or inappropriate, explosive expression), self-injury (cutting skin or scratching until it bleeds), dissociation (noticed especially in class), and amnesia for traumatic events. Although the children, collectively, were able to describe some of the events sufficiently to provide evidence, all had blank episodes, which they were unable to describe. It was, unfortunately, two years before the children could be placed in permanent foster homes and another year before they felt supported enough for their therapy to begin. Many of the children, especially the older ones, felt shame, guilt and self-blame. Fintan felt he should have protected his younger sisters and castigated himself for not doing so. All the children were afraid of the power of the perpetrators and attributed magical powers to some of them. They felt they could be seen wherever they were and that they would be punished for telling the secrets.

Damage caused by sexual abuse

Children who have suffered prolonged childhood abuse have been likened to long-term prisoners who have been tortured. Such children are held captive within their families just as surely as if they were imprisoned. They are tied first by the physical impossibility of survival outside the family for a young child. Second they are held by the emotional bonds that children form with their carers or those who give them some attention, even when that attention is abusive.

Children who have been abused by those from whom they expected protection, whether these people are family members or 'friends of the family', exhibit all the symptoms of post-traumatic stress disorder (PTSD). This has been clearly recognized by the American Psychiatric Association which has added the detailed manifestation of PTSD symptoms in children to their diagnostic criteria (1994).

The feminist psychiatrist, Judith L. Herman (1998), herself one of the committee who formed the diagnostic criteria for PTSD, has stated that in survivors of prolonged abuse the symptom picture is far more complex than that shown in simple PTSD. She points out that 'there are often characteristic personality changes, including deformations of relatedness and identity'. She also says that survivors of abuse in childhood are, in addition, 'particularly vulnerable to repeated harm, both self-inflicted and at the hands of others.' She has called the symptoms seen in such survivors 'Complex PTSD' (pp.118–122) and gives a complete classification. Those who work with children will note that the symptoms in children often become manifest in their play, especially the reliving of experiences and their repeated search for a rescuer.

Herman points out that other clinicians who work with survivors of childhood abuse have also refined the definition of post-traumatic stress disorder to include two categories of 'simple' and 'severe'. Through long experience of working with sexually abused children I have recognized the difference in presentation between children who have been abused repeatedly, by a trusted adult, and children who have suffered a short-lived traumatic event. The former usually feel that they had no one to support them. They are often completely isolated and have no idea that others may be suffering in the same way. They are like hostages who are unable to communicate with anyone other than their captors.

The difficulties that such children have with identity and relationships may be connected to dysfunctions in their attachment process. Developing children need to form attachments to their primary carers. As Bowlby (1953) showed, these attachments are crucial to satisfactory development. Children appear to need these bonds so much that they will seek to make them even with abusive and uncaring parents. Those who work with child sex abusers are aware of the way in which the abusers deliberately encourage the attachment process. They do this by 'grooming' the child gradually, so over-coming the child's resistance (Finkelhor 1984). The attachment process is distorted by the fact that the abuser–child relationship is not mutually bene-ficial but is detrimental to the child. Although the procedure of building a relationship with a child, as described by abusers, is undoubtedly coercive, they rationalize that it is mutual and so the dysfunctional attachment is made.

Individual and group treatment

In the early days of research into suitable treatment for those who had been abused in childhood, the focus was on adults rather than children. Possibly as a result of the damage to the attachment process, adults who have been multiply abused in childhood often have relationship difficulties. Hence, during the last two decades, there has been much research to show that the most common treatment for adults is often within the therapeutic group (van der Kolk 1987). For a discussion of group treatment and also individual treatment of adult survivors of child sexual abuse see Sheldon and Bannister (1998). As an extension of this work with adults, group treatment for ado-lescent survivors of abuse has also been advocated. Since peer support and approval is usually more important to adolescents than that of adults, treatment of young people in small groups has often been shown to be suc-cessful. (Blick and Porter 1982, Bannister and Gallagher 1995).

However, many abused adults and adolescents have benefited from indi-vidual therapy, especially in the early stages of their recovery, and likewise children have often been treated on a one to one basis, with good results (Bannister 1992 and 1997; Cattanach 1992). Children are very close to their traumatic events and their coping behaviours are less well developed. Sometimes they have not been able to form any kind of attachment to a non-abusing adult. The formation of such an attachment, to an individual therapist, often marks the start of an improved ability to relate better to peers.

Children who have received some individual therapy may be ready to move on to a therapeutic group where they can experience the support of other children and their isolation can be reduced. They can learn to relate better to others and can practise different ways of behaving in the safe environs of the group.

There are, however, problems in the safe management of a group for younger children suffering from complex post-traumatic stress disorder. There needs to be a high ratio of therapists to children and, because of developmental differences, there should be a small age range between the children. There may, therefore, be difficulties in setting up such groups and those that have succeeded have often been short term and have concentrated on self protection and social skills (Silovsky and Hembree-Kigin 1994).

However there is evidence to show that longer-term groups have more lasting benefits (Reeker and Ensing 1998). The use of open, ongoing groups is generally not advocated with sexual abuse survivors because a time-limited, closed group will feel safer. Such a group can be carefully structured so that work on painful issues can be done after a long period of consolidation and trust-building. Sufficient time can then be allowed for safe closure and containment before the group finishes.

Assessment for suitable treatment

The management of younger children in such a group is further complicated by the need for thorough assessment to ensure each child's readiness to work in this way. The following checklist may be useful for workers assessing abused children for inclusion in groups.

Coping mechanisms

Some children cope with the trauma by exhibiting behaviour that is sexually abusive and therefore dangerous to other children. However, this behaviour in young children is often ignored or condoned by adults (Bannister and Gallagher 1996). The person who referred the child to the group may not reveal such behaviour unless specifically questioned and therefore a careful assessment should be made to see whether the child is behaving in very controlling ways. Such a child could be a danger to other children in the group and may respond better to individual treatment. A child who is abusing others may respond well in a small group of similar children, where the emphasis is on behavioural modification.

Relationships with others

Since the abuse is likely to be relatively recent, children may be completely unready to hear about the abuse of others in the group and may become overwhelmed. A child who has only a dysfunctional attachment to an abusing adult will find it difficult to make appropriate attachments to the group workers and to other children. It is important, therefore, that children in a therapeutic group have already had the opportunity to make an attachment to at least one non-abusing adult. This may be done in a short period of individual therapy.

Developmental levels

An abused child already has a sense of difference from others, so special care should be taken to ensure that a fairly narrow age range and developmental level exists in the group. With pre-puberty children it is possible for both boys and girls to be included and, indeed, it is often helpful for children to see that both genders can be abused. A balance between the numbers of boys and girls works best. Children who have learning disabilities (even if these are severe) can be admitted to a group of children with similar problems. This is no barrier to therapeutic treatment.

Priority of sexual abuse issue

Some children who have suffered a short period of sexual abuse, outside the family, may have become more vulnerable to such abuse because of temporary family difficulties. At such times parents who are normally supportive may have become unavailable and the child could have been easily seduced by a powerful perpetrator. Such a child may need help in exploring the family difficulties, with the family, rather than becoming a member of a group where sexual abuse is the focus. Assessment should therefore follow the child's agenda at all times so that children are able to express feelings about anything which is worrying them.

During the assessment period of several weeks, therapists should also ensure that children are reasonably secure in their family environment and that carers are able to support the children during the period of their therapy.

Therapeutic Methods

This chapter will describe a small therapy group for four sexually abused children, two boys and two girls, which ran for 20 weeks. The children were aged eight or nine. I am a psychodramatist/dramatherapist who has worked with sexually abused children for many years, and my three co-workers are social workers experienced with sexually abused children. They had also received some training in creative play methods.[1]

In a small group which runs for 16 to 20 weeks there is opportunity to repair some of the developmental damage which may have been done, and to build new relationships. Each child will have been uniquely affected so a flexible form of therapy is required which can be adapted for each child. Children often have difficulty in ascribing meaning to their abusive experiences. The therapy must allow them to replay events, whether metaphorically or more directly, so that they can make sense of their experiences in the safe company of their peers and their therapist. They often need witnesses to reassure them and help them to recreate events. Creative play therapy, which incorporates psychodrama, dramatherapy and, possibly, art and music therapy is a most suitable approach for these young people.

Psychodrama

In addition to the damage to development caused by dysfunctional attachments, multiple abuse may cause damage to the child's sense of identity and ability to empathize with significant others. Moreno described this developmental process in a psychodrama session, which he gave to nursing students in 1952 (see Fox 1987). He suggests three stages of child development:

- finding a separate identity;
- recognising the self;
- recognising the other.

Psychodramatic techniques directly compare with methods which a parent or carer uses to help a child to develop. The technique of doubling in psychodrama helps people to express feelings, and through that maybe to find their own identity. The technique of mirroring helps people to see themselves as others see them and therefore to recognize themselves. The technique of role reversal is most helpful in enabling people to understand and recognize the differences in others. It seems reasonable to suggest a hypothesis that a thera-

---

1   I am indebted to my colleagues, Louise Brown, Steve Towers and Janice Wilson, my
       co-workers in the pilot group described here. Without their expert contributions the
       group would not have existed.

peutic procedure which specifically uses the techniques of doubling, mirroring and role-play, could be helpful for pre-puberty children who have been multiply sexually abused. The omissions and distortions of an early abusive experience could be mitigated by a positive replay of the developmental process.

In a psychodrama group with adults a protagonist may be doubled by the director, by a trained auxiliary, or by another group member. This person normally stands alongside the protagonist and, using skills in assessing body language, or using tele (the two-way empathic response between people) the double speaks aloud that which is unspoken. This can be corrected or confirmed by the protagonist.

However in this group with severely abused children the technique of doubling was used only by the therapists, who stood or sat alongside a child who seemed to be having difficulties in expressing feelings or proclaiming identity. The child was usually enabled to be more forthcoming and perhaps to make sense of conflicting feelings.

Also in a psychodrama group with adults the director may suggest that a potentially painful scene be done 'in mirror' so that the protagonist watches the scene with someone else in his or her place. In the group with children such scenes were run 'in mirror' by using puppets which the workers operated. The children also used puppets and joined in the action when they felt able. The use of puppets is often recommended with children (Carlson-Sabelli 1998). It may be that this form of projection helps to distance the action and also that the 'miniaturization' makes the action more manageable.

Role-reversal is a frequently used technique with adults in a group, often used to enable the protagonist to see the other's point of view. It is also used to expand the role repertoire of someone who seems to be restricted in this way. In the children's group there was much role-reversing, both with the puppets and in 'dressing up' games where the children devised scenes of fantasy, often taking several roles. They also directed others to take roles, especially the therapists, and they were then invited to reverse roles with the therapists, when they were ready.

These techniques from psychodrama were combined with dramatherapy and play therapy methods to provide a flexible, effective way of working which the children enjoyed.

Dramatherapy

Dramatherapy utilizes a developmental model of play. Children's first play is 'embodiment'. Children play with their own bodies, or bodily excretions; they suck or grab the fingers of adults and later they will dabble in water or push sand or soil around. They are experiencing the world through all their senses, including touch and taste. This stage may last for a year or two and children will frequently revisit the stage throughout life. A child who has suffered trauma during this stage may find it difficult to play in a messy way or, alternatively may be obsessively stuck in the stage and unable to move on. This stage is comparable with the 'identity' stage of development as suggested by Moreno in psychodrama (see Fox 1987).

The second stage of play is projective, in which children project feelings onto toys or people. By allowing the feelings to be expressed by a toy, children may receive confirmation of their own feelings. For example by telling mother that 'Teddy is feeling sad today', and receiving mother's sympathy, the child may be more able to experience the effect of his or her own feelings on others. This stage may be compared with the second stage of development which Moreno termed 'recognizing the self', or 'mirroring'.

The third stage of play is role-play and by the age of three or four most children are playing different roles constantly. Often the first roles are those of mother or father but soon animals and fantasy figures join the extensive role repertoire of most healthy young children. This third stage is, of course, comparable with Moreno's 'role-reversal' stage.

This developmental theory of play was first suggested by Peter Slade (1954) and further refined by Sue Jennings (1995). Both these drama-therapists have been inspired by the play of children in their work, just as Moreno was.

Dramatherapy utilizes metaphor so that problems are acted out through fairy stories and legends. The group was consistently child-centred so the stories that were acted out were frequently taken from the television programmes which the children had been watching. Since young children appear to use metaphor consistently in their play the therapists in this group were careful to stay within the metaphors which the children chose, unless the children themselves chose to make the metaphor more explicit.

For example one child had, during the life of the group, suffered a humiliating and painful court case where a jury found his abuser not guilty. This boy began his storytelling with some wise birds who got everything wrong. This was acted out with puppets. Eventually the story changed into a judge and jury who were severely punished for not getting things right. This too was acted out with the puppets and so the metaphor became clear. This gradual move from metaphor to reality protected the children from becoming overwhelmed by re-enactments of traumatic events. In this case the boy was then able to enact further scenes from his abusive experiences.

Staff group

The four therapists, three women and one man, had a weekly changing rota in which two of them ran the children's group and one ran a concurrent group for the mothers of the children. The fourth therapist was present as an observer in the children's group, and recorded the process in writing. This was helpful in that it provided an element of supervision for the therapists running the group. Observations were shared within the staff group who met immediately after the session for 45 minutes. They also met immediately before the session for planning purposes. Once a month one of the therapists ran a concurrent group with the mothers of the children during which information was shared with the mothers (within the limits of confidentiality) and questions were answered. It is important in a group for children who have been sexually abused by men (as in this group) that the male workers in the group are not seen as the most powerful figure (Herman 1998). In front of the children, the workers were careful to assume equal status although there were significant age and experience differences between them. I was the only qualified therapist and provided training and coaching for the social workers. The workers needed no encouragement to take roles and to use puppets and other materials since they were already experienced in such techniques.

Process of the group

All the therapists, and children, attended the first session and the information about the workers' rota and the observer was shared with the children. The children decided that the group should be named 'The Friendly Group', and they drew up the 'group rules' which were written out on a large sheet of paper which was signed by all group members, including therapists, and was affixed to the wall before each session.

The therapists had wondered if the children would be uncomfortable with the role of the observer, who took no part in the session, merely recording the action, but this was not the case. The observer was ignored throughout the session except at break time when a child would courteously offer the observer a drink and a biscuit.

The same structure was followed in each session. An energetic game of tag was introduced at the start, where the 'wolf' tried to catch the 'sheep'. One person used a wolf puppet and tried to catch the others. The children soon brought in rules about 'safe places' in the room and suggested 'elbows' as safe areas to tag someone. This theme of 'the wolf' was originally suggested by the workers but was taken up by the children and 'the big bad wolf' from fairy stories was used frequently by them in stories and pictures. This game may be seen as equivalent to a 'warm-up' in psychodrama.

After the children had expended some energy they were ready for puppet play. A large selection of animal puppets was provided and children were simply invited to 'tell how the puppets were feeling'. At first the workers also used simple drawings of faces to help the children to identify feelings but very quickly these were not needed. The children were able to talk, through the puppets, about their current hopes and fears. This section continued the 'warm-up' onto a more intimate level. Some children had favourite puppets, which they used constantly and others chose their puppets according to their mood.

A pause for refreshment followed, in which the children brought in a ready prepared tray of drinks and snacks and more informal sharing and trust-building continued throughout this part of the session.

After the food was cleared away the more formal 'action' part of the session began. At first the group was offered clay and paint to begin embodiment play and to experience this together. One boy, 'James' (not his real name), who had been abused when he was very young, found it difficult to play with the art material offered. He said he did not want to play with clay. A worker who had noticed that he was worried about getting clay on his clothes doubled him. 'Maybe I'll get into trouble if I get a mark on these pants,' she said, sitting alongside the boy. 'I used to get hit with a stick,' said James. 'And I did too,' volunteered one of the girls. The clay was pounded as all the children shared their feelings about the injustice of being beaten.

The children often chose art materials in the early stages and it may be that these were more familiar, from school. However they soon began to have extended scenes with the puppets and with small figurines (projective play) and to have elaborate role-playing, using the dressing-up clothes.

The therapists suggested a group saying or slogan, which was introduced during the first session (Corder, Haizlip and Deboer 1990). The children soon learned it and repeated it vigorously, with actions, which they devised, towards the end of each session. It ran:

I'm a good person,
I'm proud of me,
I've been through a lot,
Look how strong I've got!

The final part of the session could be likened to the final sharing part of a psychodrama session with adults. The children threw a ball to another group member, whilst thanking that person for something they had appreciated during the session. They chose to thank each other and the workers for 'doing a good painting', 'making a great model', 'listening to my story', 'helping me when I was stuck', and so on.

Content of Sessions

This psychodramatic model of a three-stage group session, 'warm-up', 'action' and 'sharing', was followed throughout the 20 weeks of the life of the group. However, the content of the sessions changed each week and the action was changed and refined mostly by the children. The initial game of tag changed little although the children made up special rules frequently. One interesting innovation was that the children began to carry the large floor cushions around and remarked that 'you can take your safe space with you'.

The projective work with the puppets was sometimes superficial but occasionally it became much deeper and this section moved imperceptibly into the action of a psychodrama. On one occasion James said that his puppet was a doctor who could 'mend broken hearts'. One girl, 'Jenny', holding a dog puppet, said, 'All my puppies have died'. Another boy, 'Patrick', said that a man came in to steal the puppies and they fought him and got 'ripped to pieces' in the fight. The action of the play became frantic as the mock fight continued and eventually all the puppies (puppets) lay still on the floor. James came on the scene as a doctor and found some life in one of the puppies. Gradually, and much to his satisfaction, he restored life into the puppies and also healed the broken heart of the dog who rejoiced as her puppies were saved. This session seemed to be a turning point for James. During the final sharing session he threw the ball to himself saying, 'I'm thanking me for being a good person'.

Part way through the group the therapists introduced dressing-up clothes as an alternative to working with clay or paints. By this time all the children were using the clay and paint in a comfortable way and were producing work which they found acceptable. Patrick had made a two-sided clay cup or mug. One side had a happy face, which, he said, was the side which people saw. The other side had a sad face, 'which was usually turned to the wall'. Other children showed their feelings through painting and drawing.

The dressing-up clothes invited role-play and became extremely popular. Mostly long scarves and belts, hats, gloves and jewellery were used. These could be placed on top of clothes so that no removal of clothing was necessary. One of the boys had been sexually abused, together with his older brother, by a male family friend, and he appeared to be worried about his masculinity. He frequently dressed as a woman in role-play but this was totally accepted within the group and gradually his worries about his sexuality seemed to fade.

After about eight weeks it became apparent that there was a group theme which concerned anger and frustration about mothers who were unable to protect their children. Continuing the theme of 'the Big Bad Wolf', I introduced a group story, based on the fairy tale of 'The Three Little Pigs'. In this therapeutic story 'Mr Wolf', whom the mother pig invited into their home, misled her. He was cruel to the little pigs and their mother did not believe them when they told her. Mr Wolf helped the little pigs to rebuild their house of straw to become a house of sticks and eventually a house of bricks. This was a twist in the original story in which the pigs had built the house of bricks to keep the wolf out. In this case the wolf was within and was building fences to keep the little pigs inside. Eventually, by banding together, the little pigs were able to send Mr Wolf on his way and they and their mother remained safe in their house of bricks.

This story was extremely popular in the group. The children spontaneously made houses of bricks with the clay, and made drawings of pigs and Mr Wolf. The most enjoyed activity was probably acting out the whole story, complete with costumes which they devised themselves. In this, of course, the children were acting out an appropriate ready-made metaphor. This gave them confidence and they then devised another story, which was acted out by the group under the joint direction of the children.

A female worker was taking the role of 'a mother who has lost her children'. The worker cried appropriately and searched unsuccessfully for her children. A girl in the group, 'Jenny', took the role of the daughter who was lost. She moved to the far end of the large group room at maximum distance from the mother. The mother continued to weep and wail. At this point Patrick took charge and informed the mother that in order to find her children she must 'wrestle with her conscience'. He drew an imaginary circle on the floor and stepped inside it, assuming a fighting posture. The mother cautiously stepped inside the circle and another worker took over the direction to ensure safety in the mock battle, which followed. Patrick, as 'conscience', and the worker, as 'mother', prowled around each other with mother defending herself from the threatening gestures which Patrick made. The worker playing 'mother' said she felt sorry for what had happened. At this point Jenny called out, 'I'm here, mother', and she and 'mother' ran the length of the room to be reunited.

Both Jenny and Patrick appeared to benefit considerably from this work. Jenny's behaviour became less angry and more appropriately assertive. Patrick gained confidence and self-esteem.

Results

The children completed B/G-Steem tests (Maines and Robinson 1988) at the beginning and at the end of the group. This test measures self-esteem and locus of control in children. The workers chose this test because low self-esteem is frequently a symptom of children who have been sexually abused. All the children registered 'low' on the self-esteem scale at the beginning but moved to 'normal' or 'high' after the group had finished. The same test measures the children's perception of their locus of control. Because abused children, who are suffering from PTSD, usually show changes in their relationship with others, the B/G-Steem test was also deemed particularly suitable for them. The children in the group either showed a tendency to control others or they had repeated failures to self-protect. At the beginning all the children perceived themselves to be powerless, without any control, or, alternatively, to have excessive power over others. The changes, which were registered in their locus of control, meant that they were less inclined to bullying behaviour and much more inclined to protect themselves from further victimization.

The primary carers of the children, in this case mothers, were also asked to complete a test (Naglieri, Le Buffe and Pfeiffer 1993) regarding their child's behaviour, before and after the group. The results of this test obviously depended on the children's relationships with their mothers. Unfortunately the parallel group for the mothers, which met monthly, had only spasmodic attendance because all the mothers suffered severely disruptive events during the course of the group. These events included hospitalization, court cases and unplanned relocation of homes. This meant that attendance was less than regular. The group had been designed to share information with the mothers but also to provide them with support. In the event, all the mothers were offered a support group after the children's group had finished.

Despite this, the results of the tests showed some consistency in that all the mothers rated the children's self-esteem and creativity highly at the end of the group. One of the mothers, whose relationship with her child had been particularly problematic, noted significant improvement in this relationship. Two other mothers were particularly impressed with their child's new, self-protective attitude. All the mothers also rated the depression suffered by the children to be very much improved.

The behaviour of the children within the group was also discussed and recorded by the workers at their weekly meetings. In the early days there were frequent recordings of inappropriate sexual behaviour, especially in the puppet play. Most children, through the puppets, appeared to show feelings of loss. For example, the puppet animals were often described as 'feeling sad because they have no daddies', or 'feeling bad because their mummy was very ill'. Puppets frequently asked their 'brother' or 'sister' or 'friend' for assistance and often failed to get either help or protection.

Later on the change was marked when puppets felt 'good' or 'strong' and helped each other or received help from others. Spirituality was brought into the puppet play through one boy who felt that 'God was not fair' and the puppets had a dialogue with God in which they expressed their anger, first against God, then against more secular power figures. With two sessions remaining the workers led a session where puppets were asked to 'say anything they needed to say before leaving'. This led to a projective scene in which the children used small plastic figures (animals, monsters and fantasy figures). The children played and worked together on a scene in which a large eagle taught all the other animals to fly.

As part of the closure work, two weeks before leaving, the children were given attractive folders in which to place their art work, copies of the group story and slogan and so forth and these folders were taken home to show their mothers. In the final two sessions they were able to collaborate happily on making a collage, in the form of a banner, celebrating the 'Friendly Group'. One boy made a 'coat of arms' with swords and shields to protect all the group members. A girl made a garland of flowers to entwine around all the members to keep them safe.

Themes of 'keeping safe' are common in short-term focused groups for children who have been sexually abused. There are many descriptions of such groups (Simpson 1994). Their purpose is to educate these vulnerable children so that they are less likely to become victims again. The children are taught strategies for safety such as 'Say no!' or 'Run and tell!' However, in our group such a theme had never been introduced directly by the therapists. There was no learning of strategies for safety. Such strategies may easily be forgotten (Simpson 1994) but we believe that the theme of safety was integrated in a more meaningful way.

At a final, formal leaving ceremony, the children were presented with certificates of attainment and there was a prolonged 'sharing session' which was particularly successful. Everyone enjoyed the final party, with special food, chosen by the children.

Discussion

This pilot group was set up to look at any significant changes in the behaviour of severely sexually abused eight to nine-year-old children over the course of 20 weeks. The group was too small to generalize from the results and a further group is to be set up in the near future. Finkelhor and Berliner (1995) in their review of research on the treatment of sexually abused children found that groups often had very small numbers and comparisons of different groups was difficult because of differing measures used in each group. In addition, Carbonell and Parteleno-Barehmi (1999) recently evaluated the effectiveness of psychodrama groups with traumatized middle-school girls. Comparisons of treatment and control group members' pre- and post-intervention adjustment revealed significant decreases in group participants' self-reported difficulties in withdrawn behaviour and anxiety/depression.

Study of the literature shows that most studies do not differentiate between children who are exhibiting symptoms of complex post-traumatic stress and children who have fewer and less intrusive symptoms. Various treatment methods have been tried from anxiety reduction strategies to psychodynamic therapies. Monck (1997) looked at 144 children who had been attending various treatment groups. She reported improvements in the Child Depression Inventory and in the Child Behaviour Check Lists.

However, long-term benefits have not yet been assessed because research on treatment groups has not been in existence for long enough.

I have used psychodrama and dramatherapy with severely sexually abused children, mostly on a one to one basis, for 20 years. Others (Cattanach 1992; Ryan 1995; Hoey 1997) have used similar techniques, also with individual children. There is a need to look further at the efficacy of groups for severely sexually abused children, using creative therapy techniques. This pilot project marks a small beginning.

References

American Psychiatric Association (1994) *Diagnostic and Statistical Manual of Mental Disorders:* DSM-IV. Washington DC: AMA.

Bannister, A. (ed) (1992) *From Hearing to Healing: Working with the Aftermath of Child Sexual Abuse.* Harlow, Longman and Chichester, John Wiley (Reprint 1998).

Bannister, A. (1997) *The Healing Drama: Psychodrama and Dramatherapy with Abused Children.* London: Free Association Press.

Bannister, A. and Gallagher, E. (1995) 'Group work in child protection agencies.' In K. Wilson and. A. James (eds) *The Child Protection Handbook.* London: Balliere/Tindall.

Bannister, A. and Gallagher, E. (1996) 'Children who sexually abuse other children.' *The Journal of Sexual Aggression 2,* 2.

Blick, L.C. and Porter, F.S. (1982) 'Group therapy with female adolescent incest victims.' In S.M. Sgroi (ed) *Handbook of Clinical Intervention in Child Sexual Abuse.* Lexington, MA: Lexington Books.

Bowlby, J. (1953) *Child Care and the Growth of Love.* Harmondsworth: Pelican Books.

Carbonell, D.M. and Parteleno-Barehmi, C. (1999) 'Psychodrama groups for girls coping with trauma.' *International Journal of Group Psychotherapy 49,* 3, 285–306.

Carlson-Sabelli, L. (1998) 'Children's therapeutic puppet theatre – action, interaction and cocreation.' *The International Journal of Action Methods, 51,* 3, 91–112.

Cattanach, A. (1992) *Play Therapy with Abused Children.* London: Jessica Kingsley Publishers.

Corder, B.F., Haizlip, T. and Deboer, P. (1990) 'A pilot study for a structured, time-limited therapy group for sexually abused pre-adolescent children.' *Child Abuse and Neglect 14,* 243–251.

Finkelhor, D. (1984) *Child Sexual Abuse: New Theory and Research.* New York: Free Press.

Finkelhor, D. and Berliner, L. (1995) 'Research on the treatment of sexually abused children: A review and recommendations.' *Journal of the American Academy of Child and Adolescent Psychiatry 34,* 11, 1408–1423.

Fox, J. (1987) *The Essential Moreno.* New York: Springer.

Herman, J.L. (1998) *Trauma and Recovery: From Domestic Abuse to Political Terror.* London: Pandora.

Hoey, B. (1997) *Who Calls the Tune?* London: Routledge.

Jennings, S. (1995) *Drama Therapy with Children and Adolescents.* London: Routledge.

Maines, B. and Robinson, G. (1988) *B/G-Steem: A Self-esteem Scale with Locus of Control Items.* Bristol: Lucky Duck.

Monck, E. (1997) 'Evaluating therapeutic intervention with sexually abused children.' *Child Abuse Review 6,* 163–177.

Naglieri, J.A., Le Buffe, P.A. and Pfeiffer, S.I. (1993) *Devereux Behavior Rating Scale: School Form Manual.* San Antonio: Harcourt Brace and Co.

Reeker, J. and Ensing, D. (1998) 'An evaluation of group treatment for sexually abused young children.' *Journal of Child Sexual Abuse 7,* 2.

Ryan, V. (1995) 'Non-directive play therapy with abused children and adolescents.' In K. Wilson and. A. James (eds) *The Child Protection Handbook.* London: Balliere/Tindall.

Sheldon, H. and Bannister, A. (1998) 'Working with adult female survivors of child sexual abuse.' In A. Bannister (ed) *From Hearing to Healing: Working with the Aftermath of Child Sexual Abuse.* Harlow: Longman and Chichester: John Wiley.

Silovsky, J.F. and Hembree-Kigin, T.L. (1994) 'Family and group treatment for sexually abused children: A review.' *Journal of Child Sexual Abuse 3,* 3.

Simpson, L. (1994) *Evaluation of Treatment Methods in Child Sexual Abuse: A Literature Review.* Bath: University of Bath.

Slade, P. (1954) *Child Drama.* London: University of London Press.

van der Kolk, B.A. (1987) 'The role of the group in the origin and resolution of the trauma response.' In B.A. van der Kolk (ed) *Psychological Trauma.* Washington, D.C: American Psychiatric Press.

CHAPTER 7

The Use of Psychodrama in the Treatment of Trauma and Addiction

Tian Dayton

It is estimated that seven out of ten people in the USA are in some way affected by addiction. Researchers have well established the connection between trauma and addiction and suggest that trauma survivors often develop alcohol or other drug problems as a result of their attempts to 'self medicate' (APA 1988; van der Kolk 1996; Danieli 1984). Added to this group are the many people who suffer deep emotional and psychological pain through living with addicts and who are vicariously traumatized by the experience.

Studies of populations with substance abuse consistently report childhood histories of abuse and neglect in much higher proportions than are found in the general population. In traumatized adults, high rates of alcohol and drug abuse have been documented (van der Kolk 1996).

The connection is clear. People who are in emotional and psychological pain and who lack the inner resources and support systems to tolerate this pain often seek chemical solutions. They learn lesson number one of addiction: 'I can make my pain go away with a drug. When I use, I feel better.' But this 'feeling better' slowly erodes their inner world, their social network and locks them into the fatal disease of addiction.

The broad scope of therapeutic issues inherent in the treatment of both trauma and addiction requires effective and individualized approaches. Traumatized people are frequently misdiagnosed and mistreated in the mental health system. Because of the number and complexity of their symptoms, their treatment is often fragmented and incomplete. In addition, they are vulnerable to becoming re-victimized by caregivers because of their characteristic difficulties with close relationships (Herman 1992).

Because of the unpredictable and uncontrollable nature of substance abuse and addiction, people who are chemically dependent – or those in the family system – experience some form of psychological damage.

Individuals in addictive systems behave in ways consistent with psychological trauma. An addictive environment where there is chronic tension, confusion, unpredictable behaviour and abuse can create traumatic symptoms. A person who is abused or traumatized may develop survival roles, a set of defensive behaviours designed to keep themselves safe. Trauma victims often develop 'learned helplessness' – a condition in which a person loses the capacity to appreciate the connections between their actions and their ability to influence their lives (Seligman 1975).

Centuries ago, an Italian proverb observed that when: 'The mind is hurt the body cries out.' A trauma survivor may self-medicate with chemicals such as drugs or alcohol or try to alter their brain chemistry by bingeing, purging or withholding food. These may be attempts to affect the pleasure centres of the brain, enhancing 'feel good' chemicals to minimize pain. Scientific advances, mainly in neurobiology, have produced significant studies of PTSD. Findings through brain imaging report that trauma can affect the body and brain much more than had previously been understood: 'People have been aware of a close association between trauma and somatisation since the dawn of contemporary psychiatry' (van der Kolk 1996, p.194).

Psychodrama is one of the earliest methods of body psychotherapy. Moreno (1964) taught that the body remembers what the mind forgets. He understood the wisdom of involving the body in therapy and hypothesized two types of memory: content (mind) and action (body). Content memory is stored as thoughts, recollections, feelings, and facts. Act memory is stored in the brain and also in the musculature as tension – holding, tingling, warmth, and incipient movement. The best route to recapturing act memory is through expressive methods that use the whole person (mind and body) in action (Moreno 1964).

The link between psyche and soma is well supported by the current research of neuroscientist Candace Pert who discovered the opiate receptor. Pert explains that the memory of trauma is stored by changes at the level of the neuropeptide receptor: 'Intelligence is located not only in the brain, but in cells that are distributed throughout the body' (1998, pp.269–271).

Addiction

Alcoholism is a fatal disease. Ten per cent of the drinkers in America will become alcoholics (Johnson Institute 1980). The significant characteristics of the disease concept of alcoholism are that it is primary, progressive, chronic, and fatal. The Johnson Institute describes the stages from drug use to drug dependence as:

1. Initial drug experience (pre-symptomatic phase) may be experimental, socially motivated, and provide relief from tension. An individual learns that the use of the substance can change a mood and through experience develops a relationship with the substance.

2. The onset phase comes when the drugging is no longer recreational, but rather medicinal, with an increasing preoccupation with a drug of choice. The individual seeks the mood shift; this stage may be accompanied by 'blackouts' in which the addict loses memory of specific events.

3. The next phase of harmful dependence comes with excessive use and loss of control when the person picks up the drug. This phase is accompanied by a progressive deterioration of self-image, acute phases of self-destructive behaviour, and distorted emotional and psychological attitudes.

4. In the chronic phase that follows, a person needs to use just to feel normal. Being a progressive illness, this phase often results in death.

As of 1995, the cost of substance abuse to society was about $276 billion and the cost of drug abuse and addiction itself was about $110 billion (AAAP Newsletter 1999). There have been multiple attempts to define addictions over the last hundred years, and the definitions have ranged from moral failures to diseases to pharmacologically mediated brain dysfunctions (Gray 1999). The National Institute on Drug Abuse recently cited between 50 and 70 risk factors for drug abuse that are found in the community, the individual's peer cluster, the individual's family, and within the individual himself. The largest risk factor for drug abuse is an untreated childhood mental disorder (Gray 1999). Two reasons that people take drugs are to awaken a 'feel good' sensation in the brain (sensation seeking), or to feel better (self-medication) (AAAP Newsletter 1999). Years of brain studies on addiction by the National Institute on Drug Abuse suggest a common biological thread to all addictions, revealing that drug use alters brain chemistry.

Trauma

Trauma has been defined as a rupture in an affiliate bond (Lindemann 1944), the result of which is a loss of trust and faith, a loss of connection with self and others, a loss of the ability to dream, to picture mentally and take steps toward manifesting desired life choices. The work of Bessel van der Kolk has addressed the developmental, biological, psychodynamic, and interpersonal aspects of how a person is impacted by trauma. His research elucidates how trauma and disruptions in attachment bonds can affect a person's development throughout the life cycle. According to van der Kolk:

> A traumatised person does not have access to the left hemisphere of the brain which translates experience into language, therefore they can't make meaning out of what is happening to them or put it into any context. The right hemisphere evaluates the emotional significance of incoming information and regulates hormonal responses. Traumatised people have been known to have trouble tolerating intense emotions without feeling overwhelmed and thus continue to rely on disassociation. This interferes with their ability to utilise emotions as guides for action. They go from stimulus to response without being able to figure out what makes them so upset. They overreact, shutdown, or freeze. (1996, p.193).

Many trauma victims present with somatic symptoms. Psychosomatic patients often show an apparent intellectual inability to verbalize emotions or feelings. 'Trauma may lead to "speechless terror" which in some individuals interferes with the ability to put feelings into words, leaving emotions to be mutely expressed by dysfunction of the body' (van der Kolk 1996, p.193).

Addicts and those who have lived with addicts exhibit behavioural cycles of intensity versus shutdown or withdrawal; that translates to what is commonly referred to as black and white thinking. The origins of this may be found in the trauma set up.

The basic psychological response to trauma is a bi-phasic reaction of protest and numbing. The protest phase in response to an uncontrollable event may be marked by anger, verbal hostility, or acting out. In time the initial reaction is followed by numbing, a state of emotional and interpersonal withdrawal from active participation in one's environment. The signs of numbing include complications of the victim's cognitive capacity to solve problems, social withdrawal, and isolation (Flannery 1986).

Trauma victims may attempt to control their internal state of hyper-arousal, social withdrawal, emotional pain, and anger through the use of substances that quiet their inner struggle and restore a sense of control over their tumultuous inner world. The substance becomes a reliable source of mood management that temporarily masquerades as a restoration of the trauma victim's equilibrium.

For example, heroin has powerful effects on muting feelings of rage and aggression, whereas cocaine has significant antidepressant action. Alcohol is probably the oldest medication for the treatment of post-traumatic stress (van der Kolk 1996, p.191).

This method of mood management, however, actually has the effect of denying trauma victims access to their own inner world, rendering them emotionally illiterate. The information gleaned from tuning in on emotional states that would allow trauma victims to comprehend and come to terms with their internal struggle are medicated and thus distorted. Trauma victims gain the temporary relief that they are seeking but at the expense of self-knowledge and their potential for self-mastery.

To complicate matters further, the addictive process comes to have a life of its own. The withdrawal from authentic emotion and alienation from the self that the drug use induces leaves trauma victims helpless before their own internal world. The 'learned helplessness' (Seligman 1975) of the trauma victim is reinforced. When the substance wears off, they are again overwhelmed with the pain that they have medicated which now has added to it further isolation, shame, and unresolved issues. Hence, the need for a substance to assuage a stormy inner world is now all the more pressing.

And so the trauma victim enters a vicious cycle of pain–medication– sobering up–more pain–more medication and so on. The addictive process takes over and births a life of its own, rendering the trauma victim more and more helpless with each sinister turn of the wheel of addiction (see Figure 7.1).

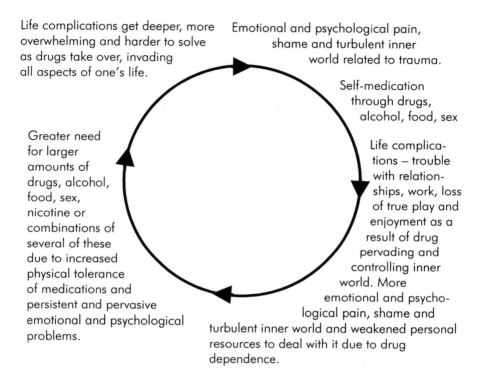

You can start anywhere on the wheel

Life complications get deeper, more overwhelming and harder to solve as drugs take over, invading all aspects of one's life.

Emotional and psychological pain, shame and turbulent inner world related to trauma.

Self-medication through drugs, alcohol, food, sex

Greater need for larger amounts of drugs, alcohol, food, sex, nicotine or combinations of several of these due to increased physical tolerance of medications and persistent and pervasive emotional and psychological problems.

Life complications – trouble with relationships, work, loss of true play and enjoyment as a result of drug pervading and controlling inner world. More emotional and psychological pain, shame and turbulent inner world and weakened personal resources to deal with it due to drug dependence.

Figure 7.1: The wheel of trauma and addiction (Dayton 2000)

Psychodrama with trauma

Psychodrama is part of a triadic system, which includes sociometry, psychodrama and group psychotherapy. Because trauma represents ruptures in relationship bonds, healing needs to occur in the relationships. The current treatment model of choice for both trauma and addiction is group therapy, because both disorders affect a person's ability to form relationships (Dayton 2000).

Group therapy helps trauma survivors and addicts and their families to regain trust, a sense of connection, and community. Psychodrama allows for a clinical rather than a self-destructive 'acting out' of repressed memory. Working through early traumas with real people and understanding how they fit into the overall life pattern gives a lost context back to the survivor (Dayton 1994). The primary concepts of Moreno's personality theory – namely warming-up, role-playing, spontaneity, and creativity – can be applied in transformative and restorative work with the survivor of trauma and addiction. The methods available in a psychodrama group can concretize the complex internal world of a client, provide a safe arena in which issues can be explored, and offer corrective and reparative experiences.

How can psychodrama help to resolve and rebuild these damaged areas?

Psychodrama places clients at the centre of their own drama, their own life story, and their own psychological and emotional processes. Protagonists can use stand-ins, if they choose, to represent themselves as they witness the content of their own drama. They can move in and out of the scene through role reversal. They also have the opportunity with the director to freeze the scene so that they can step back and get a deeper look at what might have been going on for them at a given juncture in their lives. The fact that psychodrama is a role-based method allows a client to explore damage that may have occurred in a particular role, say that of daughter, while preserving strength and resilience that may still be present in other life roles.

Built into the method of psychodrama are many therapeutic opportunities that are useful in examining and restoring injured relationship patterns that have been internalized into the self-system. Psychodrama can help an individual have a corrective experience and gain mastery and control over their environment. This counters the trauma victim's sense of learned helplessness.

In Moreno's concept of personality development, he theorized that the self emerges from the roles that are available to a person (Moreno and Moreno 1969). When we work with a role, we address the internalized criteria and attached feelings, as thinking feelings and behaviours are role specific. 'The role is the enactment of a status within the system. Consequently, any role work is by nature a systems intervention' (Siroka, quoted by Dayton, 1994, p.41).

The psychodrama therapist has available a variety of sociometric and psychodramatic interventions which can encourage a protagonist to make new choices and expand his or her role repertoire. Role training is especially important for a trauma survivor and/or addict who has felt disenfranchised and disempowered and who, therefore, needs to retire, modify, transform, discover, expand, rehearse, and/or build new roles.

On the following pages I shall describe three tools that I have developed to work with trauma and addiction: the Trauma Resolution Model for the Creative Arts Therapists; the Trauma Time Line; and the Living Genogram. Also included are three ways in which I have adapted the Social Atom for use with this population. (For further exploration, see Dayton 2000).

Psychodrama methods for trauma and addiction

Trauma model for experiential therapies (Dayton 2000)

1. Warm-up to the trauma story. Use appropriate techniques to warm up the group and help clients get in touch with their own story or personal metaphor of their trauma experience.

2. Enact the story with the group as witness. Using whatever experiential therapy is your speciality – psychodrama, gestalt therapy, dramatherapy, art therapy, or music therapy – concretize the trauma story experientially with the witness of the group.

3. Offer corrective experience. Simply concretizing the story with the group as witness is corrective and empowering. Also, it is possible for the protagonist to recreate a scene as they wished it had been. This should provide an opportunity to create a corrective memory that can be internalized, giving the client a blueprint of health to draw from stored within them so that the trauma memory is not the only memory.

4. Separate the past from the present. Link the current behaviour or re-enactment dynamic to past trauma wounds. Identify the present-day re-enactment dynamic that is creating a life problem and link it up to the originating wound, loss, or trauma. Analyse ways in which the past is getting in the way in the present.

5. Create a new narrative. Reintegrate the trauma back into the overall context of life, along with newly gained insight and meaning. Begin with the time of life before the trauma began and move to the present day. Trauma tends to be decontextualized within the self-system – it needs to be reintegrated as part of one's overall life pattern.

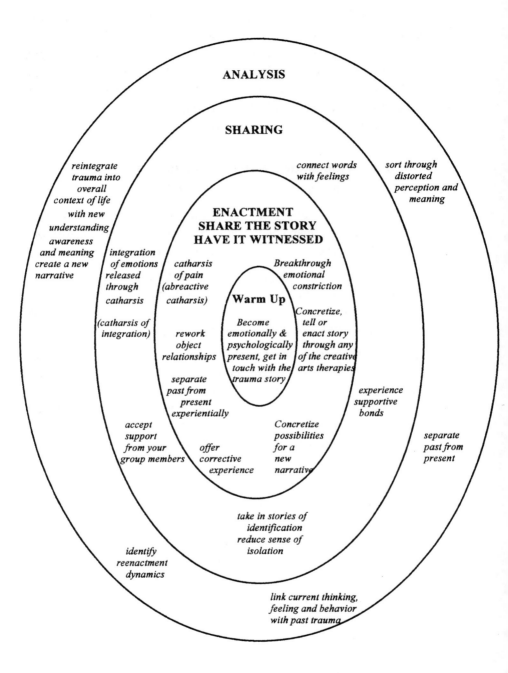

Figure 7.2: Trauma Resolution Model for the Creative Arts Therapies (Dayton 1996).

The Trauma Time Line (Dayton 2000)

The losses due to trauma and addiction are multiple and substantial. Part of the task facing any clinician who works with addicts, trauma survivors, or family members is to assist in identifying and sharing long-repressed memories and feelings and encouraging the essential grief work. Recovery and healing from both trauma and addiction involves a grief process (Dayton 1997).

The Trauma Time Line is a paper and pencil technique that can be used exclusively in this manner or can also lead to psychodramatic exploration. The Time Line can be laid out across the floor with markers at five year intervals. Role players can represent the protagonist at the various points of development. The protagonist can talk 'to' themselves or reverse roles and speak 'as' themselves whenever they feel the need. They can identify themes that weave through their time lines in the form of trauma re-enactment dynamics and can trace them back to their origins. Patterns of addiction become evident as to where they began, how long-lived they are, and so forth. Clients are able to identify how traumas may bunch up during a particular period of their lives or, conversely, how certain traumas are cumulative and persist over long stretches of time.

The Trauma Time Line helps the client get a handle on how trauma may have affected their overall life pattern, leading to a greater sense of mastery over what can be an overwhelming and indistinguishable series of events. The client can enact psychodramatic scenes exploring issues related to any part of the time line to which he or she feels warmed up. The Trauma Time Line is also useful in creating a context so that traumatic events that feel split off can be recontextualized within the client's life span. In this way, working with the Trauma Time Line can be part of the 'trauma narrative' (Herman 1992).

TRAUMA TIME LINE NARRATIVE

Alice is a child of an alcoholic. When she was ten years old her parents divorced. Her father remarried a woman with two children with whom he involved himself more than with his own children. Alice and her two siblings were raised primarily by their alcoholic mother and each other. When her older siblings left for college within two years of each other, Alice felt again abandoned. Her grandmother, who was a powerful surrogate figure and who put Alice through college, died before she graduated. Another loss containing guilt and sadness was that Alice's grandmother could not see her

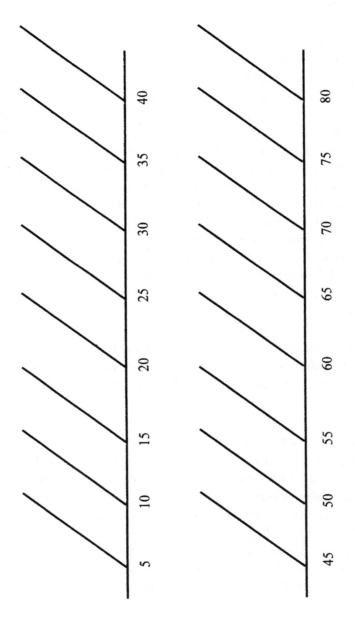

Figure 7.3: Your personal timeline (Dayton 1996).

graduate. Sad and alone, Alice fell in love and married someone whose character felt familiar to her and had two children. She did not connect the beer in his hand with alcoholism, as that disease had never been openly addressed in her family. Alice eventually joined Al-Anon, left her alcoholic husband, went back to college, remarried and blended her family with her husband's two sons. Much of Alice's life improved through her recovery work. Her awareness of alcohol increased tenfold and she was helpful in steering her children away from it. Their father's alcoholism grew worse. However, the underlying trauma in their family system went largely unaddressed. Hence, the children went on to their own trauma re-enactments, the son, by becoming a sex addict, and the daughter by marrying a man who was unavailable to her and who had multiple affairs.

When Alice saw the trauma of her life laid out on a time line she was able to wrap her mind around her own life and the lives of her children. Themes of trauma and addiction emerged and the re-enactments became clear. Seeing her life on paper she began to develop some compassion for herself which helped to lift the shame she had carried most of her life. After a considerable amount of grief work, Alice felt less threatened by hearing her own children's pain. Toward the end of her life she was able to use the time line to experience a Life Review (Erickson 1988) through which deep healing took place for herself and her relations.

The Living Genogram (Dayton 2000)

Substance abuse decreases the ability of a family to provide a healthy environment for its individual members where bonding, growth and development can occur. Relationship traumas tend to get passed down through the generations. It is no new fact that children of alcoholics are at five times higher risk of becoming alcoholics themselves and frequently marry alcoholics or ACOAs (adult child of alcoholics).

The genogram is an instrument from the family systems field that can illuminate patterns such as trauma and addiction that get passed down through generations. 'The development of the genogram was greatly influenced by Moreno's concept of the social atom' (Marineau 1989, p.158). I have adapted the genogram to psychodrama, that is, moved it from the paper to the stage as the 'Living Genogram.' The 'living' aspect is that once the genogram is completed on paper it is then put into psychodramatic action allowing not only the history to become conscious, but also its emotional and psychological content. For too long the solution to family addiction was seen as

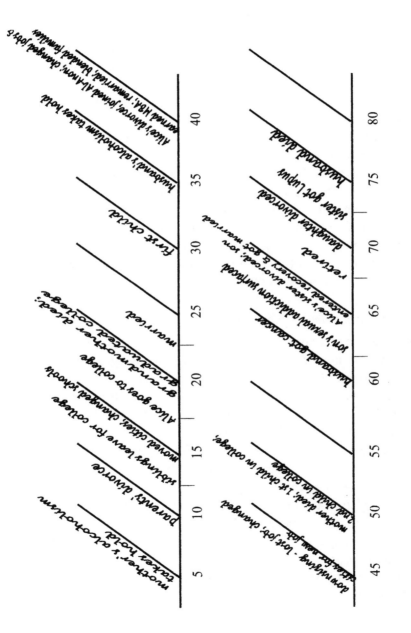

Figure 7.4: Trauma Time Line – Birth through 80 years – Alice's Trauma Time Line example

getting the alcoholic to sober up, assuming that this would clear up the problem in the family system. This approach ignored the underlying family pain and pathology that both contributed to and resulted from years of living with addiction.

The Living Genogram is a genogram brought to life through the use of role-play in the same way that a social atom becomes an action sociogram. It combines the family systems tool of the genogram with the psychodramatic method of role-play. It brings what was on paper into space, giving it concrete form and dimension, allowing clients to obtain a three-generational visual picture of the family system that they grew up in. The full genogram need not become an action sociogram in one session. It can act as a treatment map that both brings into focus areas that need work and provides a way of understanding how issues of trauma and addiction have manifested through generations of unhealthy dynamics.

The Living Genogram acts as a segue between the field of psychodrama and the broader mental health field connecting family systems theory with psychodrama. It brings the genogram to the psychodramatic stage where its contents can be made visible through the casting of role players to represent people in the genogram. The Living Genogram provides for a visual picture of a personal history along with the further option to move into psycho-dramatic enactment. The client can choose someone to play or represent him or herself then move in and out of the picture through role reversal. This provides a stand-in (mirror) so that if protagonists are at risk of becoming flooded or re-traumatized, they can locate themselves at a safe distance. The Living Genogram allows the client to give concrete form to the family that lives in imagination or surplus reality and to get a visual picture of the inter-generational family system. The Living Genogram provides a venue through which the protagonist can tell a story of trauma through action, have it witnessed, and resolve open tensions and act hungers.

When clients are permitted, through the use of the Living Genogram, to see the whole picture, they can sense where their unfinished business lies by noticing which parts of the sculpture or picture they are drawn to. This gives them an opportunity to make a sort of mental time line for where they need to go in their personal work. They get a sense of the origin of their trans-ferences, family alliances, triangles, act hungers, and open tensions. By actually taking a walk through or revisiting their own pasts, they get an opportunity to de-personalize what may actually be generational dys-function. Thus, they may be freed from the pathological grip of a dysfunctional, pain-filled or petrified system. At the same time, through self-defining and separating, the client can view a system now separate with perspective and compassion.

The Living Genogram provides an overall map, which can guide psychodramatic, group and individual therapy over time. When the genogram is put into action, it can be done so in its entirety or through vignettes. Some of the questions to be asked are: 'Where are some of the triangles in this family system? Along what generational lines do family addiction and dysfunction seem to travel? And, what does that indicate in terms of risk categories? What are the types of addiction in this family? What are some of the strengths that continue to show up through the generations? How did the gender roles in this family system get played out? How does it feel to look at your Living Genogram, to look at your family? Where are you most comfortable and most uncomfortable? Where do you feel that you have unfinished business? Who do you wish to talk to in this genogram? And, who do you feel you do not wish to talk to?'

The therapist can ask the client to rearrange this genogram so that it reflects dyads, triads, clusters, alliances, and cut-offs. Exploring the protagonist's feelings, the therapist may ask: How might the dynamics you observe be playing out in your life today? How does the path of addiction run through this family? Who do you feel close to, distant from, affectionate towards, antagonistic towards? Where is your positive or negative tele? The therapist can then ask the client to rearrange this genogram so that it reflects the way they wish it had been.

LIVING GENOGRAM NARRATIVE

In Russell's genogram we see how addictive life patterns are being passed down through three generations. Addiction breeds addiction. The genogram helped Russell to get a grasp of how addiction in two generations above him (that we know of) may have set him up for his own addiction problems. Both of Russell's parents, Melissa and James, grew up in alcoholic families. Though Melissa and Miranda avoided drinking, Miranda became an overeater at age eight while Melissa was tacitly assigned the role of 'family hero.' In essence, her personal likes and dislikes, wishes and desires were placed second to constant and diligent work at 'maintaining the family honour'. She was a class president, cheerleader, on the debate team, and a top student. Though these were indeed estimable accomplishments, she felt that without them she would not be a welcome, valued member of the family. In a

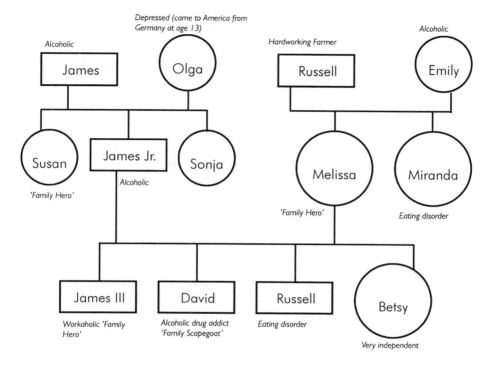

Figure 7.5: Russell's Genogram

sense, her job became to act out the spoken values of the family and Miranda's and eventually Russell's jobs were to act out the unspoken ones.

James, on the other hand, became an alcoholic. He took his first drink at age eleven and he liked it. It calmed his inner world and restored a sense of equilibrium. He carried on the father's name and the father's disease. His sister, Susan, was their family hero and James married someone quite like her.

When Russell was able to see his family patterns laid out in this manner, he felt less burdened with unspoken family history and he understood that his addiction problems came from somewhere. This was the beginning of his getting a 'handle on his own disease'.

The social atom with trauma and addiction (Dayton 2000)

Survivors of trauma, addicts, and people from addicted homes live in two different worlds. For the person who has experienced a sudden loss, there is life before the trauma and after the trauma. After a trauma a person's sense of a predictable and orderly world can feel shattered. Their inner world can be consumed with thoughts and feelings related to the trauma. Life after the trauma can feel different. Bad things can and do happen. Suddenly, the world can feel like a potentially threatening place and relationships with people can be anxiety provoking – people are neither perfect nor permanent.

For the ACOA and co-addict, there are two distinct realities, the wet one, and the dry one, or the one while the addict is using and the one when the addict sobers up. Each world has its own method of operation, its own mode of functioning. Rules and morality are different for each. Relationships and relating styles are unique to each world, and what works in one world does not necessarily carry over to the other. Consequently there is a shift in object relations, but in the case of addictions that shift may move regularly back and forth. This is why children from alcoholic families can feel 'crazy' or develop a powerful need for control. They may have trouble integrating one reality. Because the environment changes, the child internalizes two homes and two modes of functioning.

The social atom is a diagram or picture that represents the nucleus of all individuals toward whom a person is emotionally related. The social atom is useful both in individual therapy and in the group context. A person is asked to place him or herself on a piece of paper and then locate significant relationships as close or distant and in the size and proportion that feels right, using circles to represent females, triangles to represent males and broken lines to represent anyone who is deceased. There follow examples of three different ways to use the social atom: a trauma atom, an ACOA atom and an addict's atom.

Carolyn did a psychodrama of a never-talked-about incident in her life that she imagined had been 'over' long ago. When she was three, her baby sister suffered a cot death. Not only did she lose her sister, but also she was

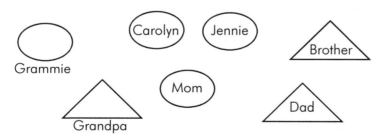

Figure 7.6: Carolyn's social atom before trauma

the one who discovered her lying lifeless in her crib. In her psychodrama she began to weep and stomp her feet, 'Wake up, Jennie, wake up'. After her psychodrama work, Carolyn was asked if she could draw a social atom. One was representing her family of origin before the trauma and one representing them after it. This is what she drew.

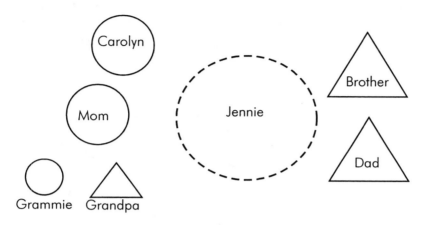

Figure 7.7: Carolyn's social atom after trauma – sudden death

Carolyn was asked to draw an atom of life after the trauma in order to see if it had changed.

Clearly, the first notable change is that the size of the symbols was greatly enlarged on the second atom. The implosion of powerful emotion that occurs in trauma can make one's internal world feel hyper-extended. It is as if the inner and outer worlds of a person no longer match. The second notable feature is that some of the relationships changed in placement. The object

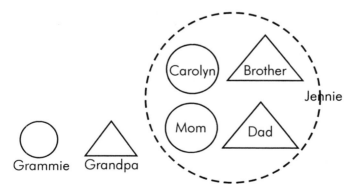

Figure 7.8: How I'd like our family to be.

relations shifted through her trauma. Carolyn's father began to drink heavily after the loss of his daughter, Jennie.

Next Carolyn was asked to draw an atom representing how she wished it would be as a corrective experience. She represented her baby sister through a broken line which she explains: 'Jennie is with us in our family but not as if she's still alive, if you know what I mean. We are all equal in status, close but not overlapped, everyone gets along with everyone, and it's comfortable. Jennie is with us but she doesn't take up a space that keeps the rest of us apart.

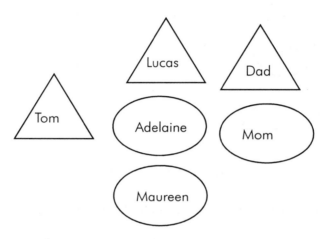

Figure 7.9: ACOA sober atom

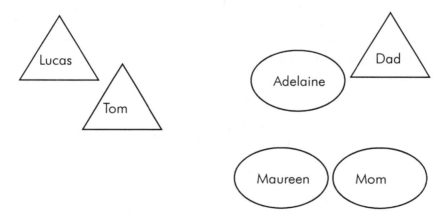

Figure 7.10: ACOA non-sober atom

She's in our hearts, but we're the family that's living and we're not stuck in the past.'

Still another version of two different worlds reveals itself in Adelaine's social atom of her world when her father was drinking and her world when her father was sober, two realities that all ACOAs internalize as they grow up. As we see in Adelaine's atoms, the object relations shift significantly when Dad is using. Mom and Dad grow distant, Maureen aligns with Mom, and Adelaine loses her place with Mom who is now preoccupied with Dad's drinking and is unavailable except to Maureen, who becomes her comfort. Lucas withdraws for protection staying out of the house as much as possible and Tom gets lost in the middle.

To complicate matters further because no one talks about the 'elephant in the living room', namely Dad's drinking, the non-sober world becomes a shadowy and murky place. Everyone lives it but it tends to be denied and repressed, leaving family members 'guessing at what normal is' (Woititz 1980). This shadow world vibrates beneath the thin membrane of the ACOA's or co-addict's world and all of the emotion, thinking, and behaviour associated with it threatens to erupt at any time when it gets triggered.

Until this world is made conscious and seen for what it is – a secondary reality with its own code of ethics and behaviour – it is difficult to sort out and understand what a normal life feels like and how it operates.

The last social atoms we shall look at here will be those of a mother of three called Theresa. Notice how the relationships of the addict shift

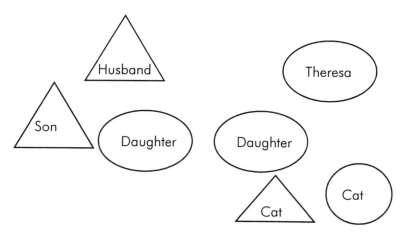

Figure 7.11: Addict's sober atom

according to her relationship with her substance. When the pull and use of the substance is most intense there is less room for anyone or anything else.

Theresa smokes pot. It helps her to feel less lonely and isolated as a mother of three young children. She is stressed, her husband works long hours, and the demands of her children can overwhelm her. She has a weak social support network due to living long distances from family and her own timidity about getting involved with community, making friends, and reaching out. Pot makes her feel less frightened and alone; it seems like a solution.

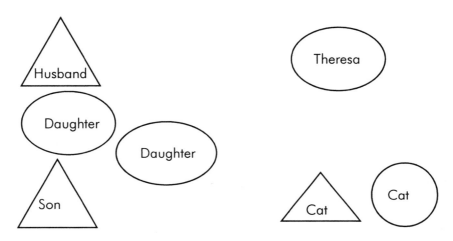

Figure 7.12: Addict's using atom

When Theresa is using and unavailable as a parent, her oldest daughter takes over that role. Now her daughter has less time and energy for school and friends and becomes increasingly preoccupied with what's going on at home, taking charge of a home that feels as if no one is in charge. The daughter's developmental needs are less well met and her parents' now distant relationship leaves her feeling frightened and insecure. She deals with this loss of family equilibrium by becoming increasingly absorbed in the needs of her younger siblings. Her sense of self is more and more derived from her role as surrogate mother. Her younger siblings feel both grateful for her attention and resentful over her control and authority. The siblings move between fused for a sense of belonging and protection and withdrawn due to the pain they're experiencing at the loss of their family and parental care.

Social atoms can be adapted in a variety of ways, such as those we have discussed here, in order to address issues related to trauma and addiction.

Conclusion

Any of the symptoms due to trauma can contribute to the erosion of inner life, producing a loss of the ability to form healthy bonds, modulate emotional states, believe in a positive future, take methodical steps toward building and sustaining personal relationships, and building a career. A psychodrama group with its adjunctive methods provides a supportive family-like (group) structure for sharing experiences, particularly loss and deprivation, as well as providing the moral solidarity of healing within the company of suffering others (Herman 1992).

Similar to Moreno's philosophy of group members being co-therapists and healing agents, the addictions field has long recognized the power and healing potential, through support and identification, that lies within the group. The broad fabric of relationships in a recovery group provides a supportive net of healing surrogates as group members bear witness to each other's stories.

It is likely that substance abuse treatment of traumatized individuals can be more effective if the issue of recurrent post-traumatic problems during withdrawal is vigorously addressed. Self-help groups such as AA seem to have grasped this issue intuitively and, with extraordinary insight, seem to have incorporated effective post-traumatic treatment in their Twelve Steps (van der Kolk 1996).

Psychodrama can facilitate each step of the recovery process as protagonists mourn past losses, develop new behaviours and attitudes, and integrate, reorganize and reorient themselves within the context of their own lives. Person by person, group by group, the connection to self and to others is reignited.

The techniques of The Trauma Model for the Creative Arts Therapies, The Time Line, The Living Genogram, and the social atom offer ways for a protagonist safely to explore personal material, revisit traumatic past events, bring past scenes toward resolution, link present day problems with their origins, and make new choices as to how to behave. All of these techniques employ psychodramatic methods to help protagonists re-contextualize and reintegrate previously split-off traumatic memories. With the use of warm-up, action, sharing, spontaneity training, creativity, role reversal, doubling, mirroring, ego auxiliary, reformed auxiliary, reconstructive scenes, abreactive catharsis, catharsis of integration and role training, the protagonist is able to resolve trauma and re-empower a disempowered self-stance.

From a psychodramatic point of view, trauma and addiction are illnesses of the system, the core unit of which is the individual. The system needs to be re-evolved sociometrically, that is, one individual will heal another then another and so on. As the individual becomes stronger and develops greater self-determination, the larger system or community transforms also.

References

All graphs taken from Dayton, T. (2000) *Trauma and Addiction*. Deerfield Beach, FL: Health Communications.

Danieli, Y. (1984) 'Psychotherapists' participation in the conspiracy of silence about the Holocaust.' *Psychoanalytic Psychology*, 23–42.

Dayton, T (1994) *The Drama Within*. Deerfield Beach, FL: Health Communications.

Dayton, T. (1997) *Heartwounds*. Deerfield Beach, FL: Health Communications.

Dayton, T. (2000) *Trauma and Addiction*. Deerfield Beach, FL: Health Communications.

Erikson, J.M. (1988) *Wisdom and the Senses*. New York: W.W. Norton.

Flannery, R.B. (1986) 'The adult children of alcoholics: are they trauma victims with learned helplessness?' *Journal of Social Behavior and Personality 1*, 4, 497–504.

Gray, R.M. (1999) *Addictions and the Self: A Self-enhancement Model for Drug Treatment in a Group Setting*. Presentation at NASW Addiction Conference, New York.

Herman, J.L. (1992) *Trauma and Recovery*. New York: Basic Books.

Johnson Institute (1986) *Intervention*. Minneapolis, MA.

Lindemann, E. (1944) 'Symptomatology and management of acute grief.' *American Psychiatrist* 141–149.

Marineau, R.F. (1989) *J.L. Moreno*. New York: Routledge.

Moreno, J.L. (1964) *Psychodrama, 1*. Beacon, New York: Beacon House.

Pert, C. (1998) *Molecules of Emotion*. New York: Scribner and Sons.

Seligman, M.E.D. (1975) *Helplessness: On Depression, Development, and Death*. San Francisco: Freeman Press.

van der Kolk, B.A. (1996) 'The complexity of adaptation to trauma.' In van der Kolk, B.A., McFarlane, A.C. and Weisaeth, L. (eds) *Traumatic Stress: The Effects of Overwhelming Experience on Mind, Body, and Society*. New York: The Guilford Press.

Woititz, J. (1980) *Adult Children of Alcoholics*. Deerfield Beach, FL: Health Communications.

CHAPTER 8

Psychodrama with Adolescent Sexual Offenders

Marlyn Robson

A 17-year-old boy was referred to us for having had sex with a 12-year-old girl without her consent. After having been in treatment for nearly 18 months, he feels sure about his progress and wants to leave the group. One of his safety rules is that he should only have a relationship with a girl who is the same age as or older than himself. Therefore, his first step should be to ask a girl her age before dating her in order to see if she is over 16 (the legal age for sexual activity in New Zealand). The boys and girls in the group are instructed to enter a role-play of going to a party. We then create a scene in which one of the girls seductively slinks over to a boy and starts chatting him up. He is totally mesmerized by her, but says nothing. In role reversal, the role of the girl is expanded, but nothing new is revealed. The boy is then asked to observe a re-run of the enactment from outside with another boy playing his role. From that position, he says calmly, 'I could not ask her age. I guess I have still some more work to do.' This short vignette provided him with some action-insight into his actual behaviour with girls. It also revealed how shy he still is with girls of his own age and that he will not be safe at parties until he can control this behaviour.

Most treatment programmes for sexual offenders around the world are based on the premise that a programme should be highly structured, specifically focused, and generally based on cognitive behavioural therapy (Hall 1995; Marshall and Barbaree 1990). If the clients gain insight and understanding of themselves and their difficulties, how they arose and how they can be changed, then they may develop the strategies and resources to change their offensive behaviour. The theory is that sexual offenders have developed both a victim and a perpetrator role in response to the various traumas that they have experienced in their own lives. In response to certain stressful life experiences, they tend to revisit these traumatic events in their minds and sometimes re-enact the roles of victim and perpetrator in real life in an attempt to gain mastery over them.

The purpose of this chapter is to describe how psychodrama is used with adolescent sexual offenders at SAFE, a community programme for the treatment of sexual offenders in Auckland, New Zealand. The adolescent programme started about nine years ago at the Leslie family therapy centre and as the need for treatment increased, it joined with the adult programme at SAFE network. In this treatment programme we try to make it *safe* to re-experience feelings of being a victim and a perpetrator. This includes an active attempt to address the shame, to develop empathy, to enhance responsibility, to restructure distorted cognition, to control deviant fantasy and to develop relapse prevention strategies. In this work, we have found that the psychodramatic techniques of role-playing, concretization, mirroring, doubling, modelling and role reversal are useful.

Theory and research

It is a myth that all offenders were once victims of sexual abuse. Research shows that only approximately 30 per cent of offenders have been sexually abused themselves (Finkelhor 1986). However, while the majority of sexual offenders may not have been sexually abused, there seems to be increasing evidence suggesting a link between a history of physical abuse and sexual offending behaviour in adults and adolescents with over half of them having suffered some form of physical abuse (Awad and Saunders 1991; Fehrenbach *et al.* 1986; Ryan *et al.* 1996). Despite all these research findings, there seem to be no clear and simple answers to the question of why someone becomes a sexual perpetrator. Apparently, many influences are involved. For example, sexual offending appears not just to be about sex, but sex in relation to violence, power and control. Similarly, Malamuth (1986) found that while no single predictor is likely to result in the development of sexual aggression, the interaction of two independent paths – hostile masculinity and sexual promiscuity – seem to be essential contributing factors.

Approximately 99 per cent of the adolescents with whom we work are males. Adolescent offenders are not just younger or more impulsive adults. They think, feel and perceive the world in a manner different from their older counterparts. From a theoretical perspective, Miner and Crimmins (1997) used social control theory, differential association theory and peer theories to explain the development of delinquency. In addition, many adolescent sexual offenders seem also to suffer from some degree of attachment deficit. Marshall, Hudson and Hodkinson (1993) argue that offenders are likely to have formed anxious-avoidant or anxious-ambivalent relationships that result in an inability to form intimate relationships. This may cause emotional loneliness that may then result in the development of aggressive interpersonal behaviour.

Schwartz (1995) developed an integrative dynamics of sexual assault model for use with adult offenders which has some implications also for adolescents. In addition, Gould (1997) found that developmental disabilities and brain injuries were present in a large number of such cases. High levels of

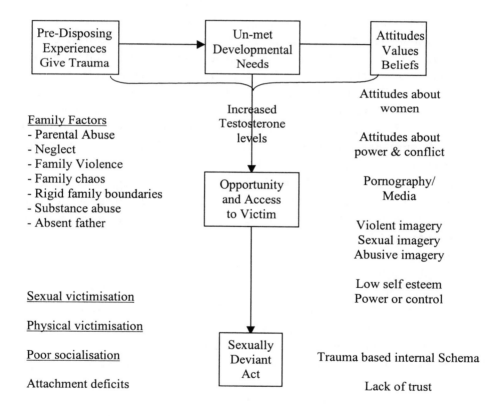

Figure 8.1: Development of sexual deviance

stress in the year prior to the most recent offence as well as use of drugs and alcohol were also present. Obviously, all such factors resulted in some impairment of impulse control. Research in this field is ongoing and all that is clear is that the causal factors are varied. In many cases, there will apparently be some predisposing trauma (sexual, physical, and/or emotional) as well as developmental deficiencies, distorted attitudes and a largely increased hormonal activity that will give rise to sexual thoughts and feelings. Some or all of these factors may prevent the adolescent from socializing properly with his peer group making age appropriate sexual experimentation unavailable. As such, he might become a social outcast and a loner who watches from afar the interpersonal activities of others. If there is then some access to younger siblings, cousins or neighbours who can satisfy his needs, sexually deviant acts may occur in a violent fashion. Such development of sexual deviance is illustrated in Figure 8.1.

From its inception and throughout its development, the team at SAFE has incorporated psychodramatic theory and practice within a cognitive behavioural approach in its treatment programme (Lambie, Robson and Simmonds 1997; Robson and Lambie 1995; Robson 1998). It is our experience that, used in a safe and mindful way, psychodrama can help to create the capacity to be mindful of current experience and to create symbolic representations of past traumatic experiences with the goals of taming the associated terror and of desomatizing the memories (Van der Kolk and McFarlane 1996). For example, it is possible in a psychodrama group to concretize a scene from the past when a boy is being beaten by his father and encourage him to observe the scene from outside in order to process cognitively and assimilate emotionally the traumatic event. Thus, he may be helped to remember more fully his past and learn how it affected him in the development of his own personal offending cycle.

Obviously, there are some special problems when working with groups like this. For example, according to the focal conflict theory of Whitaker and Lieberman (1964), groups like this tend to be stuck in a position of conflicting tensions. While there may be a wish for change (because they are in trouble with the police, they have been removed from home, they have been expelled from school, and so forth), there is also a reactive fear to change because that would involve adopting new behaviour that is unusual and strange to them. The disturbing motive and the reactive fears both need to be acknowledged and explored for enabling solutions to be found.

Cognitive behavioural therapy is based on the assumption that what we think influences what we do (Beck 1995). Thus, if we can change the way we think we will perhaps also be able to change our behaviour. Concerning sexual offenders, this is easier said than done partly because it is difficult to discover what they actually think about. The nature of their offences is based in part on secrecy and they resist openly discussing their offences. Because of fear and shame, they may act as if they comply while they are in fact only putting on a show to please everybody and to avoid facing the truth. In addition, their beliefs about what they have done are so distorted that they may find it hard to understand what was wrong in the first place. Finally, because of their invariably painful early experiences of life, they have problems identifying, discussing and coping with their overwhelming and tumultuous emotions. Because of these problems in affect regulation, they have difficulties in differentiating between feelings and expressing them in an appropriate manner. They will in addition tend to convert any unrecognized feeling into a well-known sexual feeling that they are more familiar with and can cope with better, but that they will not admit to having. Sexual offenders in particular have difficulties naming other feelings than anger. A primary task is therefore to discover the hidden feelings that are often masked by the expression of anger. For therapy to be successful with this population the process of self-discovery needs to include a catharsis of integration that touches upon the emotional, cognitive, and behavioural levels of a person at one and the same time.

Why use psychodrama with sexual offenders?

Psychodrama offers a powerful opportunity to change old self-defeating patterns through the creation of new learning experiences. Psychodrama as an experiential therapy works on four levels, according to Dayton (1994): the emotional, cognitive, behavioural, and spiritual. In addition, such therapies give participants an opportunity to discriminate between past and present, to discover and own their experience, to generate a hypothesis about the origin of their beliefs and to evaluate the tenability of that strongly held belief (Greenberg, Watson and Leitaer 1998). All this may be subsumed in the achievement of action-insight. Such psychodramatic action-insight, however, 'cannot be handed over from one person to another and cannot be given to the client by the therapist in the form of an interpretation,' according to Kellermann (1992, p.88). It has to be an actual personal learning experience.

In our programme, such experiential learning experiences happen in short vignettes to long dramatizations. For example, as we concretize bullying on the playground some action-insight may occur about the various roles that allow for different choices to be made in the future. Enacting a scene of rebellious behaviour with mother may provide some insight into how much anger has been displaced from the absent father. Creating a scene of a family celebration with numerous aunts, uncles and cousins may help a boy remember the abuse he repressed for a long time. The working through of this memory may in turn help him take more personal responsibility for his own offending behaviour.

While sexual perpetrator therapy sometimes attempts to understand the past, it mainly concentrates on changing the behaviour of the present and the future. This is in agreement with Kellermann who suggested that 'the process of self discovery must be complemented with an element of foresight in the enhancement of anticipatory awareness to be used in future coping behaviour' (1992, p.86). In the treatment of sexual offenders this emphasizes the importance of learning to gain enough insight to look ahead and make different choices for the future. Moreno (1972) proposed that an increase in spontaneity and creativity would bring about the formation of new roles. Such new roles may include different thoughts, beliefs, feelings and actions. With the use of simple role-playing and concretization techniques, we try to build such new roles. As the spontaneity level rises in these boys, we can observe new roles developing that are positive and creative in their expression. This work often gives new psychological strength that can be used to work through their own past traumatic events and to begin to make better choices in life.

Spontaneity is expressed when there is a new response to an old situation, or an adequate response to a new situation. In his spontaneity theory, Moreno (1972) suggested that in the development of a person there can be original moments, truly creative and decisive beginnings. This is exactly what is looked for to help change sexually offending behaviour. Moreno also talked of spontaneity being creative, original, and dramatic and having an adequacy of response. It is the energy that drives the creative act. When anxiety or resistance is high, as it often is in our groups for reasons that have already been described, then spontaneity is low and the chance of new role development is low. At these moments, we work to increase the warm-up in order to encourage creative responses to emerge from the boys.

Warm-up

The concept of warm-up is very important with adolescent boys. Like athletes warming up before a race in order to achieve their full potential, clients also need to warm up to being in a group, to the leaders and to the idea of change. For traumatized individuals, the process of warm-up may help their bodies to remember what their minds may have forgotten. Whether staunch, terminally cool, or just plain stubborn, participants are actively encouraged by various activities to use their bodies. By doing so, their emotions are stimulated, bringing about a balance of action and feeling in their warming-up process. The fun involved assists a great deal in lowering anxiety and facilitating an environment where trust can be reborn.

The level of increased spontaneity will determine how people will react to new situations. Van der Kolk (1996) suggested that after trauma, individuals respond to high levels of emotional arousal with an inability properly to evaluate and categorize the experience, or to make sense of it. They have difficulty taking in and processing arousing information and with learning from the experience. Van der Kolk states that their altered psychobiology may cause them to react with aggression or withdrawal. The warm-up process therefore needs to be carefully monitored as too much can result in rage, fragmentation of the group or someone storming out. The director has the task of regulating the warm-up so that participants can tolerate the intensity of the enactment.

Any game that gets the participants moving will increase warm-up and spontaneity. Walking games, tag, fantasy and adventure journeys are some examples of the endless variety of games that can be used. Obviously, these games will be more effective when used with a purpose. Some games are used for physical warm-up, such as Slalom. Some stimulate the mind and improve concentration, such as Zip Zap Bop. Other games encourage creativity, such as speaking in funny voices or passing an object around and trying to find new functions for it. The skill involves selecting the precise moment to produce the maximum result.

Slalom is an example of a game which is very physical. It requires a certain amount of thought, as well as the ability to contain intense emotions. It is a visualization game where the boys stand an arm's length apart, all facing in one direction, like slalom poles in a ski race. The boy at the end looks carefully at where everyone is and attempts to memorize this, as he is then blindfolded. Using skiing movements, he then tries to zigzag as fast as he can between the poles to the end. Everyone has a turn and each boy gets something different out of it. This is a tremendous test, for most of these boys have never learned to trust anyone about anything in life. Boy A has to trust totally the group to stay where he visualizes them. Boy B has to stay in line and play fair. In life, he has learned always to be one step ahead. Boy C does not dare to be blindfolded but agrees to participate if he can choose to close his eyes by himself without the blindfold. Boy D is small and timid and wonders if he can legitimately bump into the others in the group without getting hit by them.

Care has to be taken in order for the game not to get too violent. If that happens, fragmentation may occur. Therefore constant assessment of the warm-up is needed by noticing voice levels, interruptions, body movements and general anxiety level. Games can also be introduced to slow the process down, help them to concentrate and to access self-control, which is a new concept for many of the boys. The old trust game of one person in the middle of a small circle with their eyes closed being moved around by the others, can be useful here, if the instruction is really to care for this person, and act lovingly and gently in the way you yourself would liked to be touched.

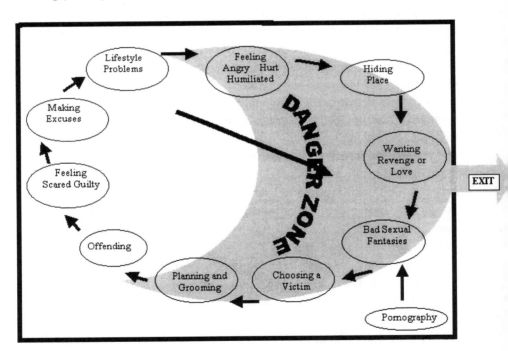

Figure 8.2: Cycles of offending. Courtesy of SAFE

Most of therapy is conducted in weekly groups, with about eight to ten boys in each group, which continue for about a year on average. These groups give an opportunity for boys to learn about where they might personally fit within the offending cycle, as illustrated in Figure 8.2, and to find ways to exit from that cycle.

Further learning is also provided through the training of social behaviour and communication skills. Deviant sexual fantasies are discussed as well as possible uses of pornography. An important part of the programme is to teach a relapse prevention model, as illustrated in Figure 8.3 which aims to help participants to discover their own high risk situations and to make more appropriate choices when such situations arise.

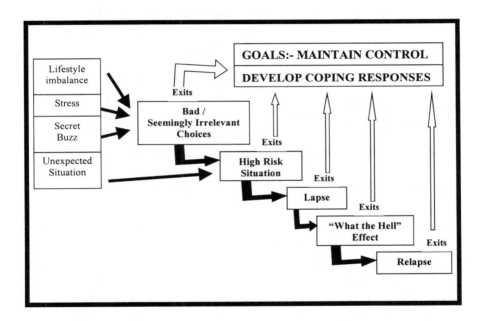

Figure 8.3: The relapse process. Courtsey of SAFE

The group process

Safety issues usually arise at the beginning of groups such as these, together with feelings of shame, fear and the protagonists' efforts to keep their inner world secret from others and from themselves. Warm-up games are introduced to prepare them for some more experiential activities and short concretizations of everyday life events are enacted when the time is ripe. Physical awareness of the manifestation of feelings is encouraged at this stage. As trust increases, the concretizations become vignettes and then enactments that include full dramatizations of life events and include the use of the technique of role reversal.

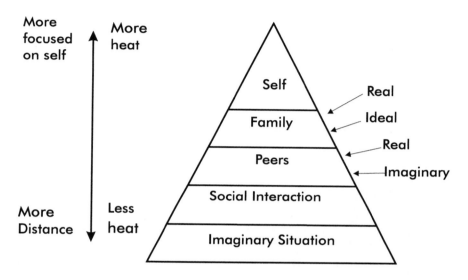

Figure 8.4: How to choose the therapeutic moment. Courtesy of John Bergman.

Each boy seems to need a different warm-up and a flexible approach to psychotherapy. One boy may only be able to tolerate a fantasy journey through an enchanted forest and explore the feelings he experiences there. Another may have enough self-esteem to enact a small psychodrama about a high-risk situation in his everyday life and his choices around that. Invariably, however, all boys are hypersensitive to criticism, shame and embarrassment and are terrified of being exposed and isolated and humiliated. Attempting to help them to disclose their hidden worlds in the open is a constant challenge. 'What do they fear?' 'Do they remember their own abuse?' 'Are they plotting revenge?' 'Do they ache for love and someone to care for them?' The use of masks, pictures and strange toys is sometimes very helpful in this work of revealing the secret or shameful parts of themselves. In addition, the use of mirroring is an important tool in helping to delineate progressive and functional roles which may increase self-esteem (Clayton 1994).

As illustrated in the initial example, the use of psychodramatic enactment may also be diagnostic. A boy may have trouble remembering just how much force he used to rape his little sister. Setting the scene in the group allows him to warm up sufficiently truly to recreate the offence. The force displayed is often shockingly strong, as are the threats used to keep the victim quiet, none of which would be revealed by only talking about it. Such re-enactments, however, are delicate manoeuvres and should be handled with caution. For example, in order for the young offender not to become too sexually aroused by the memory, he is asked to show what happened using a cushion, rather than repeating the scene with another group member who would play the role of victim.

A very useful and simple exercise for role development that we use is 'New Me versus old Me.' Using a 'good' voice and a 'bad' voice, we try to recreate what messages both voices give the young offender in high-risk situations. We ask: 'What does the bad voice say?' 'What can we do to strengthen the good voice?' 'Who can help?' Setting a scene of a high-risk situation may be very helpful to help practise new role behaviour for the future. We especially inquire about possible supportive people and role models who can be of help in such situations. When a particular boy has never experienced any such good role models in life, we search for other, more creative role models that they might look up to. Boys may then choose such film or TV stars as Superman, Obi wan Kanobi, William Wallace or Indiana Jones.

Social atom repair

Initially, it is too threatening for the adolescents to go too far with social atom repair because these boys come from incredibly dysfunctional families and they are holding in so much pain. We set out family sculptures to highlight the relationships within the family system, asking the boys to place people as close or as far away from them as they actually feel towards these people. Sometimes enough insight is gained by just seeing who is positioned where in the family. At other times it is possible to express powerful sentiments towards one or many of these significant people. Such direct encounters with family members seem to add an increased awareness beyond what we see in family therapy. In addition, it gives the opportunity to express feelings that they have kept in for a long time. The opportunity to experiment with expressing what could never be expressed directly in the family can be explored safely within playful enactment. If such enactments become too hard, a boy can always leave the scene and observe the situation from outside. From that distant position, he is then encouraged to get a different awareness of what took place. Boys can explore being enormously angry with an absent or violent father and say directly what they feel which would not be safe in real life. They can also learn to clarify what might have been good in their families, which may be important to remember and use at a later stage in the process of the group. Diagnostically, such an act may be very useful since it helps to highlight resources in the family that we can later encourage.

The containing double

The concept of the containing double (Hudgins and Drucker 1998) is very helpful in our work. Many of our boys may have missed out on the developmental stage in their life that emphasizes such an empathic significant other. In addition, the 'therapeutic spiral model' with trauma survivors (see Chapter 13 in this book) has been a central part of our understanding. While only about 30 to 40 per cent of boys treated in our programme have been sexually abused, all are survivors of traumas, including physical and emotional abuse and severe attachment deficits.

There are three steps in developing the containing double. The first is learning to reflect on the process or on what is happening at any given moment. This ability to observe is frequently absent in our boys who commonly say that the offence 'just happened'. The second step of development is learning to express the containing statement 'I am OK, I can handle this, I do have some skills'. The third step is the anchor in the here and now, for example, being aware of changes in the body. Young offenders become sexually aroused almost without awareness and have little skill to calm down and sublimate their sexual urges. It is incredibly empowering for them to become aware of the fact that they do not necessarily have to act upon their arousal and that there may be other ways to defuse their libido. Using these three steps in developing the containing double provides a sense of having a strong, accepting and loving mother beside you that notices what is happening and totally believes in you, but still keeps you from doing things that you are not in control of. As such, the containing double becomes a helpful role relationship that makes it safer to face their own traumatic experiences.

Victim empathy

Empathy training is an important element of many treatment programmes around the world (Thomas 1992) including our own. The assumption is that if an offender has a better understanding of what it is like to be treated as a victim, then it may prevent him from repeating his offence. Recent studies have shown particular intervention programmes to be effective in raising the empathy scores of adult offenders (Hogue 1994; Pithers 1994; Schewe and ODonohue 1993). For example, Daniels and Thornton (1998) used psycho-dramatic role-play for this purpose with adult offenders in a large-scale trial in British prisons. Similarly, our team at SAFE has used psychodramatic role reversal for the increase of victim empathy ever since we started our programme (Robson and Lambie 1995). It is interesting that a recent study by Monto (1998) found that offenders were not significantly less empathic than a comparison population of urban high school students.

Rather than explaining their offence with a lack of empathy, this study suggests that some perpetrators might not see their offence as harmful. An alternative explanation may be that they have the idea that their victim was a willing participant. Finally, their offence might be understood as a lack of impulse control and judgement. At the crucial moment of offending, they were simply too turned on to care about the consequences or what the victim might have felt. This might have been true even for boys who themselves had been previously abused and who, one would have expected, should have known better.

Our method of attempting to increase victim empathy includes both cognitive and affective components. Cognitively, we introduce experiential exercises around the effects of sexual abuse on others. 'How would they know someone is being abused?' By looking at pictures of people, we try to help them recognize feelings of, for example, fear, horror and pain. In addition, they are taught some basic assertiveness training principles in terms of people's right to say 'No!' even though the other person may be a sibling, cousin or friend who might be older than them.

Affective experiential exercises include sculptures around power and control situations, such as situations of domestic violence or bullying at school. We do not recommend doing role reversals at this initial stage, only sharing of feelings. Masks may be first used to portray what feelings were inside them at the moment before offending and what feelings the victims might have been feeling. Initially, their responses are frighteningly blank. Dolls and puppets can also be used to set up the offending scene, as well as drawings, since this might give some distance to that which is hard to look at directly. Gradually, the young offenders find their own ways to enact the difficult moments of their lives, showing in action what they remember and role reversing with the people present and later sharing about their own victimization.

To role reverse truly is a very complex skill requiring clear perception of and an ability to imitate the other. Obviously, sex offenders will have great difficulties in this because of their tendency to distort and misunderstand what they see. In fact, the basic empathy required in role reversal seems to be largely lacking in many of these boys.

Therefore, when these boys are asked to role reverse they are only able to take the other role in a superficial manner, sometimes as an act of trying to please the leaders but without any deep understanding of the other person. This is in line with Kellermann's notion that 'Complete role reversal is impossible. We can never fully conceptualise the feelings, attitudes and motives of another person, much less reproduce what we perceive in action' (1994, p.267). However, some glimpses of understanding of how it is to be in the role of the other may help the adolescent to make a different choice at a crucial moment.

When participants are ready to re-enact their offence, the scene is set and the protagonist is invited to choose group members to be actors in his drama. The enactment usually goes through three stages, starting with the scene before the offending incident, moving on to the moment of the actual offence and then providing an opportunity for emotional and cognitive integration. We do not fully enact the actual scene of victimization since this might lead to re-traumatization and too much arousal of the offender and other group members. At one point or another, the perpetrator is asked to role reverse with the victim and, in order to concretize the power dynamics involved, the victim may be kneeling. In this role of victim, the protagonist will be encouraged to connect with how he has felt previously at powerless moments in his life. This may have to be done several times before he can feel something of what it was like to be his victim. In the sharing afterwards, other group members might be warmed up to re-enact their own memories of abuse and victimization.

Andrew

Andrew was referred to SAFE as a 14-year-old boy who had admitted to various incidents of indecent assault, abduction, attempted rape, actual rape of a four-year-old girl, and rape of his younger sister who was then ten years old. There were also two incidents of arson. Further assessment revealed that he had serious learning disabilities and was functioning at the level of a six-year-old. He was reported to have been sexually abused by his father, although he had no memory of this. However, he remembered being severely physically abused by his mother. His father had been absent from his life since he was three years old and he had lived since then with his mother and two younger siblings. Initially, Andrew was sullen, closed off and difficult to engage. He did not want to interact with other group members but loved to draw and liked to talk about his drawings when encouraged.

Andrew has now been in the programme for about three years. He is small for his age but strong and physically fit with good hand-eye co-ordination. He loves active games and is excellent at them. In games such as 'red light-green light', 'tag' and 'touch rugby' he has gained a sense of mastery. He has also improved his connection with others in the group and, as a result, seems to feel better about himself. In the slalom game described above he found it was hard to be blindfolded but loved to visualize the positions of the others and get through the obstacles successfully. Initially, when asked about his family dynamics, he would close off and become silent. Gradually, however, sculptures and concretizations in pairs around phrases such as 'You have done it again', 'It's all your fault' and 'Come here!' triggered him to respond and express some of his hitherto kept-in anger towards his powerful mother.

He also gained a better understanding of the different behaviours of 'old Me' and 'new Me' and became able to set up a continuum of all the roles involved. Through role-play, he seemed to have gained enough insight to understand when he had slipped back to 'old Me' and what he needed to do then. Because Andrew could neither read nor write, it was important for him to experience and internalize voices that gave him messages that he could access at appropriate times. Role-plays were an essential part of developing these voices with various people that he respected. Thus, some simple messages were internalized, such as 'No parks, no schools and no shopping malls', 'Don't do it!', 'Have respect for little kids', 'I care about you and I believe that you can make good choices', 'call SAFE to get help when you need'.

In a 'victim empathy drama', Andrew was incredibly clear about his pattern of offending. The scene included his mother asleep in front of the TV.

He was angry with his sister for taking his stereo. He had been looking at pornography in his own room. He had became sexually aroused and had entered the room of his sister and abused her under threat. When role reversed into his sister's role, he gained enough insight to display a sadness that he had rarely shown. Later, he seemed to have integrated the experience sufficiently to talk about it and show some understanding of his sister's sadness. These are just small parts of action over an intensive three-year period of therapy with a very low-functioning boy. We were impressed, however, that even a boy who was as defiant and closed off as Andrew was able to learn from this experience and started to understand the consequences of his own behaviour.

Conclusion

Perpetrators of sexual abuse are experts in secrecy and do everything to keep therapists away from revealing the truth. The challenge is to get under their skins without causing more traumatization. Because of their dislike of anyone who is in a position of authority, adolescents are particularly difficult. Experiential therapy can be an effective adjunct to cognitive behavioural therapy in this work. While the mind might try to lie, the body cannot. Psychodrama is very visual; as a scene is set out, a body moves, a voice speaks. We can see what is mirrored back: the truth is here.

References

Abel, G.G., Mittelman, M.S. and Becker, J.V. (1985). 'Sexual offenders: results of assessment and recommendations for treatment.' In M.H. Ben-Aron, S.J. Hucker and C.D. Webster (eds) *Clinical Criminology: The Assessment and Treatment of Criminal Behaviour.* Toronto: University of Toronto.

Awad, G.A. and Saunders, E.B. (1991) 'Male adolescent sexual assaulters: clinical observations.' *Journal of Interpersonal Violence 6,* 446–460.

Beck, J. (1995) *Cognitive Therapy: Basics and Beyond.* New York: Guilford Press.

Clayton, M. (1994) 'Role theory and its application in clinical practice.' In Holmes, P., Karp, M. and Watson, M. (eds) *Psychodrama Since Moreno: Innovations in Theory and Practice.* London and New York: Routledge.

Daniels, M. and Thornton, D. (1998) 'Using role play to develop victim empathy: experience from a large scale trial.' Presentation at A.T.S.A. 17th Annual Research and Treatment Conference, Vancouver.

Dayton, T. (1994) *The Drama Within: Psychodrama and Experiential Therapy.* Deerfield Beach, FL: Health Communications.

Fehrenbach, P., Smith, W., Monastersky, C. and Deisher, R. (1986) 'Adolescent sex offenders: offender and offence characteristics.' *American Journal of Orthopsychiatry 56*, 225–233.

Finkelhor, D. (1986) 'Abusers: special topics.' In D. Finkelhor (ed) *A Sourcebook on Child Sexual Abuse*. Newbury Park, CA: Sage Publications.

Gould, M.A. (1997) 'An empirical investigation of floodgates factors in child sexual abuse.' In B.K. Schwarz and H.R. Cellini (eds) *The Sexual Offender: Corrections, Treatment, and Legal Practice*. Kingston, NJ: Civic Research Institute.

Greenberg, L.S., Watson, J. and Leitaer, G. (1998) *The Handbook of Experiential Psychotherapy*, 509–532.

Hall, G.C. (1995) 'Sexual offender recidivism revisited: a meta-analysis of recent treatment studies.' *Journal of Consulting and Clinical Psychology 63*, 5, 802–809.

Hogue, T.E. (1994) 'Sex offense information questionnaire: assessment of sexual offenders and perceptions of responsibility, empathy, and control.' *Issues in Criminological and Legal Psychology 21*, 68–75.

Hudgins, M.K. (1998) 'Experiential psychodrama with sexual trauma.' In L.S. Greenberg, J.C.Watson and G. Lietaer (eds) *Handbook of Experiential Psychotherapy*. New York: Guilford Press.

Hudgins, M.K. and Drucker, K. (1998) 'The Containing Double as part of the Therapeutic Spiral Model for treating trauma survivors.' *The International Journal of Action Methods, 51*, 2, 63–74.

Hudgins, M.K., Drucker, K. and Metcalf, K. (2000). 'The Containing Double: Preliminary research results with PTSD.' *British Journal of Psychodrama and Sociodrama 15*, 1, 58–77

Kellermann, P.F. (1992) *Focus on Psychodrama: The Therapeutic Aspects of Psychodrama*. London: Jessica Kingsley Publishers.

Kellermann, P.F. (1994) 'Role reversal in psychodrama.' In P. Holmes, M. Karp and M. Watson (eds) *Psychodrama Since Moreno: Innovations in Theory and Practice*. London: Routledge.

Lambie, I., Robson, M. and Simmonds, L. (1997) 'Embedding psychodrama in a wilderness group programme for adolescent sex offenders.' *Journal of Offender Rehabilitation 26*, 89–107.

Malamuth, N.M. (1986) 'Predictors of naturalistic sexual aggression.' *Journal of Personality and Social Psychology 50*, 953–962.

Marshall, W.L. and Barbaree, H.E. (1990) 'Outcome of comprehensive cognitive behavioural treatment programmes.' In W.L. Marshall, D.R. Laws and H.E. Barbaree (eds) *Handbook of Sexual Assault*. New York: Plenum Press.

Marshall, W.L., Hudson, S.M. and Hodkinson, S. (1993) 'The importance of attachment bonds in the development of juvenile sex offending.' In H.E. Barbaree, W.L. Marshall and S.M. Hudson (eds) *The Juvenile Sex Offender*. New York: The Guilford Press.

Miner, M.H. and Crimmins, C.L.S. (1997) 'Adolescent sex offenders' issues of etiology and risk factors.' In B.K. Schwartz and H.R. Cellini (eds) *The Sexual Offender: Corrections, Treatment, and Legal Practice*. Kingston, NJ: Civic Research Institute.

Monto, M., Zgourides, G., Wilson, J. and Harris, R. (1998) 'Empathy and adolescent male sex-offenders.' *Perceptual and Motor Skills, 79*, 1598.

Moreno, J.L. (1972) *Psychodrama, Volume 1*. New York: Beacon House.

Pithers, W.D. (1994) 'Process evaluation of a group therapy component designed to enhance sex offenders' empathy for sexual abuse survivors.' *Behaviour Research and Therapy 32*, 565–570.

Robson, M. (1998) 'Action insight: the treatment of adolescent sexual offenders.' *Journal of the Australian and New Zealand Psychodrama Association 7*, 41–57.

Robson, M. and Lambie, I. (1995) 'Using psychodrama to facilitate victim empathy in adolescent sexual offenders.' *Journal of the Australian and New Zealand Psychodrama Association 4*, 13–19.

Ryan, G., Miyoshi, T.J., Metzner, J.L., Krugman, R.D. and Fryer, G.E. (1996) 'Trends in a national sample of sexually abusive youths.' *Journal of the American Academy of Child and Adolescent Psychiatry 35*, 17–25.

Schewe, P.A. and Donohue, W. (1993) 'Sexual abuse prevention with high-risk males: the roles of victim empathy and rape myths.' *Violence and Victims 8*, 339–351.

Schwartz, B. K. (1995) 'Theories of sex offenders.' In B.K. Schwartz and H.R. Cellini (eds) *The Sexual Offender: Corrections, Treatment, and Legal Practice.* Kingston, NJ: Civic Research Insitute.

Sternberg, P. and Garcia, A. (1989). *Sociodrama: Who's In Your Shoes?* New York: Praeger.

Thomas, D.W. (1992) *A Special Report on Juvenile Sex Offenders.* Pittsburgh, PA: National Centre for Juvenile Justice.

Whitaker, D.S. and Lieberman, M.A. (1964) *Psychotherapy Through the Group Process.* New York: Atherton Press.

van der Kolk, B.A. (1986). The complexity of adaptation to trauma. In B.A. Van der Kolk, A.C. McFarlane and L. Weisaeth (eds) Traumatic Stress: The effects of overwhelming experience on mind, body, and society. New York: Guilford Press.

van der Kolk, B.A. and McFarlane, A.C. (1996) 'The black hole of trauma.' In B.A. van der Kolk, A.C. McFarlane and L. Weisaeth (eds) *Traumatic Stress: The Effect of Overwhelming Experience on Mind, Body, and Society.* New York: Guilford Press.

CHAPTER 9

Time's Distorted Mirror
Trauma Work with Adult Male Sex Offenders

Clark Baim

> In the desert
> I saw a creature, naked, bestial,
> Who, squatting upon the ground,
> Held his heart in his hands,
> And ate of it.
> I said: 'Is it good, friend?'
> 'It is bitter – bitter,' he answered;
> 'But I like it
> Because it is bitter,
> And because it is my heart.'
>
> Stephen Crane, 'In the Desert' (1895) (Miller 1991)

It is mid-way through the psychodrama and Warren, the protagonist, is trying to understand how he came to commit his offence – the rape of an acquaintance from work – and to gain a sense of empathy for others, particularly his victim. From the role of his victim, a woman in her twenties, Warren says, 'I feel trapped. I'm afraid he'll kill me'. Soon after this, Warren takes on the role of the rape victim's eight-year-old son, who witnessed the rape, and then of his own nine-year-old son, whom Warren had beaten many times. In the role of his own son, Warren asks, 'Why does Dad beat me? Why doesn't he just talk to me? I love him and I hate him!'

The director asks Warren if these suffering voices sound familiar to him. Back in role as himself, Warren shakes his head disconsolately. 'I'm just like my father,' he sighs. He is sitting on the floor, his arms folded around his knees and clasped to his chest. 'How old do you feel?' asks the director. Warren responds, 'I feel ten years old.'

The psychodrama moves back in time to when Warren was ten. At first, the role of ten-year-old Warren is played in mirror by another member of the group, with Warren standing at the edge of the stage and looking in at the scene. Gradually, and with an increasing sense of reality, the scene recreates the daily ritual of Warren's father beating him and his brothers with a belt, while mother is looking on. Every day, at the same time, the ritual is performed. As he lashes out with the belt, Warren's father tells him that the beating is his own fault, it is meant to teach him a lesson.

In a later, frenzied scene, Warren receives the worst beating from his father, who uses a stick this time, the blows landing so hard on Warren's head and back that he is certain he will die. Only at the last minute before he loses consciousness does his mother intervene. When this scene is replayed in mirror, Warren begins to cry. He spits out the words, 'Oh, shit, shit it hurts!'. Warren continues to watch and narrate the scene in mirror, as his ten-year-old self is left shivering and locked in a dark coalbunker in the cellar. As he looks at himself in the coalbunker, Warren says that this was the moment when he decided that he would never have feelings again.

Introduction

People who become sex offenders have often experienced severe trauma, child abuse, neglect and exploitation themselves. The abusive behaviour of offenders may be understood as a distorted mirror image of early traumatic experience that remains unprocessed in their mind, too painful to look at or work through (Jefferies 1991 and 1996; de Zulueta 1998; Schwartz, Galperin and Masters 1993). This distorted mirror has an insidious power to infiltrate all aspects of human function, creating distorted views of self and other and disabling the ability to regulate affect and tolerate painful feelings. Even with the passage of time, the toxicity of the abuse remains. It will not fade without deliberate attention and working through which allows the trauma victim to add symbolic meaning to the trauma and achieve relief through catharsis, grieving, new understanding and adaptation (Winn 1994; Goldman and Morrison 1984; Briere 1996; Scheff 1979; Langs 1999).

This chapter describes my psychodramatic practice in addressing trauma issues with adult men who have committed acts of sexual abuse, including adult rape, sexual abuse of children and sexual murder. The work takes place in a special prison which is run as a therapeutic community and which provides essential support and a safe context for the psychodrama sessions. In this chapter, offenders are referred to as male, as the theoretical material and programme descriptions are based on work addressing male offenders.

Using psychodrama as a method of choice with this population provides a highly accessible, concrete and effective method for moving back and forth through time, simultaneously addressing the individual's offending behaviour and its origins. Underpinning the work is the belief that sexual offending is a learned behaviour (Jefferies 1991 and 1996) and is in most cases a symptom of the perpetrator's maladaptive thinking, feeling and behaviour patterns developed largely in response to earlier trauma.

Post-trauma work with sex offenders does not differ significantly from trauma work done with any group of trauma victims. The key differences are in the context of the trauma work, the risk factors involved which impact on public protection and confidentiality and, finally, the timing of the trauma work. Bearing in mind the exigencies of working within the criminal justice system and, by extension, within the broader framework of public protection, it is crucial that work on the offender's own trauma history is never undertaken when there is a risk that the offender will use his traumatic experience to justify his crimes or absolve himself of culpability. Balancing these two therapeutic imperatives demands enormous resources of human tolerance and the considered application of evidence from the fields of psychobiology, psychology, trauma counselling, sociology and criminology (van der Kolk 1994a, 1994b; Kipper 1998).

Prevalence of trauma histories among sex offenders

Most sex offenders have suffered significant sexual, physical or emotional abuse, neglect, exploitation or traumatic disruption to primary attachments when young, to such a degree that they develop a distorted and corrupted trauma-based emotional system (Schwartz et al. 1993 and 1995; Briere 1996; Wallis 1995). One recent study, for example, found that 93 per cent of a group of sex offenders had been sexually abused when they were children (Briggs 1995, p.xii). Grubin (1998) summarises studies showing rates of sexual abuse histories among offenders of 18 to 79 per cent. This compares with a generally agreed consensus of research that indicates a 10 per cent prevalence of sexual abuse among male children in the general population. This percentage includes only sexual abuse, and not other forms of abuse.

In light of these and other findings consistently cited in the literature (Salter 1988; Morrison, Erooga and Beckett 1994) it is reasonable to use as a working assumption that individuals who have committed self-motivated and repeated sex offences have experienced significant and debilitating trauma, whether it be from physical or sexual abuse, prolonged neglect or major disruptions in early primary attachments. When one is working with such individuals, one is most often working with someone whose core experience of being alive is that of being unvalued, powerless, excluded, detested, exploited, dehumanized or shamed – in short, being a victim. This principle applies whether or not the offender consciously understands his own trauma as damaging. Many, in fact, will see their abuse as being a good thing, that 'it did me no harm' (Briggs 1995; Burt 1980; Marshall and Maric 1996; Salter 1988).

This experience of damage that occurs early in the life of offenders should be taken into consideration in offender treatment, despite common reservations about approaching such issues out of fear of being seen as collusive. As Jefferies (1991) has pointed out, the abuse committed against these individuals is often far worse than that which they later perpetrate. For the sceptic who may dismiss such an approach as collusive or soft on offenders, it is important to point out that the degree of trauma being referred to is far beyond the normal trauma of infancy and childhood. These are the traumas of, for example, the boy beaten over the head with a thick stick by a mother shouting at him that she wants him dead; the boy who, throughout his childhood, repeatedly witnesses his father brutally raping his mother, often while holding a knife to her throat; the boy who is repeatedly raped by a group of men and then forced to watch as the men inject other boys with muscle relaxants prior to raping them; or, as in the case of Warren, the trauma of the boy beaten every day, until one day he decides he will never have feelings again.

These are among the most horrific atrocities, committed in secret and behind closed doors against silenced children. As long as these horrors remain unspoken of, they retain their debilitating power. The fact that these boys later grow into men who commit further offences makes it all the more crucial to acknowledge their pain and begin the process of healing in the hope of helping them develop and practise safe behaviour.

Looking through the distorted mirror: from victim to victimizer

What is the process by which a victim of abuse and trauma may then go on to commit acts of abuse in later life? It is crucial first to stress that most individuals who suffer severe stresses or childhood trauma will not go on to abuse

(Briggs 1995; Tedeschi and Calhoun 1995; Webb and Leehan 1996; Wallis 1995). While trauma will increase the likelihood of future psychological disturbance, including abusive acting out, a number of factors will assist healing. These may include a loving and protective network of family and friends, the opportunity to talk through and attribute accurate meaning to the trauma, the social and internal ego development of the trauma victim at the time of the trauma, and biological and genetic factors (Bannister 1991; Tedeschi and Calhoun 1995; Whitfield 1995).

Even when healing never occurs, and the trauma victim continues to live within a trauma-based emotional system, this will not necessarily lead to offending behaviour. A wide range of coping and compensating behaviours may be used in lieu of abusive acting out. These may include denial, repression, avoidance or various forms of self-harm and self-destruction such as substance abuse, to name just a few of the strategies that may be used (see Chapter 13 of this book by Kate Hudgins; Langs 1999).

Concentrating on the aetiology of offending, the fields of neurobiology and attachment theory have much to say about how the effects of childhood trauma may lead, in some cases, to future offending. Research within the field of neurobiology explains that overwhelming incidents of sexual and physical trauma and other terrifying experiences have the effect of freezing our normal biochemical, physical, perceptual, cognitive, emotional, psychological and behavioural processes (Kipper 1998). Primate research and research with human infants demonstrates that severe and prolonged trauma overwhelms the brain's capacity to process information, forcing the individual to cope with trauma by dissociating, psychically numbing and blocking off feelings in order to survive (van der Kolk 1994a). Langs has observed that these coping responses may indeed be deeply embedded in evolutionary selection as a means of self-preservation. In order to survive, the brain uses a strategy of knowledge reduction as opposed to knowledge acquisition or retention (Langs 1999).

As a result, the memory of these early traumatic experiences is not coded and given meaning as most experience is, but is rather stuck on the sensorimotor level of memory. This creates what Hudgins describes in Chapter 13 as 'trauma bubbles', which contain the sensory information and emotions related to the experience, but which are often out of reach of conscious, intellectual or verbal understanding and explanation. Some of these pockets of energy contain memory of sounds, fragments of voices, some contain memory of smells or sights or touch.

The confusion about their own abuse is often paralleled in offenders by their confusion about their own offending. It is common for offenders to state that they wish to discover the reasons why they offended. Given the degree to which so many offenders learned at an early age to dissociate and separate physiological sensation from mental understanding, it is not surprising that they should be confused or even mystified about their own offending. Indeed, it is often the case that offenders dissociate while offending. The re-enactment of their own abuse remains unconscious, and will continue to be so until they are helped to understand the links between their offending and their victim experience (Schwartz *et al.* 1993).

Studies in neurobiology have also found physical evidence that trauma causes profound damage to neural pathways and the structure of the brain. For example, parts of the cerebral cortex and limbic system are on average between 20 and 30 per cent smaller in children who have been abused compared with non-abused children (Perry and Pate 1994). The effects on the limbic system are particularly noteworthy, as this area is associated with emotional regulation and attachment. These children also show reduced brain stem regulation and fewer synapses in affected areas of the brain. Furthermore, a study of brain activity in abused children found that 55 per cent had an abnormal EEG, compared with 27 per cent in a control group of non-abused children (Ito *et al.* 1993).

For many individuals so traumatized, the slightest stress may unleash an over-abundance of cortisols and other stress hormones, leading to impulsive acting out, heightened anxiety, diminished concentration, self-destructiveness and general loss of self-control. In those instances where life events trigger a powerful release of the toxic memory, an adrenaline-induced fight or flight response will lead to a chronic dysregulation of affect and behaviour (Hunter 1995; van der Kolk 1994a and 1994b).

In order to cope with such chronic dysregulation, many trauma survivors adapt by avoiding feelings entirely. They become psychically numb in order to anaesthetise the entire system and so minimize the chances of feeling pain and losing control (Greenberg and Paivio 1998). In sex offenders, their inability properly to regulate their emotions leads them to override their internal inhibitions. This is one of the prime deficiencies in sex offenders and is one of the major areas stressed in cognitive behavioural programmes (Finkelhor 1984; Beckett 1994). It is interesting that most offenders do understand on a cognitive level, even at the time of their offending, that what they are doing is wrong. This is why it is often superfluous to teach offenders why sex offending is wrong. Such an approach has only limited benefit if the underlying problem, the dysregulation which allows the offender to over-ride his inhibitors, is not addressed directly (van der Kolk 1994a).

Attachment theory provides further insights that help to explain how victims of abuse can later become offenders. Attachment theory points out that, during traumatic experiences, the defensive regression to a primitive level of functioning creates a powerful attachment need, equivalent to the need for protection of the infant in relation to its mother (Bowlby 1988).

The trauma-induced regressive state would ordinarily demand that the mother, or carer, acknowledge the distress of the infant, and show emotional signs that parallel and feed back these emotions in a safe, contained and much diminished form, such that the infant internalizes a means by which profoundly distressing affect can be regulated (van der Kolk 1994a).

When, however, the source of the trauma is the very person who should ordinarily be protective, nature plays its cruellest trick, which is to increase the need for and attachment to the very source of the terror (Bowlby 1984). This same pattern applies even when the abuser is not the ordinary caregiver, but has managed to manipulate the child and the environment around the child such that the abuser is the person to whom the child feels greatest attachment – a well known strategy of child sexual offenders (Finkelhor 1984). As a result, some victims of child abuse staunchly defend their abuser, based on the distorted belief – often inculcated during the grooming process by their abuser – that they deserved what happened to them because of their own badness, or that they liked what was being done to them and that their abuser is really looking out for their best interests.

In those cases in which the victim goes on to abuse, this distortion becomes a rationalization and justification for their acts of abuse against others: 'That child liked it, I really loved her.' Or, 'He deserved it!'. These are frequently heard distorted beliefs or justifications used by offenders. Such a distorted belief system has been described as identifying with the aggressor (van der Kolk 1989; de Zulueta 1998). It may also be seen as a maladaptive coping strategy which allows the offender to avoid the most distressing and painful of his memories of his abuse by turning them around and making himself the abuser.

To recover from trauma, people make use of the resources available within their culture. When, however, there is no moral sense to the trauma, if there is no access to proper support, and if the trauma victim has been corrupted and groomed, leaving him with reserves of suppressed rage against his abusers, then one way of providing alleviation for this suppressed rage is sexual offending. Power and sex become the means of feeling alive, and feeling better. In the child victim's experience, 'there are only two kinds of people in the world: victims and offenders. When he can no longer stand being a victim, his only choice is to become an offender' (Sanford 1993, p.12). Miller (1995) has also described how the perpetrator may re-enact the wickedness done to him in the hope of a better outcome, the lesson being that within the offence, which is a symptom of an underlying need, there is the need to re-enact the early experience of being, among other things, despised as children.

Trauma work in the context of sex offender treatment programmes

The field of sex offender treatment is currently dominated by the cognitive behavioural approach, which focuses on helping offenders to alter their distorted beliefs, increase their victim empathy, take responsibility for their actions and control their behaviour while maintaining a healthier lifestyle (Beckett 1994; Barker and Morgan 1993; Simpson 1994; Clark and Erooga 1994; Jenkins 1997). Many programmes also focus on decreasing the offender's sexual attraction to the target victim and the target act of sexual aggression (Wyre 1999). While the state of the art of sex offender treatment has unquestionably come very far within the past 15 years, the field is still young. While the cognitive behavioural approach has shown much merit, it is crucial to continue the development and widen the therapeutic approach, avoiding an unjustified notion that the right approach has been perfected (Hanson 1999).

Bearing this in mind, it is important to note that the mainstream literature on sex offender treatment has in general failed to incorporate more than four decades of research into the effects of trauma, post-traumatic stress reactions and the resulting effect on self-regulation. Moreover, much of the literature has historically warned against focusing on early trauma with offenders because of the danger that this will be seen as justification for their own crimes, an exoneration from culpability, or a pity party (Samenow 1984; Jenkins 1997; Salter 1995).

Yet focusing on offending behaviour while denying historical links with early trauma can damage the therapeutic relationship and treatment prognosis. Indeed, in many cases, ignoring or downplaying the offender's trauma history is to bypass the key factor influencing his decision to offend and the development of his distorted, offence-focused mental schema (Schwartz *et al.* 1993). With any other client group, a therapist would be considered negligent for ignoring or dismissing the relevance of early severe trauma in a client's life history, or insisting that the debilitating emotional effects of that trauma are not relevant to the modification of the client's current behaviour. Such an approach carries with it the high risk of re-abusing the offender by re-silencing him.

It is too often the case that offenders leave cognitive behavioural treatment with a treated profile – that is to say, they have been compliant in treatment, learned to 'talk the talk' (Salter 1988) and managed to show improvements in psychometric tests – only to go on to later re-offend. This must at least be partly due to the fact that the offender has not been helped to recover from his own trauma. Until he is helped to do so, therapy is likely to offer him coping strategies to control his offending impulse, rather than diminishing the impulse itself. Put another way, cognitive behavioural therapy is usually most effective in helping offenders cope with and intervene in their offending cycle of behaviour, whereas trauma work will in most cases diminish the potential for the offending cycle to re-start in the first place.

Working through emotions: the advantages of using psychodrama to address trauma histories in sex offenders

In the published literature, there are very few references to the importance of allowing and working through the feelings resulting from traumatic experiences specifically as this relates to adult male perpetrators of sexual abuse (Jefferies 1991 and 1996; Schwartz *et al.* 1993 and 1995; Baim *et al.* 1999; Corsini, 1951a and 1951b). Greenberg and Paivio (1998) point to what may be the key reason for this shortcoming when they write that the transformation that occurs in allowing painful feelings has been one of the most undocumented processes of psychological healing.

While most programmes for sex offenders make reference to the importance of gaining an intellectual understanding of the early life experiences of the offender (Beckett 1994; Erooga 1994), in particular experiences of abuse and neglect, there is a distinct lack of emphasis on emotional working through, and no mention whatsoever of the need for emotional re-experiencing in the here and now which has become a central tenet of work with survivors of traumatic incidents or abuse (Hudgins and Drucker 1998; Schwartz and Masters 1993).

A mistaken assumption that is often made in the literature is that the early abuse is accessible on the level of verbal and intellectual understanding, and that the offender would be capable of analysing and drawing lessons from the abuse without first working through the experience on an emotional level. As Greenberg and Paivio (1998) point out, the meaning of a traumatic event normally does not alter for the victim until the victim can first access the memory of the event – which may be problematic in itself – and then allow and accept the painful feelings associated with the experience of trauma. Kellermann supports this view when he writes, 'Repetitive action and re-enactment of repressed experiences are necessary in order to secure recall and translate some of the most unacceptable, unconscious fantasies into conscious thoughts ... [with] ... the aim of narrowing the gap between conscious experience (of motor and affective discharge) and the unconscious meanings of these same actions' (1992, p.129). Van der Kolk summarizes this point when he writes, 'As long as the trauma is experienced as speechless terror, the body continues to keep the score' (1994a, p.9).

Given the degree to which the memory of trauma may be hidden within the body's memory and inaccessible to cognitive awareness, sexual offending may be understood in part as a projecting-out of the intolerable and unresolved painful feelings associated with the early trauma (de Zulueta 1998; Jefferies 1991 and 1996; Miller 1995; Sanford 1993). Until the painful feelings are re-experienced in a safe and contained setting, where compassionate understanding and accurate labelling can occur, the victim (now the offender) can remain permanently traumatized and emotionally disabled. Therefore it can be seen as over-optimistic to suggest that a survivor of childhood abuse, who has later gone on to abuse others, should be able to see how he learned maladaptive lessons and attitudes, when indeed he may still be in a traumatized or indeed a fully groomed state of mind.

In order for maximum healing to occur, it is necessary that victims of abuse have their suffering acknowledged and respected by others. Beyond such validation, however, there must also be resolution, by revisiting the scene of the trauma in a structured way and providing a comforting and empowering new experience which helps to tame the terror and allow grieving and adaptations which make the memory more tolerable.

Going back in time also serves as an opportunity for directly addressing and modifying the destructive urge to abuse. The role of the perpetrator must be tracked back to its precipitating source, its 'locus nascendi' (Moreno 1946; Bustos 1994), and addressed and modified at that source. Both the perpetrator and victim roles derive from the same originating event(s), which is why it is so crucial to track back the damaging role to its point of origin and promote a freeing of the log jam of emotional repression which has contributed so greatly to the offending behaviour (Corsini 1952).

Ideally, offence-focused work and post-trauma work should co-exist within a single psychodrama session. When psychodrama is conducted in this manner, the role of offender and the role of victim can be given equal credence. This strategy also addresses the general misgivings about trauma work with sex offenders, namely that they will be allowed to focus on their own abuse to the exclusion of work on taking responsibility for their crimes. In this format, they are asked to hold both roles in mind at the same time.

Clinical applications: technique and intervention

In order to begin a module on post-trauma work in a group for adult male sex offenders, you can begin by asking the group members to create sociodramatic sculpts, or frozen pictures, of hypothetical families. The group members can be divided into small groups and asked to create images of a family that communicates well and supports each other, and a family where anger and fear are always present. The sculpts can then be processed to look at issues regarding what helps and what damages the children. The images can be moved forward and backward through time, to gain an awareness of how behaviour and attitudes are passed down generation to generation.

Inevitably, the group members will make connections with their own upbringing. These sculpts can also be used to demonstrate the principles of functional and dysfunctional attachment (Jefferies 1991 and 1996). For example, 'looking at this father and son, what happens to their relationship if the father is abusing his son, but the son can't tell his mother?' Where appropriate, encourage the group members to make links with their own behaviour as an adult as well as their behaviour as a child. This strategy can be highly useful in reducing the amount of denial and shame in group members, as they learn the ethos of the director's approach when the group are discussing the fictional families.

Warming up to role reversal

Role reversal – the psychodramatic technique whereby the major participants in an interaction exchange roles – has been described as the engine which gives power to psychodrama. It is the quintessential skill needed by group members, and serves as a powerful tool for developing empathy (among other uses) as it encourages participants to move beyond the 'habitual limitations of egocentricity' (Blatner 2000, p.175).

Clinicians can introduce the technique of role reversal by interviewing the group members while they are in role as 'someone who has a stake in my doing well on this programme, whose opinion I value and respect'. Where appropriate, have each group member create a personal flip chart sheet with that person's name on it in large letters. Putting these pieces of paper on the wall can become part of the opening procedure of each therapy session, reinforcing the idea that each man has a personal witness and an observant container here in the room with him.

Once group members are familiar with the process of entering into role and responding 'in character', they will be more able to proceed with full role reversals.

The victim to offender psychodrama sequence

This is a sequence of three psychodramatic encounters. They need not be undertaken in the exact sequence shown, but should rather inform an underlying structure for all psychodramatic work with sex offenders. In other words, at some point in his treatment, each sex offender should have the opportunity to have each of the following conversations (Taylor 1999, personal communication): 1. a conversation between me as a victim of abuse, and those who perpetrated against me; 2. a conversation between me as a perpetrator of abuse, and those who perpetrated against me; 3. a conversation between me as a victim of abuse, and the victims I have perpetrated against.

The above conversations are facilitated with the emphasis on allowing the offender's own best self and own best critic to emerge. Regardless of the sequence, the conversations must be facilitated in such a way as to allow the offender to feel that he is being heard and not judged. It is suggested that at some point each conversation be viewed by the protagonist in mirror, standing back and gaining a more objective understanding of how the various roles fit together and how they have influenced each other over time. In effect, he will be learning how his distorted mirror developed.

Where appropriate, the offender can be encouraged to apologize (psychodramatically) to those he has harmed, and to forgive himself for his actions, in order that he may move on (Miller 1995). In the context of the above sequence of three conversations, this would be a fourth: 'a conversation between me as a perpetrator and the victims I have abused.' In addition, internal conversations such as 'a conversation between myself as a victim of abuse and myself as a perpetrator of abuse,' or 'a conversation between the part of me that wants to offend and the part of me that doesn't,' may encourage motivation and the sense of self-determination and choice.

Confronting the perpetrator role

When facilitating a psychodrama in which the offender is in role as his perpetrator self, the director can engage with the perpetrator as with any maladaptive role. That is to say, the facilitator can allow the protagonist to feel safe in portraying this side of himself, without fear of judgement and without fear that this role will be targeted for elimination. After all, aspects of the role were once necessary for the protagonist's survival, so the threat of eliminating this role may create an understandable resistance (Metcalf 1997). By bringing this role into the light of day, exploring its origins, and allowing safe role completion, the energy and heat are diminished and the role loses its power and ultimately dissipates (Kipper 1998).

There is, however, a real risk of re-traumatizing the offender when he enacts his own perpetrator role. Many offenders are terrified that they will over-identify with their perpetrator role, and somehow get stuck again in the role. Others carry profound shame in relation to the role. Therefore a structured progression should be followed which will minimize the likelihood of such traumatization by allowing the protagonist to control the degree of identification with the role (see Hudgins, Chapter 13). The following stages are a useful guide.

1. After the protagonist identifies his intrapsychic, interpersonal and transpersonal strengths (see Hudgins, Chapter 13), and after he has the support of a containing double, have him describe the perpetrator role. 2. The protagonist places the role in the space (for example, the scene of the offence) by identifying and describing his physical position and actions at the time. 3. The protagonist anchors the role with object(s), placing the object(s) in the space. 4. Continuing to stand out of the scene, the protagonist provides a voice-over, repeating the words he used at the time. Where appropriate, this may be done using auxiliaries. 5. The protagonist enters the scene and takes his own role, enacting his perpetrator role and certain key moments of the offence. Through the use of role reversals with his own current self, with his victim, and with other internal and external roles, the protagonist is helped to diminish the strength of his own perpetrator role and achieve a healthier internal role balance.

Post-test – role training using 'Mr Self-Aware'

After the offence-focused work and post-trauma work has been successfully addressed, it may be useful, as part of the role training aims of the offender programme, to ask the group members all to take on the role of 'Mr Self-Aware'. This is the role of a hypothetical man who has committed sexual offences in the past, but has now undergone a full treatment programme. He is as self-aware as he possibly can be. He knows his high-risk situations, he has his coping strategies rehearsed, and he is able to make age-appropriate friendships in the community. Crucially, he is not a Mr Goody-Two-Shoes. Rather, he is more like an older, life sentence prisoner who has played all the games in the past, thinking he was tough enough and clever enough to get past the system, or beat it. Now, Mr Self-Aware has devoted his energies to being low risk, and maintaining a balanced, healthy lifestyle free of offending. Allow the group members to take on this role and practise being Mr Self-Aware for long periods of time. I have occasionally asked group members to stay in role as Mr Self-Aware all week, until the next session. In some cases, this practice of a new way of being in the world can be a profound experience for the offenders.

Case study

The following clinical example is typical of psychodramas I have directed with adult male sex offenders. These psychodramas always relate the effects of the offender's core trauma experience to his later offending, taking precautions to ensure the offender does not reinforce his victim stance but rather removes it entirely by allowing him emotionally to work through his victim experience. The psychodramas have as their central strategy to trace back the roles of victim and perpetrator to their point of origin in order to provide a psychodramatic modification of the events precipitating the two roles. The psychodrama below was directed by the author according to the principles and methods of 'classical' psychodrama (Moreno 1946; Hollander 1978), the psychodrama spiral (Goldman and Morrison 1984) and the therapeutic spiral (see Hudgins, Chapter 13) a model designed specifically for psychodramatic work with survivors of trauma.

Biographical details have been altered for reasons of confidentiality.

Adrian

Adrian, 47, was in prison for sexually abusing a girl (distantly related) who was aged between 9 and 11 during the abuse. Before joining the psycho-drama group, he had already been through a prison sex offender treatment programme, and had what he described as a good understanding of his offending cycle. He was in the psychodrama group to address early events in his life, most particularly violent abuse from his father. He reported having large gaps in his memories of his childhood.

Adrian put himself forward to work on the issue of his physical abuse from his father. He wanted to look again at a particular incident that happened to him at age eight, when he had been playing with his friends and had torn his shirt. He cried all the way home, because he knew his father would beat him severely.

Before going back in time to this early scene, it was necessary to anchor Adrian in the present in order that he would have a concrete reality to return to. This was particularly important in that Adrian had by all indications used dissociation as a means of coping with the abuse at the time, and so there was a risk that he would dissociate at some point during the psychodrama. This indeed turned out to be the case at a few key moments. Adrian identified several personal, internal strengths that could help him return to this episode of abuse. He identified his care and concern for others, his desire to know his own true self, his ability to listen, and his ability to make friends as strengths. He also identified his mother as his key interpersonal strength. Time was taken to ensure that mother's presence was fully there for him in the psycho-drama, and that this version of mother would not be afraid to do what she needed to do in order to protect her son. Adrian also chose to have the role of Dr Martin Luther King Jr. present in the room, as he took a great deal of spiritual strength from his knowledge of Dr King. In role as Dr King, Adrian spoke of the importance of finding out the truth and protecting all oppressed people, including children abused by their fathers. After this, Adrian chose a group member to act as a containing double (Hudgins and Drucker 1998), who would be there by his side throughout the scene of trauma in order to provide support and to help Adrian contain his dissociation and tendency to regress when riddled by the toxic shock of his memories.

The scene then moved to the children playing on a broken tractor, and Adrian tearing his shirt. As he walked home as his eight-year-old self, Adrian began to have flashbacks, which seized him and caused his body to heave and contort. He lowered himself to the ground in tears. After an intervention by the director and containing double which stopped him from going into uncontrolled regression, Adrian was able to narrate the events in the front room of the house, where he received a severe beating from his father, which included punches to his face and kicks to his stomach from his father's boots. He repeated in a powerful and threatening voice the words of his father. As he said the words, he heaved with sudden bursts of memory. He was in very great distress, but wanted to continue.

The next stage of the re-enactment had Adrian listening to two auxiliaries play out the scene of abuse. At this time the director intervened and gave a label to what was going on in that room, explicitly calling it an act of horrific violence. Adrian also named and labelled the abuse for what it was, as did all of the group members, so there was total agreement that this was a scene of abuse and in no way a scene of reasonable punishment. As he continued to cry, and listen to his containing double, Adrian felt able to go to the next stage, which was to witness the two auxiliaries play out the scene of violence. He was put in charge of the scene by being allowed to stop and start the scene, as he felt able to cope with the next bit. He used the stop/start button several times. He could hardly stand looking at the scene. When he saw his eight-year-old self thrown to the floor and kicked in the head, he spontaneously rushed to help the boy, and led him to the safety of the mother's chair. Several swift role reversals had Adrian in role as his mother, lending the young Adrian comfort, then Adrian in role as his young self, being comforted by mother. At this point he grabbed hold of the group member playing the role of his mother, and broke down into heaving sobs. He allowed himself to be held and comforted, and spoke of his pain at what had happened.

Adrian was then able to enter the scene of the abuse himself, as his eight-year-old self, in order to re-experience and re-integrate the scene of his core trauma in such a way that it could be relived in a contained way but also re-invented with a different outcome. In order to separate the surplus reality scene from the actual scene of abuse just witnessed, a hypothetical scene of a similar beating was created. Before entering the scene, Adrian reviewed what strengths were available to him, and what the various roles were around him. A reformed version of mother was created who would have the strength to protect her son. Adrian entered the scene, and in the midst of the horrific scene of violence, was rescued by the new, strong and righteous mother (played by another inmate). The mother took him far away from the scene of abuse. She hugged him and allowed him to cry, saying that if she had known about the violence against him, she would have protected him. Adrian cried and cried, and put his head into the shoulder of the group member playing the role of mother.

After this catharsis, Adrian was able to stand with his strong mother and tell his father about how much this had hurt him. Adrian then played out a future projection scene, where he told his father that he would actually like to talk with him again (father is still alive) and to try to talk about the past and about his father's own life story, even though he knew his father would probably never be able to admit the full scale of the harm he had done to Adrian.

It was important that an auxiliary was brought in to represent Deborah, Adrian's victim. Adrian said in the midst of his talk with father, 'I was a defenceless child, and that was reflected in what I did to Deborah, who was also a defenceless child. You had no right to do what you did to me, and I had no right to do what I did to her. I was trying to make her feel as bad as me.'

During the next several months, Adrian increasingly became more active in assisting other inmates with their own therapy, and was less withdrawn and preoccupied. He reported that he was much more relaxed and far less afraid of his own memories and feelings. In particular, he no longer felt afraid of his father. He also felt that there were very few gaps in his memory of childhood. More than one year after supervised release, he continued to make improvements and maintain a non-abusive lifestyle.

Conclusion

Trauma work will never be the only or even the main mode of treatment for sex offenders. Even so, it will be relevant for a large percentage of serious and repeat offenders. Research into therapeutic work with victims of prolonged and inescapable childhood trauma suggests that psychodrama should be an integral part of standard sex offender treatment. Psychodrama can assist in addressing and modifying offenders' victim stance, external locus of control and affect dysregulation, and the effects of early abuse, traumatic sexualization, maladaptive learning and functioning and poor attachment history. Psychodramatic trauma work also complements the goals of standard cognitive-behavioural approaches by directly addressing cognitive distortions, victim empathy and relapse prevention (Baim *et al.* 1999; Robson and Lambie 1995)

It may be difficult for some even to consider addressing the personal trauma history of the abuser – at first glance; this seems the greatest injustice to his victims. Nevertheless, if we treat the offence as a symptom, we can often see that the offence acts as a distorted mirror, or an affect bridge (Schwartz and Masters 1993), through time, bending and reshaping earlier experience into new episodes of abuse. It does not particularly matter that the perpetrator was once on the other side of the mirror, for through time the mirror distorts, like a Möbius strip, so it is all one surface. For roles are reciprocal; the bond passes in both directions, from one person to the other. Good parenting may lead to good parenting, a good manager will serve as a model for workers when they become managers, and the effective abuser, whatever his strategy, whether it be kindness, threats, or sheer brutality, will also pass on the knowledge of how to commit his particular brand of abuse. This is why looking at the offence, or at the fantasies of the abuser, may be the most powerful clue to the underlying trauma.

Therapeutic work with sex offenders must be soul work, because in almost all cases the offenders themselves have suffered grievous damage to their souls before going on to attempt to destroy the souls of others. A very basic quality of human nature is that we find it hard to feel sorry for others who are in pain when it seems that no one feels sorry for our pain. We need that acknowledgement in order to free us up and satisfy a fundamental demand of the ego: to be heard, seen and respected (Miller 1995). Otherwise we resort to anger and resentment, or internalize the anger and become depressed or anxious. At its most extreme, if feelings are ignored completely, there may be a lack of empathy even for those one has directly hurt. The same principle applies: 'I don't care about you because no one cares about me.' It is rooted in the offender's early trauma, in experiences where he was unable and denied the ability to say 'no'. Post-trauma work will help him to take back that 'no', in the knowledge that when we can say 'no', there is no place for anger or violence.

References

Baim, C., Allam, J., Eames, T., Dunford, S. and Hunt, S. (1999) 'The use of psychodrama to enhance victim empathy in sex offenders: an evaluation.' *The Journal of Sexual Aggression* 4, 1, 4–14.

Bannister, A. (1991) 'Learning to live again: Psychodramatic techniques with sexually abused young people.' In P. Holmes and M. Karp (eds) *Psychodrama: Inspiration and Technique.* London: Tavistock/Routledge.

Barker, M. and Morgan, R. (1993) *Sex Offenders: A Framework for the Evaluation of Community Based Treatment.* (Report to the Home Office). Bristol University: Faculty of Law.

Beckett, R. (1994) 'Cognitive-behavioural treatment of sex offenders.' In T. Morrison, M. Erooga and R. Beckett (eds) *Sexual Offending Against Children: Assessment and Treatment of Male Abusers*. London: Routledge.

Blatner, A. (2000) *Foundations of Psychodrama History, Theory and Practice*. (4th edition). New York: Springer.

Bowlby, J. (1984) 'Violence in the family as a disorder of the attachment and caregiving systems.' *The American Journal of Psychoanalysis 44*, 9–27.

Bowlby, J. (1988) *A Secure Base: Clinical Applications of Attachment Theory*. London: Routledge.

Briere, J. (1996) 'A self-trauma model for treating adult survivors of severe child abuse.' In J. Briere, L. Berliner, J.A. Bulkley, C. Jenny and T. Reid (eds) *The APSAC Handbook on Child Maltreatment*. Thousand Oaks, CA: Sage Publications.

Briggs, F. (ed) (1995) *From Victim to Offender: How Child Sexual Abuse Victims Become Offenders*. St Leonards, New South Wales: Allen and Unwin.

Burt, M.R. (1980) 'Cultural myths and supports for rape.' *Journal of Personality and Social Psychology 38*, 2, 217–230.

Bustos, D. (1994) 'Wings and roots: locus, matrix, status nascendi and the concept of clusters.' In P. Holmes, M. Karp and M. Watson (eds) *Psychodrama Since Moreno: Innovations in Theory and Practice*. London: Routledge.

Clark, P. and Erooga, M. (1994) 'Groupwork with men who sexually abuse children.' In T. Morrison, M. Erooga and R. Beckett (eds) *Sexual Offending Against Children: Assessment and Treatment of Male Abusers*. London: Routledge.

Corsini, R.J. (1951a) 'Psychodramatic treatment of a pedophile.' *Group Psychotherapy, Journal of Sociopsychopathology and Sociatry 4*, 3, 166–171.

Corsini, R.J. (1951b) 'The method of psychodrama in prison.' *Group Psychotherapy 3*, 4, 321–326.

Corsini, R.J. (1952) 'Immediate therapy.' *Group Psychotherapy 4*, 322–330.

de Zulueta, F. (1998) *From Pain to Violence: The Traumatic Roots of Destructiveness*. London: Whurr Publishers.

Erooga, M. (1994) 'Where the professional meets the personal.' In T. Morrison, M. Erooga and R. Beckett (eds) *Sexual Offending Against Children: Assessment and Treatment of Male Abusers*. London: Routledge.

Finkelhor, D. (1984) *Child Sexual Abuse – New Theory and Research*. New York: The Free Press/Collier Macmillan.

Goldman, E. and Morrison, D. (1984) *Psychodrama: Experience and Process*. Dubuque, IA: Kendall/Hunt.

Greenberg, L.S. and Paivio, S.C. (1998) 'Allowing and accepting painful emotional experiences.' *The International Journal of Action Methods: Psychodrama, Skill Training and Role Playing 51*, 3, 47–61.

Grubin, D. (1998) 'Sexual offending against children: Understanding the risk.' *Police Research Series, Paper 99*. London: Policing and Reducing Crime Unit – Research, Development and Statistics Directorate.

Hanson, K. (1999) 'Work with sex offenders: a personal view.' *The Journal of Sexual Aggression 4*, 2, 81–93.

Hollander, C.E. (1978) *A Process for Psychodrama Training: The Hollander Psychodrama Curve.* Denver, CO: Snow Lion Press.

Hudgins, M.K. and Drucker, K. (1998) 'The containing double as part of the therapeutic spiral model for treating trauma survivors.' *The International Journal of Action Methods: Psychodrama, Skill Training, and Role Playing 51,* 2, 63–74.

Hunter, M. (1995) *Child Survivors and Perpetrators of Sexual Abuse: Treatment Innovations.* London: Sage.

Ito, Y., Teicher, M.H., Glod, C.A., Harper, D., Magnus, E. and Gelbard, H.A. (1993) 'Increased prevalence of electrophysiological abnormalities in children with psychological, physical and sexual abuse.' *Journal of Neuropsychiatry and Clinical Neurosciences 5,* 401–408.

Jefferies, J. (1991) 'What we are doing here is defusing bombs.' In P. Holmes and M. Karp (eds) *Psychodrama: Inspiration and Technique.* London: Tavistock/Routledge.

Jefferies, J. (1996) 'A psychodramatic perspective.' In C. Cordess and M. Cox (eds) *Forensic Psychotherapy.* London: Jessica Kingsley Publishers.

Jenkins, A. (1997) *Invitations to Responsibility – The Therapeutic Engagement of Men who are Violent and Abusive.* Adelaide, South Australia: Dulwich Centre Publications.

Kellermann, P.F. (1992) *Focus on Psychodrama.* London: Jessica Kingsley Publishers.

Kipper, D. (1998) 'Psychodrama and trauma: implications for future interventions of psychodramatic role-playing modalities.' *The International Journal of Action Methods: Psychodrama, Skill Training and Role Playing 51,* 3, 113–121.

Langs, R. (1999) *Psychotherapy and Science.* London: Sage.

Marshall, W.L. and Maric, A. (1996) 'Cognitive and emotional components of generalized empathy deficits in child molesters.' *Journal of Child Sexual Abuse 5,* 2, 101–110.

Metcalf, K. (1997) Role theory and eating disorders. *Psychodrama Network News,* newsletter of the American Society of Group Psychotherapy and Psychodrama, January 1997.

Miller, A. (1995) *The Drama of Being a Child.* London: Virago.

Miller, J.E. (ed) (1991) *Hertiage of American Literature, Vol. 2.* New York: Harcourt Brace Jovanovich.

Moreno, J.L. (1946) *Psychodrama, Vol. 1.* Beacon, NY: Beacon House.

Morrison, T., Erooga, M. and Beckett, R. (eds) (1994) *Sexual Offending Against Children: Assessment and Treatment of Male Abusers.* London: Routledge.

Perry, B.D. and Pate, J.E. (1994) 'Neurodevelopment and the psychobiological roots of post-traumatic stress disorder.' In L. F. Koziol and C.E. Stout (eds) *The Neuropsychology of Mental Disorders: A Practical Guide.* Springfield, IL: Charles C. Thomas.

Robson, M. and Lambie, I. (1995) 'Using Psychodrama to Facilitate Victim Empathy in Adolescent Sexual Offenders.' *Journal of the Australian and New Zealand Psychodrama Association 4,* 13–19.

Salter, A. (1988) *Treating Child Sex Offenders and Victims.* London: Sage.

Salter, A. (1995) *Transforming Trauma – A Guide to Understanding and Treating Adult Survivors of Child Sexual Abuse.* London: Sage.

Samenow, S. (1984) *Inside the Criminal Mind.* New York: Times Books/ Random House.

Sanford, L.T. (1993) *Strong at the Broken Places – Overcoming the Trauma of Child Abuse.* London: Virago.

Scheff, T.J. (1979) *Catharsis in Healing, Ritual and Drama.* London: University of California Press.

Schwartz, M.F. and Masters, W.H. (1993) Integration of Trauma-based, Cognitive Behavioural, Systemic and Addiction Approaches for Treatment of Hypersexual Pair-Bonding Disorder. In Carnes, P.J. (ed) *Sexual Addiction and Compulsivity, Vol. 1.* London: Brunner Mazel.

Schwartz, M.F., Galperin, L.D. and Masters, W.H. (1993) 'Dissociation and treatment of compulsive re-enactment of trauma: sexual compulsivity.' In M. Hunter (ed) *The Sexually Abused Male, Vol. 3.* Lexington, MA: Lexington Books.

Schwartz, M.F., Galperin, L.D. and Masters, W.H. (1995) 'Sexual trauma within the context of traumatic and inescapable stress, neglect, and poisonous pedagogy.' In M. Hunter (ed) *Adult Survivors of Sexual Abuse.* London: Sage.

Simpson, L. (1994) *Evaluation of Treatment Methods in Child Sexual Abuse: A Literature Review.* Bath: University of Bath and Dorset Area Child Protection Committee.

Tedeschi, R.G. and Calhoun, L.G. (1995) *Trauma and Transformation – Growing in the Aftermath of Suffering.* London: Sage Publications.

van der Kolk, B. (1989) 'The compulsion to repeat the trauma: re-enactment, revictimisation and masochism.' *Psychiatric Clinics of North America 12,* 389–411.

van der Kolk, B. (1994a) 'Childhood abuse and neglect and loss of self-regulation.' *The Bulletin of the Menninger Clinic 58,* 2, pp.1-14.

van der Kolk, B.A. (1994b) 'The body keeps the score – memory and the evolving psychobiology of post-traumatic stress.' *Harvard Review of Psychiatry 1,* 3, pp.253-265.

Wallis, K. (1995) 'Perspectives on offenders.' In F. Briggs (ed) *From Victim to Offender: How Child Sexual Abuse Victims Become Offenders.* St Leonards, NSW: Allen and Unwin.

Webb, L.P. and Leehan, J. (1996) *Group Treatment for Adult Survivors of Abuse – A Manual for Practitioners.* London: Sage.

Whitfield, C.L. (1995) *Memory and Abuse – Remembering and Healing the Effects of Trauma.* Deerfield Beach, FL: Health Communications.

Winn, L. (1994) *Post-Traumatic Stress Disorder and Dramatherapy.* London: Jessica Kingsley Publishers.

Wyre, R. (1999) *The Aware Culture* and *Arena of Safety.* Milton Keynes: Ray Wyre Associates (unpublished manuscript).

CHAPTER 10

Psychodramatic Treatment of Dissociative Identity Disorder[1]

Kerry Paul Altman

Expressive therapies have been used to provide both diagnostic information and direct treatment for individuals diagnosed with multiple personality disorder (MPD) and dissociative disorders (Cohen and Cox 1989; Chess 1990). Several writers have proposed the role of expressive therapy as a primary treatment for adults recovering from the impact of childhood traumatic abuse (Chu 1991). While psychodrama has long been associated with the expressive therapies and has been used effectively in many treatment settings (Buchanan and Dubbs-Siroka 1980), specific reports of psychodramatic treatment of individuals diagnosed with multiple personality disorder (MPD) or a dissociative disorder is absent from the literature. Since the autumn of 1990, psychodramatic group psychotherapy has been an integral part of the total treatment approach in an in-patient programme focusing exclusively on the treatment of adults recovering from childhood traumatic abuse, the majority of whom are diagnosed with MPD or a dissociative disorder. This chapter presents a preliminary report on the application of psychodrama to work with this in-patient population, and is intended as an introduction to the use of psychodrama in the treatment of MPD and dissociative disorders.

Historical overview of psychodrama

Before examining the specific applications of psychodrama to work with this specialized population, some general information may be helpful. Psychodrama was the creation of Jacob Moreno, M.D., a Viennese psychiatrist who

1 First published in *Dissociation*, Volume 1, No. 2, June 1992. Reprinted with kind permission of the publisher, Ridgeview Institute.

emigrated to the USA in the 1920s (Fox 1987). In Europe and the USA, Moreno explored new areas of the emerging mental health field and was a pioneer in the development of role theory, sociometry, and action methods in psychotherapy (Moreno 1961). In 1931, he coined the term 'group psychotherapy' while continuing to develop his theory and practice of psychodrama (Blatner 2000). At the request of Dr William A. White, Moreno helped establish the psychodrama section of St Elizabeths Hospital in Washington DC in 1937, which remains a major centre for psychodrama training (Buchanan 1981).

Psychodrama employs action methods to provide an opportunity for group members to explore issues in an interactive way. Moreno's role theory is an essential element of the psychodramatic approach, and a variety of techniques including role reversal, doubling, and mirroring are often used to explore an individual's repertoire of existing and potential roles (Z. Moreno 1959). The use of group members as active therapeutic agents is another element of the psychodramatic approach (Buchanan 1984; Z. Moreno 1965). A full description of psychodrama theory and methodology is beyond the scope of the present chapter, and the reader is encouraged to consult one of the available texts for a more comprehensive view (Blatner 1989; Fox 1987; Moreno 1946).

Psychodramatic Structure

All psychodrama sessions consist of three parts. The first part of the session is known as the warm-up, and involves a verbal exploration of individual issues and concerns. During the warm-up, themes emerge and a central concern is developed for exploration in the second phase, the action. During the action phase, the central concern is explored using specific auxiliary ego techniques. Most often, one individual emerges as the protagonist and explores a personal manifestation of the central concern. If the warm-up portion is thorough enough, each group member is emotionally attached to the central concern and benefits vicariously from the work of an individual protagonist (Buchanan 1980).

Group members often assume supportive roles in psychodrama sessions, enhancing group cohesion and furthering awareness of the repertoire of personal roles. Occasionally, a group-centred psychodrama session involves all members in a more sociodramatic or generic exploration of a central concern (Sternberg and Garcia 1989). The final phase of the group is the sharing, in which group members are given the opportunity to express personal reactions, associations, or other feelings stimulated by the work during the action phase. De-roling is an important aspect of the sharing phase in which group members are encouraged consciously to disengage themselves from roles assumed during the action, protecting against role contamination and enhancing role and ego integrity (Holmes and Karp 1991, pp.12 and 58; Altman and Hickson-Laknahour 1986).

Expression versus restraint

One common misconception of psychodrama is that the action orientation of the method encourages more and more expression with little regard for the need of individuals to contain and develop appropriate roles for release of strong emotions (Z. Moreno 1965). In fact, while psychodrama is indeed a powerful therapeutic tool, cathartic emotional expression is only a small part of the psychodramatic approach. Before an individual's issues or concerns are explored in action, careful attention is paid to the development of an action structure, that is, a scene and general form for the exploration of an issue (Blatner 1989).

In work with dissociative abuse survivors, the action structure often provides the boundaries necessary to proceed with therapeutic work in an organized manner. An advantage of psychodrama is that these boundaries are symbolically externalized and become quite tangible on the 'stage' or in the space provided for the psychodramatic work (Williams 1989). For example, an individual struggling with introjected mixed messages from an abusing parent can be given an opportunity to create an action structure in which each of these conflicting messages can be concretized and acknowledged through the use of other group members as role takers or auxiliary egos. Once the action structure is established the internal conflict is given tangible form, and safe, thoughtful therapeutic work can occur within agreed upon boundaries (Williams 1989). Thus, while psychodrama provides an opportunity for expression of repressed affect, it also provides a structure for containing the emotional expression within safe and therapeutic parameters (Z. Moreno 1965).

Act hungers and open tension systems

A principle of psychodrama that has direct relevance to therapeutic work with survivors of childhood trauma is the concept of act hungers and open tension systems (Buchanan 1980; Sternberg and Garcia 1989). Moreno theorized that the desire or 'hunger' to act is a basic element of the human experience (Williams 1989). Act hungers include the most basic human actions such as the need to laugh, cry, or otherwise react appropriately to emotional stimuli.

Complex act hungers of abuse survivors may involve a need to create a sense of safety, a wish to tell about an abuse experience, or any desire to act in a way that alleviates emotional discomfort. When an act hunger is repeatedly unfulfilled, the result is an internalized system of complex emotions coalescing around the frustrated act hungers known as an open tension system (Sternberg and Garcia 1989). Anyone who has worked with survivors of repeated abuse knows the extent to which frustrated act hungers ultimately result in open tension systems, which limit spontaneity and inhibit the potential for emotional growth and development. For example, a child who is repeatedly frustrated in attempts to find safety may experience a generalized fear of people and experiences in adult life. The unexpressed 'need to tell' of an abused child may lead to pathological secrecy and mistrust in potentially intimate relationships in adult life (Courtois 1988).

The action orientation of psychodrama provides a setting for entry into a survivor's reality on the level of act hungers and open tension systems. By beginning with a specific scene and addressing act hungers in action, the psychodramatic approach begins the process of challenging the accepted reality of a survivor's open tension systems. Long-held act hungers can be safely expressed in a psychodrama session, inviting empowerment through new responses to internalized belief systems.

Case studies

The following examples are based on my experience directing psychodrama groups in an in-patient abuse recovery programme. The first example is chosen to illustrate how psychodrama is used to facilitate internal communication in an MPD patient, with minimal emphasis on cathartic expression. The second example demonstrates how psychodrama can be used to facilitate emotional expression and controlled abreaction in a safe, supportive setting. The group from which these examples are drawn meets twice weekly for 90 minutes each session. The psychodrama group comprises a maximum of eight patient members and the therapist, traditionally called the 'director' (Holmes and Karp 1991, pp.2, 5, 8 and 9). An additional staff therapist often attends sessions, serving as a co-therapist and professional role taker, or auxiliary ego, as needed. In the following case studies, names and minor demographic facts have been altered to protect the anonymity of the patient.

Jean

Jean is a 41-year-old woman who was hospitalized to address issues of anxiety, confusion and depression related to internal conflict between emerging alternate personalities. During Jean's hospitalization one year earlier, she had begun to acknowledge the reality of sexual abuse by family members during childhood. In the intervening time, Jean had been involved in intensive out-patient treatment, which led to the diagnosis of MPD. At the time of her recent hospitalization, Jean acknowledged the reality of her MPD but had difficulty working therapeutically with alternate personalities without becoming overwhelmed, which invariably led to feelings of depression, some self-injurious behaviour, and a general sense of hopelessness with suicidal ideation. During her recent three-week hospitalization, Jean focused her work on enhancing internal communication and cooperation to better facilitate her outpatient work.

Discharge was planned for two days following her final psychodrama session, and Jean's available alters, that is, the dissociated ego states that the patient is able or willing to access at a given time, had signed a paper assuring personal safety and agreeing to avoid self-injurious behaviour. Jean attended her final psychodrama group with seven other group members, most of whom had been in the treatment programme for two to three weeks. The theme during the warm-up phase focused on the issue of problems with self-acceptance in light of past events, which group members experienced as shameful. Jean raised a personal concern involving her fear that an alter who had signed her safety commitment could not be trusted to keep her word and avoid self-harm. The feared alter, Alice, was identified as an angry woman who had inflicted superficial lacerations on Jean in the past. The group supported Jean's request for help on this issue, and Jean was selected as protagonist. A verbal contract was established between Jean, the psychodrama director, and the group, establishing the stated goal for the session as an increased sense of personal safety.

Jean selected a volunteer group member to assume the role of her alter, 'Alice'. Jean described Alice as a woman who was always angry, verbally aggressive, and threatening toward Jean. After describing her perception of Alice, Jean was asked to reverse roles with the group member assuming the role of Alice by physically switching places and talking to the group as she imagines Alice would talk, describing Alice in the first person, and discussing Alice's relationship with Jean.

It was the director's experience that assumption of the role of an alter by a host or other personality often facilitates the accessing of the alter personality. In order to avoid the protagonist's sense of being tricked into switching or deceived by the director, this likelihood is always discussed with the protagonist in advance of the action work, and the protagonist is always given the option to discontinue or renegotiate the session contract. However, it is notable that protagonists rarely opt to discontinue the work and are invariably able to assure the necessary safety boundaries for the work to continue.

Upon assuming the role of Alice, Jean quickly accessed her alter, Alice, and was able to express her concerns to the director and the group. Briefly stated, Alice strongly expressed her anger at Jean for denying Alice's existence and refusing to accept the painful memories of sexual abuse from Jean's childhood. Alice's perception was that she alone has had to suffer with the memories, and she expressed resentment and anger at Jean for her refusal to accept the truth.

The director again called for a role reversal, inviting the protagonist to return to her original role as Jean where she could listen and respond to the role player presenting Alice's concerns.

Since each role reversal essentially invites switching between personalities within the system, the director's attention to the protagonist's experience is of paramount concern, and issues of pacing, timing, and clarity of role assumption must be individually addressed with each protagonist.

Through a series of role reversals, Jean engaged in a heated dialogue with Alice in which each one's concerns became more fully expressed. In addition, their essential interdependency to achieve the goals of the overall system became more evident to each. Alice's anger at Jean for non-acceptance of her abuse history was expanded and Alice's frustration, loneliness, and exhaustion became clear. The fear underlying Jean's apparent non-acceptance was more fully expressed, as was her well-developed sense of denial as a strategy for coping with past abuse.

During the role reversal exchange, therapeutic doubles (Hale 1985; Buchanan 1980) were chosen to encourage expression and to support the value-free reality of each polar position. The action portion of the session concluded with a self-negotiated arrangement between Alice and Jean in which Jean agreed to begin to acknowledge Alice's presence and the reality of Alice's memories, and Alice agreed to stop her cutting behaviour and act in a less frightening manner toward Jean.

Jean's general treatment goal of enhanced internal communication was addressed, as was her session goal of an increased sense of personal safety. The sharing phase of the session provided an opportunity for group members who had assumed important auxiliary roles to de-role, and for all members to discuss personal reactions, feelings, or thoughts raised by the session. As is usually the case, issues raised in sharing were related to specific issues raised in the session as well as the central concern, which emerged during the warm-up, in this case involving issues of self-acceptance.

Sandy

Sandy is a 35-year-old married mother of three who was hospitalized for treatment of acute depression. While recently diagnosed with MPD, Sandy has a history of hospitalizations and other psychiatric diagnoses dating back several years. Previous diagnoses have included affective, organic, and psychotic disorders, although one of the goals of her present hospitalization was to clarify the diagnostic picture. Treating psychiatrists had recently speculated that she had been misdiagnosed in the past and that MPD was the appropriate diagnosis. At the time of her admission, Sandy was taking high dosages of a combination of antidepressant, anti-anxiety, and anti-psychotic medications and efforts were under way gradually to remove her from medications.

It was hypothesized that excessive medication may have accounted for her rigid gait and blunted affect, which gave her the appearance of a chronic schizophrenic. At the onset of her second psychodrama session during the first week of her admission, Sandy surprised the group by requesting to use psychodrama to work on issues related to repressed anger, which was the emerging central concern of the session. Sandy stated that she had observed another group member's psychodrama session a few days earlier, and she thought that the approach would help her deal with some angry feelings about her mother. The group was very supportive of Sandy, and a contract was established with the goal of providing an opportunity for Sandy safely to acknowledge and express long-withheld feelings regarding her mother's abuse of her.

Despite her rigid physical presentation and apparent constricted affect, Sandy spoke freely and openly about past abuse by her mother. She reported a good working relationship with her internal system of personalities, with a high degree of co-consciousness. She was able to assure both intrapersonal and interpersonal safety and appeared eager to promote her healing through her work in psychodrama.

In the warm-up to action, Sandy described a typical scene from her childhood in which her mother would return home late at night. Sandy reported that her mother was always drunk and verbally abusive and insisted that nine-year-old Sandy fix dinner, serve her alcoholic drinks, and meet her every demand. The punishment for refusal or slow response was physical abuse, although the threat of abuse of Sandy's toddler-age sister was reported as the most frightening aspect of the recalled event. Group members volunteered to assume the various required roles for re-enactment of the traumatic scene.

Sandy described the physical features of her home and used the group room furniture to simulate the space in which her encounter with her mother would take place. She then described how her mother would return home, make demands and threats, and terrorize young Sandy and her sister. Sandy was encouraged to give specific information to the group member assuming the role of her mother, describing voice tone, body gestures and specific verbalizations.

Several psychodrama techniques were used to enhance the accuracy and appropriate emotional intensity of the assumed roles. Following the warm-up to space and roles, the scene was replayed with little interruption. Sandy quickly accessed the anxious and fearful emotional state that characterized her childhood interactions with her mother. Sandy's voice tone, childlike verbalizations, and body movements were consistent with those of a frightened child, and she reported that she had switched to a child alter who had experienced similar events. The scene was stopped and Sandy expressed feelings of shame, sadness, and fear that she associated with the scene. To honour the original contract, Sandy chose to revisit the scene with the option of expressing some of the previously unexpressed anger about her mother's treatment of her. A staff role player served as double to support Sandy's safe expression of anger. Sandy was able to access an alter personality who was more directly in touch with appropriate anger. In the replayed scene, Sandy's angry alter directly confronted her mother, strongly expressing long-withheld angry feelings about physical abuse, abuse of her younger sister, and forced sex with her mother's male friends. The action phase of the session ended with Sandy acknowledging the appropriateness of her anger and identifying areas for further work in ongoing treatment.

Despite the loud expressions of anger during the session, all group members reported feeling safe throughout the psychodrama. Support for Sandy's work was offered and led naturally into the sharing phase of the session. The sharing focused on group members' personal issues with unexpressed anger, as well as the role of fear in the recovery process.

The preceding case examples were chosen to illustrate two distinctly different aspects of the psychodramatic approach to working with individuals diagnosed with MPD. The first example demonstrated how the method could be used to encourage internal communication and development of a cooperative internal system that supports the overall goals of treatment. The second example focused on the use of psychodrama for the safe expression of powerful emotions in a controlled abreactive setting. In these examples, it can be seen that psychodrama provides a structure and setting for the protagonist's work which establishes clear boundaries for an agreed upon action therapy experience.

Summary and recommendations

This chapter has described how psychodramatic group psychotherapy has been effectively used in the treatment of abuse recovery. Some very broad and general theoretical principles were introduced to provide a framework for understanding the methodology. Undoubtedly, the chapter has raised a number of questions regarding theoretical, technical, and practical considerations for the use of psychodrama with adult survivors of childhood traumatic abuse. Specific descriptions of psychodramatic techniques are available in a number of texts and articles (Z. Moreno 1959; Blatner 1989; Fox 1987). However, it is important to recognize that psychodrama is much more than a collection of techniques, and extensive training, experience, and evaluation is required for certification by the American Board of Examiners in Psychodrama, Sociometry, and Group Psychotherapy. Psychodramatic treatment of this challenging population should be conducted by certified or closely supervised psychodrama therapists.

Controlled research is needed to evaluate more fully the specific advantages and possible contraindications of the psychodramatic approach with this population. Research and anecdotal reports are also needed to further determine the variations and adaptations of traditional psychodrama methodology necessary for work with in-patient and out-patient abuse recovery groups.

Psychodrama has been used effectively with a wide range of in-patient and out-patient populations. While there does not appear to be a therapeutic rationale for withholding psychodrama treatment from any patient population per se, treatment goals vary according to the population served, and adaptation of techniques may be necessary for work with special populations (Holmes and Karp 1991, chapters 6, 7, 9 and 10). It is important to bear in mind that psychodrama is a form of group psychotherapy, and all of the concerns regarding a patient's ability to participate in and benefit from a traditional psychotherapy group are equally important in a psychodrama group (Yalom 1985). Similarly, while psychodramatic treatment is appropriate for individuals at all stages in the process of recovery from traumatic abuse, potential group members should be considered in light of their individual needs and psychological functioning. Patients with acute generalized social fears, an inability to tolerate very minor interpersonal conflict, or extreme narcissism may lack the ego strength necessary for action oriented group work. Such patients may require a more individualized treatment approach before being referred to a psychodrama group. In any event, concurrent individual psychotherapy is recommended for this population.

References

Altman, K. and Hickson-Laknahour (1986) 'New roles for psychodramatists in counter-terrorism training.' *Journal of Group Psychotherapy, Psychodrama, and Sociometry 39*, 2, 70–77.

Blatner, A. (2000) *Foundations of Psychodrama: History, Theory, and Practice.* New York: Springer.

Blatner, A. (1996) *Acting-in: Practical Applications of Psychodramatic Methods.* New York: Springer.

Buchanan, D. (1980) 'The central concern model, a framework for structuring psychodramatic production.' *Group Psychotherapy 33*, 47–62.

Buchanan, D. (1981) '41 years of psychodrama at St Elizabeths Hospital.' *Journal of Group Psychotherapy, Psychodrama and Sociometry 34*, 134–137.

Buchanan, D. (1984) 'Psychodrama.' In T.B. Karasu (ed) *The Psychiatric Therapies: Part 2, The Psychosocial Therapies.* Washington, DC: American Psychiatric Association.

Buchanan, D. and Dubbs-Siroka, J. (1980) 'Psychodramatic treatment for psychiatric patients.' *Journal of the National Association of Private Psychiatric Hospitals 11*, 27–31.

Chess, J. (1990) 'Creative arts: keys to remembering, exploring, and regulating early traumatic memories.' Paper presented at the International Society for the Study of Multiple Personality and Dissociation Conference, Chicago, IL, November 11, 1990.

Chu, J. (ed) (1991) 'Critical issues task force report: the use of expressive therapies in MPD.' In *International Society for the Study of Multiple Personality and Dissociation Newsletter 9*, 4, 6–8.

Cohen, B. and Cox, C. (1989) 'Breaking the code: identification of multiplicity through art productions.' *Dissociation 2*, 3, 132–137.

Courtois, C. (1988) *Healing the Incest Wound: Survivors in Therapy.* New York: W.W. Norton and Company.

Fox, J. (1987) *The Essential Moreno.* New York: Springer.

Hale, A. (1985) *Conducting Clinical Sociometric Explorations.* Roanoke, VA: Royal Publishing Company.

Holmes, P. and Karp, M. (eds) (1991) *Psychodrama Inspiration and Technique.* London and New York: Tavistock/Routledge.

Moreno, J. (1946) *Psychodrama: Volume I.* New York: Beacon House.

Moreno, J. (1961) 'The role concept, a bridge between psychiatry and sociology.' *American Journal of Psychiatry 118*, 518–523.

Moreno, J. (1965) 'Therapeutic vehicles and the concept of surplus reality.' *Group Psychotherapy 18*, 4, 211–216.

Moreno, Z. (1959) 'A survey of psychodramatic techniques.' *Group Psychotherapy 5*, 1, 12–14.

Moreno, Z. (1965) 'Psychodramatic rules, techniques, and adjunctive methods.' *Group Psychotherapy 18*, 1–2, 73–86.

Sternberg, P. and Garcia, A. (1989) *Sociodrama: Who's in your shoes?* New York: Praeger Publishers.

Williams, A. (1989) *The Passionate Technique: The Strategic Psychodrama with Individuals, Families, and Groups.* London and New York: Tavistock/Routledge.

Yalom, I. (1985) *The Theory and Practice of Group Psychotherapy.* New York: Basic Books.

CHAPTER 11

Appearance and Treatment of Dissociative States of Consciousness in Psychodrama

Grete A. Leutz

Dissociative states of consciousness may arise as an adaptive response to intrusion of Holocaust memories. This chapter will describe how such states may appear and be treated within psychodrama. Such an approach is based on the vision of the significance of spontaneous scenic representation of the patient's life situations and their integration, as suggested by J.L. Moreno (1923, pp.76-77), and from the English translation (Moreno 1973):

> The persons [protagonists] play before themselves, as they did once out of necessity in self conscious deceit, the same life again. The place of the conflict and of its theatre is one and the same. Life and fantasy become of the same identity and of the same time. They do not want to overcome [split off] reality; they bring it forth. They re-experience it; they are masters of their true existence. Because it is just this which they do. The whole of life is unfolded, with all its mutual complications, not one moment, not one instance is extinguished from it; each question, every fit of anxiety, every moment of inner withdrawal, comes back to life. It is not only that they come back and re-enact their dialogues, but their bodies, too, come back rejuvenated. Their nerves, their heartbeats ... All their powers, deeds, and thoughts appear on the scene in their original context and sequence; replicas of the phases through which they have once passed. The whole past ... arrives at a moment's call ... But this manifestation of life in the domain of illusion does not work like a renewal of suffering, rather it confirms the rule: every true second time is the liberation from the first. (1973, pp.90–91).

In addition, this approach is also in agreement with the clinical literature on the treatment of post-traumatic stress disorder (PTSD) 'which repeatedly cites the importance of recovery and integration of traumatic memories with their associated affects' (van der Kolk 1987, p.119).

Dissociative states are characterized by significant alterations in the integrative functions of memory for thoughts, feelings, or actions and significant alterations of self (Ludwig 1983; Nemiah 1981). According to Putnam

> they have long been recognised as adaptive responses to acute trauma, because they provide: (1) Escape from the constraints of reality, (2) Containment of traumatic memories and affects outside of normal conscious awareness, (3) Alteration or detachment of sense of self (so that the trauma happens to someone else or to a 'depersonalised' self), and (4) Analgesia (absence of pain) (1989, p.53).

In the cases described below, dissociation occurred very unexpectedly. As such, they may be understood as adaptive responses to trauma, that is to intrusion of traumatic memories of the Holocaust.

Case study: Ruth

Ruth, a good-looking woman in her forties, widow of a physician, mother of a grown-up daughter, practising psychologist, participated in a five-day psychodrama workshop which I conducted as continued psychotherapeutic education for staff members of a Swedish State Hospital. She impressed me as a warm, intelligent, serious person. Toward the end of the workshop, Ruth reported in obvious distress that on the third day, she began to slip into a steadily growing extraordinary state which until then she had only known from a recurrent dream but never experienced awake. In the dream which she had repeatedly related before without association in her analysis, she walks aimlessly, endlessly on a bridge in thick fog. 'Since yesterday, except when watching psychodrama, I am more and more often in that state of neither recognizing my environment nor myself. Even at night in the streets I am in "thick fog" and have a hard time finding home. It is frightful. I am telling it because I need help.'

Needless to say, this symptom of dissociation required immediate psychodramatic crisis intervention. With the consent of Ruth and the group we began to concretize the dream in scenic action. Applying the double technique I walked behind Ruth on the imagined bridge and phrased unfinished sentences which referred to her environment, such as:

Grete: When I am looking to my right I see ...

and Ruth completing the sentence, went on:

Ruth: ... fog, dense fog.

So I continued:

Grete: To my left there is ...

Ruth: Only fog.

Grete: And in front?

Ruth: Also.

Grete: The bridge leads to ...

Ruth: Nowhere.

Grete: But it comes from ...

Ruth: Nowhere.

Grete: Behind me I feel ...

Ruth: Nothing but fog.

Grete: Under the bridge ...

Ruth: ... as well.

Grete: And over my head...

Ruth: Fog, only fog.

For the first time I felt totally lost in psychodrama and thought, I have to give up. As a last intervention, I turned Ruth physically through 180 degrees, while doubling.

Grete: At the beginning of the bridge, I now see ...

and Ruth, as if struck by a thunderbolt, tears in her eyes, continued:

Ruth: My mother and my little brother Sam.

Grete: But where are you?

Ruth: I am still on a board that bridges a little brook outside the fence of the Warsaw Ghetto, taking off with two men unknown to me, Polish collaborators of the Nazis whom my mother has bribed with jewellery to take me away.

Spontaneously reaching out in the direction of her mother and brother, she burst out in a torrent of tears.

Ruth: Mother, mother, I won't leave, no, no, no, I don't want to. Why did you arrange for this?

And then still with strong emotion:

Ruth: But this is your last wish, I must go.

The next moment she whimpered again in despair.

Ruth: I left without knowing what would happen to you. I should have
stayed. You had no right to send me away. What do I live for?

After this outburst, I continued to double by mentioning facts of Ruth's life,
with Ruth responding, e.g:

Grete: I live for my family.

Ruth: Untrue – my husband has died as well.

Grete: But my daughter needs me.

Ruth: No, she gets on well without me.

Grete: I can do much for my patients.

Ruth: So what?

Grete: I have friends.

Ruth: So what?

The protagonist was so shaken by her survivor guilt that I had to support her
with my arm. At that moment, two psychodramatically experienced group
members in silent communication with me placed themselves on a chair in
front of Ruth. They assumed the roles of Ruth's mother and brother. The
younger man, his head on the older man's shoulder, said: 'What a miracle,
mother, that you could help Ruth to get out.' Whereupon, in order to have the
reply emerge in spontaneous action from Ruth's unconscious, I asked her to
reverse roles.

After a moment of silence, the young man put his head again on the
mother's – now Ruth's – shoulder and repeated his statement. In the role of
her mother, Ruth stroked the young man's head and quietly replied: 'Yes, this
gives us peace.'

Back in her own role, Ruth appeared calmer. I therefore ended the action
phase of the session and invited her to leave the stage and lie down. Placing
myself behind her I then began to quote in German from Herman Hesse's
poem *walking in fog*. When I came to the lines which read something like: 'Full
of friends was the world in my youth. Now, that the evening falls, I have but
the blues…' Ruth sprang up in a frenzy. Laughing, weeping and jumping
about, she exclaimed: 'Leaving the ghetto, I haven't walked into nowhere. I
have found a new world, my friends, my family, my work, myself. I am sure
that's what mother and Sam had hoped for. I am sure. I have fulfilled their last
wish! I am truly sure of it.'

During the closure of this session the group members, with tears still in their eyes, expressed how close they felt to Ruth.

The following day Ruth communicated her relief to the group: 'I cannot understand what happened yesterday. How could I see my mother and brother in two totally different looking men? But I did. Yet, today I know that you have gone with me through the most horrifying moments of my life, the moment of separation from my doomed mother and brother. A few days ago you were still strangers to me. Now you are the only people who know what I have gone through. Before, I had never been able to communicate this experience to anyone, not even to my husband and daughter. As a matter of fact, I hardly remembered it myself. Only sometimes, I had that nightmare of walking on the fogged-in bridge, the endless bridge that led to nowhere. Yesterday I penetrated the fog. I have arrived.'

The group continued at long intervals for over three years. Ruth's dream of walking aimlessly and endlessly in the fog never reappeared. Neither did any symptoms of PTSD.

Discussion of Ruth's case

First, we feel compelled to ask what had released Ruth's dissociative state of consciousness in the form of the recurrent dream of walking without orientation in thick fog and in form of the 'daydream' with the same image.

Psychodramatists don't feel the need to interpret such images because, according to Moreno, 'interpretation is in the act itself' (1969, p.244). Consequently, Ruth's psychodramatic action led to the crucial scene on the primitive bridge across the brook separating her for ever from her most beloved ones. Thus, recovery of the original trauma underlying her painful memories, which before had to be walled off by dissociation, took place. Yet, psychodramatic action accomplishes still more than this.

Ruth's role-reversal with her mother liberated her of the fixated role of 'illegitimate survivor.' Drawing from the 'co-unconscious' (Moreno 1959, p.59), when in her mother's role, Ruth literally became able to look at herself and her life through the eyes of her mother. This resulted in a change of attitude toward herself. Back in her own role, the painful affect of guilt was replaced by the gratifying affect and knowledge of having fulfilled her mother's last and deepest wish. This consequently made integration of the trauma into Ruth's life-history possible. But how was the re-activation of affects brought about?

Most likely, it was triggered off by the emotional impact that the first psychodramas of our workshop had on Ruth. Those plays of other protagonists revolving around family issues must have re-activated repressed memories of her early family life. Concomitant with those memories however, were the traumatic ones of Ruth's separation from her closest relatives who were murdered in the Holocaust. Later, the traumatic memories were so painful that Ruth could neither talk nor think of them. As 'an adaptive response to trauma' they had to be split off from consciousness by dissociation.

In Ruth's case, the present trauma had not been her memories on the cognitive level but the re-experiencing of affects which had accompanied the original trauma of thirty and more years ago. Van der Kolk (1996, p.296) explains this process as follows: 'Traumatic memories come back as emotional and sensory states with little verbal representation. This failure to process information on a symbolic level which is essential for proper categorisation and integration with other experience, is at the very core of the pathology of PTSD' (1996, p.296). And further, he refers to Janet's clear distinction between traumatic and ordinary memory, according to which 'traumatic memory consists of images, sensations, affective states and behaviour that are invariable and do not change over time. In contrast narrative (explicit) memory is semantic and symbolic according to social demands' Janet (1925). Such memories can be expanded or contracted.

The importance of psychodrama in the treatment of PTSD lies exactly in the fact that traumatic memories need not be described by the patient but are first acted out within the structures of the scene that is re-enacted on stage. This safe setting is containing the patient's physical, emotional and mental expressions simultaneously and this helps the protagonist to re-experience the scene holistically. However, any affective memory, while enacted in psychodrama, also gets verbalized, that is, processed on a symbolic level. This fusion will then become integrated. Thus, 'fusion/integration' as the ultimate goal of therapy of dissociative disorders of consciousness (Putnam 1989) is achieved through psychodrama therapy.

Case study: Birgit and Selma

In another newly formed psychodrama group that I led years later over several days in Sweden, a colleague conducted the first session for organizational reasons. During its warm-up phase, a young woman named Birgit related how difficult her relationship to her twelve-year-old son had become since her husband's suicide by hanging. She expressed her hope that psychodrama might help better the communication with her only child. The group shared her concern and Birgit became protagonist of the following psycho-drama.

Before starting, she chose an auxiliary ego for the role of her boy. In spite of the presence of several younger men in the group, her choice, strangely enough, fell upon Selma, a lady psychiatrist in her fifties unknown to her.

The scene began with Selma in the boy's role sitting at his desk doing homework. When his mother, the protagonist Birgit, gently laid her hand on the son's shoulder and in quivering voice said: 'I must tell you something extremely sad, your father is no longer alive!' Selma, in the role of the 12-year-old child, seemed shocked but remained silent. For a while, her behaviour appeared adequate. But when Birgit continued to talk without receiving an answer, the therapist and group members realized that Selma's condition had changed profoundly during these first minutes of psycho-dramatic interaction. This must have been even more surprising since Selma had known Birgit's story beforehand and, as a psychiatrist, undoubtedly had had to deal with suicides many times before. Nevertheless, enacting the boy's role produced amnesia in Selma as to where she was, why she was here, and with whom. Obviously Selma, the auxiliary ego in Birgit's play, had become the major protagonist of an unknown event.

As immediate crisis intervention, the therapist stopped the psychodrama and returned with Selma and Birgit from the meta-reality of play to the here-and-now-reality of the group. Together with the group members, she tried to re-orient Selma by recapping on what had happened since they had entered the room, but with no result. An emergency check-up of Selma did not yield any organic findings. Still, the therapist asked a group member to share Selma's room and let her go to sleep.

The next morning when I had to take over, Selma's condition was unchanged, the group was in a state of alarm and I, needless to say, felt uneasy as well. After all, Selma's symptoms indicated that she had slipped into a state of dissociation of consciousness.

Owing to the fact that this had occurred on stage when Selma had been acting as Birgit's auxiliary ego in the role of her son, I felt that crisis inter-vention should be carried out in the meta-reality of psychodramatic play rather than in the here-and-now-reality of the group. I requested to set up the stage as the night before and led Selma back to the boy's desk and role. When Birgit again informed her son of his father's death, Selma reacted with a slight change in posture. I gently put my hand on her shoulder and asked her to close her eyes, to stay with her feelings, and to give a description of the situation in which she saw herself. In response to my doubling of unfinished sentences like, 'I see myself...' Selma described seeing herself in a standing train crowded with children. She was twelve, her brother nine. Because of boards nailed to the train windows, she could not see her parents outside.

These details were given in response to my careful doubling. In order to elicit further information, yet not to disturb the interdependent state between protagonist and double I continued by referring to the preparation of the trip when still at home, which Selma seemed to like to re-experience in psychodramatic interaction.

The familiar living room set up on the stage, as well as the technique of role reversal, soon exerted their impact. Selma seemed to 'feel at home'. In role reversals with the members of her family she vividly portrayed each relative in words, gestures and motion: the indifference of the brother and the hectically packing mother. In her grandmother's role, she put a photograph of the family on top of the open suitcase and had her granddaughter promise often to look at the picture, together with her little brother, when away from home. Finally, taking the role of her father who sat as if 'stoned' in an armchair, she was overcome with heavy crying.

When I went up to her, Selma fell out of the role and said in tears, 'After this I did not see my father again. He died in a concentration camp. The train was the last one taking Jewish children from Vienna to Sweden.' Having slowly calmed down and appearing relieved, Selma left the stage with me and returned to the reality of the group for closure of the session. After her cathartic experience in psychodrama she was as present and coherent as she had been before her dissociation. The group was moved and deeply impressed, and some members shared own painful losses of close persons during their childhood.

The third phase or closure of any psychodrama session is of special importance. A balance between the needs of the protagonist and the needs of the group members must be established. It is best accomplished by the sharing and is particularly indispensable after a cathartic psychodrama on trauma. On the one hand it supports the protagonist, while on the other it reveals the conditions of the group members, especially of those particularly affected. They, at some other sessions, may want to play and further investigate the experiences they shared. Last but not least, sharing strengthens mutual confidence and the cohesion of the group as a safe place for victims.

Discussion of the case of Birgit and Selma

The unexpected and sudden dissociation of consciousness occurred in Selma when she, as auxiliary ego to Birgit, in the role of Birgit's son, was informed of the father's cruel death. In view of the fact that, before assuming this role, Selma had been informed of Birgit's story and had not shown any extraordinary reaction, the dissociation was obviously precipitated by the power of the set-up of that scene (the den of Birgit's 12-year-old son) on stage and of the role, namely the role of the boy in interaction with his mother, during which he experienced the loss of his father. Scene, role and interaction in psychodrama are the agents which, in contrast to cognition, induce images, sensations, affective states, behaviour and – last but not least – catharsis. In fact, they are the very reasons why in ordinary life we do not content ourselves with the knowledge of a written drama, but let its theatrical performance fascinate us.

Psychodramatic crisis-intervention in the case of Selma consisted of creating a safe situation in which there was a deliberate repetition of the dissociation-precipitating scene. In addition, it was most likely also created by my hand on Selma's shoulder, which seemed to reinforce the suggestion of Putnam that 'the patient must experience the therapist as caring and sensitive to the recovered material and its effect on therapy' (1989, p.250). In this situation of safety, stepwise age regression in the service of trauma recovery and integration was facilitated by application of the psychodramatic double technique, enabling the protagonist to recover the original trauma on an 'affect-bridge' as Watkins (1971, pp.21–27) calls comparable procedures of hypnotherapy.

As Selma's own role feedback revealed, role reversal with her grandmother had the effect of making her aware of the everlasting positive influence her family has had on her, while role reversal with her beloved father induced her catharsis. Psychodramatic role reversal cannot be appreciated highly enough in the recovery of dissociated material. On the one hand it offers the protagonist the same mechanisms of 'adaptation to trauma' as dissociation of consciousness does. On the other hand, it promotes fusion/integration due to the protagonist's simultaneous emotional experience of the usually split-off traumatic memories while still in the role of the other.

General discussion of dissociation of consciousness in psychodrama

In more than 30 years of experience with psychodrama, I have witnessed only three dissociative states which occurred unexpectedly during a session, if I do not consider the many more psychosomatic reactions as related events. Like dissociations, such psychosomatic reactions generally do not occur in protagonists, but in group members watching protagonist centred plays, such as in the first case presented above.

I have seen dissociation in an auxiliary ego only in the second case described in this chapter. However, transitory feelings of confusion of auxiliary egos as to their age adequate identity, upon return from the meta-reality of psychodramatic play to the here-and-now-reality of the group, should not be overlooked. Such feelings may occur if the de-roling of an auxiliary after the play is forgotten or insufficiently done.

The various sharings given by these people to the protagonist generally reveal astonishing correspondences between scenes and roles that they have experienced themselves at some time in their lives and the roles that they enacted in the protagonist's psychodrama. Owing to its semantic and symbolic presentation, immediate sharing relieves them of their affective symptoms. In contrast, members of the audience who react with psychosomatic symptoms to a specific psychodrama enactment usually cannot give any substantial sharing, although they mention or complain of their physical sensations. This behaviour is very similar to what many authors describe as the alexithymia ('there are no words for feelings') characteristic of psychosomatic patients.

Dissociative reactions, as well as psychosomatic ones, may likewise occur in members of the audience when a certain scene and role is presented by the protagonist. This may be caused by a resonance of split-off or repressed traumatic memories of corresponding scenes and roles that the affected person has experienced in his or her own life. In my experience, when recovering their trauma in psychodramatic crisis-intervention, and when the client has accepted and integrated it as an event of the past, the dissociative or psychosomatic reactions will disappear as fast as they appeared. I attribute this effect largely to reversal of the 'adaptive responses to acute trauma' so that there is an active re-entering into the traumatic constraints instead of an escape from them, an active re-experiencing of the traumatic memories instead of containing them outside of normal conscious awareness and catharsis and regaining of the sense of self instead of analgesia and of having the trauma happen to a depersonalized self (Leutz 1996).

References

Janet, P. (1925) *Psychological Healing 1-2*. NY: Macmillan.

Leutz, G.A. (1996) 'Uber den psychodramatherapeutischen Umgang mit dissoziativen Stoerungen' (Remarks on the psychodramatherapuetic approach to dissociative disorders.) In U.H. Peters, M. Schifferdecker and A. Krahl (eds) *150 Jahre Psychatrie. Band 1*. Koln: Martini.

Ludwig, A.M. (1983) 'The psychological functions of dissociation.' *American Journal of Clinical Hypnosis 26*, 93–99.

Moreno, J.L. (1973) *The Theatre of Spontaneity*. Beacon, NY: Beacon House.

Moreno, J.L. (1959) *Psychodrama, Volume 2*. Beacon, NY: Beacon House.

Moreno, J.L. (1969) *Psychodrama, Volume 3*. Beacon, NY: Beacon House.

Nemiah, J.C. (1981) 'Dissociative disorders.' In A.M. Freeman and H.I. Kaplan (eds) *Comprehensive Textbook of Psychiatry*. Baltimore: Williams and Wilkins.

Putnam, F. (1989) *Multiple Personality Disorders*. New York and London: The Guilford Press.

van der Kolk, B. (1987) *Psychological Trauma*. Washington DC: American Psychiatric Press.

van der Kolk, B. (1996) 'The body keeps score: approaches to the psychobiology of post-traumatic stress disorder.' In B. van der Kolk, A.C. McFarlane and L. Weisaeth (eds) *Traumatic Stress: The Effects of Overwhelming Experiences on Mind, Body and Society*. New York: Guilford Press.

Watkins, J.G. (1971) 'The affect bridge: A hypnoanalytic technique.' *International Journal of Clinical and Experimental Hypnosis 19*, 21–27.

CHAPTER 12

Psychodrama with Survivors of Traffic Accidents

Jörg Burmeister

Talking about trauma is not enough: trauma survivors need to take some action that symbolises triumph over helplessness and despair (van der Kolk 1995b, p.12)

Severe injuries of body and psyche generate a biopsychological chain reaction that improves the chances of survival. This reaction includes not thinking about it, not remembering it, not talking about it, not identifying with it and feeling the same terror again. It also means being under the effect of a constant physiological hyper-arousal which informs the person instantly about a possible repetition of the traumatic experience. All these reactions tend to stabilize and give rise to harmful emotions which are connected with the trauma: shame, guilt, anxiety (including nightmares), depression and other more severe changes in personality.

While the development of PTSD after terrifying experiences is among the most common of psychiatric disorders (van der Kolk 1995a), retraumatization may also occur as a result of the treatment itself, especially in those interventions which are centred around groups and actions. Naturally, not all traumatic incidents provoke PTSD and many 'normal' coping reactions have similar features to PTSD (Horowitz 1993, pp. 49–60).

This chapter will introduce the basic requirements of an integrative trauma therapeutic approach with special emphasis on psychodramatic elements. I will explain some of the basic neurobiological foundations of the disorder and specifically focus on the application of this model on the treatment of car accident victims, giving a review of core concepts, specific strategies, questions of setting and relevant literature. Different stages of the treatment model will be related to distinctive aspects of the concerned population and illustrated with case studies.

As psychodrama therapy investigates three main principles – action, imagination and cooperation (Buer 1989) – it reveals a prominent role in the integrative model of trauma therapy. It is not only one of the basic approaches of group psychotherapy but it also focuses specially on the creative aspects of human nature which are of special interest in the framework of trauma therapy.

Symptoms and neurobiological foundations of PTSD

Post-traumatic stress disorder is an anxiety disorder (e.g. ICD–10) whereby an unexpected, unpredictable and uncontrollable in its consequences, terrifying experience could not be integrated appropriately into the biopsychosocial framework of an individual. Despite the great variability of traumatic origins and individual responses, post-traumatic stress disorder so far encompasses intrusions, avoidance behaviour, and physiological hyper-arousal. In addition, people with PTSD may have major changes in their sense of identity. Moreover, they tend to process information in such a way that they are prone to expose themselves again to situations reminiscent of the trauma.

If the PTSD is complicated by or originates from extreme stress (Herman 1992, van der Kolk, McFarlane and Weisaeth 1996), it can also be associated with affective and impulsive dysregulation (anger, self-destructiveness), damaged identity concepts (permanent guilt and shame), interpersonal disorders (unspecific revenge feelings) and a general loss of a sense of meaning (hopelessness, lack of values and convictions).

The traumatic experience interferes with the normal information processing system. The evolutionary younger parts of the brain (specific cortex areas with complex functions like abstract thought or processes of symbolization) will be disconnected by the extreme anxiety and its impact on the whole central nervous system. On the contrary, the evolutionary older parts (brain stem, mid-brain and limbic system) store the information at a sensorimotor and affective level usually assigned as implicit memory system (Squire 1994; Schachter 1987; Le Doux 1992; van der Kolk 1994). During extreme emotional arousal, higher hippocampal memory functions cease to work and the individual may start to dissociate. This mechanism will be reproduced on behalf of coping needs and increases the probability of developing PTSD (van der Kolk 1995). PET measurements of neuronal activity in the recalling process of traumatic events clearly demonstrate the higher implication of right-brain structures and the much lesser activity of left-brain 'symbolizer' areas. These neurobiological findings stress the importance of therapeutic approaches like psychodrama, which specifically involve motor, sensual and affective aspects together with a higher right-brain onset during its application.

I will here describe a model of an integrative therapeutic approach to PTSD with special emphasis on action-centred, psychodramatic interventions. The model summarizes the experience of more than 15 years of treatment of single clients and groups suffering from PTSD. It has also taken into account different references to PTSD treatment (Antonovsky 1987; Herman 1992; van de Kolk 1995b and 1996; Williams and Sommer 1997).

The model encompasses four basic stages. The first stage of preparation is dedicated to reassure client and therapist about the basic requirements of the therapeutic encounter before entering the treatment process itself. The following stage contains three target areas:

1. To stop the feeling of insecurity and loss of self-determination. This is the phase of empowerment.

2. To control the effect of the traumatic stress and to integrate it into a system of personal coherence. This is the phase of rescription of the traumatic experience.

3. To redefine its consequences for the victim and the world. This is the phase of re-evaluation of roles and social network as well as the re-establishment of trust and intimacy.

Table 12.1 gives an overview of the model while more detailed information on the treatment of accident victims will follow.

TABLE 12.1: Integrative treatment model for PTSD

Phase I: Preparation

1. Guarantee safety

2. Information/education

3. Cultural framing and assessment

4. Establishing therapeutic relationship –

- acceptance, empathy, validation, no neutrality;
- speed determined by client;
- drama triangle – supervision, self-experience necessary

5. Therapeutic planning on consent

Phase II: Safety, empowerment

1. Deconditioning by relaxation techniques

2. Self-management and self-control:

   - exercises to choose;
   - echo in the group;
   - control and effect on situations;
   - self-determined body experience;
   - symbolizing and creative;
   - non-verbal expression: music, dance, painting, voice;
   - narration of a healing myth;
   - specific magic shop

3. Hope, regulation of anxiety and aggression (breath, visualization, objects

4. Framing and validation of spontaneous images of the client

Phase III: Re-organization of the traumatic scene

1. Establishing the safety place: restoring pre-traumatic resources, images, objects, symbols, people, feelings, atmospheres, music, smell, movie stars, etc. by actional, symbolic and/or imaginary/hypnotic assessment

2. Anchoring with sensual markers and reinforcement

3. Management of cognitive changes. ABC scale – provoking event, accompanying belief/conviction/cognition, consequences, sense and alternative cognition. Five target areas: safety, confidence, power/influence, auto-estimation and intimacy

4. Establishing of rescue fantasies

5. Re-exposition step by step, armouring in the safe place. Special deconditioning techniques. Sensual markers, chorus with self-given positive/alternative cognitions, control by role-triggered approximation.

6. Introduction of change, new power distribution and new exit

7. Level of aggression varies (loyalty)

8. De-roling of group and auxiliary ego

9. Sharing on different levels including archetypal and spiritual dimension

10. Difference between role-feedback and capacity to protect the protagonist

Phase IV: Re-connection with the living world

1. Social network inventory: new roles? Old roles modifying?

2. Inviting the family (inter/transgenerational issues)

3. New therapeutic issues: psychosomatic disorder? Affective dysregulation?

4. Witness/survivor report

5. Topic of justice

6. Taking a mission

7. Existential, spiritual level

Traffic accident victims

More than two million traffic accidents take place in Germany every year. More than 500,000 people are injured, of whom more than 100,000 are severely injured. The consequences of these accidents transcend the mere economic and physical damage. Following recent studies, between 20 and 30 per cent of the victims may develop psychic impairments which range from PTSD, phobic avoidance, other anxiety disorders and depression to organic syndromes (Malt 1988). Public health care systems usually underestimate the incidence and the degree of the resulting psychic damages (Green et al. 1993; Mayou 1993; Stallard 1998). The incidence of a complete PTSD syndrome after traffic accidents amounts to 18.4 per cent; subsyndromal PTSD (only one or two categories of the B, C and D categories of DSM-IV are fulfilled) even occur in 29 per cent of all cases (Frommberger et al. 1997). In another survey the incidence of PTSD after traffic accidents runs about 41 per cent while it declines to 21 per cent after six months (spontaneous recovery; Blanchard et al. 1995). Between 10 and 30 per cent of all victims affected by PTSD after traffic accidents develop chronic PTSD (Taylor and Koch 1995). On average 35 per cent of children exposed to a traffic accident will develop PTSD, especially in the role of witnesses (Stallard 1998). Besides PTSD, chronic pain and depressive syndromes, particularly in combination with a whiplash injury or other more severe brain injuries, may complicate the psychic outcome of the accident survivor (Smith 1989). The onset of the symptoms is early and independent of the severity of the somatic trauma (Mayou and Radanov 1996).

Clients complain about intrusive memories of the accident. This is especially common when they are re-exposed to stimuli connected with the accident itself. For example, when they are driving along the same or a similar highway, under weather conditions similar to the time of the accident, approaching a car similar to the ones involved in the accident; media reports about accidents and the anniversary date of the accident can have the same effect. Nightmares may provoke sleep disorder. The perception of normal traffic is imbued by feelings of anxiety and menace. Constant alert reactions, irritability and less frustration tolerance accompany the traffic performance of accident victims (Burstein *et al.* 1988). Feelings of guilt determine the psychic outcome of the accident victim when he or she accepts responsibility for the accident. On the other hand the permanent loss of body integrity (for example, loss of limbs, loss of cognitive or other brain functions) or the loss of family members or friends in the accident complicates the processing of the psychic impairments of the accident victim in a decisive way, especially if there are still unresolved juridical implications. Therapeutic strategies must be able to assess and to work on these differential issues of the accident survivor in a flexible way.

Assessment and diagnostic issues

Assessment as a process accompanies the whole treatment while it explores the wishes, expectations and needs as well as the deficiencies and the resources of the client on a multidimensional scale of personal and interpersonal criteria. Psychodrama monitors a specific 'humanistic' attitude in this process while appointing the role of the guiding protagonist and giving control over the process to the client explicitly (Kellermann 1992).

Concerning the scientific validation of diagnostic manuals, the works of Foa and Cashman (1996) and Gunkel (1996) merit special attention (Maercker 1999). At a psychodramatic level the assessment of the social network (for example, 'The social networks inventory' by Treadwell, Leach and Stein 1993) and of role charts (Clayton 1994; Williams 1989) will give basic information for a conjoint psychodramatic treatment planning. But assessment in accident victims cannot focus on PTSD alone. Seventy-two per cent of the victims of natural disasters also develop other psychiatric disorders apart from PTSD, particularly depression (McFarlane 1989). Confrontative techniques diminish PTSD, but fail to diminish depression (Keane 1989; Boudewyns 1990).

Dissociation as a repairing or at least protecting biopsychic arrangement is not applicable to the majority of accident victims. The dynamic of extreme loss and mortification might therefore often hit victims directly. The therapy must deal with phenomena of pathologic grief reactions; with depressive and/or unresolved aggressive features; with special guilt implications – the victim and perpetrator may be one and the same (if the accident was provoked by the victim – with or without terrifying consequences for others); with somatic injuries; with severe impairments and pain; with psychological disturbance; and also with open juridical issues. Cognitive impairments particularly reduce life quality in the long run (Oddy 1985).

The following table tries to outline some of the main issues which are valid for the assessment process. If some of the features are present the treatment plan must establish carefully the appropriate order of approaching them. Some of the following case studies inform about concrete criteria to decide upon the strategy of choosing. The consent of the client always conditions the ongoing process.

Table 12.2 Assessment of comorbid influences on accident victims besides PTSD

Indicator for

- severe/prominent loss:
- body functions
- specific emotionally relevant persons?

with

pathologic grief reaction and:

- depression?
- unresolved anger/aggression?
- anaesthetic, dissociation?

guilt dynamics

cognitive impairments/somatic pain

open juridical claims

Treatment: Studies and setting

There are no controlled studies about the effectiveness of psychotherapy on PTSD after accidents. Some case studies, however, indicate successful interventions by cognitive behavioural methods such as relaxation techniques, systematic desensitization, cognitive restructuring or exposition in sensu and in vivo (McCaffrey and Fairbank 1985; Kuch, Swinson and Kirby 1985; Muse 1986; McMillan 1991; Horne 1993; Horton 1993). These studies prove the effectiveness of the treatment even in chronic types of PTSD, in cases with comorbid depression, pain syndrome or neuropsychological impairments, and also that still pending juridical claims for damages could not interfere with the positive outcome of the treatment. All case studies use individual settings for the psychotherapeutic intervention. The following paragraphs discuss, as well as the individual setting, two different types of setting for the therapeutic approach of PTSD after accidents: working with homogenous groups of victims and working with families. Some case studies describe in addition individual interventions in the context of heterogeneous groups.

Treatment: Psychodrama theory and specific efficacy

Psychodrama as a whole reconstructs experiences at different role and reality levels. Psychodrama mobilizes through action not only manifest role behaviour but causes associated scenic memories to resonate internally (role cluster, scenic memory: Petzold and Matthias 1982) while it activates all role dimensions (Burmeister and Schwinger 1995). Action therefore may enable and reinforce the power of scenic rescription in the PTSD treatment setting, increasing the impact of emotions and forming a pathway for cathartic reactions. Working with the body incites implicit memory functions more specifically than a mere verbal dialogue, which cannot activate nor change them. Restoring the body with action-based exercises (including dances like flamenco, moving exercises like t'ai chi or self-defensive methods like karate) as well as replacing intrusive images by visualization based exercises at the imaginary level can form the basis for a healing transformation. And catharsis, lastly, facilitates processes of mourning and separation as well as the integration of aggression.

Individual setting – first stage: Establishing the therapeutic relationship

The therapeutic relationship is of crucial importance for the whole treatment process and must be established carefully. The power gradient between the role of the therapist and the client imitates the traumatic experience of being powerless. Although the trauma type does not correspond with a man-made disaster, the difference of power may disturb the treatment of accident victims if not addressed appropriately. One of the standards for the trauma therapist therefore is to revise her or his own power complex at the self-experience level. Nevertheless, the therapist can easily receive the role of the victim or of the aggressor her or himself while the traumatic experience is constantly present and re-staged on different levels in the context of the therapeutic encounter (Reddemann 1998). Therefore permanent supervision should be another standard during the treatment process.

The relationship must guarantee right from the beginning safety, trust building, reliability, respect and empathic kindness. The therapist witnesses the traumatic experience not in a neutral but in an active, validating way which includes the role of the ally with clear emotional boundaries. This attitude can easily oscillate between active listening, validating the meaning of the traumatic experience, framing spontaneous images of the client and active doubling in the later treatment stages. The client regulates the speed of the treatment process – too much pressure from the role of the therapist may only lead to a blockage of the whole treatment. An anxious and avoidant communication style in the client often reflects a spectrum of difficult emotions: the shame of exposing a 'personal defect', feelings of guilt (not having been able to prevent it) and anxiety about suffering from traumatic experiences again. Thus, the therapy and the therapist need time to enable the client to gain sufficient trust in the therapeutic relationship.

But accident victims also usually lack information about the nature of PTSD while they are suffering from its consequences. So far, giving information about PTSD after confirming its presence (complete, complicated or subsyndromal) should be one of the first interventions in the treatment process itself. Research data support the beneficial effect of giving such information (Broda and Muthny 1990). Finally, clients are informed about the possible therapeutic strategies and stages of therapy in relation to the given model of the PTSD. They are asked to give their consent to a decided period of treatment. If accident victims present a more complicated clinical feature with more prominent issues of loss (body function, family members or friends), these aspects must be addressed separately. Planning the treatment then means deciding with the client where to go first. Although the PTSD treatment may disclose other issues, they are usually not chosen as the presenting problems. If the client comes from another cultural background, the cultural meaning of loss and grief for the client must be clarified as well as the existence of specific coping or healing rituals (Williams and Sommer 1997).

Apart from the subject of a separate prominent loss or PTSD, the accident victim always traverses a psychodynamic level of mourning. Such a level includes a mortification of the own 'narcissistic' self and forced dependency after the accident (Burmeister 1991). A large amount of research has clearly demonstrated that the fear of losing autonomy may even exceed the fear of dying itself. Therefore, the loss of freedom and self-determination must be addressed prior to the work of learning how to cope with the loss. In her wonderful book *Meeting with Terminal Patients* Frede (1992) describes how it can be hurtful for a person if this is not respected.

Case study 1: First stage

A 19-year-old Swiss man suffered a car accident that was his own fault. Owing to a severe neural injury, his right arm remains partly paralysed. During the first appointment four months after the accident, he complains of constant headaches, nightmares in connection with the accident and generalized anxiety in ordinary traffic situations, which lead him to avoid driving. Moreover he shows clear depressive symptoms with lack of energy, sleeping disorders and loss of a sense of meaning with his life. He talks about his handicapped right arm in an angry and embittered way. His social life has changed very much after the accident. He can no longer do his former job and needs rehabilitation to find a new occupation. He is withdrawn and keeps his distance from others. He also isolates himself from his peer group because he feels worthless and ashamed of his handicap. It is not easy to establish a therapeutic relationship while the therapist activates and increases the mortification of the physical damage by not being handicapped.

Case study 2: First stage

While walking on the street, a 27-year-old Muslim woman from Croatia is hit by a car through no fault of her own. She recovers without major somatic injury but develops a clear case of PTSD with vivid intrusions, nightmares, flashbacks of the accident, fears of leaving home and constant 'nervousness' as if she were being threatened by 'nearly everything'. Her husband accompanies her to the first appointment three months after the accident as a translator. Because of the cultural background, a female translator must participate in the sessions while no other man with the exception of the therapist is allowed to listen to the words of the woman. Although the therapist suspects a marital conflict, the cultural background and a conflict of loyalty prevents a straightforward immediate exploration of the topic. However, the therapist and the client reach a mutual agreement about starting treatment of PTSD already in the second session.

Individual setting – second stage of empowerment

Traumatic experiences shatter the trust in a stable and predictable environment. To the same degree they weaken the belief in one's own capacity to determine situations and to protect oneself and/or to be protected against any threats to corporeal or psychic integrity. The biological chain reaction of the traumatic impact in fact initiates the psychological one. The phenomenon of the secondary affecto-cognitive processing of the trauma even seems to prevail in the scope of recent investigation on long-term trauma consequences (van der Kolk 1995b). Therapy should encompass the 'searching out of the dissociated fragments of the patient's personal identity, raising them into consciousness and facilitating the emotional abreaction of the pathogenic memories' (Nemiah 1995, p. 305). On the other hand traffic accident victims tend to exhibit the impact of the trauma on their concept of their own abilities to protect themselves, on the vision of their destiny and on the sense of meaningfulness of their life. One of the most common questions asked by traffic accident victims is 'Why me?' thus jeopardizing convictions about one's own person and its traumatic history.

Besides establishing a positive and validating communication, relaxation and breathing techniques (Basler 1989), the basic strategy in the second stage of the treatment process encompasses exercises and interactions which foster the ability to choose, to decide, to have a real influence and to be effective again (Burmeister and Diebels 1999). The onset of the action-centred interventions always depends on the client's approval and may be prepared by imaginary interventions. Other starters for opening up the spontaneous level of the process promote the deliberate variation of distance and closeness of emotionally relevant relationships, symbolized by tiny objects (Ziegler 1987) or chairs, or the application of a specific variety of the magic shop where wishes will be fulfilled without any service in return ('anti burn-out method'). Often enough the feeling that there is at least one choice is difficult to achieve. In these cases, connection with the past and past moments of choice contribute to the actualization of the existential modus vivendi of the choice and thereby the experience of self-efficacy. This approach to the treatment of trauma and the basic strategies in the treatment of depression thus often go side by side as they usually also fit together in the clinical practice (depression and psychodrama e.g. Burmeister and Diebels 1999).

Case study 1: Second stage

The issue of the meaning of the impairment for the young man is approached by careful doubling, as well as offering a clear model of PTSD. Almost in the second appointment the client is able to admit that he really hates his paralysed arm as being of no worth any more. The self-reported symptom analysis of his headache (a written form with exploration of symptom-related scenes as homework is easy to transform into action vignettes) reveals that it changes under stress and is triggered particularly by feelings connected with the right arm. His social network, portrayed with symbols, confirms his almost complete isolation after the accident due to hostile reaction to the 'healthy others'. Only his brother is accepted still (imaged as a knight on a horse). The client symbolizes the aim of the therapy (psychodramatic assessment of therapeutic goals also at a symbolic level) by wiping away a dark animal which is persecuting him. While formulating the therapy plan the client prefers first to work on the topic of his 'damned' right arm and only afterwards on the PTSD.

Case study 2: Second stage

At the beginning of each session the client is invited to designate a colour representing for her the expected mood of the session. Then the client actively recalls memories of her birthdays as a child, associating wishes from the past. This issue brings back the cultural dimension and reinforces this level of identity which was dissipated by the immigration. She also imagines her favourite landscape, also situated in her country of origin, introducing the smell of the field and the changes of the seasons. She forms a trans-generational network with tiny objects, which she has taken from home and which remind her of her own culture. Finally the client and the therapist listen together to the client's favourite piece of music. The cultural dimension serves as a useful guard, connecting the stage of empowerment with the stage of the safe place. Instead of remaining an obstacle, it transforms the therapeutic relationship into a real encounter. The client always refuses to move forward to action exercises as it provokes too much shame against the background of cultural and gender issues. Nevertheless, the 'psychodrama en miniature' works excellently. Thus it is possible to advance in a very natural and organic way towards the stage of the reconstruction of the safe place.

Individual treatment – third stage: Safe place technique

Traumatic experiences tend to contaminate the meaning of other experiences in the total life span of the individual. Although even safe experiences are apparently extinguished and disappear because of the overwhelming emotional consequences of the trauma, at least some of these experiences potentially still keep their safe and undamaged significance. The action-centred approach of the reconstruction of the safe place stimulates good, non-spoiled experiences in the individual's present and past situations by the use of body, imaginary or symbol-based exercises. The safe place could contain body sensations, sensual experiences on different levels of perception, emotionally relevant situations or scenarios and significant interpersonal relationships even if they are wishful or fantasy ones (for example, favourite fairy tale hero, literature or movie character, historical characters and so forth).

The elaboration of the safe place requires the same thorough management that is otherwise implied in case history work. Sometimes a list may help to address all relevant topics (Bisbey 1998). Yet the resources evoked in the process of reconstruction of the safe place and by its undeniable existence are sometimes even strong enough to overcome the consequences of less severe PTSD. This type of resolution depends first of all on the severity of the traumatic experience (for example, torture victims need much more time for warming-up in order to recollect the experiences), second, on the degree of comorbid depressive syndromes (depression also inhibits the active remembrance of positive experiences), and third, on the degree of interfering processes of loss and mortification (especially triggered by a pre-existing unstable personality or by real harm to body functions with a bad prognosis for rehabilitation). Traffic accident victims often also suffer from the latter consequences. While the aggressive affect is primarily directed towards the individual or environment, perhaps as resentment, it may disturb even in a hidden way the recollection of positive experiences, in a passive-aggressive manner. The role of loss and aggression must therefore be acknowledged accurately during treatment assessment and planning (see section on assessment and case report 1).

Case study 2: Third stage

The client reconstructed the safe place by introducing some of the elements she had already picked up during the empowerment stage: significant relatives like her grandmother and her brother, the fragrance of her favourite landscape and a small lute as a symbol of the music of her place of origin. In addition to the objects she had already chosen she elected a former mystic king of Croatia, represented by an invulnerable knight, in order to protect her and to restore the feeling of safety and trust. It became quickly evident for her that the assigned colour of this king and the assigned colour of her husband were very similar. Following this perception the relationship between them and its emotional link was strengthened again and intimacy improved very much. After just four sessions and without approaching the trauma directly she had recovered completely from all PTSD symptoms. In the follow-up after six and twelve months the result proved to be stable.

Individual treatment – third stage: Rescription (or re-writing) of the traumatic scene and replacement by a therapeutic altered version

The outcome of the work in the safe place and its resolution on the role level could be transformed or anchored by body, sensual and image modalities. In combination with relaxation or breathing techniques it enables the individual to control physiological arousal. A gradual approximation to the traumatic experience contributes towards the flexible handling of the dimension of closeness and distance itself. The monitoring of the body and interactional reactions during the re-approximation by the therapist is vital for the guarantee of safety during the re-framing stage of trauma (Reddemann 1998). The protagonist should never directly approach the scene psychodramatically as this would compromise or surpass his capacity to control the experience, but should gradually go into the scene, starting from a safe place in the room (director or mirror position). After being able to witness the performance of the traumatic sequence and/or by introducing new elements, the protagonist re-experiences the scene with less physiological and emotional arousal. This corresponds to the main principles of confrontative therapeutic interventions (Foa and Cashman 1996). Intermediate steps in the approach to the scene might focus upon object roles inside the scene (for example, a table, a picture). The physiological and emotional reactions must be followed and checked by the therapist at all times in case dissociation or overwhelming emotional responses occur. Then relaxation techniques, often triggered by conscious breathing patterns and scenic redistancing must be applied immediately. Excessive arousal interferes with the acquisition of new information. The protagonist should control and maintain empowerment over the re-exposure of the trauma as the main goal of this stage. Otherwise, retraumatization might rupture the therapeutic and healing effect of the work. A chorus instructed with verbal messages from the safe place of the protagonist may encourage him or her during the rescription of the traumatic sequence. This rescription often takes advantage of the fact that trauma victims might be able to bear the impact of the trauma for the first time without avoiding it or dissociating from it. By mastering the experience the victim may proceed towards the new representation.

In the case of strong violent man-made traumatic experience a new character or role often enters the scene, changing the power balance in favour of the victim and stopping the trauma. During the re-experience of the trauma strong body reactions may occur. They range from different pain syndromes to vomiting, dyspnoea or hyperventilation. These body reactions often signal deeper interpersonal conflicts on the level of loyalty, guilt or mistrust. They must be addressed and clarified afterwards only if they persist in the absence of the traumatic experience.

The protagonist should never take the role of the aggressor; it contravenes the establishment of clear boundaries and may even facilitate identification with the aggressor (Dhawan 1992). If the victim is acting in his or her own role he or she could be assisted by at least one auxiliary ego in another new role (out of the rescription of the traumatic scene, for example, a fairy: Reddemann 1998). If the victim likes, he or she could also take the new role of the defender, managing to stop the trauma by him or herself. The choice to do so should be offered in an open way and protagonists should never be pushed towards it. Only on those rare occasions when there is no resolution of the torturing feeling of guilt mediated by the process of identifying with the aggressor is it necessary to work through the two sides of the aggressor. In such work, the apparent split between the good and the evil side of the aggression is acknowledged, but without this role being taken on. This can be done through sensitive doubling by the therapist from behind an empty chair. This arrangement provides the same therapeutic structure that is recommended for process-experiential psychotherapy .

The basic dimension of the therapeutic strategy helps the protagonist to bear its scenic representation. It is vital to encounter the death-threatening dimension of the experience on the one hand, but also to connect with the feeling of having overcome it on the other. The latter aspect provokes a cathartic reaction that helps to integrate the whole experience. But the gratitude for having survived may be damaged if other people were killed or seriously injured at the same time. The topic of unresolved guilt requires a special approach of dialogue between survivor and the other person (see section on pathologic grief). If it was a very severe accident it may be necessary to re-experience it several times in order to reduce anxiety and to control the emotional response (Bisbey 1998; Shapiro 1989). Thus, besides the cathartic experience of having survived, often cognitive restructuring and re-evaluation of important self or object concepts promote the therapeutic process (see section on the fourth stage of individual treatment, p.216).

In the individual setting the therapist also shares and validates the experiences by focusing on the content of the outcome. The personal sharing of the therapist is possible and even desirable but at the same time difficult as it may dissipate the clear role structure of the therapeutic encounter and may even correspond with the therapist's own unresolved conflicts. However, it might also reinforce the therapeutic alliance in a very significant way for the victim.

Case study 3

A 13-year-old teenager was nearly killed in a car accident. She was in a coma for two weeks and clinically dead for more than 12 hours. Before the accident happened, she was a very successful and charming but also over-adapted girl. Following the accident and recovery phase she radically changed, exposing herself to a series of very risky situations without taking care of herself or considering the possible disastrous outcome. She changed her interpersonal behaviour and acted in a very pronounced, independent way, freeing herself from the considerations and expectations of others. At the age of 15 her school career collapsed and she suddenly fell into a state of deep anxiety and depression about life and her future. Because of the very prominent symptoms of these clinical features she was admitted to a day clinic. Although she always claimed that the accident had changed her life completely it was not considered to be the origin of her crisis.

While PTSD diagnosis could be established, the working on the issue of the safe place clarified two main tendencies and empowering roles: the role or object of her former childhood teddy-bear on the one hand and the role of a nun, a traumatized female pianist who survived by 'taking it all'. The teddy bear was reassuring the protagonist with 'soft skills' of warmth, understanding and acceptance while the nun was encouraging the protagonist to act directly for the sake of her own soul. The nurturing role of the male and the more fighting role of the female character reflected her own family background on one level, with a strong and aggressive mother and a 'soft' father. After establishing these 'safe' objects on the stage (having prepared them beforehand during individual sessions) she mentioned her accident, which she could not recollect directly. Seeking the right distance from the scene, she looked from outside while she was hit and smashed during the accident then transported away by the ambulance. She was overwhelmed and cried looking at the scene. The teddy bear gave her support and warmth while the nun encouraged her to 'see it again'. She did that, now applying breathing techniques more consciously and holding the teddy bear in her arms. After the closure of the second rehearsal she suddenly asked to see it again a third time but also giving to it a new end: her discharge from the hospital. Just by looking at it she was saying to herself: 'Now it's over! I have survived and I am so thankful.'

As a result of this process, her relationship with her parents improved very much and in the later period of the therapy her attitude towards herself and others could also be reconstructed. It had been inspired for such a long time by the idea of 'taking it all' and surviving while there was no safe place and every moment could be the last one, but she changed it. In the follow-up after one year she was able to renew her college studies and approach her parents more independently. She guarded the experience of surviving as an 'inner wisdom' (her own words) that protected, but also guided her in difficult situations.

Individual treatment – fourth stage: Reconnection with life

After the direct trauma work and its hoped for effect of altering the outcome of the traumatic experience (fulfilling the criteria of manageability and comprehensibility as proposed by Antonovsky 1987) the last, but often equally decisive, part of the therapeutic process starts. The new insights into the nature of and new attitudes towards, the traumatic experience might touch and disturb all related concepts of the person's interactive patterns and concept of life in the world. It may even initiate a metamorphosis of all these aspects. The meaning of the cathartic and scenic integration of the traumatic emotions which were expelled in the previous stage is connected with the fact that emotions structure our adjustment to expectations of ourselves, others and the world (Krystal 1978). The patient's 'repeating' the trauma in action is the forerunner to his 'remembering' and symbolizing it in words, which in turn is the precursor of and accompaniment to his 'working through' of the emotional experience (van der Kolk and Fisler 1995).

The social network inventory is a powerful medium for concretising the new evaluation of existing relationships. New expectations as well as needs or wishes for change may arise within such explorations. In addition, past relationships might be revitalized. This emphasizes the importance of also doing a social network inventory relating to before the accident. An acknowledgement or reassurance of a new 'meaning' may in itself create a first step in the restoration of the individual's personality. Furthermore, specific role charts may explore the change process in terms of the roles played, while it may also help to integrate an axiomatic perspective (Frede

1992). But if the trauma was very severe, as for example in torture victims, this might be insufficient. In these cases the therapist might choose to underline his support for the victim by testifying a witness report or even promote political actions which try to defend and to restore the human dignity of the victims. For example, the Pinochet trial may outweigh hundreds of hours of therapy for a former victim of the Pinochet regime.

PTSD and comorbid pathologic grief reactions

According to Worden (1982) and Bowlby (1980), normal grief processing contains four tasks: first, accepting the permanent loss of the deceased by expressing open anger and sadness; second, experiencing the pain of the loss of the deceased; third, adapting to an environment where the deceased is missing; and fourth, withdrawing emotional energy from the deceased and reinvesting it in a new relationship. Pathologic grief reactions increase if the loss is sudden and unexpected, if there is no social support system available, if there are pre-existing vulnerabilities in the bereaved and if the nature of the relationship with the deceased is complicated. Accident victims are prone to develop pathologic grief when losses hit them unexpectedly and individual responses are determined by a conflict between wishes of autonomy and the obvious restrictions in autonomy caused by the accident. If there is no acceptance of the loss and this manifests itself in depressive or aggressive behaviour patterns (which might even increase if there are ongoing judicial issues regarding the accident, including especially the question of indemnity for the victim) the resolution of this dimension of the trauma must obviously come first during the proper therapy of PTSD.

Work with the experiences of loss and accompanying emotions in psychodrama follows a structured procedure:

1.   addressing and validating the existence of the feeling at an emotional and somatic level, reinforcing this process by doubling and empathic mirroring;

2.   advocating an encounter with the difficult emotions on the interpersonal level and transformation into an interpersonally significant scene;

3.   staging a scene which leads towards cathartic abreaction of the difficult emotions;

4.   creating space and time for the separation process, ending by giving a concrete space for the memory of the deceased in the scene;

5.   reconnecting with life and reality and assessing the consequences of the loss (Espina-Barrios 1992; Filgueira Bouza 1995; Burmeister 1994).

Case study 1: Fourth stage

In the individual work with the young client, a body map was drawn in which the handicapped right hand was painted in black and the good spot was placed on the heart and coloured with red. Describing the spot of the heart, he mentioned that it was especially hot, fiery and very strong, but also hurtful, explosive and passionate. Looking at his hand he yelled bitterly, saying that this hand was now of no worth, that it was now ugly and disgusting. The therapist suggested that he give them more concrete evidence by putting them on stage. After accepting this proposal, the client placed two chairs, one for the heart and one for the hand. Starting to dialogue with his handicapped hand, he was blaming it in the same way that he had before. In role reversal with his handicapped hand, he said that he really feared being no use and that this felt very sad. It was even more sad to listen to the harsh words. After making the role reversal again, the client said: 'Yes it's true! I really want you to feel even more sad and to make you suffer like I suffer because of you.' Then the therapist doubled, 'Yes it is very important for me to make you feel how I suffered. Nobody had pity for me either.' Making the role reversal again, from the role of the hand, the client said: 'Yes, I see why you need to talk to me like that. But don't you understand that I also suffer a lot, that nobody loves me any more, not even you!' As himself, the client responded: 'Yes it's true, I'm also feeling lonesome so often, but the only way I can cope with it is to hate you. You are the guilty one. I hate you for being dependent on others so much.' Reinforcing this in doubling, the therapist said: 'Yes, I like to be independent. Yes, I like to make my own life.' In the role of the hand, the client responded: 'Yes, I understand. I'm sorry that I cannot be of much value for you now. But if you carry on beating me and punishing me like this it will be very painful, not only for me but for you too, and for your head.'

Back in his own role, the client for the first time gained experiential insight into the relationship between the emotional pain concerning his hand, the pain manifested in his headache and his own attitude towards them. His yearning for more social and emotional autonomy resonated with childhood memories of being treated badly by his parents. Thus, it required a lot from him to accept the partial loss of this capacity. Instead of going on to be mortified by his hand, he was able for the first time to mourn his loss, which also changed the image of his heart, as later manifested. Most importantly, from having directed most aggression towards himself, he now started to direct his aggression against destiny and God, who in his eyes were the ones responsible for allowing such tragic events to happen. He developed a kind of heroic defiance, which allowed him to reconnect with his social relevant environment with less self-destructive anger. However, the psychosomatic pain reactions did not diminish. At the two year follow-up, he had accomplished most of the relevant rehabilitation tasks at the social level, but still received long-term psychodynamic psychotherapy to support his process of long-lasting grief that is not yet finished.

Working with homogeneous victim groups

In a homogeneous group setting with severely injured accident victims, the group process focuses on the improvement of the multiple impairments into a new rebuilt identity by social and emotional sharing. The sharing quality increases the tele factor, which is of a healing nature for the self. The effectiveness of group therapy is confirmed by various studies (Lating, Everly and Boyle 1999) and is regarded as a treatment of choice for patients with trauma histories (van der Kolk and Fisler 1995). Even if there are cognitive or speech impairments, severely injured accident victims may benefit from the solidarity and self-help potential of groups. The therapeutic goal in such groups is often based on finding a way of accepting the altered destiny and in finding individual solutions to each difficult situation. Most importantly, the sharing of traumatic experiences may be very intensive. For this to happen, however, there must be a stable framework in which there is a sense of holding and containing. For example, participation should be prepared and confirmed by an individual interview before the first group meeting. Such a preparatory interview should include not only assessment, but should also address motivational aspects. The chosen group model (open, slow open, closed) should respect a positive resonance in accordance with the needs of the institution. If possible, a constant stable group over six to eight weeks with two sessions a week should deliver the best setting for such kind of group work.

If cohesion and confidence is established in the group, the traumatic content will appear and be manifested. If this does not happen, a transforming myth, such as a fairy tale or an old cultural legend, may be introduced to speed up the process of disclosure. During the rehearsal of the myth and the taking and acting out of the roles included, there may be profound emotional sharing of personal experiences. After the performance, other beneficial influences may result from the therapeutic project to reinstall the new identity.

One of the essential topics which almost always arises in accident victim groups is the question: 'Why me? Why do I have to cope with this traumatic event?' If this question does not emerge, therapists may introduce it as a ritual half way through the course of treatment. Answers frequently touch upon existential convictions, axiomatic quarrels, and especially include reference to their relationship with higher powers such as God. While group work in itself may differ a lot from the individual sequence of trauma therapy, group members almost expect to clarify the ultimate meaning of the trauma for themselves and, connected with that topic, to approach the role of God. The direct encounter with God, put on an empty chair as for example described by Frede (1992), may clarify some of the relevant existential issues. Furthermore, such a dialogue with God may help to envision a new creation (Burmeister 1994) and may illustrate some of the many possibilities of how to address the topic in the group with action-centred methods. Whatever technique is used, the basic question, 'Why me?' is not resolved by logical means. It needs to be explored through experiencing confidence and belief in a higher meaning, for example within the existential framework of the group process.

If there is a psychodramatic staging of the traumatic experience, the de-roling of the auxiliary egos is of extreme importance because they have usually taken upon themselves very negative roles and may be partly involved in the aggressive action of the traumatic sequences. The sharing then not only restores the integrity of the victim but also reconnects the individual, group and universal dimension of the experience into a holistic view of life in general. Topics like the injustice of life, the value and limitations of human existence, the connectedness beyond death and especially the protection felt by being part of a living community or brotherhood of mankind constitute an important part of this work. During role feedback the therapist must guarantee the safety of the protagonist while emotional impact may lead some of the group members to give feedback about the destructive experience of being accused by the victim.

Integrating the family

Traumatic incidents alter not only the life of the victim but may change the victim's entire socio-emotional network at a secondary level. Expectations, wishes and hopes connected with the future perspective of the victim can become invalidated by the impact of the trauma. As the outcome of the rehabilitation and restoring process of the trauma depends directly on the mitigating qualities of the socio-emotional support systems, intervention on the family level is a necessary ingredient in the model of any integrative rehabilitation process of the victim. Following the traumatic incident, the emotional and social investment in the family system grows dramatically. The victim's change of perspective requires a process of adaptation and mourning for the whole family which also has an impact on the therapeutic results for the victim himself. The issue of guilt particularly seems to reach beyond intergenerational and even transgenerational boundaries in the family system and needs a very careful assessment when addressing the family system.

All the relevant members of the system first and foremost require all information about a working model of PTSD, about personal changes in interpersonal behaviour of the victim and their bio-psycho-social source and about possible strategies for coping successfully with these changes within the relationship. Special problems in the interaction concern the control over relationships, such as issues of mistrust, anticipation and rejection of closeness, self-devaluation, the feeling that treatment is superfluous or lacking in progress, or that it is all meaningless (Ziehlke 1996). Not only the victim, but also the relatives tend to ignore the chronic impairments and their consequences (Romano 1974; Brooks 1984; Prigatano and Schacter 1991). As a consequence, integrating the family directly improves the prognosis of healing.

After the first consultation, the family is invited to enter a special programme on a voluntary basis. As well as individual family meetings about every six weeks, a special group for relatives of car accident victims and long-term self-help groups is offered to family members. Action-centred elements increase the quality of the information obtained at an interpersonal level by introducing the dimension of self-efficacy for all family members. Family statues, allusion to values and expectations and emotional links between the family members emerge as key elements in the frame of an action-centred approach. So motivation and engagement usually increase. Moreover, analogue communication may provide relevant information about relationships (Bateson 1983; Watzlawick *et al.* 1974). It is conveyed by images, especially when concretized in space and metaphor and is processed in the right brain area. This connectedness induces representation systems that specifically attach to traumatic experiences in a more appropriate way than mere verbal reflection can do (implicit memory system). Special techniques introduced by Satir (1988) and Hellinger (1994) complete the basic action-centred approach of psychodramatic family therapy elaborated lately by Williams (1989) and Farmer (1995).

Case study 4

Walter, a 54-year-old-man, participated in a self-experience group based on action-centred methods related to the topic of PTSD. Walter shared with the group that his sister had drowned 42 years earlier in a swimming accident in which an aunt had been negligent. Walter, his two other sisters, and his parents were at home when the bad news arrived. After receiving the tragic information, the whole family system changed and would never completely recover. The aunt in particular was never able to talk about the event and lived isolated from the rest of the family in the following years. But also Walter's parents could not bear the loss and Walter and his sisters were isolated themselves. Walter became a well-known physician who specialized in treating psychosomatic disorders with traumatic aetiology. Because of his exceptional sensitivity and awareness, he was able to detect forgotten traumas of his clients and therefore become a very effective therapist. During the self-experience work on the death of his sister, he became able to understand for the first time the impact of the death of his sister on the whole family system, including the role of the hated aunt. He could also recognize that other intimate relationships still presented features of anxiety and mistrust, which he directly attributed to the traumatic experience of losing his sister. After gaining insight in this link he started to change his behaviour towards his wife. In the follow-up the emotional quality of his relationship with his wife considerably increased.

Final comment

Recovery from trauma may become a life-long project on different existential levels. Besides the mere psychotherapy, the rehabilitation process must address all other dimensions of the human being including explicitly also the spiritual field.

References

Antonovsky, A. (1987) *Unravelling the Mystery of Health*. London: Jossey Bass.

Basler, H.D. (1989) Psychologische Schmerztherapie. Z. Klin. Psych. 18(3), 203–214.

Bateson, G. (1983) *Okologie des Geistes*. Frankfurt: Suhrkamp.

Bisbey, S.L. (1998) *Brief Therapy for Post-Traumatic Stress Disorder. Traumatic Incident Reduction and Related Techniques*. Chichester: Wiley.

Blanchard, E.B., Hidding, E.J., Mitnick, N., Taylor, A.E., Loos, W.R., Buckley, T.C. (1995) 'The impact of severity of physical injury and perception of life threat in the development of PTSD in motor vehicle accident victims.' *Behaviour Research and Therapy 33*, 529–534.

Boudewyns, P.A. (1990) 'Physiological response to combat memories and preliminary treatment outcome in Vietnam veteran PTSD patients treated with direct therapeutic exposure.' *Behaviour Therapy 21*, 63–87.

Bowlby, J. (1980) *Attachment and Loss*. London: Hogarth Press.

Broda, M. and Muthny, F. (1990) *Umgang mit chronisch Kranken*. Stuttgart: Thieme, Stuttgart.

Brooks Brenneis, C. (1996) 'Memory systems and the psychoanalytical retrieval of memories of trauma.' *Journal of the American Psychoanalytical Association 44*, 1165–1187.

Brooks, N. (1984) 'Head injury and family.' In *Closed Head Injury: Psychological, Social, and Family Consequences*. New York and Toronto: Oxford University Press.

Buer, F. (1989) Morenos therapeutische Philosophie. Zu den Grundideen von Psychodrama und Soziometrie. Opladen.

Burmeister, J. (1991) Psychodynamik und handlungsgest tzte Begleitung von schweren Unfallopfern. Vortrag an der SUVA-Rehabilitationsklinik, Bellikon/CH.

Burmeister, J. (1994) Pathologische Trauer und Psychodrama. Vortrag an der Psychiatrischen Klinik Hard, Embrach/CH.

Burmeister, J. and Diebels, E. (1999) *Antrag zur wissenschaftlichen Anerkennung des Psychodrama*. Unpublished Manuscript.

Burmeister, J. and Schwinger, T. (1995) 'Psychodrama und konstruktivistische Erkenntnistheorie.' In: Buer, F. (ed) *Jahrbuch für Psychodrama, psychosoziale Praxis und Gesellschaftspolitik*, Leske und Buderich, Opladen. 159–182.

Burstein, A. (1989) 'PTSD in victims of motor vehicle accidents.' *Hospital Community Psychiatry 40*, 295–297.

Burstein, A., Ciccone, P.E., Greenstein, R.A., Daniels, N., Olsen, K., Mazarek, A., Decatur, R. and Johnson, N. (1988) 'Chronic Vietnam PTSD and acute civilian PTSD: a comparison of treatment experiences.' *General Hospital Psychiatry 10*.

Clayton, M. (1994) 'Role theory and its application in clinical practice.' In P. Holmes, M. Karp and M. Watson (eds) *Psychodrama Since Moreno*. London: Routledge.

Cramon, D.Y. von and Matthes-von Cramon, G. (1992) 'Reflections on the treatment of brain-injured patients suffering from problem-solving disorders.' *Neuropsychol Rehab 2*, 207–229.

Dhawan, S. (1992) 'Psychodrama in der therapeutischen Arbeit mit politisch Verfolgten.' *J Systema 6*, 37–49.

Espina-Barrios, J.A. (1992) 'El Cuerpo Muerto – Psicoterapia del Duelo: Individual, de Pareja, Familiar y Grupal.' *Informaciones Psiquiatricas, 2° Trimestere No 132*. 275–285.

Farmer, C. (1995) *Psychodrama and Systemic Therapy*. London: Karnac Books.

Filgueira Bouza, M.S. (1995) 'Psicodrama focal del duelo patologico.' *Informaciones Psiquiatricas 140*, 237–251.

Foa, E.B. and Cashman, L. (1996) *The Validation of a Self Report Measure of PTSD: The Post-traumatic Diagnostic Scale (PDS)*. Philadelphia: Medical College of Pennsylvania and Hahnemann University.

Foa, E. and Rothbaum, B.O. (1996) 'Posttraumatische Belastungsstoerungen.' In *Lehrbuch der Verhaltenstherapie, Band II*. Springer, Heidelberg pp. 107–120.

Frede, U. (1992) *Behandlung unheilbar Erkrankter*. Weinheim: Beltz.

Frommberger, U., Nyberg, E., Stieglitz, R.D. and Berger, M. (1997) Psychotherapie und Psychopharmakotherapie in der Behandlung Posttraumatischer Belastungsstoerungen.

Green, M.M., McFarlane, A.C., Hunter, C.E. and Griggs, W.M. (1993) 'Undiagnosed post-traumatic stress disorder following motor vehicle accidents.' *Medical Journal of Australia 159*, 529–534.

Gunkel, S. (1996) *PTSD-Fragebogen*. Berlin: Freie Universitet, Abt. fur Sozialpsychiatrie.

Hellinger, B. (1994) *Ordnungen der Liebe. Ein Kurs Buch*. Heidelberg.

Herman, J. (1992) 'Complex PTSD: A syndrome in survivors of prolonged and repeated trauma.' *Journal of Traumatic Stress 5*, 377–391.

Hofmann, A. (1996) 'EMDR: Eine neue Methode zur Behandlung posttraumatischer Belastungsstoerungen.' *Psychotherapy 41*, 368–372.

Horne, D.J. (1993) 'Traumatic stress reactions to motor vehicle accidents.' In Wilson and Raphael (eds) *International Handbook of Traumatic Stress Syndromes*. New York and London: Plenum.

Horowitz, M.J. (1993) 'Stress response syndromes: a review of post-traumatic stress and adjustment disorders.' In J.P. Wilson and B. Raphael (eds) *International Handbook of Traumatic Stress Syndromes*. New York: Plenum.

Horton, A.M. (1993) 'PTSD and mild head trauma: follow up of a case study.' *Perceptual and Motor Skills 76*, 243–246.

International Classification of Diseases: World Health Organisation. Tenth revision of the international classification of disease (ICD-10). Geneva: WHO, 1993.

Keane, T.M. (1989) 'Implosive (flooding) therapy reduces symptoms of PTSD in Vietnam combat veterans.' *Behaviour Therapy 20*, 245–260.

Kellermann, P.F. (1992) *Focus on Psychodrama*. London: Jessica Kingsley Publishers.

Krystal, H. (1978) 'Trauma and affects.' *Psychoanalytic Study of the Child 33*, 81–116.

Kuch, K., Swinson, R.P. and Kirby, M. (1985) 'PTSD after car accident.' *Canadian Journal of Psychiatry 30*, 426–427.

Lating, J.M., Everly, G.S. and Boyle, S.H. (1999) 'The effectiveness of psychological debriefing with vicarious trauma: a meta analysis.' *Stress Medicine 15*, 4, 229–233.

Le Doux, J.E. (1992) 'Emotion as memory: anatomical systems underlying indelible neural traces.' In S.A. Chistianson (ed) *Handbook of Emotion and Memory*.

Maercker, A. (ed) (1999) *Therapie der Posttraumatischen Belastungsstoerungen*. Heidelberg and New York: Springer.

Malt, U. (1988) 'The long-term psychiatric consequences of accidental injury.' *BJP 153*, 810–818.

Mayou, R. (1993) 'Psychiatric consequences of road traffic accidents.' *International Review of Psychiatry 4*, 647–651.

Mayou, R. and Radanov, B.P. (1996) 'Whiplash neck injury.' *Journal of Psychosomatic Research 40*, 461–474.

McCaffrey, R.J. and Fairbank, J.A. (1985) 'Behavioral assessment and treatment of accident-related PTSD: two case studies.' *Behaviour Therapy 16*, 401–416.

McFarlane, A.C. (1989) 'The aetiology of post-traumatic morbidity: predisposing, precipitating and perpetuating factors.' *British Journal of Psychology 154*, 221–228.

McMillan, T.M. (1991) 'PTSD and severe head injury.' BJP 159, 431–433.

Moreno, J.L. (1954/1974) *Die Grundlagen der Soziometrie.* Opladen: Westdeutsche Verlag.

Moreno, J.L. (1959/1973) *Gruppenpsychotherapie und Psychodrama.* Stuttgart: Thieme.

Muse, M. (1986) 'Stress related post-traumatic chronic pain syndrome: behavioral treatment approach.' *Pain 25*, 389–394.

Nemiah, J.C. (1995) 'Early concepts of trauma, dissociation and the unconscious: their history and current implications.' In D. Bremner and C. Marmar (eds) *Trauma, Memory and Dissociation.* Washington DC: American Psychiatric Press.

Oddy, M. (1985) 'Social adjustment after closed head injury: A further follow up seven years after injury.' *Journal of Neurology and Neurosurgical Psychiatry 48*, 564–568.

Perry, B. (1999) 'Memories of fear: how the brain stores and retrieves physiologic states, feelings, behaviours and thoughts from traumatic events.' In *Splintered Reflections: Images of the Body in Trauma.* New York: Basic Books.

Petzold, H. and Matthias, U. (1982) *Rollenentwicklung und Identitat.* Paderborn: Junfermann.

Petzold, H. (1990) *Die neuen Kreativitatstherapien. Handbuch der Kunsttherapie.* Paderborn: Junfermann.

Piper, W. (1992) *Adaptation to Loss through Short Term Group Psychotherapy.* New York and London: Guilford Press.

Prigatano, G.P. and Schacter, D.L. (1991) *Awareness of deficit after brain injury. Clinical and theoretical issues.* New York: Oxford University Press.

Reddemann, L. (1998) 'Zur Psychotherapie von Vergewaltigungsopfern. Ein ressourcen orientierter tiefenpsychologisch fundierter Ansatz.' *Psychotherapy, 42*, 146–150.

Romano, M.D. (1974) 'Family response to traumatic head injury.' Scandianarian Journal of Rehabilitative Medicine. 6, 1–4.

Satir, V. (1988) *Familientherapie in Aktion. Die Konzepte von Virginia Satir in der Praxis.* Paderborn: Junferman.

Schacter, D.L. (1987) 'Implicit memory: History and current status.' *Journal of Experimental Psychology, Learning, Memory and Cognition 13*, 510-518.

Schneider-Gurewitsch, K. (1998) 'Hirnverletzte Menschen. Gerettet und dann?' *Gazette Medicale 16*, 743–746.

Shapiro, F. (1989) 'Efficacy of the eye movement desensitization: a new treatment for post-traumatic stress disorder.' *Journal Behavior Ther. Exp. Psychiatry 20*, 211–217.

Smith, R. (1989) 'Psychological trauma following automobile accidents: a review of literature.' *American Journal of Forensic Psychology 7*, 5–20.

Smucker, M. and Niederee, J.L. (1992) 'Imagery rescripting: a multifaceted treatment for childhood sexual abuse survivors.' *Innovations in Clinical Practice 13*, 73–86.

Squire, L.R. (1994) 'Declarative and non-declarative memory. Multiple brain systems supporting learning and memory.' In D.L. Schacter and E. Tulving (eds) *Memory Systems.* Cambridge, MA: MIT Press.

Stallard, P. (1998) 'PTSD in children.' *British Medical Journal 317,* 1619.

Taylor, S. and Koch, W.J. (1995) 'Anxiety disorders due to motor vehicle accidents: nature and treatment.' *Clinical Psychology Review 15,* 721–738.

Treadwell, T., Leach, E. and Stein, S. (1993) 'The social networks inventory: a diagnostic instrument measuring interpersonal relationship.' *Small Group Research 24,* 2, 155–178.

van der Kolk, B.A. (1994) 'The body keeps the score: memory and the evolving psychobiology of post traumatic stress.' *Harvard Review of Psychiatry 1,* 253–265.

van der Kolk, B.A. and Fisler, R.E. (1995a) 'Dissociation and fragmentary nature of traumatic memories: Overview and exploratory study'. *Journal of Traumatic Stress 9,* 505–525.

van der Kolk, B.A., van der Hart, O. and Burbridge, J. (1995b) 'Approaches to the treatment of PTSD.' *Trauma Information Pages,* Articles, p.12.

van der Kolk, B.A., McFarlane, A. and Weisaeth, L. (1996) (eds) *Traumatic Stress: The Effects of Overwhelming Experience on Mind, Body and Society.* New York: Guilford Press.

Watzlawick, P., Weakland, J. and Fish, R. (1974) *Change: Principles of Problem Formation and Problem Resolution.* New York: Norton.

Williams, A. (1989) *The Passionate Technique. Strategic Psychodrama with Individuals, Families and Groups.* New York: Tavistock/Routledge.

Williams, M.B. and Sommer, J.F. (1997) 'Towards the development of a generic model of PTSD treatment.' *Handbook of Post-Traumatic Therapy.*

Worden, J.W. (1982) *Grief Counseling and Grief Therapy: A Handbook for the Mental Health Practitioner.* New York: Springer.

Ziegler, G. (1987) 'Psychodrama en miniature.' *Integrative Therapie 1,* 36–53.

Ziehlke, M. (1996) 'Sexueller Missbrauch: Das stille Leiden als besondere Herausforderung an Selbsthilfegruppen, Psychotherapeuten und Aerzte.' In *Handbuch Stationare Verhaltenstherapie.* Weinheim: Beltz.

PART 4

Experiential Models of Healing

CHAPTER 13

The Therapeutic Spiral Model: Treating PTSD in Action

M.K. Hudgins

Six months into a weekly psychodrama group, a protagonist and director walk around the stage. The protagonist, 'Greta', tells the group she wants to confront her grandfather who sexually abused her and rescue the 'five-year-old stuck inside me who is still screaming for help'. She starts to cry, voice changing to that of a little girl, body beginning to shake and her mind starting to dissociate from her feelings. She grabs the director's hand and looks helpless and scared. It is clear to all that she is shifting to the role of the child who was hurt right before our eyes. Someone else in the group gets up and walks around the room in angry agitation. Another group member feels the beginning of a flashback starting and says quietly, 'no, no, no,' over and over.

This is the moment of decision. How do you direct this psychodrama at this clinical point? How to prevent retraumatization? How to use the healing power of psychodrama? You 'direct the drama', first and foremost, as a clinician making directing decisions to structure conscious and controlled regression. Then, in the case of the therapeutic spiral model, you follow a step by step guide for safe use of experiential methods with trauma survivors. To demonstrate, this chapter follows Greta as she uses this experiential model of healing in her personal journey of recovery from sexual trauma.

Overview of the therapeutic spiral model

The therapeutic spiral model (TSM) was developed to provide clear clinical guidelines and action intervention structures for psychodrama with trauma survivors. In this way, the pace and intensity of experiential therapy can be clinically controlled so that regression is chosen, conscious, and always in the service of the ego.

This model was developed over 20 years of clinical and training practice using experiential methods with survivors of severe sexual and physical abuse. It is a clinically structured method of using classical psychodrama in order to prevent retraumatization. Unique structures teach containment, clinical decision points and intervention modules to increase treatment effectiveness when treating trauma with action methods. The therapeutic spiral model intends to provide:

1. client-friendly constructs of experiential self-organization for trauma survivors;

2. clear clinical structures for safe experiential psychodramatic psychotherapy; and

3. advanced action intervention modules for containment, expression, repair, and integration of unprocessed trauma material.

Research on experiential psychotherapy and trauma

In 1997, a noted Harvard researcher on trauma, Bessel van der Kolk, was the keynote speaker at the American Society of Group Psychotherapy and Psychodrama. He stated that body-centred, experiential methods are a 'treatment of choice' for these patients, and called for more research to demonstrate the claims of psychodrama. Moreover, van der Kolk (1996) states:

> Prone to action, and deficient in words, these patients (trauma survivors) can often express their internal states more articulately in physical movements or in pictures than in words. Utilising drawings and *psychodrama* may help them develop a language that is essential for effective communication and for the symbolic transformation that can occur in psychotherapy (1996, p.195, emphasis mine).

In fact, recent empirical research indicates that experiential psychotherapy can be equally as effective as psychodynamic, cognitive behavioural, and behavioural theories of psychotherapy in studies with a variety of psychiatric diagnoses (Bergin and Garfield 1994; Greenberg, Elliott and Lietaer 1994; Greenberg, Lietaer and Watson 1998; Greenberg and Paivio 1998). Post-traumatic stress disorder (Elliott, Davis and Slatick 1998; Elliott *et al.* 1996; Hudgins and Kipper 1998), anxiety disorders (Wolfe and Sigl 1998), and borderline personality disorder (Eckert and Biermann-Ratjen 1998) have all shown therapeutic change using experiential methods of psycho-therapy.

Although research in classical psychodrama has been less prolific for many reasons, current studies also suggest effectiveness (Blatner 1997; Kipper 1989; Wilkins 1997). In addition, there are a number of texts on psychodrama that provide ample clinical documentation of the usefulness of psychodrama with trauma (Kellermann 1992; Moreno 1953; Moreno and Blomqvist 2000; Moreno and Moreno 1969; Holmes 1992).

Specific studies show the use of psychodrama with PTSD (Baumgartner 1986; Burge 1996; Hudgins, Drucker and Metcalf 2000; Hudgins and Kipper 1998), sexual abuse (Bannister 1990, 1991 and 1997; Hudgins 1998; Hudgins and Drucker 1998; Karp 1991), somatization disorder (Kellermann 1996), eating disorders (Hudgins 1989; Widlake 1997), bor-derline personality disorder (Sidorsky 1984), and dissociative identity disorder (Altman 1992 and 1993; Raaz, Carlson-Sabelli and Sabelli 1992; Reynolds 1996).

A composite client

While the therapeutic spiral model becomes easy to understand when dem-onstrated in practice, like all action models of healing, it needs 'a guide' to help convey the story in writing. This chapter uses the composite image of Greta to portray many of the clients who have worked on sexual abuse using this model. Thus, confidentiality is maintained for all individuals through these examples.

Greta is a 35-year-old woman who was referred to psychotherapy by her physician. Married at 18 to a violent alcoholic, she was divorced after three years and has a 15-year-old son from that marriage. Greta remarried six years ago and she and her husband have a four-year-old daughter. Greta sought treatment when she found herself responding to her son's adolescent aggression and anger with fear, tears, and uncontrolled regression. She reported a history of childhood sexual abuse by her grandfather and said she 'wondered if that might be what the problem is.'

Greta spent about three months in individual experiential therapy using this model and is followed here as she begins a TSM psychodrama group for sexual abuse survivors.

Experiential self-organisation: 'client-friendly' constructs

Even psychologically sophisticated clients can have a hard time under-standing and communicating the helplessness and distress they feel from chronic symptoms of PTSD. Perceptual distortions, intense feelings, body memories, flashbacks, primitive defences, addictions, and even compulsive repetitions of early trauma can haunt the adult survivor of childhood abuse (Ellenson 1986 and 1989; Gelinas 1983; Young 1992). Clients report 'feeling crazy', 'thinking I'm nuts', 'not knowing whether I'm five years old or an adult woman!' and 'not being in my body'. Medical diagnoses such as dissociative identity disorder (DID), borderline personality (BPD), func-tional psychosis, depression and anxiety disorders can often confuse the picture even more. To help clients communicate this internal distress, this model uses three client-friendly descriptions of experiential self-organi-zation. Two graphic representations – the spiral image and trauma bubbles – become 'shorthand' symbols to organize unprocessed trauma in words clients can understand. In addition, the trauma survivor's intrapsychic role atom is a clinical map for director, team, group and protagonist to follow during enactments of personality structures.

The therapeutic spiral image

The spiral shape was chosen for several reasons that are relevant to experi-ential clinical practice with trauma. The internal chaos and interpersonal distress many survivors experience often feels like a tornado. Providing the image of a therapeutic spiral gives the client an alternative image to the uncontrolled energy of a tornado. Clients can learn to move up or down the spiral as needed, rather than being buffeted by the chaos of the tornado.

The indigenous cultures with whom our teams have had contact – Native Americans, Australian Aborigines, New Zealand Maori, South Pacific Islanders, South American and Korean shamans – all have the spiral incorpo-rated into their healing symbolism. In Western medicine, the physician's staff, the caduceus with its entwined snakes, resembles a spiral and means 'do no harm'. As TSM regards safety as well as spiritual healing as primary, the use of the spiral image appropriately fits.

Finally, in classical psychodrama theory the development of the action goes from 'the periphery to the centre' in what has been called a psy-chodramatic spiral (Goldman and Morrison 1984). Enactment proceeds from assessment scenes in the present life of the protagonist and moves into connected scenes from the past.

Description of the three strands of the spiral

The spiral image was then divided into three strands to further clarify the survivor's internal representation of trauma. It provides an easy checklist for both therapist and client. Simply addressing the questions, 'Does the client need to increase or decrease energy? What role needs to be more consciously experienced? What meaning is there?' can provide an easy way to talk about self-organization with trauma survivors.

Imagine a three-dimensional image of a spiral shaped like a DNA model with three strands, each one a different colour. Purple is for energy, teal symbolizes experiencing, and pink is the colour designated for new meaning. In healthy functioning, one moves up and down each strand or moves from one strand to another in a conscious journey of healing repair. When trauma happens, the overall flow of the strands becomes blocked, distorted, restricted, and compartmentalized from each other.

Figure 13.1 The Therapeutic Spiral Graphic

Energy

The first strand is called 'energy'. Energy is defined as an ever-renewable state of spontaneity and creativity from classical psychodrama. It is embodied in a sense of physical vitality and aliveness. It connects human beings to each other. In psychodrama, it is also called the 'godhead' (Moreno 1915), and in TSM it is a sense of spirituality. Energy can be collective as well as personal, and is accessed through a rich source of historic, familial, gender, racial, cultural, and spiritual roles. Greta described her energy as 'contact with a higher power and a belief that I'm supposed to be here on earth at this time'. During different dramas, she further concretized energy into roles such as her guardian angel, physical strength, and connection to HP (the Higher Power in a 12-step construct for God) and used them to help her break through blocks along the way.

Experiencing

The second spiral strand is called 'experiencing'. Active experiencing includes awareness of sensations, perceptions, non-verbal behaviours, intuition, and emotional nuances. Conscious experiencing of the unprocessed images, body memories, distorted thoughts, and dissociated feelings is structured so as not to affectively overwhelm the protagonist and trigger uncontrolled regression.

Greta soon learned how to communicate when she was feeling emotionally vulnerable and on the edge of being triggered during experiential work. She could say, 'Help, I need to go up the spiral to feel less and think more.' When she reconnected to her energy and positive roles, she could then experience more of the thoughts and feelings that were dissociated from her childhood experiences with her grandfather in a safe manner.

Meaning

The third strand is called 'meaning'. People live their lives based on the meaning that they have made of past experience. Personal narratives guide lives. When cognitive meanings are attached to accurate experiencing, these symbolic representations create realistic goals and expectations about self and others. However, when trauma distorts belief systems, it is important to spend time sorting out a new personal narrative based on personal experience, not introjected meaning.

A particularly important psychodrama led Greta to the realization that her son's hostility was what was triggering her in their interactions. When she heard the hostile voice tone she would 'hear her grandfather'. In action, she was able to discriminate this transference and learn new roles for relating to her adolescent son as a mother. In later psychodramas she was able to work through this transference and express her feelings of hate, rage, and terror toward her grandfather, rather than at her son.

Trauma bubbles

As one client said, 'there are no words to express what happens to you when you are sexually abused.' So, one of the first steps in understanding the impact of trauma is to have words to describe what happens to the self. Whereas the spiral image provides shorthand for healthy functioning, trauma bubbles are a quick way to describe the systemic changes that occur in conscious awareness due to trauma.

An image of bubbles, filled with visual, sensory, auditory, and emotional fragments of trauma, makes sense for the trauma survivor. Experience is split into different trauma bubbles. Rigid psychological barriers form against trauma, but, like a bubble, they can be popped unexpectedly. When triggers happen, unconscious trauma material disrupts the present, as the air inside a

Figure 13.2 The Trauma Bubble Graphic

balloon releases with force when popped. Providing this image to trauma survivors gives them a tool for communication, as well as the beginning of a measure of control over unprocessed material. Greta found this image particularly useful. She could easily describe how trauma bubbles would hang around her head with images of herself at five, locked in a closet in one bubble, but the screams she hears inside were held in a different bubble. Her grandfather's rageful face was stored in yet another trauma bubble. She could see how her experience was split and needed to be reconnected to make sense in the present.

The trauma survivor's intrapsychic role atom (TSIRA)

Clients can get lost trying to understand 'parts of self', 'alters', 'sub-personalities' and 'personalities' and become over-identified with diagnoses such as DID or BPD. Role theory, a contribution of classical psychodrama, normalizes the internalization of trauma into 'roles' and gives clients a non-shaming way to talk about their self-experience. The earlier template for the present role atom can be found in the three-child model of recovery (Hudgins and Sheridan 1990), which categorizes roles into adult-child, wounded-child, and sleeping-awakening child.

Description of role atom

The trauma survivor's intrapsychic role atom (TSIRA) is a clinical map of the essential roles in the personality structure of a trauma survivor at any given moment (Hudgins 1998; Toscani and Hudgins 1996). It is divided into 1. prescriptive roles, 2. trauma-based roles, and 3. transformative roles.

   In this section, Greta presents her role atom, and then these roles are used to describe the vignettes of dramas throughout the rest of the chapter.

Prescriptive roles

To prevent retraumatization and uncontrolled regression, TSM prescribes a number of positive roles that first need to be established for safety. These prescriptive roles are concretized prior to progressing down the spiral into active re-experiencing and affective release work. Prescriptive roles serve three main psychological functions for the protagonist: 1. restoration, 2. containment, and 3. observation.

Purpose: To build and sustain an integrated state of spontaneous learning.
Cossa and Hudgins (1998) have created this table to summarize the TSIRA (Toscani & Hudgins, 1996). Yorke (1997) introduced the term "spontaneous learning state".

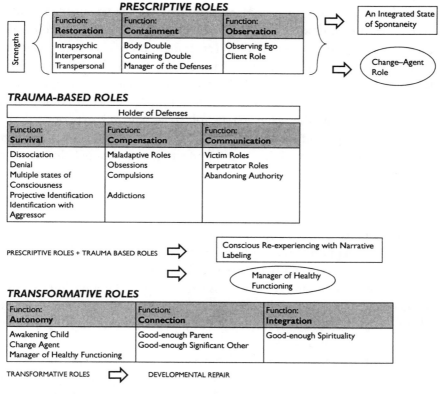

Figure 13.3 The Trauma Survivor's Intrapsychic Role Atom: TSIRA (Cossa and Hudgins, 1999)

Restorative Roles

The cluster of restorative roles focuses on filling up the depleted trauma-based self, so that change can occur. They help clients to feel more resilient and connected to others. These roles help the client access energy and the state of spontaneity. For the protagonist to be spontaneous and supported, restorative roles must be available at all levels: personal, interpersonal, and transpersonal strengths.

The director concretizes positive, restorative roles early in a 'trauma-drama' so that they are on the stage when needed. Even if the protagonist does not spontaneously suggest positive roles of restoration during the initial enactment, the director prescribes these clinical roles for safety.

When Greta contracted to confront her grandfather, the first scene was to concretize her restorative roles. At that moment of decision when Greta was beginning to decompensate, the director did not follow her to the trauma scene. Instead, the director asked Greta: 'Who or what do you need to be with you during this confrontation so you can stay safe and in your adult roles? We don't want to go to that scene until you are stable and can choose to go there.'

In scene 1, Greta chose a group member, Susan, to play her best friend from childhood (interpersonal), Mike to be her 'courageous lion' (personal), and Linda to be her guardian angel (transpersonal). As each restorative role was introduced on the stage, Greta role reversed and experienced the infusion of energy and spontaneity from these positive roles. She no longer felt alone. She walked with her best friend and guardian angel. She had the courage to continue.

Containing Roles

Containment is a psychological term to describe a sense of emotional 'holding' and support for clients to stay in the present moment. Containment provides flexible yet solid boundaries. Containing roles attempt to create a safe and conscious awareness of what is happening, without having to resort to unconscious primitive defences to protect against overwhelming feelings. There are three containing roles: the body double, the containing double, and the manager of defences.

The body double speaks in the first person and focuses on positive sensations, non-verbal behaviours and physical awareness to keep people in their body. The containing double also speaks in the first person and puts narrative labels to overwhelming experience to make it more manageable. The manager of defences directs the use of higher order adaptation and healthy functioning, rather than relying on primitive defences. As with the other pre-scriptive roles, the containing roles are assigned or directed at the clinician's assessment.

Scene 1 continued with these roles. As soon as Greta began to be overwhelmed by her terror and started to regress, the director asked her to pick a containing double. She chose Jeanne, who made statements, such as 'I can feel how scared I am as I think of confronting my grandfather. And, yet … I can take a deep breath and hold the hand of my guardian angel, and know I'll be OK.' A body double was assigned to a team member to anchor her into staying in the present. The body double stated: 'I can feel my breath going in and out and feel my feet on the floor. My eyes are looking at the eyes of my best friend. I can breathe.'

Observing roles

The third set of prescriptive roles addresses the need for observation during conscious re-experiencing of trauma scenes. When trauma survivors start to become emotionally overwhelmed, they need a place to step aside and objectively see what is happening to them. Then, they can make informed decisions about how to respond based on information in the present. There are two observing roles that can be assigned by the director as needed: the observing ego and the client role.

The observing ego is a clinical term for a role that remains emotionally neutral to what is happening and can simply 'collect the facts' and 'see the data without judgement'. The client role was created as separate from the protagonist role specifically to work with people in a dissociated state. This role remains stable and focuses on the whole scene, while the protagonist role reverses as needed. The client role provides stable object relations in three-way role reversals in victim and perpetrator roles.

To finish scene 1, Greta was asked to choose a role that could observe her confrontation with her grandfather and be there to see and record what happened. She asked Tommy to be her 'keeper of the records' and to write down what she says to her grandfather as a witness to her work that day. At this point Greta was able to stay conscious of her thoughts and feelings in her adult state and was ready to progress down the spiral into conscious re-experiencing and developmental repair.

Trauma-based roles

In addition to the clinically prescribed roles, the TSIRA provides a clinical map of traumatic experience and includes roles of defensive structures and internalization of the trauma. Defensive structures are divided into the role of the 'holder of defences' and the roles of the defences themselves. These roles seek to protect the client from the experience of trauma. Victim, perpetrator, and abandoning authority roles represent the internalization of trauma, and keep the trauma alive until it is processed. These roles serve to communicate the experience of past trauma into the present.

As noted, trauma-based roles are only concretized and enacted by the protagonist after the prescriptive roles are established and group support is present, in order to prevent uncontrolled regression and retraumatization. Even if a protagonist spontaneously sees his or her victim self or perpetrator role on the stage, the director has a clinical responsibility to make sure the prescriptive roles are stabilized before further enactment of these trauma roles.

Defences

The experience of severe trauma overwhelms even the most well-functioning person. The violence and unpredictability of catastrophe shatter cognitive beliefs about self and other. Intense feelings flood the body and the mind. When this happens, ego defences are automatically engaged to prevent psychological death. The spirit is depleted. This model looks at three levels of defence: primitive, addictive and maladaptive.

Primitive defences, which are necessary at the time of trauma, include dissociation, denial, idealization, multiple states of consciousness, projective identification, and identification with the aggressor. Obsessions, compulsions, and addiction form as these defences become more ingrained in the personality and are role locked. Maladaptive roles can include the caretaker, the controller, the over-achiever, the adult-child, the rescuer, and so on.

Holder of the defences

This role evolved from the experience of concretizing dissociation with trauma survivors and finding that both the protagonist and auxiliary then dissociated. So, a role was created to control or hold the dissociation so that it could be used if needed, but not happen automatically in a trauma drama. Later, the role was expanded to be 'the holder of defences' as it serves this rigid function no matter what defence is used.

As Greta began to set up a scene from her childhood, she started to dissociate and forget for a moment where she was. She became still and looked around in a dazed fashion. The auxiliaries in the prescriptive roles spoke their lines and offered an anchor into positive states. However, it was as if Greta had floated away and could not hear nor see them. Thus, the director decided to concretize the dissociation floating around the room and had a trained auxiliary take the role of the holder of dissociation. Colette, a team member, spontaneously took up the role and started drifting around the room with a white scarf. She swished it in the air and said:

'I can pick up and hold all the dissociation in the room. Greta, help me gather it together so I can keep it here. You can have it back if you need it, but I think it's safe right now to see what's happening.'

The director followed this team intervention and said: 'Yes Greta, pick up the pieces of fuzziness that are floating around the room and put them concretely in the white scarf there. Tell the holder what to do with them.' Greta responded, 'I don't need to be fuzzy right now, but you can stand over there in the corner with your scarf just in case I get too scared.'

Internalization of trauma roles

Clients easily understand this category of trauma-based roles, although some are more familiar than others. This model divides internal representation into victim, perpetrator and abandoning authority. For many trauma survivors, either the victim or perpetrator role seems to have dominated their lives. They can recognize dysfunctional thoughts, feelings, and re-enactment of these roles. The role that is subtler is that of the abandoning authority. This role of the abandoning authority may be the parent that did not intervene, but can also represent school, church, or government that did not provide safety and help. Often the abandoning authority role needs to be changed before either of the other trauma-based roles can be addressed.

Often, trained members of the action trauma team initially enact these roles in order to prevent retraumatization of clients. As they are ready and it is clinically indicated, clients themselves are directed to take these roles for deeper levels of experiencing. Victim and perpetrator roles can be enacted, explored, and experienced in the safety of the model in order to complete memory retrieval, express dissociated feelings, and regain a sense of mastery over the past. Abandoning authority roles can be seen and changed as part of the internal reorganization of self. Usually, a psychodrama explores one of these roles rather than all three, again to provide a sense of boundaries and containment.

In this session, Greta said she wanted to 'take my own authority and stop the screams of my five-year-old'. For scene 2, the director asked her to set up an image from her head that kept getting stuck that included the screaming five-year-old role. Greta described a scene with her grandfather when she was five years old. In this scene, she stated that they were in the barn when he physically backed her up against a stall where some baby calves lived. Then he forced her to perform oral sex on him, left her there, and walked off.

As she first witnessed this scene and started to feel powerless, the director asked her, 'where is your authority to save this child?' She said she didn't know and began to cry. So, the director said, create 'an authority' from the group and see how you can get some help to stop the screaming. The trauma-based scene froze on the stage, while Greta created 'a spirit of compassion' out of three group chairs. One chair held a gold scarf and was 'compassion'. The second chair was covered with yellow and was called 'light'. And the final chair, which sat behind the other two, was 'action' and was concretized as a glowing spirit. As Greta was role reversed and became her glowing spirit, she picked up her light and compassion and rescued her screaming five-year-old. This spirit of compassion could stop the grandfather and comfort the screams of the child.

Transformative roles

When prescriptive roles are enacted with the trauma-based roles, new spontaneity is added. New individualized roles emerge that are named the transformative roles in this model. There are three psychological functions that these new roles serve for healthy functioning: self-initiative/autonomy, connection with others and integration.

Given that these roles are unique to each individual it is hard to provide categories of enactment. Most often, however, it appears that transformative roles include at least one of the following: a change agent, the sleeping-awakening child, a good-enough mother or father, and a good-enough God.

When Greta changed her sense of helplessness into the role of 'spirit of compassion' she created a transformative role that allowed her to take new actions toward herself and others. Over time, Greta internalized her experiences of having a containing double into the role of 'my own ally', which was a unique, personalized role that promoted integration and connection to others in a healthy way.

Clinical structures for safety: Action guides

Clinical structures provide another level of safety using experiential psychotherapy with trauma survivors. These structures seek to prevent uncontrolled regression and to promote narrative labelling of unprocessed thoughts, feelings, and behaviours when working with trauma. The structures are: action trauma team, circles of scarves, types of re-experiencing dramas, and principles of conscious re-experiencing.

Action trauma team

Over the years of using psychodrama with trauma survivors, it became obvious that the safest and deepest work can only be done with a trained clinical team. Except in very few cases, full conscious re-experiencing of core trauma scenes needs the support of a team trained in the nuances of trauma symptoms and the skills of classical psychodrama. This is why it is called an action trauma team; team members integrate knowledge of action methods and apply them competently to trauma. Each team includes a team leader/director, an assistant leader, and a minimum of two trained auxiliaries.

Director/team leader

The director assesses protagonist's and group members' strengths and vulnerabilities. He or she makes directing decisions based on clinical knowledge of diagnosis, adaptive functioning, treatment planning, timing, and goals of the session. He or she contracts with protagonist and group for the type of re-experiencing drama (Hudgins 1993). In addition, the director establishes safety precautions needed for enactment and expression of intense emotion and dissociated material prior to action. The director then concretizes trauma scenes using the step by step principles of conscious re-experiencing and developmental repair (Hudgins 1993).

Assistant leader

It is a team effort to allow the protagonist to enact the chaos of the inner symbolic world while integrating group members who may become triggered into their own unconscious material. The role of assistant leader was developed to provide extra clinical support to the director, protagonist and other group members when working with trauma survivors in a group setting. The assistant leader assesses group members' levels of personal safety, positive roles, and interpersonal support throughout the drama and intervenes with group members for containment if needed. He or she co-directs the trained auxiliary egos to implement the director's interventions through use of the team. The assistant leader also integrates spontaneous auxiliary roles from group members and team members and makes therapeutic role assignments.

Trained auxiliary egos

Trained auxiliaries are a rich resource for protagonist and group alike when re-experiencing past core trauma scenes. These clinicians promote adaptive release of primary affect and developmental repair from their roles in the dramas or as support to group members. Trained auxiliaries provide support for group members, and enact projective identifications as needed. They are also required to take all trauma-based roles as directed, and to process their own personal responses during team time.

Support

As Greta began her drama, and a second group member was triggered into a flashback, the assistant leader asked a trained auxiliary to sit next to the client as she said, 'No, no, no'. The auxiliary took on the role of a containing double (CD) and used the client's experience to ground her in the present session. The group member's CD said: 'That's right, I want to say "No, no, no," to this flashback. I can say "No!" right now and take a look around and see I am in the psychodrama theatre of protection. I can look at Greta and remember that she wants to say no to her grandfather as well.'

Emotional expression of dissociated affect can result in time distortion and uncontrolled regression, placing the trauma survivor at risk of retraumatization. To prevent this, an auxiliary stands beside the protagonist or group member and supports a level of conscious awareness with statements from a cognitive role when directed to do so. For example, Greta's CD often made cognitive statements such as: 'I can feel my feelings ... my terror, my anger ... and I can still think about what I want to say today. Today I am an adult, not a kid. I can feel kid feelings and I can express them as an adult.'

Enacting projective identifications

Trained auxiliaries also enact projective identifications that are recognized during a trauma drama. These can then be integrated into the drama rather than floating around and triggering group members. This happened when Colette spontaneously enacted the role related to holding the dissociation. Rather than letting the group get caught in the sense of dissociation, she therapeutically used it to change the energy of this defence into positive containment.

Enacting trauma-based roles

It is in the roles of victim, perpetrator, or abandoning authority that clients are most at risk for uncontrolled regression and retraumatization. These roles hold all the unconscious and unprocessed trauma material that needs to be communicated for healing. Full developmental repair can result when these roles are accessed, information shared, emotions released, and new meanings made. However, this all must be done in a clinically controlled structure to prevent uncontrolled regression.

Thus, team members taking these roles provide safe structures for the protagonist to interact with trauma-based roles. They follow the director's lead, make interventions that create containment rather than expansion, and only exert enough action demands on the protagonist as needed. When the protagonist is ready, he or she can then take these roles with the trained auxiliaries as support.

Greta chose Ann, a trained auxiliary, to play her five-year-old self in the conscious re-experiencing scene of her sexual abuse. After Greta had rescued her five-year-old from the role of 'spirit of compassion', Greta chose to experience the five-year-old role to release her own scream. In this victim role, protective auxiliaries in the prescriptive roles surrounded her so she was not alone. As the auxiliary playing her grandfather began to move toward her, five-year-old Greta felt her terror and screamed and screamed into the arms of the spirit of compassion. Held and protected she could experience the depth of her childhood pain in a conscious and controlled regression through the use of an action trauma team.

Circles of scarves

To experientially teach boundaries and containment, each and every clinical and training session in TSM begins as follows.

Containment/experiencing circle

Scarves of various colours, textures, and sizes are put in the middle of the circle of chairs as the group begins. Each group and team member picks at least one scarf to represent a strength they bring to the group today. Strengths can be targeted at themes each week; for example, what strength is needed to look at defences? What strength is needed to enact childhood scenes? Then, each person stands up, stating the strength and placing the scarf to make a physical circle or container.

This container then becomes the 'experiencing' circle and the group learns that the trauma material can be enacted safely in this circle. Over time this structure becomes a consistent reminder of the importance of boundaries, and how to build them in different ways. The group Greta was in began that session by putting out strengths that would allow them to 'go deeper into the feelings of the past', which created a warm-up for Greta to become protagonist.

Trauma / healing circle

The group can also concretize a second circle if trauma material is breaking through into the present. The group can repeat the above process to create a second circle, the 'trauma circle', to contain the unprocessed images, sensations, thoughts, feelings, and behavioural urges. Strengths and defences are chosen to create this second circle and fragments of trauma are concretized and put into this trauma circle for healing. When contained in this 'trauma/healing' circle, the trauma material is narratively labelled and can be chosen to work on or to be left alone during the session. If Greta had not been able to re-compensate with the help of prescriptive roles in scene 1, the director could have intervened by asking the group to create this trauma/healing circle before moving on. Then protagonist and group members alike could put scarves, objects, and chairs to concretize flashbacks that were disrupting their present experiencing. Often this circle is created as part of the warm-up so it is ready as needed.

Types of re-experiencing dramas

Another risk of retraumatization can occur when psychodrama scenes slip from the present to childhood memories without conscious consent by the protagonist. To control the seductive pull of unconscious trauma material, TSM delineates six types of dramas to promote clear boundaries during the action sequences (Hudgins 1993; 1998). Contracting with protagonist and group is an important step in informed choice and conscious re-experiencing of core trauma scenes.

Restoration and renewal

These dramas focus on concretizing and experiencing the prescriptive roles to restore a sense of depletion so trauma work can be done. Energy is unblocked and resiliency is restored. Prescriptive and transformative roles can be enacted to increase personal renewal at any point in the therapy process: at the beginning of therapy, as fuel for uncovering and working through trauma memories and for celebration at termination.

Dreams and metaphors

These dramas concretize the abstract symbols often found in dreams, myths, and other metaphors. The important structure in this type of drama is that the director sticks to the contract to explore abstract symbols, even if the dreams or metaphors appear to have unconscious trauma material in them. This boundary protects the protagonist from being surprised by victim and perpetrator roles when he or she thought it was only a fairy tale being enacted.

Initial discovery and accurate labeling

These dramas concentrate on putting narrative labels to previously unknown trauma material. While trauma-based roles will be enacted in this type of drama, the contract is for cognitive meaning, not emotional expression. An example of this type of drama would include enacting a fragmented memory to discriminate what actually did happen. Interventions would direct the protagonist toward meaning making rather than emotional expression, which would be completed in a later drama.

Uncovering and exploring core trauma

These trauma dramas provide a framework to consciously re-experience scenes of the past complete with dissociated affects being expressed. Prescriptive roles are stabilized in scene 1. Then the unconscious experience and meaning of trauma-based roles can be consciously re-experienced through controlled regression and team support in additional scenes. Dissociated feelings can be accessed and expressed from the victim role. Identification with the aggressor can be explored through enactment of the perpetrator role. New meanings emerge out of accurate experiencing of the past.

Conscious re-experiencing with developmental repair

These specific dramas provide structures for controlled regression into the past following the principles of conscious re-experiencing. Step by step the director and action trauma team direct the safe and conscious re-experiencing of core trauma scenes. The final scene in these types of dramas is always one of developmental repair. The self integrates. The bad mother reforms and apologizes. The group is trusted with self-disclosure.

Greta's drama to confront her grandfather and to rescue her screaming five-year-old would be a contract for conscious re-experiencing with developmental repair. As shown in this chapter, Greta first concretized her prescriptive roles. When she was stable, she was able to role reverse into her trauma-based child role and enter a controlled regression to identify and express her screams of terror. However, she was not alone, but experienced repair as she was surrounded by her internal positive roles and held in the arms of her spirit of compassion.

Letting go and transformation

These dramas typically center on role training new behaviours to replace old roles. Often future projections are directed to test the development of new transformative roles prior to having to use them in the world. These types of dramas can be conducted as a group using either a central concern model or a sociodramatic framework, as well as with individual protagonists.

Each type of conscious re-experiencing drama has a contract, clinical session goals, and action descriptions to guide psychodrama to prevent uncontrolled regression.

Principles of conscious re-experiencing

The principles of conscious re-experiencing were developed to further guide the action sequence when the contract is for exploration and repair of core trauma scenes (Hudgins 1993). There are six steps in self-disclosing and enacting trauma scenes, which guide the director and protagonist. These are talk, observe, witness, re-enact, re-experience and repair.

Talk

First the protagonist verbally describes the trauma scenes that will be enacted in the drama. Verbal sharing allows for assessment of protagonist and group in terms of support for the re-experiencing work. Talk also allows group members to know ahead of time the horror, pain, and so forth, that they will see. Greta first described the scene of forced oral sex in the barn before it ever began to be enacted.

Observe

The protagonist sets up a trauma scene while maintaining a safe, therapeutic distance through observing ego roles. Auxiliaries walk through the scripted scene without additional spontaneity. This gives the team and director a chance to continue to assess safety needs and the level of adaptive functioning and to make interventions as needed. Greta first observed the scene for accuracy as the trained auxiliaries walked through the described actions of violence and sexual abuse. When she became paralysed, she was directed to create her own authority and the spirit of compassion was concretized.

Witness

The protagonist is in a witness role while the scene is being enacted with an increase in spontaneity and affective expression. Often the protagonist will spontaneously rescue the victim-self from the trauma. This provides empowerment and expands the role repertoire. Witnessing provides both experience and observation of the trauma in the moment. When Greta was role reversed into the spirit of compassion she was able to reach in and stop the abuse and offer comfort to the five-year-old, demonstrating her ability to witness the story in a new way.

Re-enact

When clinically ready the protagonist goes through the scenes of trauma in close connection with the director and all support roles. This role parallels that of observing, though it is done from one of the trauma-based roles, so it is re-enactment. The protagonist in the role of victim, perpetrator, or abandoning authority walks through this experience so the director can assess for containment before full experiencing of core trauma. Greta walked through her experience as the five-year-old once before she was directed to complete the conscious re-experiencing of this victim role as well as its scream.

Re-experience

The protagonist consciously re-experiences the scene of trauma from all the roles that are clinically indicated – victim, perpetrator, 'absent' mother, enemy and so forth. This is conscious regression in the service of the ego. With the support of the prescriptive and transformative roles on the stage, the protagonist can re-experience the depth of dissociated feelings and new knowledge from trauma based roles safely. Greta was able to re-experience and express her childhood scream of terror so that it would not keep going around and around in her head.

Repair

The final step in conscious re-experiencing is always developmental repair. Controlled regression is directed to enable repair scenes to be enacted to change old trauma patterns. Repair scenes can focus on the self, model group (family of origin) relationships, significant others in the present, members of the group, or transpersonal symbols as healing agents for the core trauma experience. In the role of the spirit of compassion, Greta could stop the abuse and find comfort.

Advanced intervention modules: Steps in action

While this chapter cannot present the entire list of modified psychodramatic techniques that are part of TSM, one will be presented as an example: the containing double. Other techniques present additional intervention modules, including:

- the body double
- manager of healthy functioning
- concretizing defences
- the client role
- three-way role reversal
- enacting victim/perpetrator/abandoning authority roles safely

The containing double

This intervention module has been standardized and operationally defined in a three-session application for research and clinical practice. In an initial study, the containing double has been shown empirically to decrease dissociation and avoidance (Hudgins and Drucker 1998; Hudgins, Drucker and Metcalf 2000). There are three simple steps in completing the containing double intervention module:

1. Speaking in the first person, the CD makes a reflection of the process, content, affect, intensity, defence structures and so forth that the protagonist is experiencing at that moment. For example,

Greta's CD said: 'I am really really scared of being anywhere close to my grandfather.'

2. Still speaking in the first person, the CD makes a statement that labels the ability to contain and manage the reflected process, content, feeling and so forth into conscious awareness. As Greta's CD continued, she said: 'I know I am really scared right now and feel like a kid ... and I know that I can take a deep breath and get curious why this is happening now. What's going on for me that I'm losing my adult role?'

3. Anchor the reflection and containment into the here and now through time references, sensory data, and/or interpersonal connections. Greta's CD stated: 'I can feel the director's hand and look around the group here. These people are here to support my drama. I am safe in the here and now even as I think about my grandfather.'

As standardized, the CD can be used to train clinicians and students in the use of one experiential intervention to increase containment. It can be taught to clients in individual therapy or used over time in group sessions. As the CD is experienced again and again, it becomes internalized and adds to the resiliency of clients as they live in the world.

Conclusion

While the therapeutic spiral model presents a comprehensive clinical model of using experiential methods with trauma survivors, much work remains to be done to verify and validate the effectiveness of this model. Research has begun to demonstrate the effectiveness of the intervention module of the containing double with PTSD. Additional studies are in progress testing other modified interventions and constructs.

TSM integrates the power of classical psychodrama with the clinical structures learned from recent trauma theory to produce a safe and effective system for treating trauma survivors. It is unique in its step by step clinical directions that can be broken down into single interventions or guide all encompassing dramas. This chapter has provided a summary of the major innovations of this model in experiential self-organization, clinical structures and advanced intervention modules. A composite case guided the reader gently through the abstract concepts.

In conclusion, psychodrama can be a treatment of choice with trauma survivors. However, the methods of classical psychodrama must be used to promote containment as well as expression to provide safe treatment using experiential methods. It is the hope that the therapeutic spiral model addresses many of the questions of how to conduct psychodrama without triggering uncontrolled regression or risking retraumatization. Most of all, it is the hope that trauma survivors can heal rapidly and with compassion.

The therapeutic spiral model has been co-created with the clinicians who have been on the action trauma teams of the Center for Experiential Learning over the past 15 years, including (but not limited to) Colleen Baratka, Jeanne Burger, Mario Cossa, Mimi Cox, Karen Drucker, Peter Dummett, Kathleen Fimmell, Colette Harrison, Kathy Metcalf, Mary Anna Palmer, Rebecca Ridge, Francesca Toscani, Trish van Peursem, and Cathy Wilson in the USA; Julia Howell and Francis Batten in England; Charmaine McVea and Penny Crawley in Australia; Jacqui Gough, Estelle Mendelsohn, and Miriam Hammond in New Zealand, and George and Irene McDermott in Canada.

I also want to thank the many protagonists who have shared their stories of personal and collective trauma with me at The Psychodrama Theatre of Protection in Black Earth, Wisconsin, USA, and at workshop sites around the world. With your help, TSM has become a powerful tool for healing trauma. Thank you for your courage and risk taking. It is with faith and hope that the therapeutic spiral model carries forth what we have learned together over the years. As J.L. Moreno (1953), the founder of psychodrama, said, we have found ways to 'teach them (trauma survivors) to dream again!'

References

Altman, K.P. (1992) 'Psychodramatic treatment of multiple personality disorder and dissociative disorders.' *Dissociation 5*, 2, 104–108.

Altman, K.P. (1993) 'Psychodrama in the treatment of post trauma syndrome.' *Treating Abuse Today 2*, 27–31.

Bannister, A. (1990) *From Hearing to Healing: Working with the Aftermath of Child Sexual Abuse*. Chichester: John Wiley.

Bannister, A. (1991) 'Learning to live again: psychodramatic techniques with sexually abused young people.' In P. Holmes and M. Karp (eds) *Psychodrama: Inspiration and Technique*. London: Tavistock/Routledge.

Bannister, A. (1997) *The Healing Drama: Psychodrama and Dramatherapy with Abused Children*. London: Free Association Books.

Baumgartner, D. (1986) 'Sociodrama and the Vietnam combat veteran: a therapeutic release for a wartime experience.' *Journal of Group Psychotherapy and Sociometry 38*, 31–39.

Bergin, A.E. and Garfield, S.L. (1994) 'Overview, trends, and future issues.' In A.E. Bergin and S.L. Garfield (eds) *The Handbook of Psychotherapy and Behavior Change.* New York: John Wiley and Sons.

Blatner, A. (1997) 'Psychodrama: the state of the art.' *The Arts in Psychotherapy 24*, 1, 23–30.

Burge, M. (1996) 'The Vietnam veteran and the family "both victims of post traumatic stress" – a psychodramatic perspective.' *Australian and New Zealand Psychodrama Association Journal 5*, 25–36.

Cossa, M. and Hudgins, M.K. (1999) Workshop handout. Keene, NH: ACTING OUT Program.

Eckert, J. and Biermann-Ratjen, E.M. (1998) 'The treatment of borderline personality disorder.' In L.S. Greenberg, J.C. Watson and G. Lietaer (eds) *Handbook of Experiential Psychotherapy.* New York: Guilford Press.

Ellenson, G. S. (1986) 'Disturbances of perception in adult female incest survivors.' *The Journal of Contemporary Social Work 67*, 149–159.

Ellenson, G.S. (1989) 'Horror, rage, and defenses in the symptoms of female sexual abuse survivors.' *Social Casework: The Journal of Contemporary Social Work 12*, 589–598.

Elliot, R., Davis, K.L. and Slatick, E. (1998) 'Process-experiential therapy for posttraumatic stress difficulties.' In L.S. Greenberg, J.C. Watson and G. Lietaer (eds) *Handbook of Experiential Psychotherapy.* New York: Guilford Press.

Elliot, R., Suter, P., Manford, J., Radpour-Markert, L., Sigel-Hinson, R., Layman, C. and Davis, K. (1996) 'A process-experiential approach to post-traumatic stress disorder.' In R. Hutter, G. Pawlowsky, P.F. Schmid and R. Stipsits (eds) *Client-centered and Experiential Psychotherapy: A Paradigm in Motion.* Frankfurt: Lang.

Gelinas, D.J. (1983) 'The persisting negative effects of incest.' *Psychiatry 46*, 312–333.

Goldman, E.E. and Morrison, D.S. (1984) *Psychodrama: Experience and Process.* Dubuque, IA: Kendall/Hunt.

Greenberg, L.S., Elliott, R.K. and Lietaer, G. (1994) 'Research on experiential psychotherapies.' In A.E. Bergin and S.L. Garfield (eds) *Handbook of Psychotherapy and Behavior Change.* New York: John Wiley and Sons.

Greenberg, L.S., Lietaer, G. and Watson, J.C. (1998) 'Experiential therapy: identity and challenges.' In L.S. Greenberg, J.C. Watson and G. Lietaer (eds) *Handbook of Experiential Psychotherapy.* New York: Guilford Press.

Greenberg, L.S. and Paivio, S.C. (1998) 'Allowing and accepting painful emotional experiences.' *The International Journal of Action Methods 51*, 2, 47–62.

Holmes, P. (1992) *The Inner World Outside: Object Relations Theory and Psychodrama.* London: Tavistock/Routledge.

Hudgins, M.K. (1989) 'Experiencing the self through psychodrama and gestalt therapy in anorexia nervosa.' In L.M. Hornyak and E.R. Baker (eds) *Experiential Therapies for Eating Disorders.* New York: Guilford Press.

Hudgins, M.K. (1993) *In Videotape: Healing Sexual Trauma with Action Methods.* Madison, WI: Digital Recordings.

Hudgins, M.K. (1998) 'Experiential psychodrama with sexual trauma.' In L. Greenberg, G. Lietaer and J. Watson (eds) *Experiential Psychotherapy: Foundations and Differential Treatment Approaches.* New York: Guilford Press.

Hudgins, M.K. and Drucker, K. (1998) 'The containing double as part of the therapeutic spiral model for treating trauma survivors.' *International Journal of Action Methods 51*, 2, 63–74.

Hudgins, M.K., Drucker, K. and Metcalf, K. (2000) 'The containing double to prevent uncontrolled regression with PTSD: A preliminary report.' *The British Journal of Psychodrama and Sociodrama 15*, 1, 58–77.

Hudgins, M.K. and Kipper, D. (1998) 'Action methods in the treatment of trauma survivors.' *International Journal of Action Methods 51*, 2, 43–46.

Hudgins, M.K. and Sheridan, M.S. (1990) *The Three-Child Model of Recovery*. Workshop handout and unpublished monograph. Charlottesville, VA: The Center for Experiential Learning.

Karp, M. (1991) 'Psychodrama and piccalilli: Residual treatment of a sexually abused adult.' In P. Holmes and M. Karp (eds) *Psychodrama: Inspiration and Technique*. London: Tavistock/Routledge.

Kellermann, P.F. (1992) *Focus on Psychodrama: The Therapeutic Aspects of Psychodrama*. London: Jessica Kingley Publishers.

Kellermann, P.F. (1996) 'Concretization in psychodrama with somatization disorder.' *The Arts in Psychotherapy 23*, 149–152.

Kipper, D.A. (1989) 'Psychodrama research and the study of small groups.' *International Journal of Small Group Research 5*, 4–27.

Moreno, J.L. (1915) *Words of the Father*. Beacon, NY: Beacon House Press.

Moreno, J.L. (1953) *Who Shall Survive?* Beacon, NY: Beacon House.

Moreno, J.L. and Moreno, Z.T. (1969) *Psychodrama: Volume 3*. Beacon, NY: Beacon House.

Moreno, Z.T. and Blomqvist, D. (2000) *Healing Through the Use of Surplus Reality*. NY: Jason Aronson.

Raaz, N., Carlson-Sabelli, L. and Sabelli H. (1992) 'Psychodrama in the treatment of multiple personality disorder: a process-theory perspective.' In E. Kluft (ed) *Expressive and Functional Therapies in the Treatment of Multiple Personality Disorder*. New York: Guilford Press.

Reynolds, T. (1996) 'Dissociative identity disorder and the psychodramatist.' *Australian and New Zealand Psychodrama Association Journal 5*, 43–61.

Sidorsky, S. (1984) 'The psychodramatic treatment of the borderline personality.' *Journal of Group Psychotherapy Psychodrama and Sociometry 37*, 117–125.

Toscani, F. and Hudgins, M.K. (1996) *Trauma Survivor's Intrapsychic Role Atom: Including Prescriptive Roles*. Unpublished manuscript. Charlottesville, VA: The Center for Experiential learning.

van der Kolk, B.A. (1997) Keynote address. Annual conference of the American Society of Group Psychotherapy and Psychodrama. New York.

van der Kolk, B.A. (1996) 'The body keeps the score: Approaches to the psychobiology of posttraumatic stress disorder.' In B.A. van der Kolk, A.C. McFarlane and L. Weisaeth (eds) *Traumatic Stress: The Effects of Overwhelming Experience on Mind, Body, and Society*. New York: Guilford Press.

Widlake, B. (1997) 'Barbara's bubbles: The psychodrama of a young adult recovering from an eating disorder.' *The British Journal of Psychodrama and Sociodrama 12*, 23–34.

Wilkins, P. (1997) 'Psychodrama and research.' *The British Journal of Psychodrama and Sociodrama 12*, 44–61.

Wolfe, B.E. and Sigl, P. (1998) 'Experiential psychotherapy of the anxiety disorders.' In L.S. Greenberg, J.C. Watson and G. Lietaer (eds) *Handbook of Experiential Psychotherapy*. New York: Guilford Press.

Young, L. (1992) 'Sexual abuse and the problem of embodiment.' *Child Abuse and Neglect 16*, 89–100.

CHAPTER 14

Cycles of Healing
The Treatment of Developmental Trauma

John Raven Mosher and Brigid Yukman

In this chapter we will present the healing circle model of therapeutic inter-ventions. This model was initially derived from correspondences between the cycle of the seasons and the cycle of human development. The model has been further elaborated in therapeutic practice as a structure for classifying behaviours. We identify four kinds of developmental trauma and four resulting personal mythologies: abandonment, betrayal, disempowerment and chaos. These personal mythologies are essentially incomplete life cycles or half-lives driven by interrupted developmental cycles. In the first part of the chapter we summarize the early childhood developmental cycle as it cor-responds to the ancient use of the quartered circle to see the human life cycle in relation to that of the seasons. We then use the quartered circle to align this developmental cycle with personal mythologies that result from the trauma. In the second part of the chapter we present narrative accounts of four actual psychodramas emerging from four personal mythologies. During each drama the director follows a particular cycle of interventions – a cycle of healing – using the quartered circle to view the relationship between the trauma and the developmental cycle as a whole.

At its simplest, the healing circle model is a quartered circle, a four-part structure for viewing the sequence of human development as a cycle that repeats and can be interrupted and altered by trauma. Once this repetition is apparent, the outlines of a life pattern come into view. As will be demon-strated in greater detail, the quartered circle is actually a set of relationships that create a system. Just as the basic grammar of a language can be used to generate thousands of sentences, the paired opposites that form the quartered circle represent a set of relationships among parts that structure many living systems, including the cycle of the seasons and human development.

Although they cannot be developed in the scope of this chapter, there are further theoretical explanations for why the quartered circle can be used to predict patterns in this way (Mosher 1999). The principle of complementarity represented by the relationships between solstices and equinoxes in the ancient use of the quartered circle helps explain why viewing development and trauma within the whole life cycle can suggest powerful, even counterintuitive interventions. When quantum physicists measure matter as waves they cannot measure it as particles; when they measure it as particles they cannot measure it as waves. Nonetheless, matter is both particle and wave. Like the wave/particle theory of quantum physics, the quartered circle brings the whole comprising complementaries into view.

The cycle of healing interventions to be discussed in this chapter can also be understood in the context of complexity theory. According to complexity science, complex dynamic systems like the human life cycle remain true to their initial conditions, show self-similarity at every scale, and self-organize in new ways as they near chaos. The healing circle model of intervention perturbs the self-similarity and predictability of individual life patterns as they repeat initial developmental trauma, pushing the client toward chaos and change.

The psychodramas described in the second part of this chapter should be seen as representative examples from a broad context. The healing circle has been developed and tested experientially as a method of working with trauma in several private practices, workshops, trainings, and presentations since 1983. While this is not a research paper, the four dramas we present should be seen as representative of many others, directed by both certified practitioners and trainees, in clinical, professional, and training settings that contributed to developing the quartered circle into the model of intervention that is the subject of this chapter.

The healing circle

The Native American Medicine Wheel and the Celtic Eight-fold Calendar are both indigenous variants of the quartered circle. Historically and metaphorically the quartered circle is tied to the cycle of the seasons. Based upon a few simple rules inferred from the orbit of the earth around the sun, the thresholds between the seasons came to symbolize rites of passage linked to the dynamics of the solstices and the equinoxes.

The figure below is a composite of many cultural variants of the healing circle, depicting the seasons, their orbital thresholds, and cross-cultural rites of passage associated with the solstices and equinoxes.

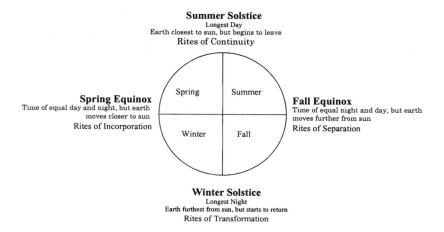

Figure 14.1: The healing circle

The seasons of human development

In Western thought, human development has traditionally been conceptualized as linear. Twentieth century research by Ames *et al.* (1979), Carter and McGoldrick (1988), Levin (1988), and Levinson (1978), among others, has demonstrated that human growth processes are also cyclical. According to these and other current theories, human beings repeat their early childhood development cycles throughout their lives at many levels.

Neither parents nor babies being perfect, human beings tend to experience trauma that affects their early development and resulting patterns of living. They store developmentally impinging trauma in their bodies, habits, dreams, memories, and stories. Furthermore, as if on a quest to set the trauma right and complete the developmental cycle, human beings continually seek out conditions in life that will enable them to replay early trauma (Fromm and Smith, 1989).

The quartered circle can be used to view our apparently linear lives as the repetition of a developmental cycle. From this perspective we can begin to investigate how developmental traumas have organized the range of behaviours or possibilities for living available to the self. The quartered circle provides a structure for mapping the transitions from one phase of development to the next, indicating where a person reliving one of the four classes of developmental trauma is likely to get stuck because he or she is without the skills or emotional experiences to make those transitions. When a particular person's life pattern or cycle is superimposed on an arrangement of the developmental stages around the quartered circle, a cycle of interventions, or a *cycle of healing* is indicated. The Healing Circle Model is an adaptation of the ancient quartered circle to the developmental cycle that suggests how to intervene therapeutically when a person is reliving a pattern of interrupted development.

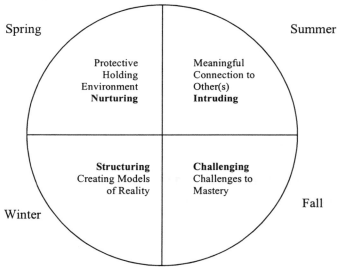

Figure 14.2: The seasons of human development

Among the many possible aspects of human development, we will focus on the relationships between the child and the social environment that are necessary for developing a self. In order for a self to emerge, as Mahler, Pine and Bergman's (1975) psychoanalytic work with infants demonstrated, the newborn requires a developing relationship with the primary caregiver or the social environment in which each stage builds upon the next. Specifically, the growing self first requires a protective holding environment, then a meaningful connection to an other, followed by challenges to mastery, and finally, structures for understanding reality. There are other schemas for identifying developmental stages, but many share the four fundamental relationships between parent and child classified by Anne Jernberg in her book *Theraplay* (1979). We have elaborated on the categories she names below:

Spring, Quadrant I: Nurturing – 'The Parent' rocks, nurses, holds, nuzzles, comforts, feeds, cuddles, envelops, caresses, lies next to, and hugs baby. An unconditional loving and touching care that simulates a womb outside the mother's body. Maintains protective holding environment. Facilitates the development of *feelings*, beginning with *trust*. Appropriate for times of helplessness, extreme need, profound confusion, and new beginnings.

Summer, Quadrant II: Intruding – 'The Parent' tickles, bounces, swings, surprises, giggles, hops at and pounces playfully, makes eye contact with baby. An energetic drawing into the world through eye contact and age appropriate play. Maintains contact. Facilitates the development of dealing successfully with *wanting* and developing *intuition*. Appropriate for clarification of boundaries, wants, spirituality, and the development of intimacy and interdependence.

Fall, Quadrant III: Challenging – 'The Parent' teases, dares, encourages, varies, chases, and sets forth age appropriate and achievable developmental tasks for the child. Leads the child to a sense of mastery. Facilitates confidence in *doing* and the experience of *sensation*. Appropriate for directing 'child' beyond perceived limits into available areas of new behaviour and knowledge.

Winter, Quadrant IV: Structuring – 'The Parent' limits, defines, forbids, outlines, reassures, speaks firmly, labels, names, clarifies, confines, holds, and restrains the child. Teaches differences and their names. Creates models of reality. Facilitates the development of *thinking*. Appropriate in times of meaninglessness and chaos as a container of generative energy.

Like most things in nature, the lives of human beings pass through seasons of unfolding, season by season, year after year. Spring is the time of new beginnings, when nature provides the nurturance and protective holding environment for new life. Summer is the time of harvests, when the relationship with the environment, whether organic or human, bears fruit. Fall is the time of preparation for the challenges of winter, when people master the tools for survival. Winter is the time for rest, recuperation, and the creation and sharing of personal and cultural stories. These seasons of life repeat as life continues.

Kinds of developmental trauma

In the course of our lives we are exposed to extreme experiences. When they are greater than our capacity to cope with them, we experience trauma. While some traumatic experiences are random and unrelated to development, the research into trauma shows that not all people have a trauma response to the same events. In other words, a person may be predisposed to experience trauma of one kind or another by a physiological, chemical, and psychological adaptation to early attachment trauma that affected further development. Four kinds of trauma relating to the stages of development within the early parent/child relationship can occur.

The first relational stage in development is symbiosis. A newborn can experience abandonment trauma when the nurturing environment fails to nurture. When this abandonment trauma occurs early enough it can affect the child's lifelong capacity for attachment, as van der Kolk discusses in his article 'The Separation Cry and the Trauma Response' (1987). As the developmental cycle repeats, the child, and later the adult, will continue to experience this trauma and create a life pattern that organizes every aspect of being.

The next relational stage in development is differentiation, or learning to relate to others as 'not me.' A child can experience betrayal trauma in response to broken, inappropriate, or extreme expectations from others. Psychodynamic theory refers to this kind of trauma as narcissistic (Miller 1981). It is not surprising that a child who is derailed at this developmental stage grows up blaming self or other for what happens and striving to be right at all costs rather than successfully differentiating.

Growing into the next stage of development and relationship, that of practising competency in age appropriate activities and behaviours, the child depends upon teachers. It may be life itself that is the teacher. At this stage of development a child is likely to experience trauma as disempowerment. Being overwhelmed can lead the child onto a path of manipulative care giving or care seeking, and a Peter Pan-like incapacity to grow up.

Finally if the social environment is adequate, the child reaches a level of competency and self-knowledge and is able to observe and create his or her own reality. Overwhelmed by experience at this stage, a child's capacity for creating meaning is itself impaired. Reality becomes meaningless because the child cannot believe he or she can impact experience. This kind of traumatic response is referred to as post-traumatic stress disorder or PTSD. PTSD might be described as a lost birthright to human consciousness: the capacity to observe and create human reality. How many times have any of us found and incorporated new information that changed our world view and as a result changed the world we view? When this process can occur, the crisis is resolved because people arrive at new meaning, and their wounds can heal. Recent research into trauma has focused on PTSD.

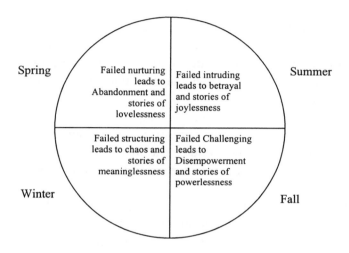

Figure 14.3: The seasons of development derailed

The personal mythology

Eventually, physiological and psychological responses to trauma, repetitions of developmental trauma, and the accumulated loss of alternative experiences, create a life pattern that is both conscious and unconscious. People make meaning of their experiences by creating stories about them. Some of these stories are public ones through which we define or seek our roles with others and our communities. Some of these stories are private ones that we keep secret out of shame. Some of these stories we forget because they are no longer relevant or because they are too painful. And some of these stories self-organize outside our awareness, and though they are the core meanings we have made of our lives, we live them unconsciously. Taken together, private, public, forgotten, and core myths are the traces of a unique individual personal mythology.

Research on memory (Siegel 1999) demonstrates that everyone has a narrative autobiography. We are referring to this narrative autobiography as the personal mythology in order to reflect that it is both conscious and unconscious and that it shapes our lives as powerfully as cultural myths once did. These stories of the self over time shape the course of our lives and seem to be powerfully affected by threats to our survival as well as our inspirations for living. People live these narratives whether or not they are conscious of doing so. People growing up in cultures untouched by psychological narratives or the contemporary Western understanding of child development would have narratives organized around alternative perceptions of developmental stages and the life cycle. To the degree that development is universal for human beings, however, developmental trauma may influence all narrative autobiography.

Though every personal mythology is unique, four types correspond to the four traumas that interrupt stages or 'seasons' of human development, as they are understood in Western culture. The characteristics of the personal myths discussed in this chapter were derived from extensive observation in long-term therapeutic settings.

Mythologies of abandonment, reflecting the failure of the protective holding environment, correspond to spring. The dominant trauma response is denial: denial of needs, feelings, and interpersonal relationships. This abandonment personal myth is often expressed as lovelessness filled with busy doing. Myths of betrayal, the failure of significant others to relate in trustworthy and appropriate ways, correspond to summer. The dominant trauma response is depression: the expectation that all experience will ultimately result in disappointment, no matter what. This betrayal personal myth is often expressed as joylessness driven by relentless, perfectionist criticism and blame of self and others. Myths of disempowerment, the failure to develop mastery, correspond to fall. The dominant trauma response is anxiety, but it camouflages anger. Any exercise of personal power is perceived through disempowerment trauma as extremely threatening and potentially humiliating, whatever the outcome. This leads to personal myths of powerlessness, driven by carefulness, care giving, and care seeking. Myths of chaos, the failure of meaning, correspond to winter. Chaos myths are the stories of post-traumatic stress disorder. They represent events that have remained undigested and unincorporated. People suffering chaos trauma can exhibit the trauma responses above as well as others like aggression against self and others, avoidance, dissociation, lack of motivation, learning disabilities, memory disturbances, over-reaction or freezing, physiological hyper-arousal, psychosomatic reactions, sleep disorders, and an exaggerated startle response (to name but a few). They lead to personal myths of meaninglessness.

The half-life of the personal mythology

People repeat the life patterns that emerge from their early development throughout their lives. When these patterns or personal mythologies are mapped out on the quartered circle, they are half circles – an image of what we term *half-lives* – because people tend to experience the same half cycle over and over again. The repetition of the pattern is extreme when developmental trauma has been extreme. In effect, when confronted with overwhelming stress that causes a person to freeze into immobility, unable to either fight or flee, the whole self-system – body, mind, emotions, and spirit – transports them out of a developmental cycle.

Repeated or extreme stress eventually results in accumulated loss of experiences at the next developmental stage. This loss in turn causes their access to the missing parts of the cycle to become even more difficult. Since the next developmental stage is inaccessible, trauma sufferers continue the cycle without acquiring all of the resources of the quadrant of trauma, or those of the next on the developmental stage. The self-system missed these stages even though time moved on. Under subsequent periods of stress, which become categorized in the terms of the initial trauma, they continually repeat a half circle, returning to the developmental cycle via compensatory behaviours, the path of least resistance, until, encountering stress again, they repeat the half-life cycle. And yet, Jung (1968), for one, argued that the missing experiences become part of the unconscious and will consequently keep leading us back to the crisis situation until the wound is healed or the cycle can be completed.

To summarize then, when our personal mythologies are mapped on the quartered circle, both the quadrant in which the trauma occurred and the next quadrant represent the uncompleted developmental experiences. They also point to a cycle of healing that must occur to complete the developmental cycle and alter the personal mythology.

The figures below identify the quadrants of trauma in relation to the half-life of each personal mythology.

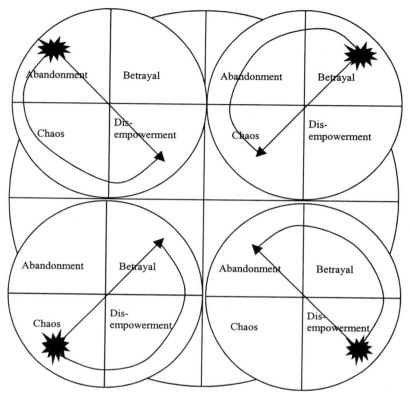

Figure 14.4: Categories of personal trauma

In the cycle of healing each quadrant has a significant relationship to the quadrant of trauma. As an example, the chaos half-life chart (Figure 14.5) shows the relationship of the other quadrants to chaos trauma. The Home Base is the quadrant of overt, compensatory behaviour under stress. The original traumatic experience is quite specific (abandonment, betrayal, disempowerment, or meaninglessness), but in time any significant stress will lead us to rely upon the same defensive behaviours. Because these strengths have been used to compensate for missing experiences, they are compromised. People often enter therapy when their Home Base behaviours fail to calm them effectively any longer.

The Starting Point is the last successful stage on the path of development before derailment. We are strongest in resources of this quadrant because we have the greatest access to behaviours of this 'season' of living. As will be discussed later in relation to directing psychodramas, for example, this is usually the quadrant in which the director can best join the protagonist and 'start' the cycle of healing.

Ground Zero is the quadrant of early childhood trauma, complementary (a dynamic opposite) to the Home Base. Developmental trauma occurring in this quadrant lays the ground for the personal mythology. When people flee the horror and helplessness of the Ground Zero quadrant into the complementary Home Base quadrant, they entirely miss the next quadrant, the Doorway, which holds unexplored possibilities for the self. Until we have integrated the traumatic experience into a fuller view of reality, access to this quadrant is underdeveloped, because it is unknown to us. These relatively unavailable experiences are the Doorway to the complete developmental cycle, and consequently to spontaneity and the wholeness of the human life cycle.

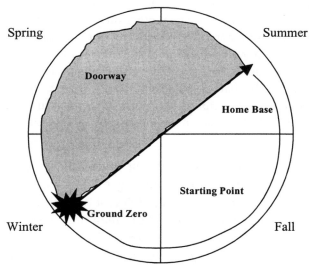

Figure 14.5: The half-life of chaos

When development is seen as a cycle, it becomes apparent that the developmental timing of trauma more than the event itself determines the parameters of a personal mythology. An exception to this link between developmental trauma and an emergent personal mythology can be trauma that is so severe it destroys the victim's ability to make meaning, no matter when or at what developmental level it is experienced. In general, early conclusions about life will determine reactions to trauma unless the traumatization is so devastating it bypasses the personal mythology.

Differential directing with the healing circle

The cycle of development leads to a particular life cycle or half cycle. Ideally, in the unfolding of the client's personal mythology, the therapist or director can make inferences about developmental trauma and together with the client proceed towards completion of the developmental cycle and transcendence of the personal mythology half-life. When the relationships between the developmental cycle and the personal mythologies are viewed on the quartered circle, a cycle of interventions is suggested. Of course many other therapeutic models reflect the need for more than one method of intervention. The appropriateness of shifting the role of director in relation to the client's process was first discussed by Moreno. He recognized a typology of clients and reciprocal therapies. He went further to say:

> One has to have an open, flexible mind; at times there may be an indication for using an authoritarian, at other times a democratic method, at times it may be necessary to be more direct or more passive, but one has to be willing to move gradually from one extreme to the other if the situation requires. Just as there is a choice of therapist there may be a choice of vehicle, couch, chair, or stage, and there may be a choice of which system of terms and interpretations a patient needs, until a system is formulated which is able to attain the consensus of all (Moreno and Moreno 1975, p.3).

Warner (1980) introduced the phrase 'differential directing' in reference to psychodrama. He referred to a matching of directing strategies to the behaviour patterns and perceptual styles of the protagonist. Whereas Warner's differential is the symptom, the healing circle model of intervention is based upon the life-impinging trauma to the developmental cycle. The need for differential directing is suggested by placing the developmental cycle and the personal mythology on the quartered circle. Each of the quadrants calls for a different kind of directorial style based on the developmental needs of the client. Just as the developing self grows in relation to a social environment, the protagonist or client grows in relation to the social environment represented by the therapist, group, or workshop. In a psychodrama, the director and the group act as the social environment.

Two findings in the research on PTSD are particularly relevant to understanding the healing circle model of intervention. One definition of trauma is that it severs the person's relationship with the social environment. Conversely, healing happens in community. As van der Kolk points out, 'the most powerful influence in overcoming the impact of psychological trauma seems to be the availability of a caregiver who can be blindly trusted when one's own resources are inadequate' (van der Kolk and Greenberg 1987, p.32). The developing relationship between therapist and client, especially during the long-term therapy process many PTSD clients require, is a bridge to the larger social environment. The successful recreation of the sense of human interdependence and community is the surest sign that the traumatic events have been integrated into the on-going autobiographical narrative, altering the personal mythology.

Figure 14.6: Leadership styles and functions

Because early developmental trauma influences the personal mythology, the healing cycle will start and reach completion within different quadrants, depending on the developmental trauma. Accordingly, the style of most effective directing will come from different quadrants at different points in the drama. Ultimately, spring calls for nurturing; summer, for intruding; fall, for challenging; and winter, for structuring.

Using the template of the quartered circle increases the attunement between director, protagonist and group by indicating which differential leadership style will accommodate the cycle of healing at each stage of the drama. In fact, the classic analysis of leadership roles and interventions by Lieberman, Yalom and Miles (1973) aligns with the cycle of development when displayed around the healing circle:

These directorial roles correspond to parental roles in early childhood development. In effect, the director is establishing a corrective social environment so that the protagonist can complete the developmental cycle. The director is thereby pre-empting the compensatory behaviours of the personal mythology, and, with the protagonist, co-creating a new story that can affect change.

The following dramas are offered as examples of differential directing that is responsive to and anticipates the protagonist's progress around the cycle of development. The quartered circle was used as a template to determine the Starting Point, Ground Zero, Doorway and Home Base, that were indicated by the class of trauma that unfolded in the warm-up to the drama. The shifting role of the director closely interfaces with each protagonist's progress out of the half-life of the personal mythology. There are no prescribed rules or scripts for this type of directing, but the parameters of the role are indicated and bear a relationship to those the parent takes in early childhood development. The practice of differential therapy allows the therapist to attune to the client's process despite the contradictory and conflicting extremes of trauma responses. This attunement assures that the client-therapist bond, a fundamental requirement for successful healing, is sustained through a complete developmental cycle. In other words, the director's relationship with the protagonist in a drama that completes a cycle of healing provides a safe and accepting holding environment (quadrant 1), intrusion and play that reflect encouragement to claim self fully through self expression of needs and wants (quadrant 2), appropriate challenges that teach mastery and competency (quadrant 3) and meaning attributions that establish revised models of reality (quadrant 4).

The details of each drama and the protagonists' names and gender have been changed. Because directors' experiences with the protagonists have a wider context than can be presented here, their intuitions cannot be accounted for entirely. Shifts in directorial styles are not only changes in the direction of the drama. When shifting directorial roles, the director changes his or her tone of voice, choice of words, style of contact (touch/no touch), eye contact, and other behaviours. What is important to observe about these four dramas is the way the director relates to the protagonist. Some of the director's approaches may seem counter-intuitive because they are indicated by the cycle of healing rather than symptoms the protagonist exhibits.

The abandonment cycle of healing: Mary

In a weekly psychodrama therapy group Mary, a 35-year-old chief executive officer of a small business, asked for time to 'get rid of' her anxiety. Agitated, Mary told the group about how she had driven herself to the emergency unit of a hospital the day before, afraid that she was going to die.

This information suggested that Mary was re-experiencing abandonment trauma. Regular panic attacks, thinking that one can 'get rid of' anxiety, and hyperactivity are characteristic of the abandonment personal mythology. The healing circle model indicates that the Starting Point for the abandonment cycle of healing is the directorial role of meaning attributor. But in this case, Mary was too warmed up, too anxious to access her spontaneity. The director, hypothesizing that Mary was unable to get to her Home Base, quadrant 3, elected to help her get there by relating to her through the director style. He directed her to set up the scene of her drive to the hospital. This direction moved her from her Ground Zero or abandonment despair to her Home Base of doing.

By having her describe and set up the scene of driving her car to the hospital, the director helped Mary to cool down rapidly. The director then shifted to the role of meaning attributor, the Starting Point for healing an abandonment personal myth. As meaning attributor, the director focuses on structure, thinking and meaning. Following direction, Mary described the new model Lexus she had purchased earlier in the week. She was immensely proud of this new car though she was not really sure why she had bought it. Sitting in the driver's seat, she remarked: 'I feel like I'm sitting in a womb, safe and quiet.' To attribute meaning, the director decided to concretize the metaphor.

Mary was asked to pick someone to play Mary and then to become the voice of the womb herself. This direction drew upon Mary's ability to play a self-observing role. In terms of the developmental cycle, she was enacting a containing structure, or structure for reality, as the parent does in the developmental stage represented by quadrant 4. Living an abandonment personal mythology, Mary had some strengths in this quadrant, her Starting Point.

The ensuing scene depicted a frantic auxiliary/Mary, unreachable by the voice of the womb/Mary. The story of her birth then emerged. Her mother's father had died as Mary was being born. Just hours after Mary's birth her mother turned her newborn baby over to a wet nurse so that she could travel to another state to bury her father. Mary's mother was gone for six months. As she told this story, Mary was completely devoid of feeling, still in quadrant 4, while the group, on the other hand, was profoundly affected.

The director, still in the meaning attributor role, stopped the scene, dismissed the auxiliary, and spoke to Mary as herself. Seeking to enhance the meaning of the experience, the director asked Mary why she thought she associated her car with a womb. After several valiant efforts at analysing her metaphor, Mary fell into a shocked silence.

Then, tears spilling down her cheeks, she said: 'Oh, my God! Mother!' Crying in earnest, she shared with the group that she had heard at the end of the last week that her mother had cancer of the pancreas and was dying. She had bought her womb-like car that weekend. The panic attacks had started early in the following week. Through her therapy, Mary had built a meaningful relationship with her mother; and now she was losing her. The director summarized: 'Your mother's coming death activated your deepest abandonment wounds. No wonder you were afraid you were dying.'

'I need to talk to Mom,' Mary declared. Mary picked a group member who had played her mother many times during her earlier work. Entering the nurturing quadrant as caring leader, the director helped Mary set a scene with Mother where Mary was richly supported by the group and the director in expressing the fullness of her feelings of fear, despair, and loss. In role reversal as her mother, Mary gave herself a 'mother's blessing' to 'carry on your life with me in your heart'. This blessing marked the threshold crossing of a rite of continuity, from quadrant 1 to quadrant 2, where Mary claimed her full womanhood within the community of her therapy group.

After the drama, and before her mother's death, Mary married her long-time live-in partner and became pregnant. Mary believes that the spirit of her mother lives on in her daughter. As shown in the chart below, the process of this healing cycle went from 'spring' to 'fall' to 'winter' to 'spring', and ended in 'summer', completing a developmental and life cycle. Mary stepped through the Doorway of her personal mythology into experiences of differentiation, unavailable in her early childhood development.

The betrayal cycle of healing: Juliet

People with betrayal mythologies are frequently entangled in ambivalent relationships with their betrayers. Juliet had a love/hate relationship with her mother. She depended on her for approval, yet somehow never measured up

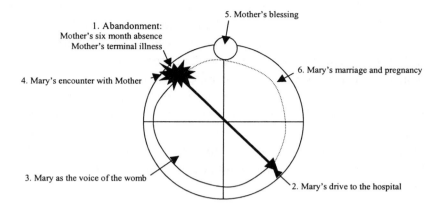

Figure 14.7: Mary's abandonment cycle of healing

to her mother's standards. Juliet had another complaint about Mom. Juliet suffered from the relatively unseen betrayal of never having her wants, goals, talents, or dreams respected or honoured by her mother. Although Juliet was a brilliant surgeon, her mother had wanted Juliet to marry well and raise a family.

During her check-in, Juliet told the group she was scheduled to meet her mother at a ski resort the coming weekend and was furious that her mother had invited a prospective husband for Juliet ('a boring oaf') to come along. The Starting Point for healing the betrayal myth is spring, the quadrant of the caring leader. The director, beginning at the Starting Point as a caring leader, joined Juliet by calming her and gently probing into the sticky dynamics of her relationship with Mother. After Juliet had exhausted herself blaming her mother for the injustices she had suffered, she became tense and silent. The leader asked: 'Juliet, what are you feeling now?' 'Scared.' 'About?' Juliet began to cry. A confession followed.

Five years earlier her aunt (her deceased father's sister) had died, leaving all nieces and nephews a sizeable inheritance. Juliet's mom, as executrix of her sister-in-law's will, delivered the money without strings attached to all the recipients except Juliet. Even Juliet's unemployed brother received his money to do with as he wished. Juliet was asked to save the money (even though she was carrying a large debt of medical student loans towards which her mother refused to contribute support). Juliet promised.

At the time of this session and drama, Juliet was starting her own practice and had decided to use the money to equip and furnish her office and pay the initial salaries of her support staff. She had not told her mother about this but was determined to do so on the ski trip. She feared that her mother would 'tear her apart'. The director as caring leader encouraged Juliet to set a scene in which she could rehearse telling her mother.

The heat went up as Juliet met her mother alone at the top of the ski lift. The director, now operating as emotional stimulator, began to encourage, cajole, tease, and demand increased emotional expression. Beginning with a tearful abject apology, Juliet became more and more furious at her mother's inflexible negativity: 'I knew I couldn't trust you,' declared Mom for the thousandth time.

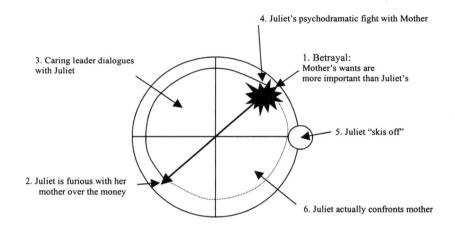

Figure 14.8: Juliet's betrayal cycle of healing

At last Juliet snapped. She told her mother off. 'I am a renowned neuro-surgeon, not a baby. I'll live my life my way and if you don't like it, you can keep it to yourself, because I will not tolerate being treated this way.' With a definitive gesture, Juliet turned and psychodramatically skied off down the slope, leaving her mother at last. The group (having witnessed many dramas with Mother that ended with Mother leaving a dejected and penitent Juliet) roared its approval.

Juliet separated and crossed over into her own competency (quadrant 3) on her own during the actual ski trip. The following week in group, she reported that she had confronted her mother about how she had denied her wants and dreams all her life rather than about spending her inheritance. After some struggle, Juliet said that she had told her mother: 'Respect me or forget me. I won't spend another minute with the only person in the world who treats me like a child.' Her mother apologized, but Juliet told the group that her attitude was that she would 'wait and see'.

The disempowerment cycle of healing: Scott

At a five-day residential workshop, Scott, a mild-mannered, likeable middle-aged man, asked for time to work on his relationship with his sister. Meeting Scott at his Starting Point, the director began in the emotional stimulator style. People wounded by disempowerment like to engage, through dialogue, conversation, intimacy, and relating to others. In this case a long dialogue ensued. Scott and his sister Helen were at odds. She was in therapy and working on 'stuff' and 'things were messed up'. What things? She was having unacceptable memories.

The Starting Point for the disempowerment personal mythology is the second quadrant, which corresponds to the developmental need for intrusion and active engagement with the parent. There is often a playful, trickster quality about this type of directorial engagement, a variation of 'peek-a-boo' between parent and child. Because disempowered protagonists are so vulnerable to humiliation, engaging at this intrusive edge successfully warms them up to empowerment – if they hold their own.

In this particular drama, Scott held his own as follows:

Director: What memories did Helen share with you?

Scott: She said she was having memories of Dad doing something to her.

Director: So?

Scott: Well, I told her I was sorry for her but I couldn't believe that happened.

Director: What couldn't you believe?

Scott: That Dad had sexually abused her (Scott begins to cry).

Director: What are you crying for? She's the one left out in the cold!

Scott: I know! (cries more).

Director: Scott, this is no time to wimp out on your sister. Knock it off!

Scott: How can you talk to me this way? Can't you see I feel bad?

Director: Not as bad as your sister.

Scott: (Standing taller) God! You're right. I have to do better.

This self-challenge was Scott's expression of readiness to move into action (and the third quadrant where he will meet the challenge of being present for his sister). The director, following Scott into quadrant 3 by shifting to the director style, helped him set up a family scene that took place at the time the abuse was supposed to have occurred. The following drama unfolded:

> Mom and Dad are fighting loudly in the kitchen. Scott, aged four, is in his bed in the room he shares with his sister, who is six. Father is very verbally abusive; mother is disempowered yet provocative. Scott has his head buried under his pillow, hiding, and Helen is hyper-vigilant. (Because he expresses the most spontaneity in Helen's role, the director eventually keeps Scott in the role.) The scene unfolds, driven by the role reversals with various family members. Mother ends the fight by locking father out of their bedroom. Father comes into Scott and Helen's room and begins fondling Helen.

The director stopped the scene at this point and placed Scott in his own role as four-year-old. As the scene was replayed, at the moment of fondling, Scott broke out of the four-year-old role and as his adult self expressed anger and outrage at his father. This was a breakthrough in Scott's ongoing therapy. The director ended the scene when Scott pushed his father out of the bedroom. Standing up to his father, who bullied him mercilessly, was a profound act of empowerment for Scott, but his challenge was not over.

Coming now from the meaning attributor style (quadrant 4), the director invited him to re-do the conversation with his sister in which she told him about the abuse, to see if this new power could transform the experience. Scott plunged into this rite of transformation, sharing his sorrow at being unable to help her when she was a child, and recently, when she first told him about the abuse. He shared with her how afraid he was of his father and how outraged he felt about Dad's treatment of her. 'To tell you the truth,' he said 'I've always wanted to kill the son of a bitch, but until now I never thought I could.'

This drama began a growth process for Scott that resulted in the successful completion of his therapy. The cycle of healing began with Scott's resorting to a Home Base (quadrant 1) behaviour: being an ineffectual caregiver for Helen. The director warmed him up by relating to him from his

Starting Point (quadrant 2), dialoguing and intruding into his process. Scott met the challenge that emerged from this engagement (quadrant 3) and claimed power in relating to his father. More importantly, he transformed his relationship with his sister and his father (quadrant 4) in relation to this issue.

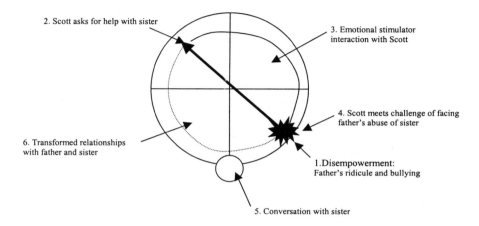

Figure 14.9: Scott's disempowerment cycle of healing

The chaos cycle of healing: Harrison

Facing the cruelties of human beings to one another is profoundly challenging. Protagonists with the half-life mythology of chaos are cut off from nurturing, often because of such cruelty, and yet they must trust again if the healing process is to begin. The afternoon that one of the authors asked Harrison for permission to use his story as a case example in this paper they went for a walk along a lakefront. As the walk came to a close, Harrison stopped and with steady eye contact said: 'You saved my life, you know'.

Harrison is the son of a career military man who physically abused him from age 2 to 15. At the age of 15 he was big enough to make his father stop. Harrison the adult returned from Vietnam with full-blown PTSD after two tours of combat duty. Years later, he came to a weekly psychodrama group both numb and hyper-vigilant. He frequently dissociated, lost the story of what happened, and verged on helplessness and hopelessness. He had to accept on blind faith that the group could be a protective holding environment. Harrison entered and left therapy four times over ten years, but was able to stay connected to the therapist. This bond made it possible for him to keep returning to the fight for himself and a meaning to his life. The psychodrama described below is an example of a chaos cycle of healing that occurred towards the end of Harrison's therapy.

In the healing cycle for chaos the Starting Point is clearly counter-intuitive. Many therapists would begin in a caring leader role, emphasizing gentleness and safety. Yet it is the director role, from which the leader challenges, questions, and generally controls the unfolding process that appears most effective. Coming from the nurturing quadrant (caring leader), the therapist would be out of attunement with the protagonist's half-life. Because of the dynamics of the half-life, nurturing is generally underdeveloped in PTSD clients, so it will not serve to dislodge them from their fright or call them back to their bodies. Typically, severe traumas cause dissociation and flight to the second quadrant. Because one of their strengths is to meet challenges, PTSD sufferers go on living as best they can, even when it is daily life itself that has become the challenge.

In this half-life, the third quadrant (mastery of challenges) becomes the strongest. Meeting the protagonists living a chaos myth in the quadrant of challenge, the director joins them in their strengths. The protagonist feels supported and perceives the Director as possessing power. Thus Harrison's work began with a challenge. One night in group, while sharing after someone else's work, Harrison told about a time that his father sent him to the store to get beer and cigarettes. He was ten, his daughter's age at the time of the drama. Harrison was in his Home Base, quadrant 2, so with great hilarity, he told the story of how he had come back with the wrong change and his father had popped him one, knocking him flat on his back. The director asked Harrison if he would be willing to watch something, and he agreed. Group members then played back the story he had just told and Harrison watched impassively. 'What's the point?' he asked.

The director then moved to the meaning attributor style and concretized the point. He instructed Harrison to watch again. In a second playback, the scene was repeated with one change. An auxiliary playing his daughter, Bernadette, replaced young Harrison. This time, when the father attempted to hit Bernadette, Harrison surged into action, enraged. He was stopped and the scene was quickly set up a third time, with little Harrison back in his place. Again, Harrison could not stand by. He rescued little Harrison and expressed appropriate anger directly towards his father for the first time in his life. After confronting his father he embraced little Harrison, holding and comforting him, expressing his commitment to taking over and caring for him, as he deserved.

In the closing phase of the psychodrama, Harrison crossed the threshold to the spring quadrant by reversing roles with little Harrison to receive the love, protection and commitment he himself had just created. The leader shifted to the caring leader style and encouraged the protagonist to take in the nurturance. The director, as caring leader, also cared for the group, facilitating the members' outpouring of nurturance and care for the protagonist or themselves. Some members had had similar traumatic experiences and the opportunities for healing that opened up for them were pursued as well. Because they have relied on the defence of dissociation, many people are quite unaware of abuses in their lives until witnessing someone else's work.

The group, identifying with the protagonist, walked the path from the second, to the third, through the fourth, to the first quadrant of the circle with Harrison, learning the same lessons of facing fear and finding meaningfulness, hope, and support. These structures for healing are more or less incorporated by each group member, the degree of incorporation depending upon the particular member's life experiences of traumatization and his or her current state of healing.

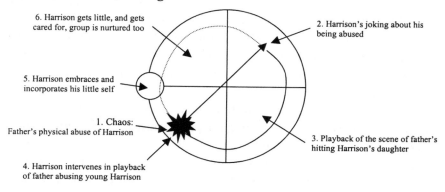

Figure 14.10: Harrison's chaos cycle of healing

This drama, one of the many over his ten-year course of therapy, proved to be the fulcrum upon which Harrison's healing turned. One evening while visiting his mother, his father became physically abusive toward her. In a flash, Harrison moved between them, ending up on the floor with his hands around his father's neck. Looking into his father's eyes, he began to weep, as did his father. Harrison had not actually harmed him. Harrison's deep conviction that he would one day kill his father was dislodged from his personal myth. Subsequently, Harrison took charge of his parents' situation, by finding a nursing home for his mother and helping his father adjust to his loss. As of this writing, two years after the drama, Harrison is on a journey with his father through the World War II battlefields of Europe. Harrison's father is returning to the scene of his own traumatization and self-part loss, and Harrison is helping him reclaim his wholeness. Father and son are being restored to one another at last.

Conclusions

The healing circle is a trauma model, not a symptom model. Various symptoms can be part of different traumatizations, confounding categories and schemas derived from symptoms. The essence of developmental trauma is in the meaning or story created to explain it. Depending on where the person is in their developmental cycle, any given trauma can be interpreted as an abandoning, betraying, disempowering, or chaotic event. This interpretation, a conclusion about reality drawn in the heat of surviving, forms the core of a personal mythology for living generated by each person. The quartered circle helps to identify the developmental trauma and corresponding mythology by clustering behaviours in meaningful patterns. The underlying simplicity of the personal myth and developmental trauma can be identified without sacrificing the complexity of each person's individual adaptation for survival. By determining the core trauma, the director or therapist can make interventions in the pattern of the half-life that create a path to wholeness.

In relation to psychodrama, differential directing allows the director to create effective warm-ups by joining the protagonist at the Starting Point of his or her cycle of healing. Shifting to the directorial style that matches the protagonist's Ground Zero process intensifies action. The catharsis is facilitated through the rite of passage between the season of trauma (Ground Zero) and the Doorway into the season of new possibilities.

According to Moreno (1951), the key to all action techniques is the warming up process. The healing circle model helps a director locate where the protagonist is stuck in the life cycle and what kind of warm-up is needed to begin an effective cycle of healing. A director can try different Starting Points if necessary, until arriving at the one that releases the spontaneity the protagonist requires to change. Thus the protagonist goes on a *walkabout*, leaving the familiar landscape of the personal mythology with its limitations and extending into new territory and potential wholeness.

References

Ames, L. B., Gillespie, C., Haines, J. and Ilg, F. (1979) *The Gesell Institute's Child from One to Six: Evaluating the Behavior of the Preschool Child.* New York: Harper and Row.

Carter, B. and McGoldrick, M. (1988) *The Changing Family Lifecycle.* New York: Garden Press.

Fromm, M. and Smith, B. (1989) (eds) *The Facilitating Environment: Clinical Applications of Winnecott's Theory.* Madison, Connecticut: International Universities Press.

Jernberg, A. (1979) *Theraplay.* San Francisco, CA: Jossey-Bass.

Jung, C.G. (1968) *Man and his Symbols.* New York: Dell.

Levin, P. (1988) *Cycles of Power.* Deerfield Beach, FL: Health Communications.

Levinson, D. (1978) *The Seasons of a Man's Life.* New York: Ballantine Books.

Lieberman, M.A., Yalom, I.D. and Miles, M.D. (1973) *Encounter Groups: First Facts.* New York: Basic Books.

Mahler, M., Pine, F. and Bergman, A. (1975) *The Psychological Birth of the Human Infant.* New York: Basic Books.

Miller, A. (1981) *Prisoners of Childhood.* New York: Basic Books.

Moreno, J.L. (1951) *Sociometry, Experimental Method and the Science of Society.* New York: Beacon House.

Moreno, J.L. and Moreno, Z.T. (1975) *Psychodrama, Volume 2.* New York: Beacon House.

Mosher, J. (1999) *The Cycle of Healing: Personal Myth, Complexity, Shamanic Psychodrama, and the Creation of Reality.* Unpublished manuscript.

Siegel, D. (1999) *The Developing Mind: Toward a Neurobiology of Interpersonal Experience.* New York: The Guilford Press.

van der Kolk, B.A. (1987) 'The separation cry and the trauma response: Developmental issues in the psychobiology of attachment and separation.' In B.A. van der Kolk (ed) *Psychological Trauma.* Washington, DC: American Psychiatric Press.

van der Kolk, B.A. and Greenberg, M. (1987) 'The psychobiology of the trauma response: Hyperarousal, constriction, and addiction to traumatic reexposure.' In B.A. van der Kolk (ed) *Psychological Trauma.* Washington, DC: American Psychiatric Press.

Warner, D. (1980) *Psychodrama Training Tips, II.* Unpublished manuscript.

PART 5

Breaking the Links

Transmission

CHAPTER 15

Health and Death
Hidden Links through the Family Tree[1]

Anne Ancelin Schützenberger

Could family patterns and problems, even traumas, be transmitted through generations as part of an invisible and unconscious, but very present, family inheritance? This is an unresolved debate over what is innate and what is acquired, which has been brought to a head by the recent development of transgenerational therapy.

Freud gave us the theory of the individual unconscious (Freud 1909), Jung the collective unconscious (Jung 1953), and Moreno the co-conscious and the co-unconscious of families and groups and we have co-discovered the anniversary syndrome and use extended family unconscious loyalties with transgenerational links.

A 'ventriloquist effect' and a 'family ghost' emerging from the 'crypt' to manifest either physically or psychically in order to be heard: this is how the psychoanalyst Nicolas Abraham sought to explain the cases of certain clients which did not correspond to a Freudian theoretical model (Abraham and Török 1978). It was as though someone else were speaking through the mouth of the patient who was in a way 'possessed' by this 'ghost' carrying a dark, hidden family secret. It was only through beginning to see, understand and disinter this secret through listening and 'holding' its manifestation that a cure could take place. Following the work of Hilgard (1989), Dolto (1971), Abraham and Török (1978), Boszormenyi-Nagy and Spark (1973), Volkan (1997) and Haley (1970), for 15 years now certain psychoanalysts and psy-

---

1   First published in *Caduceus 35*, 1997. Reproduced with the kind permission of the journal. Translated into English by Irina Kuzminskaya. Second part written directly in English by the author.

chotherapists across Europe and the USA have been working on both conscious (intergenerational) and unconscious (transgenerational) transmission. The latter may be manifested in physical, psychosomatic or psychiatric symptoms, which may express a family secret or problem or may be linked to what is known as the anniversary syndrome.

In simple terms, one instance of the anniversary syndrome would be for a similar symptom such as illness or traumatic separation to manifest itself in the descendant when he or she is of the same age as the ancestor was when a similar trauma occurred in the ancestor's life. The syndrome could also manifest itself through a link in dates or periods, so that particular symptoms such as nightmares or panic attacks will occur or begin in the same month as the original trauma sustained by an ancestor.

In 1961, the well-known psychologist and medical doctor, Joséphine Hilgard, demonstrated that in the case of adult psychosis there was a repetition of the same symptoms. For example they would be repeated when a daughter reached the age her mother was when she 'disappeared' (either through death or psychiatric internment), and when her own daughter (the third generation) reached the same age she herself was at the time of the traumatic loss of her mother.

The study, carried out on the admissions in a Veterans Administration Californian hospital over a four-year period, found this correlation to be statistically significant in cases involving mother and daughter, and frequent but not statistically significant in any other family relationship. This is an example of the working of the anniversary syndrome in psychiatry.

I have found the same mechanism in operation among certain cancer patients, in the case of accidents (going back three to five generations), and also in certain illnesses linked to the upper respiratory tract, such as bronchitis, asthma or tuberculosis. For example, patients will be 'coughing and spitting', reproducing the symptoms of a grandfather gassed in World War I at Ypres (1915) or at Verdun (1916) more than 80 years ago.

Such symptoms are a sign of 'unconscious family loyalty' and a 'symptom of the negative anniversary syndrome' which can occur in several children in the same family.

Barbara

An example of a war trauma being lived through by a descendant may be seen in the case of Barbara. Barbara had always asked herself why she had such a 'barbaric' sounding name which had not appeared previously in her family and which her classmates at her school in Normandy had always found odd.

And then, early one August, (at about the year of the commemorations of the end of the war and the entrance of the allied forces into Paris) she began to suffer from repeated nightmares, panic attacks and periods of insomnia which lasted until the beginning of September.

We began working first on the images in her nightmares and the timing, why they had started on 4 August specifically. Her nightmares were very detailed, almost of a photographic quality. In them, she could clearly see men wearing helmets pouring down the hills, dressed in grey with something pointed on their heads. 'The Prussians?' I suggested. She suddenly exclaimed, 'The Uhlans!' What she was seeing were the pointed helmets of the nineteenth century Prussian army.

We then worked on her family history and family tree and drew up a chart which I call a 'geno-sociogram' going back five generations: this is a family tree which shows the interrelationships of all members of a family, including all significant life events such as birth, marriage, separation, divorce, death, illnesses, accidents, and also studies, professions, displacements, such as moving and leaving one's home. The geno-sociogram allows the repetitions, the 'unconscious and invisible family loyalties' and cases of identification to come to light. Our research brought us to a family in the Ardennes to which Barbara was distantly related.

Having made contact, she visited them and found herself reliving vivid memories with her cousin of the war of 1870 and of the Sedan massacre of 1–2 September 1870 which occurred during the French war with Germany, Bismarck sending his Prussian troops against Napoleon III of France.

The trip brought Barbara to the ossuary at Flouing (near Sedan) and to the memory of the barbarous carnage which had taken place there: 25,000 dead, 83,000 taken prisoner, thousands of horses disembowelled, and that is without taking the civilian population into account. The basin of Sedan was flattened by 'cannon fodder' in the massacre so that the infantry could march straight across. Napoleon III could not bear what he saw and surrendered immediately.

The old memories having been revived and spoken of, and having duly mourned the past, Barbara was able to sleep normally again, her nightmares gone, although a certain remnant of pain remained. Barbara went on looking. She found out why the nightmares and the panic attacks had begun on 4 August. General MacMahon had lost the battle of Wissembourg on 4 August

1870, a battle in which several family members had taken part and one great uncle was wounded.

Even after this though, Barbara continued trying to revisit and understand her family's past.

For instance, when I asked her why she had bought a house in Normandy right near the sea, she replied: 'If the Prussians come, I shall take a boat and row to England.' But the war is over, I told her, and the Prussians from 1870 aren't about to give chase to her, and she does not have to relive the nightmarish horror of Jules, her great-grandfather, who, at the age of six, had witnessed the Sedan massacre while hidden underneath a tree, clutching the hand of his own grandfather and not daring to make a sound for fear of being killed himself.

We acted in a psychodramatic vignette the battle of Sedan with Barbara (in a role-reversal) playing the role of Jules as a six-year-old child. Jules was her great grandfather, and we hoped this would give her a real catharsis of the past.

Barbara seemed to have inherited a deep-seated fear of the 'barbarians', becoming herself a 'crypt' in which the unexpressed anguish of this suffering and these deaths had been buried over a hundred years ago for four generations. To understand the workings of this fear we worked historically, going through dates and places, particularly those linked to French and Allied defeats, from 1870 till the present. Many of these turned out to be linked to the beginning of August and of September, with Sedan figuring prominently again during World War I and especially World War II when history was repeated as the Germans invaded through Sedan, forcing the French surrender and the English evacuation at Dunkirk (1940).

Creating a geno-sociogram

The geno-sociogram is a family tree reaching back three to five generations, done initially from memory, although the search may be widened to historical records. Included are all important life events: marriages, births, deaths, separations, serious illnesses, accidents, studies (level and qualifications obtained), professions, places of residence, moving house, break-ups and losses, departures to distant places (it is a mixture of family tree and family social atom).

This allows our life scripts, our personal and professional choices and our emotional ties to be seen in the light of our conscious and unconscious family heritage.

It is a way of bringing to light the real story (often concealed) of our family over several generations: the denied family secrets, the unsaid, the repetitions which take place (sometimes useful but often harmful or even fatal), the prescribed roles (such as invalid and nurse), the traumas linked to unjust deaths, the child who takes on a trauma, the family myths and legends, certain important dates, the 'anniversary syndrome' (death, loss, success), the year or period when we are most susceptible (whether chronological age or calendar date).

There are multiple possible applications of the geno-sociogram in therapy, medicine, surgery, upbringing, education, health, in the caring professions and for our own personal or professional development.

It can be crucial in surgery for its use can often avoid complications during and after an operation, and also in schooling to avoid unnecessary failures.

In many cases, the skill of an experienced guide or therapist may be needed to 'spark' our recall of a sequence of connections.

The effect of therapy

There are many other cases in which past family traumas linked to particularly inhuman massacres and wars return to haunt a descendant (such as Ypres and nerve gas, 1915; Verdun 1916, with almost a million dead; trench warfare; the genocide of the Armenians by the Turks with two million massacred in 1915; the Jewish Holocaust, the Khmers, the Kurds and countless others).

If a trauma has not been sufficiently spoken of, acknowledged and expressed at the time of its occurrence, traces of it will remain to surface in the family even 50 or 100 years later. It is as though the family line incorporates the unexpressed horror of it to be imprinted on a descendant.

The spoken word, which is heard and properly held by a 'containing' person within a therapeutic context such as a psychodrama or group therapy session, can have the effect of freeing the individual from memories imprinted on the psyche. Speaking, crying, shouting, even hitting out from a sense of rage, hate and powerlessness are all important as they act to unblock mental structures and patterns thus preventing the conversion of psychic disturbances into somatic symptoms.

However, there are times when this is not sufficient and when there is a need for justice to be done – or at least the demand for justice to be articulated, for it is some form of reparation to have facts, wrongs and injustices recognized and not denied. That is why, for instance, it was so important for the Armenians that the genocide of their people by the Turks should be acknowledged, even 50 years after it took place.

The cold reach of the guillotine (French Revolution, 1793)

A psychotherapist consulted me after having undergone many years of throat therapy as well as psychoanalysis. Her concern for the future focused on her responsibility for her disabled younger brother François who had been dependent on her since the death of their parents. She explained that her brother was disabled after an attack of croup at the age of six months. Two throat problems: I hypothesised a connection with the gas attacks of Verdun. And indeed this was correct: her mother's father had been gassed, 'coughing and spitting', at Verdun in 1915. Having made this connection, she felt better and her breathing improved.

But something in her non-verbal communication – hand held to her throat, her short red necklace, her birth in January, her attacks of freezing coldness, similar to Reynaud's syndrome – I associated with the French Revolution and the guillotine. She denied any knowledge of such a connection, but on a hunch I insisted that she investigate this possibility further.

Returning home, she did a computerized search for her grandmother's birth certificate at her birthplace in the Vendée. By chance, or serendipity, the computer also produced a long family history and, to her shock, a picture of a guillotine with the names of five ancestors who were guillotined in 1793, and one named François, guillotined on 9 January 1793. Her brother François who was later disabled was born on 9 January 1963.

With the shock also came a sensation of release in her throat. At her next appointment with her consultant she insisted on a full examination, which revealed a striking change: her throat, which had been constricted 'permanently' since birth, was now open and normal. The consultant could offer no medical explanation for this transformation.

Three months later she reported being well, except for some terrible attacks of cold.

We looked up the battles which had taken place in the Vendée during the French Revolution, and found that one had taken place on 6 June. This was the date on which six-month old Francois had had the attack of croup which had left him disabled. We discussed the horrors of war, and the deaths. At this, the temperature of her body came back to normal.

In the past five years, I have seen about 20 similar cases of people presenting with throat problems and some dozen with Reynaud's syndrome.

Figure 15.1

The small child with asthma

Following on from a supervision training session for therapists, a young woman doctor told me that 'by the way' her four-year-old daughter had been having anxiety attacks bringing on asthma every night from the time she was born. She would wake up coughing and screaming. I asked her when she was born. The answer was 26 April 1991. I immediately thought of World War I: Gallippoli was on 25 April, whereas the Germans had first used toxic gas on the troops on 22 April. 'Do you have family at Ypres or Verdun?' I asked her. She did not know about Ypres, but Verdun was only some 20 kilometres from where her grandparents lived. A month later she was back, smiling. 'Thank you. It's a miracle, but since last time my daughter has not had any more

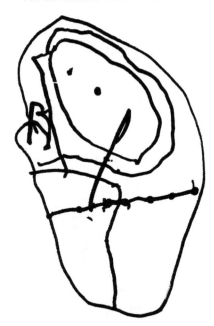

Figure 15.2

attacks, she doesn't wake up, doesn't cough … except for last night. And I did have family wounded at Ypres.' She had found that out in the Army archives.

I suggested then that she ask the little girl to draw. The mother brought along the drawing to show us. The little girl said: 'It's a diving mask with an elephant's trunk: this is the monster that has been scaring me at night.' The drawing looked like a gas mask from World War I (See Figure 15.1).

Going through the archives, the mother discovered that her grandfather's brother had been gassed and wounded at Ypres on 26 April 1915 and that her grandfather had been wounded at Verdun. The little girl has not had any nightmares now for the last two years. The coughing and the asthma attacks have also ceased. She still draws though, including things that frighten her. Figure 15.2 shows another one of her drawings, this one related to the amniocentesis her mother had had while pregnant with her. Children really are aware of everything even from before their birth and they express it, if only one really pays attention to them.

It is worth pointing out that war gases have the effect of impeding the functioning of respiratory muscles producing the same symptoms in casualties as those suffered by patients with croup, false croup, diphtheria and sometimes asthma. Following on from the recent research on the link between breathing difficulties and traumas sustained during war we encountered dozens of cases of it among the descendants of those gassed at Verdun whose symptoms either disappeared completely or showed a marked improvement when the link was made conscious.

My own working hypothesis is that when something horrifying is witnessed, often survivors do not dare to speak of it but keep the images they have seen in their mind's eye and in their heart. It is this trauma of the brush with death ('traumatisme de vent de boulet' – 'wind of the deadly cannon ball') which has shaken them to the point at which something is transmitted to their grandchildren and their great grandchildren with photographic clarity of images, and sometimes even the sensations of cold and smell.

How this occurs – whether through the shock reaching the DNA and some sort of subsequent genetic transformation, or through other somatic family links – is a subject which is at present under scientific investigation. For example, Rachel Yehuda *et al.* (1998) from the USA have found that low cortisol levels in the offspring of Holocaust survivors was associated with the tendency of these individuals to indicate distress about the trauma of the Holocaust, and to have PTSD symptoms in response to Holocaust-related events that they heard about.

Family history: two street deaths, same date, and fifty years apart

Recently a young woman came to me who was feeling guilty for the death of her sister who was trying out her new bicycle in a side street when she collided with a car. The accident was fatal and the other sister was so horrified that she lost her voice and was unable to cry for help. This accident took place on the 24 August about three years ago. The victim bled to death on the street and was revived so that her organs could be saved. The official date of her death was 25 August. It was such a shocking death that I felt that there had to be another similar death in the family.

We did research on the family tree, finding only that her father had almost drowned while staying with an uncle who was a parish priest. This uncle had died several years later, shot by the Nazis during the war. After making enquiries it turned out that the date of his death was 24 August 1944. She also found out that this great-uncle had been shot while attending to a young man who had died in the mountains. Being hard of hearing he had not heard the Germans' warning that if anyone touched this young man, they would shoot the entire village. The wounded priest was similarly left to die in the street, lingering for 24 hours. The correlation of dates was astounding: 24–25 August 1944, 24–25 August 1994.

It is interesting to see the extent to which the family reproduces the ages of marriage, procreation and death, the number of children, miscarriages, accidents and fatal accidents.

For three years now I have been doing precise research on traumas and on physical illnesses linked to grandparents who had died in tragic circumstances – in the war, by drowning, or in car accidents – and my own conclusion is that there is such a thing as 'unconscious family repetitions' and the 'anniversary syndrome'.

The Kennedy family anniversary

You could almost say that President John (Jack) Kennedy (1917–1963) contributed to his own assassination on 22 November 1963 by leaving the top of his car down during the motorcade even though he had been warned of the probable dangers of his journey. His own grandfather on his father's side, Patrick Kennedy (born 1858), had been orphaned at the age of six months, his father, also a Patrick (1823–1858), dying at the age of 35 on 22 November 1858. The father's death created many difficulties for the family at the time and it is unlikely that such an important date, 22 November, would have been unknown to the descendants, but not conscious.

Operations and the 'anniversary syndrome'

Another way in which the anniversary syndrome manifests itself is in the surprising number of operations which are fixed 'by chance' by the patient on an 'anniversary date' in the family, such as a birth, marriage or death.

A significant number of people 'choose' to have their operation on the anniversary of the death of their parents or grandparents. Not surprisingly, they often experience extreme anxiety before their operation and complications during and after. Research has been conducted on this at the hospital in Brest and at the University Hospital in Sherbrooke in Canada.

There, once the operation date was fixed, every person was questioned as to whether that date coincided with a family anniversary and if it did, the operation was rescheduled for another date. The dates did coincide a surprising number of times. And Ghislain Devroede, Professor of Surgery at Sherbrooke University, also found that once they had started to do this the incidence of post-operative complications decreased, as did the amount of anaesthetic required to operate – by 50 per cent! These are very significant findings and an important application of the anniversary syndrome.

Social class neurosis

In a different field, the sociologist Vincent de Gaulejac has given the name of 'social class neurosis' to the failures of brilliant students to pass an exam to gain a qualification that their parents do not have. He found that the parents were often putting their children into an impossible 'double bind', namely: 'don't be like me, finish your studies, I've sacrificed everything for you' – and, at the same time – 'don't leave me, don't leave your class and family background, do as I did'. The result was that the students would often unconsciously set themselves up to fail. Exposing this neurosis helps people to understand the double message their parents are sending them and the difficulty of doing better than the class they were born into. A lot of blame has been put on economic conditions for preventing certain social classes from sending their children to university.

However, Vincent de Gaulejac's theory permits us to understand better the complexities of ascending the social ladder and acquiring culture and learning. It is important to realize just how awkward it can be for children to be different from their parents, and also why therapists and especially teachers should help students to continue to feel linked to their own class background and thus to be able to fulfil their intellectual, scientific, cultural and artistic potential while not cutting themselves off from their families. Now that we have observed the problems of the third generation down of groups such as immigrants, miners, railwaymen, workers, because of loss of social background through access to learning, it is conceivably our joint collective responsibility to help the youngest generation to achieve its potential without too much psychological damage.

Clearly, in all these cases, a therapeutic situation or practice such as group analysis, psychodrama or drawing is often highly effective, bringing on catharsis and realization. However, the core of the cure is in the listening, the sense that the problem or trauma has been deposited with someone who listens (similar to Winnicott's 'holding', Winnicott 1965), hears and understands, supplementing that which is said through his or her own experience, knowledge and intuition.

The secret, the unspeakable trauma, is now deposited and contained within a tolerant and supportive context. It is vital that the message should be emitted, transmitted and received, thus heard and comprehended by the 'other,' often, though not necessarily, within a therapeutic situation.

Trauma and psychodrama vignettes

I often use short psychodrama vignettes of some 3 to 10 minutes to relive past family traumas (especially war traumas) and close 'unfinished business' of grief about losses and dramatic death.

I have worked a little with Roy Hart in Tokyo on his use of voice, shouting and singing, following Alfred Wohlfsohn's method of voice therapy. I used it for short psychodrama vignettes about intolerable sufferings of human beings and animals (especially horses and dogs) being killed in terror in wars. For memory's sake: Alfred Wohlfson could not bear the horrible sounds of hundreds of dying people in the trenches (suffocating in the mud, from wounds or from toxic gas at Ypres and Verdun) and battles of World War I and he developed a strong voice method of exploring it, and curing himself of these horrid memories, especially of cries and unearthly sounds that provoked what he called 'oral hallucinations' and that seem to be vivid, 'quasi-photographic-video' memories, with smells, sounds, heat or cold and strong moving images. Together with some other colleges in Europe and America, I actually found such memories in the nightmares of clients, especially since the commemorations of the end of the war and end of the liberation of concentration camps, and D-Day (débarquement in Normandy, 6 June 1944).

Psychodrama with traumas and post-war traumas

We use classical psychodrama and classical techniques in working through post-war traumatization, but mainly short psychodramatic vignettes. For example, acting out on stage a battle, or parts of it, with soldiers, cannons, auxiliary ego horses, friends and foes, dead and dying buddies, noise of bombs and cries of agony of dying people and horses (and of course, role reversals with these). We then add very short vignettes of surplus reality; symbolic 'good-byes' with them and also 'burials' for beloved buddies and parents.

One of the strong points is to ask the 'dead and dying' person, in role reversal, what he or she wants or needs in order to find peace. We urge the protagonist to listen to that message and to do it in psychodrama and sometimes in symbolic reality, or even in reality. It is a way to search for catharsis in the role reversal and to find closure of the tensions and symbolic reparations.

For example, the 'dead' (protagonist in role-reversal) could ask 'not to be forgotten' or to have a rose tree planted in the cemetery, or flowers thrown in the river or the sea (for people killed in the war at sea), or name a child after me, or sing a lullaby (for dead child aborted or killed).

I remember working in a demonstration workshop in Germany at a family therapy congress with a childless woman on the stage, until we came to a moment when she spoke of all the soldiers in her family, for generations back. With short vignettes of one to two minutes each, we went back in time, until we came to the Crusades. Then, on a hunch, I quoted a Muslim writer writing of crusaders hurting and killing Muslim children by taking them by the feet and crushing their heads on the city walls. She started to shout and cry then, and, after a short role reversal with a dead Muslim baby (dead a thousand years ago – the crusades took place from 1096 to 1270) she asked for a Muslim lullaby to be sung for her to be in peace. Of course, I do not speak Arabic, so I asked the audience and luckily there was a Muslim midwife in the audience who could sing a traditional Muslim lullaby and we all sang it together. After that, colour and peace appeared in her eyes. We all felt this was the closure of a very long past family transgenerational culpability that found here a completion that could permit peace of mind and peace of body, and a quiet 'turning of the page'. I prefer that term to 'wiping the slate clean' and to the 'symbolic reparations' of past traumas.

I use the same method for accidental deaths, miscarriages, and 'final fare-wells' with parents (who sometimes died without a goodbye or last message). In addition, they can be used in traumatic loss in wars, such as Sedan (1870), Verdun (1915–1916), Gallipoli (1915), the Jewish Holocaust or Armenian genocide, in the D-day disembarcation (6 June 1944), or during the retreat of armies or prisoners of war, or deported displaced persons. The same methods can also be used in the traumatic loss of a child, or beloved cat, dog, sheep or whatever, even before surgery and future loss of a limb or a breast (that has to be removed because of cancer) or other body part to be taken away. Such leave-taking rituals always help to calm the person and permit a more peaceful separation from the departed.

In our experience, the trauma is the same for the family of the killed, the family of the killer, or the family of the bystander witness (often a kind person or a friend of the dead or the wounded) who was 'brushed by the cold wind of death' ('traumatisme de vent de boulet', as it was called by the surgeons of Emperor Napoleon during the terrible retreat from Russia in 1812).

Zeigarnik effect (unfinished tasks)

In 1928, at the Berlin Institute of Psychology, Bluma Zeigarnik (still living in Moscow in 1980) worked with Kurt Lewin (gestalt theory and group-dynamics research) on finished and unfinished tasks. She demonstrated that 'unfinished tasks' (interrupted tasks that were thus left uncompleted) keep working in the mind and remain in our memories, while 'finished tasks' are stored in memory somewhere and forgotten in present lives.

I use the Zeigarnik effect theory to work with cancer patients, with their stresses and past personal, professional and family traumas, as well as 'injustices' done to them. These trigger enough worries to prevent them being in peace and able to relax. Instead they are full of stress, aggression, and anxiety. Making the connection to the unfinished tasks helps them to start working on their health problems and get much better, and often to get well completely (as in Carl and Stephanie Simonton's 'Getting Well Again', Simonton, Simonton and Creighton 1978).

I have felt that a similar process to the Zeigarnik effect of the tensions of unfinished tasks is at work with family secrets, tragic deaths or unspeakable war traumas, even generations back, in which mourning was impossible. In all such past traumas, I look at the transgenerational patterns both in traumatization and in psychosomatic and in somato-psychic illnesses that are related to this phenomenon. Thus the Zeigarnik effects and tensions from the past and hidden stresses explain for me many of the problems of 'unfinished business' with death and dying, actual unresolved fright of death, and family traumas and post-war traumas.

Conclusion

In classical or modern psychoanalysis, only the person himself is under investigation, his experiences, failings, suffering and traumas. However, in the transgenerational approach, we are concerned not only with the 'client', but with the whole cultural and family milieu which forms the framework within which the individual story unfolds.

But this work is also a family novel encompassing three to eight generations, tracing and analysing certain paths taken. A case in point was the marriage of a French-Canadian nurse Renée to a Frenchman on 28 August 1971, ten generations after her ancestor Françoise married a man called René on 28 August 1728.

Doing this kind of work allows each subject to see how their own individual path is determined by the paths of other significant members of their family, and shows to what extent the individual is the product of a family history of which they seek to become the subject. Thus the choices made and the traumas lived by the subject are determined from the start by their family's and ancestors' choices and their unfinished, unspoken traumas.

The anniversary syndrome and its effects – a kind of repetition of the same – can sometimes be clinically stopped, as I have explained. The recent chaos theory and discovery of the fractals (Mandelbrot) might open research into such infinite repetitions of the same.

Life, education, upbringing, personal development groups, psychotherapy – it is all part of a process of 'becoming'.

The 'subject' is born, grows up while appropriating her or his family history and also differentiates him or herself from parents and grandparents and from their problems, secrets and traumas. The person matures, becoming free to *be*, and to be oneself.

References

Abraham, N. and Török, M. (1978) *L'Ecorce et le Noyau*. Paris: Aubier Flammarion (Translated 1994) *The Shell and the Kernel*. Chicago, IL: Chicago University Press.

Ancelin Schützenberger, A. (1998) *The Ancestor Syndrome*. London and New York: Routledge.

Ancelin Schützenberger, A. (1991) 'The drama of the seriously ill patient: Fifteen years of experience with psychodrama and cancer.' In P. Holmes and M. Karp (eds) *Psychodrama: Inspiration and Technique*. London and New York: Routledge.

Ancelin Schützenberger, A. (1966) *Précis de Psychodrame*. Paris: Editions Universitaires. Enlarged edition 1970.

Ancelin Schützenberger, A. (1992) *Le Jeu de Rôle et le Psychodrame*. Paris: ESF.

Ancelin Schützenberger, A. (1993) *Aïe, mes Aieux, Liens Transgénérationnels, Secrets de Famille, Syndrome d'Anniversaire, Transmission des Traumatismes, et Pratique du Genosociogramme*. Paris: DDB (Enlarged edition 2000).

Ancelin Schützenberger, A. (1985) *Vouloir Guérir*. Paris: La Méridienne et DDB. (Enlarged edition 1997).

Ancelin Schützenberger, A. (1998) 'Epilogue.' In M. Karp, P. Holmes and K. Bradshaw Tauvon (eds) *The Handbook of Psychodrama*. London: Routledge.

Ancelin Schützenberger, A. (1999) 'De génération en génération, liens transgénérationnels.' In H. Calgar (ed) *Être Enseignant, Hommage à Ada Abraham*. Paris: l'Harmattan.

Ansky, A. (1917) *The Dybbuk: 'a play for Stanislavski's St. Petersburg Theater'*. (New edition 1992.) New York: Schocken Books.

Boszormenyi-Nagy, I. and Spark, G. (1973) *Invisible Loyalties*. New York: Harper and Row.

Cyrulnik, B. (1999) *Un Merveilleux Malheur*. Paris: Odile Jacob.

Dolto, F. (1971) *Le Cas Dominique*. Paris: Le Seuil. Personal communication 1955–1980.

Devroede, G. and Ancelin Schützenberger, A. (2000) 'On family trauma repetitions of sexual abuse and gastric problems.' Forthcoming publication.

Freud, S. (1909) *Family Romance. The Complete Psychological works of Sigmund Freud, Volume 5*. London: Hogarth Press, 1953.

Gaulejac, V. de (1987) *La Nevrose de Classe*. Paris: Hommes et Groupes.

Haley, A. (1970) *Roots*. London: Picador.

Hilgard, J. (1989) 'The anniversary syndrome as related to late appearing mental illness in hospitalised patients.' In S. Silvert (ed) *Psychoanalysis and Psychosis*. New York: International University Press.

Hudgins, K. and Drucker, K. (1998) 'The containing double as part of the therapeutic spiral model for treating trauma survivors.' *The International Journal of Action Methods, Skill Training and Role Playing 51*, 63–74.

Jung, C. (1953) *Collected Works*. New York: Bollinger Series, Pantheon Books.

Kipper, D. (1998) 'Psychodrama and trauma.' *The International Journal of Action Methods, Skill Training and Role Playing 51*, 112–121.

Maloof, A. (1988) *Les Croisades Vues par Muselmans*. (Crusades seen by Muslims.) Paris: Lattes.

Mandelbrot, B.B (1975) *Les Objects Fractals*. Paris: Flammarion.

Mandelbrot, B.B (1982) *The Fractal Geometry of Nature*. New York: Freeman.

Mandelbrot, B.B (1997) *Fractals, Hasards et Finances*. Paris: Flammarion.

Moreno, J.L. (1939) 'Psychodramatic shock therapy.' *Sociometry 2*, monograph number 5.

Moreno, J.L. (1946) *Psychodrama, Volume 1*. Beacon, NY: Beacon House.

Moreno, J.L. and Moreno, Z.T. (1969) *Psychodrama, Volume 3*. Beacon, NY: Beacon House.

Pikes, N. (2000) *Dark Voices: The Genesis of Roy Hart Theatre*. Woodstock, Connecticut: Spring Journal Books.

Simonton, C.O., Simonton, M.S. and Creighton, J. (1978) *Getting Well Again*. LA: Tolcher.

van der Kolk, B.A., McFarlane, A.C. and Weisaeth, L. (eds) *Traumatic Stress: The Effects of Overwhelming Experience on Mind, Body, and Society*. New York: Guilford Press.

Volkan, V. (1997) *Bloodlines: From Ethnic Pride to Ethnic Terrorism*. New York: Fahrar, Straus and Giroud.

Winnicott, D.W. (1965) *The Maturational Process and the Facilitating Environment*. New York: International Universities Press.

Zaijde, N. (1993) *Souffle sur Tous ces Morts et qu'ils Revivent*. Paris: La Pensée Sauvage.

Yehuda, R., Schmeidler, J., Elkin, A., Houshmand, E., Siever, L., Binder-Brynes, K., Wainberg, M., Aferiot, D., Lehman, A., Song Guo, L. and Kwei Yang, R. (1998) 'Phenomenology and psychobiology of the intergenerational response to trauma.' In Y. Danieli (ed) *International Handbook of Multigenerational Legacies of Trauma*. New York and London: Plenum.

CHAPTER 16

Psychodrama with Vietnam Veterans and their Families:

Both Victims of Traumatic Stress

Michael Burge

There has been much written about the effects of the Vietnam war on veterans, especially on the development of post-traumatic stress disorder. However, there has been less attention given to parallel trauma experienced by the veterans' families. Of particular note is the struggle for intimacy.

This chapter is primarily about my experiences counselling Vietnam veterans and their families. I will discuss the ways in which the Vietnam veteran's post-traumatic stress (PTSD) may infiltrate all of his family members' lives. I also attempt to demonstrate the way psychodrama, and in particular role analysis, role training, role development and role theory, can be used for the diagnosis and treatment of post-traumatic stress.

The literature

In order to maximize creativity and originality, I deliberately avoided extensive reading prior to the instigation of new psychodramatic methods in my work. My attitude to the literature is that of an explorer. My role is like that of Christopher Columbus setting out on the adventure of psychotherapy from the good spirit of psychodrama training to the literature in search of solutions and positive outcomes.

The experience in training in relation to experience generated in the provision of psychotherapy has been a flowing transition due to the overall spontaneity created. The roles of naive inquirer and systems analyst often emerge within the protagonist as I as director express these roles. For example, the role of naive inquirer assists me in becoming more spontaneous and that, in turn, assists the expression of the client's healthy roles. Spontaneity underpins all the roles and assists me to be fully in role. Reflections on my psychodrama training, presenting situations in training, and reading relevant literature are all great resources for assisting me to be more creative in discovering solutions.

In terms of reading that has been helpful for the understanding of psychodrama, I have found the following literature relevant: Moreno (1964) indicated that protagonist intra-psychic conflict can be resolved by increasing healthy roles; Williams (1989) applied this to family therapy and reported how a protagonist gets another view of the problem through interview techniques. This is particularly evident in his chapter on the systemic value of roles. For instance, a helpless child diminishes further in the face of a cruel teacher but is strengthened when the conflict or problem is viewed from the role of the supportive and protective mother.

For enhancing my understanding of role theory and practice, I found Clayton's (1993) book, *Living Pictures of the Self*, instrumental. The *Building of a Healthy Group Culture: A Psychodramatic Intervention*, by Daniel (1992), provided another useful perspective of role development, including a helpful summary of techniques and diagrams that show ways of maintaining group trust and spontaneity. Beattie (1987) put forward a useful model that demonstrates how unhealthy roles, such as rescuer, can lead to the development of similar trauma symptoms in the veteran's family.

Rosenheck (1985) described a condition that he calls 'secondary post-traumatic stress'. In one case study of a ten-year-old boy called Alan, Rosenheck noted that the boy was exhibiting a range of symptoms indicative of post-traumatic stress. Alan had difficulty sleeping, poor concentration and had frequent headaches. He was also tense and confused with numerous fears and violent behaviour in which he threatened to kill his younger brother. When he went to sleep he was worried about being killed or kidnapped. His main fear was that he would be shot as those in the war had been shot. The conclusion was that the child had gained these secondary trauma symptoms through exposure to his veteran father's reliving of the war trauma. That is, through identification and from deep involvement and preoccupation in the emotional experience of his father there was a deficiency in the child's own boundaries. Similar symptoms are reported to exist also in children of Holocaust survivors. Rosenheck (1985) also mentioned that treatment was focused on helping the boy to disentangle his own experiences from that of his father and to gain his father's approval by doing well at school rather than imitating his father's preoccupation with Vietnam and with violent behaviour.

In an extension of Rosenheck's work, Harkness (1993) investigated transgenerational transmission of war-related trauma. He reported that the impact of the father's PTSD on the second generation is contingent on how the family handles the situation. In terms of transgenerational treatment strategies, Harkness recommended considering the impact of social supports, poor familial communication skills, early childhood abuse and, in particular, preventative programmes. He considered it important to assess the family system's ability to cope as soon as possible after the traumatized veteran was reunited with his family. It is important to create a safe intervention environment, establish a 'no-violence' contract, strengthen the ego-functions of the children and teach new ways to overcome old problems.

In terms of works that reaffirm the value of psychodrama for the treatment of PTSD, Fantal (1945) provided several case descriptions whereby through psychodramatic enactment, including role reversals, the patients developed less fearful war memories. In addition, Fantal (1951) demonstrated how a soldier's civilian social atom could be taken over by his army social atom. Finally, Baumgartner (1986) indicated that sociodrama was a useful method when first treating Vietnam veterans. The method was found to help Vietnam veterans grieve the death of their buddies, improve their relationships and ventilate angry feelings connected to abuse perpetrated by the public after the war.

Shortly after the end of the Vietnam War there was a growing number of clinical descriptive reports about the unique experience of Vietnam veterans and their readjustment. Problems reported included isolation, rage, grief, blame reactions, anxiety, fear, psychic numbing and disruptive family relationships (Williams 1980). More recent research focused on the aetiology of the adjustment problems yielding significant associations between PTSD and co-existing problems such as depression, anxiety and substance abuse (Wilson 1989).

The above literature helped me to provide context and answers to questions that emerged in the application of psychodramatic methods to families suffering from trauma, and helped, in particular with the many alternatives that can be created to overcome fragmented experience.

Victims of post-traumatic stress

In terms of role theory, the essential premise is that individuals who have been traumatized can recover by tapping into and enhancing their creative and spontaneous resources, with the recognition, learning and expansion of healthy life-giving roles. The complementary nature of roles serves this purpose. That is, a role cannot exist in a vacuum; it must essentially have a positive or negative relationship with another role, such as a nurse and a patient, a teacher and a student, or a performer and an audience. The complementary nature of roles also exists within an individual's psychic system and is constantly engaging in 'self-talk', for example, a role that is encouraging versus a role that is criticizing.

As a result, during the course of intervention a therapist can assume and enact a range of roles, such as fellow explorer, supportive companion and protective coach, with the likelihood that complementary positive roles will be developed in the client. These roles provide the client with experience of power, safety, creativity, dignity, control, meaning, containment, emotional release and harmony. This experience is most often the opposite of traumatic experience and therefore forms an important part of the healing process. However, before focusing on these research and treatment issues, a brief discussion of the symptoms of post-traumatic stress disorder (PTSD) is warranted.

The most common symptoms experienced by Vietnam veterans are nightmares, flashbacks, intrusive thoughts and images, depression, anxiety, startle response, aggressive outbursts, irritability, difficulty sleeping, difficulty with intimacy and withdrawal. These PTSD characteristics could extend to the wives and children of the veteran. For instance, children often exhibit symptoms of depression, anxiety, poor self-esteem, powerlessness and behaviour difficulties. The absence of intimacy or emotional responsiveness from the traumatized veteran may leave the child feeling unloved or unwanted, or contribute to the child's depression, emotional numbness, despair or self-blame. The veteran's rages, nightmares, flash-backs, hyper-vigilance, and startle responses are more likely to lead to the child experiencing fear, anxiety, vigilance, startle responses, nightmares, and emotional isolation. That is, the child may develop a pattern of complementary PTSD symptoms to those patterns exhibited by the veteran.

There are many factors that make it difficult for the traumatized Vietnam veteran to develop intimacy with his family. First, associated with the symptoms of post-traumatic stress is fear of vulnerability or fear of being unsafe. That is, there may be concern about the risk to one's own or one's family's or friends' lives, but there is also the fear of overwhelming emotions. For example, Vietnam veterans often have memories of grief and feelings about the loss of their mates that they attempt not to re-experience. Moreover, because of the many supportive experiences among Vietnam veterans, including recruitment conditioning, the protection of the fellow soldier's life is very much akin to the protection of his own life. This can sometimes lead to over-protection of the family in later years.

Given the close bond to his fellow soldiers, the identity of the group may become incorporated in the individual soldier's intrapsychic role-system. The loss of mates and the fracture of the group identity could lead to the fractured self-identity of the soldier. The experience of the fractured identity together with the general loss can make the transition into a traumatized state rapid and enduring. If the veteran has limited coping skills and a restricted internal framework there may be too many emotions and experiences with which to deal. This has direct implications for the traumatized person's family. The veteran faces the dilemma that if he were to be vulnerable enough openly to experience intimacy, the feelings generated might open the pro-verbial 'Pandora's Box' of non-experienced and blocked emotions related to his trauma, including the unresolved grief for himself and his lost mates. In simple words, 'to risk loving is to risk losing' and as a consequence, to risk even greater disintegration of the identity.

For the Vietnam veteran in particular, although not exclusively for other types of trauma victims, the impact of unresolved family-of-origin issues and events after the war contributes to the endurance of trauma symptoms, such as poor intimacy or family enmeshment. These systemic factors are deep and complex. The patterns of withdrawal will often impinge upon the trauma survivor's capacity to recover from the trauma. After the war, many Vietnam veterans had experiences that made their traumatic conditions worse or created the traumatic condition. These experiences contributed to or created their physical and emotional withdrawal. For example, on returning home from the war, Vietnam veterans were frequently treated very poorly by the public, government and even by their own families. Rather than being welcomed home and celebrated as heroes, as warriors have been for thousands of years, they were ostracized and often stigmatized. Moreover, in many instances the partners and parents did not or could not listen to any stories about the Vietnam War, thus leaving veterans locked in their misery of unresolved grief. There was no professional debriefing and little or no family and community support. Instead, they were abandoned. The few veterans who managed to receive family and community support report that they experienced better recovery, adaptation and integration into the family and the community.

In my practice I have noted that for wives and partners of Vietnam veterans, their direct involvement with the veteran while he experiences these symptoms can be highly distressing. Frequently they report being mistaken for the enemy during their husband's nightmares and flashbacks. Sometimes the veteran, believing he was in a battle or war zone, gripped the wife's throat. Often, veterans would be in a state of numbness and then snap into aggressive outbursts with little or no provocation from their partner. In an endeavour to minimize the veterans' outbursts or mood changes, partners would spend much time focusing on the veterans' problems at the expense of their own needs. Consequently, these partners frequently became depressed, anxious or had poor self-esteem, manifesting the symptoms of secondary victimization.

Such partners of Vietnam veterans would telephone the counselling service seeking information on how to handle the veterans. Often they were desperate, indicating that they felt responsible for the veterans' problems. While some women were on the verge of leaving the relationship, others wanted couples counselling. Still others reported that they wanted to leave the marriage, but were afraid to do so for various reasons. The common factor in all such cries for help was that the family relationships were under great stress.

Due to the veteran's PTSD and inability to function, many partners live in an uncertain and fearful situation and have to bear the full burden of running the family. In addition to the feeling of the partner that she has lost her supportive husband, the veteran himself feels that his traditional role as husband and provider has been severely compromised. This exacerbates the distress and difficulties and resentments between the couple and within the whole family, which fester.

A useful model for conceptualizing and treating some of these couple and family difficulties is that of 'co-dependency'. In her book *Co-Dependent No More*, Beattie (1987) describes how wives could become so absorbed in their husband's plight that they neglected their own psychological problems or personal growth. The veteran's dependence provides his wife with plenty of opportunity to administer apparent control, rather than dealing with her own fear of losing self-control. 'Apparent' control emphasizes the volatile nature of PTSD and means less control in the family, more likely uncertainty and trepidation. In short, there is sense of control but not the real thing. Having been exposed to the distress of the veteran's trauma for many years, the wife thus develops co-dependency. I have discovered through my counselling practice that family of origin roles seems to be an important factor in this development.

The existence of these old roles can lead to the initial attraction between the veteran and a potential partner. For instance, the veteran who is helpless and fearful can choose a partner who has a need to play the role of rescuer, problem-solver, 'Mrs Fix It', warden or psychiatric nurse. In the process, the veteran may become increasingly helpless or the partner may, through numerous failed attempts at helping, become very helpless and victimized. Therefore, she may finally be the one who seeks rescuing. In some instances, there can be a rotation of these role states between the veteran and his partner (see Figure 16.1).

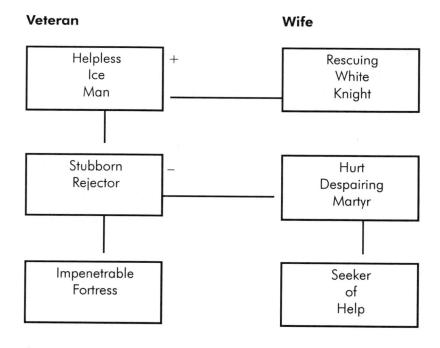

Figure 16.1 Rescuing behaviour of veteran's wife leading to her helplessness

Invariably the family-of-origin issues for the veteran and partner have to be resolved simultaneously or sequentially through couples counselling and/or individual trauma treatment. Children of Vietnam veterans can be severely affected by PTSD. The difficulty for the traumatized Vietnam veteran of maintaining intimate relationships causes major stress in the family, contributing to many secondary trauma symptoms. The ramifications for the psychological well-being of the children of the traumatized Vietnam veteran can be substantial.

If the veteran used withdrawal as a means of coping, excessive distance between family members may develop, with poor communication as a result. There is an absence of structure and authority. Alternatively, if there is too much contact, enmeshment patterns can develop in an effort to elude re-experiencing anxieties and vulnerabilities that were present during the war. In such cases, the family becomes something of a fortress, isolated and protected from a 'dangerous world.' The family members see themselves mostly in relation to their father's problems with a lack of personal autonomy and growth and with great difficulties in relationship boundaries.

Case studies

In the following two case studies, psychodrama within individual therapy is employed as a primary treatment intervention. The techniques are therefore influenced greatly by psychodramatic role theory. Foremost is the need for the protagonist to present, through enactment, his or her past problems in the here and now. Consistent with psychodrama theory, this allows the protagonist to discover through spontaneity new solutions to past difficulties.

This method is particularly useful for trauma survivors as they are often tormented by the symptoms of post-traumatic stress disorder. The traumatic past can be brought into the present through surplus reality and dealt with by the protagonist in a way that was not possible before. For example, in the past a victim of rape was completely powerless and alone. In the present psychodramatic enactment, the protagonist-victim can utilize a range of resources and support that was not accessible during the actual rape. Moreover, when the traumatic event is re-enacted, the protagonist is able to move beyond repressive influences and experience feelings that were blocked due to dissociation and psychic numbing. As a result, a state of emotional equilibrium, harmony and peace can be found. This may involve expressions of feelings such as fear, shame, humiliation, anger and then, hopefully, self-love. This process is described as 'catharsis of abreaction,' sometimes followed by a 'catharsis of integration'.

The techniques of role reversal, mirroring, doubling and coaching are very helpful in this process and may help protagonists to experience themselves more fully and gain a better perspective of the experience of the traumatic situation. For example, when the protagonist experiences sadism and anger from a perpetrator, he gets an opportunity in role reversal to re-own his own anger.

Another theoretical point needs to be emphasized here. As I have already mentioned, children of Vietnam veterans may exhibit symptoms of PTSD, such as violent anger outbursts, controlling behaviour, emotional withdrawal and fear of intimacy. The child then may grow up in a PTSD family environment and struggle to feel parental and self-love. In the cases where children are able to feel such love, their potential for resisting parental PTSD influences is good. However, in the absence of a stable parental love object, a child may create a fantasy parent of their own to help them cope. As in the case of many other abused children, these fantasies may involve imaginary friends such as storybook figures or faithful pets. However, while this may help them to adjust to the situation, it does not necessarily prevent the development of emotional difficulties, such as secondary PTSD.

It is therefore important that the therapist identifies the love objects or helps the protagonist identify them in order to provide support when confronting fears during the psychodramatic enactment. This is particularly demonstrated in the case of Caroline with her fantasized pet cat 'Felix'. I have found this concept very useful for assisting all types of trauma survivors. It is my experience that experiences of love and humanity in psychodrama can overcome traumatic adversity. The following two case studies attempt to demonstrate this process.

Caroline

Caroline was the 13-year-old daughter of a Vietnam veteran. She was reported by her teacher to have problems of disruptive behaviour at school and by her parents to be unhappy at home. During the initial assessment period, Caroline indicated that she was very much alone and alienated from the other students. She described her father as a big volcano who periodically exploded with anger (see Figure 16.2) and the relationship between her parents as very tense and full of conflicts. Caroline also indicated that her father was very controlling. There was an overt expression of guilt or responsibility for her father's difficulties. Although Caroline often mentioned that she had a yearning for a closeness to exist in the family, this was apparently absent. There seemed to be oscillation between too much separation and too much enmeshment. Her older brother had a history of getting into many fights.

In the early sessions Caroline reported having suicidal thoughts, but these disappeared through the first three sessions. Treatment consisted of mutual story telling, drawings and psychodrama. It was interesting to observe that in her drawings, when describing alienation from her peer group, there emerged a theme of her being surrounded by hostile school students with guns wishing to do her harm. The students were of different alien facial and body features. For example, she could have a round head and they would have square-shaped heads. When asked what she would need to include in her fantasy drawing in order to protect herself from the hostile students, Caroline quickly conjured up a helicopter to rescue her from above. The helicopter then transported her to a tranquil safe place with lots of trees, away from the hostility and the treachery.

The similarity of Caroline's drawings to drawings of Vietnam veterans that I have counselled was quite remarkable. Although Caroline made no direct reference to the Vietnam war in her drawing or story telling, these seemed to be overt manifestations of her largely unconscious secondary traumatization. Though it is always difficult to make definite conclusions, we cannot refrain from observing the patterns emerging from her trauma. Thus I suggest that drawing and story telling are useful means for understanding the often hidden perplexities of transgenerational trauma issues.

PSYCHODRAMA

Psychodrama was used in conjunction with art therapy. The themes and scenes emerging in the drawing are readily adaptable to psychodramatic scenes. This is also the case for developing roles recognized through role analysis (see Figures 16.2, 16.3, 16.4 and 16.5).

In the first session, Caroline indicated that she was suicidal. She felt despairing, isolated, neglected and betrayed by her friends. Caroline said that her parents and teachers described her behaviour as attention-seeking, defiant and withdrawing. Caroline said that she often felt hurt and let down by her friends even after trying to help them with their school work. During the initial interview, Caroline warmed up to conflicted roles. She described herself as alone and despairing in a barren desert. At the edge of the desert was a huge brick wall. The wall had a small hole, through which she could see a beautiful lush garden. Her trusted pet cat Felix was also in the garden, beckoning Caroline. The cat was the only one that she trusted completely. Caroline said that Felix loved Caroline and she loved Felix.

Enactment took place between the roles of Felix the cat in the garden, the wall, and Caroline abandoned in the desert. (see Figure 16.2).

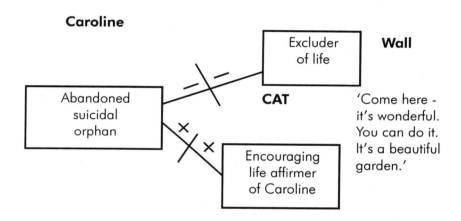

Figure 16.2: You must stay in the desert

At one point during the enactment, while attempting to climb through the wall, Caroline retreated fearful and tearful. She expressed from that role that she felt that the wall was about to explode on her and then a new scene emerged (see Figure 16.3). However, through coaching and role reversals, Caroline became aware of the cat's encouragement and strength. The cat's role evolved, taking on magical powers, which he gave to Caroline. Caroline then conjured up a whirlwind and blew the volcano out. These role developments are demonstrated in Figure 16.4.

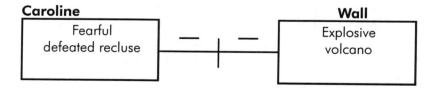

Figure 16.3

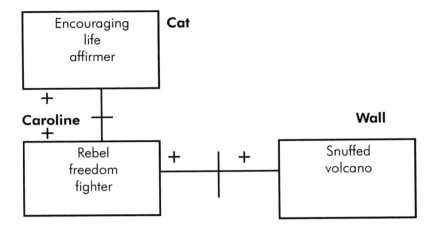

Figure 16.4

The volcano became a dormant brick wall that Caroline could easily climb through with continual encouragement from the cat. Both Caroline and the cat sat in the beautiful lush garden. The wall and the desert disappeared. The cat and Caroline sat in the garden speaking fondly to each other (see Figure 16.5).

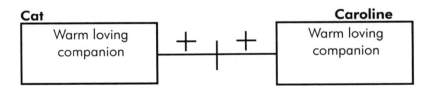

Figure 16.5

I remained continually interested, affirming and appreciative of Caroline in my role as director, producer and coach. I interchanged with Caroline's roles using doubling and mirroring. This helped maintain her warm-up to her different roles and enhanced spontaneity and creativity. When I played the role of Felix the cat, I extended that role, being particularly encouraging and supportive, that is, providing role training for Caroline, enabling her to choose the roles best able to assist in overcoming fearful and despairing roles. Caroline responded well to me playing these roles.

In the following two sessions Caroline reported feeling generally happy, not at all suicidal and was looking forward to overcoming school and home difficulties. She was feeling firm and solid in herself. Further work with Caroline included role training in order to maintain herself also in her family, for example to be aware when she is having her boundaries violated and how that can be avoided.

DISCUSSION

Analysis of the progressive role system of Caroline indicates that the playful 'lover of fun' and the 'artist' are two of her most developed progressive roles. Further development of roles such as the compassionate observer, life seeker, spontaneous actor and teacher would assist in the integration of her progressive functioning.

Analysis of Caroline's coping role system indicates that in many situations she deals with frustrations and despair by attention-seeking and deals with her powerlessness by rebelling or rescuing others. While these roles help Caroline cope at that moment, she sets herself up for disappointment and despair in the future, leading to the emergence of fragmented roles. However, I noticed that coping roles such as rebel and approval-seeker assisted in the emergence of progressive roles such as determined life-seeker, storyteller and self-appreciator.

The main role in Caroline's fragmenting role system appears to be abandoned despairing orphan and isolated child. Related to these are victim, suicidal child and fearful and defeated recluse.

'Rifle-man Rick'

'Rifle-man Rick', 42, was involved in fire support action in the late 1960s which involved him and his group securing a Vietnamese village from attack by the enemy. It was not uncommon in these actions for different members of the group to use some abandoned huts for sleeping quarters rather than tents. This was the case for Rick and three of his mates. After securing the village, Rick and his mates bedded down for the night. The area around the village seemed fairly secure and it was believed that attack by the enemy would be unlikely. However, just before retiring for the night, the village was subject to attack by Viet Cong rockets. Rick's hut sustained a direct hit causing Rick to be knocked unconscious. Nevertheless, he survived. When he regained consciousness, to his horror, he discovered that his three mates had been killed.

Furthermore his mates had been literally blown apart and some of these body parts and their blood were actually on Rick.

This traumatic experience devastated Rick, leaving him with severe and chronic post-traumatic stress disorder for well over 20 years.

Prior to the traumatic incident Rick had been well adjusted and generally happy with his life and was able to have good relationships. He reported that his childhood had been very happy. However, through the course of the 20 years' aftermath, Rick struggled in all relationships. He had had a number of marriages and tended to suffer prolonged periods of depression, including periods of dissociation. He reported that when he engaged in social functions, he had a sense of being disconnected and isolated and felt as if he was watching himself, rather than being present. He had all the characteristic symptoms of PTSD.

Perhaps most distressing for Rick was his survival guilt and the way he scolded himself for surviving the traumatic event in Vietnam. He fantasized how his dead mates, if they could, would judge him. He imagined that they would blame him for staying alive.

Rick presented for counselling in 1990 in a highly distressed state. He had recently been to his first veterans' reunion and this had made all his traumatic symptoms, including survival guilt, become intolerable. He said during the course of the initial interview that he had reached a point whereby either he had finally to join his mates or free himself from the relentless emotional pain and choose life. Evidently, Rick was making a choice between life and death.

Assessment indicated that fundamentally Rick had good ego strength. In terms of role analysis, he owned a number of healthy roles including creative explorer, storyteller, courageous adventurer and compassionate friend. I suggested to Rick that individual psychodrama would be appropriate to help him overcome his present and past difficulties. Rick liked the idea of the emphasis on creativity and spontaneity and he reflected on his creative interests of art and poetry.

PSYCHODRAMA

The first part of the intervention involved warming Rick up to the aspects of the traumatic experience that were most worrying him, especially his fantasies of being negatively judged by each of his three dead mates. Given Rick's spiritual beliefs, he was able to place each of the voices of his dead mates in the realm of the after life and, as a part of this process, the scene was set whereby three cushions were placed on the floor to symbolize his mates. I asked him which one of the three mates most concerned him in terms of the survival guilt, to which he replied that 'Joe' was the most troubling. I then asked him to talk to Joe and to keep in mind all the years of anguish, self-blame, self-loathing and guilt and shame that he had experienced in relation to Joe and the two others. At this point Rick threw himself off his chair and on to the fairly large cushion which represented Joe, hugging the cushion. He sobbed uncontrollably and continuously for about ten minutes. At different times during this process, I gently enquired what he was experiencing and he said quietly that he was sorry. Eventually, he was able to talk to Joe and express all his years of anguished guilt and shame for surviving. I then asked him to reverse roles with Joe and respond as Joe. In that role, he was surprised to hear himself saying, 'You're a bloody dickhead. I am glad and the others are glad that we all didn't get done in. Don't forget we all want each other to survive if we can and we want you to survive and we're glad you survived. It makes us feel good, so get on with it.'

There were a number of role reversals following this, including expressions of regard for each other leading to the conclusion of this scene. Rick now reported that he was feeling calm and at peace, a state that he had not experienced for years. However, he was aware of a gnawing pain in his chest. I then asked him to focus on this pain and to maximize its impact on him in terms of images, thoughts or feelings. All of a sudden Rick stood up out of his chair and said, 'The bloody bastards'. An expression of rage came over his face. I asked Rick who he meant? And he said, 'The bloody government for sending us there.' I asked Rick to choose a cushion to represent the government and to express what he felt. He chose the largest and heaviest cushion in the room to represent the government and then started to punch the cushion with almighty force and screamed a range of colourful expressions to describe his feelings. His anger and rage was so intense that the thuds against the cushion could be heard five counselling rooms away and I thought to myself that they perhaps echoed all the way to Vietnam, and certainly Canberra (this being the home of the Australian Federal Parliament which enforced conscription). Rick's expression of anger was so strong that he bit his lip and blood spilled from the cut. This enactment lasted approximately 15 minutes until his energy seemed depleted.

Taking him out of the drama into the mirror position, I then asked Rick to choose another cushion to represent him in relation to the government cushion and to express himself in terms of his feelings about his expressions to the government and his mates. He expressed regard and pride in himself for making these expressions. Taking the role of himself within the scene, Rick expressed appreciation of the mirror's regard. A number of role reversals took place during this time in which there was mutual expression of joy and appreciation. The scene was complete.

Afterwards, I spent time sharing some of my experiences of Rick's work with Rick. I mentioned that I was appreciative of his courage and disclosed some thought about the government involvement in the Vietnam War and my memories of some of the news reports of the early seventies. That concluded the session.

Rick attended another four sessions and he reported that he was having waves of emotional experiences that he had not had before. The judging voices of his dead mates had transformed into friendly companions.

DISCUSSION

The above example demonstrates how Rick was able to overcome PTSD, including survival guilt, through the use of individual psychodrama. An important part of this process involved an assessment of Rick's pre- and post-trauma ego strength and the identification of internal resources. It became apparent very quickly that Rick and I had a very good and trusting relationship and that Rick had many healthy roles that could assist him in his trauma treatment through psychodrama.

Rick was highly warmed up to the experience of his mates' death in Vietnam and was able to resolve his psychic pain and conflicts primarily through the techniques of role reversal, mirroring and coaching. He clearly experienced a catharsis of abreaction when he expressed his sorrow to his dead mates and his rage at the government for sending him and his mates to Vietnam. A 'catharsis of integration' was achieved through role reversal in which there was expression of mutual regard between him and his dead mates and between himself as mirror and himself as expressing anger towards the government. In terms of role development, Rick was able to replace self-loathing roles with roles of self-regard such as supportive loving companion, self-forgiving friend and thankful survivor. It was interesting to note that when Rick contacted me some three years later, this state of peace persisted. He was becoming increasingly involved in life-giving activities and had a new stable relationship.

From my experience in counselling traumatized Vietnam veterans and a variety of other trauma survivors I have found that there is an ongoing struggle on the part of the survivor to resolve the devastating effects of the trauma experience. Some of these struggles are destructive to the traumatized person and his family while others may facilitate healing. In addition, there are efforts to resolve the overwhelming feelings of powerlessness and victimization bestowed upon them by the 'perpetrator' or by the disaster.

The symbolic representation of the resolution process cannot be underestimated. For instance, there are many examples of Vietnam veterans engaging in counter-phobic risk, taking activities such as enlisting in foreign wars or seeking dangerous civilian jobs. These are often symbolic expressions of embracing the trauma or they may be an attempt to overcome the associated trauma fear. There are also examples of veterans having difficulty with authority figures and government institutions; the classic *Rambo* series of films symbolizes this activity.

The implication for the treatment of individuals experiencing such trauma symptoms is for the counsellor not to focus on the end behaviour roles, such as trouble-maker, racist, uncooperative actor, controller or aggressor. It may be more advantageous for the counsellor to focus on symbolic representations rather than on the acting-out behaviours because antisocial, withdrawal or other psychological or social difficulties may be attempts to resolve the trauma, that is, to help the veteran develop the role of all-seer or systems analyst in order to differentiate between the past enemy perpetrator and present shadows or reminders. In this process they can learn to develop a more trusting and collaborative relationship with the counsellor. Thus, veterans may gain a broader perspective of the influences on their reactive aggressive or self-defeating emotions and behaviour. Included in this could be the exploration of triggers, such as authority figures, aliens, or government personnel. Such exploration could move behind the triggers to uncover representations of earlier traumatic experience.

Conclusion

This chapter has attempted to demonstrate various active, expressive and experiential treatment strategies for war veterans and their families who suffer from direct or indirect exposure to trauma. The two cases presented attempted to highlight how war trauma permeates from one generation to another. The challenge for the primary trauma victim is to work through the painful and devastating experience in a way that minimises the risk of spreading the terror or despair to his family members. The treatment strategies are centred on the power of psychodrama within the framework of role theory to effect substantial resolutions in intra-psychic conflicts and emotional pain caused by the post-traumatic stress. Through a strengthening of creative and life-giving roles, the traumatized individual may be able to create peace with himself and once again feel a part of the universe.

References

Baumgartner, D.D. (1986) 'Sociodrama and the Vietnam combat veteran: a therapeutic release for a wartime experience.' *Sociometry 39*, 1, 31.

Beattie, N. (1987) *Co-dependent No More*. Blackburn, VA: Harper Collins.

Clayton, G.M. (1993) *Living Pictures of the Self. Applications of Role Theory in Professional Practice and Daily Life*. Caulfield, VA: ICA Press.

Daniel, S. (1992) *Building a Healthy Group Culture: A Psychodramatic Intervention*. Unpublished thesis, Australian and New Zealand Psychodrama Association.

Fantal, E. (1945) 'Psychodrama in an evacuation hospital.' *Sociometry 8*, 125, 3–4.

Fantal, E. (1951) 'The civilian and army social atom – before and after.' *Group Psychotherapy 8*, 1, 20.

Harkness, L. (1993) 'Transgenerational transmission of war related trauma.' In J. Wilson and B. Raphael (eds) *The International Handbook of Trauma Stress Syndromes*. New York: Plenum Press.

Moreno, J.L. (1964) *Psychodrama, Volume 1*. New York: Beacon House.

Rosenheck, R. (1985) 'Secondary traumatisation in children of Vietnam veterans.' *Hospital and Community Psychiatry 36*, 5, 538–539.

Williams, A.W. (1989) *The Passionate Technique*. London: Routledge.

Williams, T. (1980) *Post-traumatic Stress Disorders of the Vietnam Veterans*. Cincinnati, OH: Disabled American Veterans.

Wilson, J.P. (1989) *Trauma Transformation and Healing: An Integrative Approach to Theory Research, and Post Traumatic Therapy*. New York: Brunner/Mazel.

CHAPTER 17

Secondary Victims of Trauma:
Producing Secondary Survivors

Rory Remer

Sam Doe is a 47-year-old businessman with an MBA. He and Yvette, 42, have been married 18 years. She too is a college graduate, in economics. They have three children – Marla, 16, Selma, 13 and Frank, 11. Yvette was a successful buyer for a clothing store before Marla was born, but resigned her position, by mutual consent, to raise the children. Recently she has gone back to earn her Masters degree in computer science. She has been doing well, has a teaching assistantship and been encouraged to go on to obtain her Ph.D.

They live near both their families – 15 minutes from hers and about an hour from his. They see her mother and father, as well as other of her family members, more frequently than they do Sam's family members, but both she and the kids have stronger connections to his family which is larger and less formal. They have three or four close couple friends. Each of the family members also has individual friends, Marla being the most popular and Selma the shyest.

A year ago one of Yvette's closest personal friends was raped and killed. Yvette found the body when she went to her friend's apartment. As a result she started to have panic attacks at school and nightmares. Although she managed to cope, she started seeing a therapist. Consequently, she has come to realize she was sexually assaulted by a cousin starting when she was eight years old.

When she told Sam he was incredulous. He couldn't comprehend that she, and he, couldn't have known about the trauma all this time. Yvette has withdrawn from both Sam and the children. She has considered a separation, living alone in an apartment near campus. Needless to say, the family and friends are confused and concerned.

Yvette is a primary victim of trauma. But who is Sam? Just her spouse? What of Marla, Selma, and Frank? Are they just innocent bystanders? Are the family members and friends who are also affected by the havoc in Yvette's life simply observers? Each and every one is not only a resource, a potential supporter, but also suffers the ripple effects of the disruptions impacting Yvette and each other. These people are secondary victims.

Introduction

A secondary victim of trauma is any person in the social support network of a trauma victim. Included are family members, partners, and friends. In other words, a secondary victim is anyone on whose personal resources a trauma victim calls during the process of healing from trauma.

Since the size of these social support networks more often than not is of an order of magnitude larger than the number of victims (Remer and Elliott 1988a and 1988b), the effects of any trauma spread far beyond the primary victims. The toll of traumas on primary victims is staggering; the toll on secondary victims is mind-boggling.

Despite all the attention that has been paid to the healing process of primary victims recently (van der Kolk, McFarlane and Weisaeth 1996), little has been done to address the needs of secondary victims. In fact, if mentioned at all in the literature, secondary victims are usually recognized not for their own problems, but rather as needing attention because they provide resources necessary to primary victim healing or because their actions and reactions can interfere with that healing process (van der Kolk *et al.* 1996). Yet, these victims have problems of their own, some certainly linked to those of the primary victim, but many distinct. Secondary victims as well as primary victims need help in understanding their own healing processes and how these processes interface. Whether recognized as problematic or not, all victims need to be aware of their biases, tendencies and personal issues that influence and, at times, interfere with productive adaptation. They need to comprehend the difficulties they face and develop strategies and skills to address the demands of the situation. These matters must be addressed both for the secondary victims' sakes and for the good of the primary victims. The purpose of the present chapter is to focus on the healing processes of secondary victims so they may become secondary survivors applying one specific approach – sociatry.

Perspectives: useful maps

Almost all maps are helpful to some degree to someone. They both simplify and provide different views. None, however, is the actual territory being mapped. If any one was, it would not be very effective, both because it would not be serving its purpose – simplification – and because realities (territories) change. Maps, to be worthwhile, must be communicable, usable, and heuristic. Accordingly, maps employed here must be able to be explained to and understood by both victims and professionals; they must lead to effective actions; and they must allow for their own adaptation.

In particular, secondary victims (and primary victims as well) need help in coping with the complexity and the interconnectedness of the processes involved in healing from trauma. The maps employed must accommodate both aspects. They must also be mutually enhancing; that is, when superimposed (overlaid) they should bring essential features into starker relief, not obscure or muddle them.

Traumatic events are many and varied. The individuals affected are different and complicated – their personalities, histories, backgrounds, and life circumstances. The mix of all these influences makes the situations complex. To manage the intricacies, ways to organize and communicate information and to guide intervention are essential.

Many perspectives have proved useful for addressing the repercussions of traumatic events (Figley 1985a, 1985b, 1989 and 1997; Remer 1990 and 1999a; van der Kolk *et al.* 1996). Some are general theories or models of adaptation – for example, loss (Kubler-Ross 1969), cognitive development or learning (Mounoud 1976; Piaget and Inhelder 1969) or general systems (von Bertalanffy 1968). Others are specific to the area of trauma – for example, sexual assault (Remer 1984) or child sexual abuse (Chard, Weaver and Resick 1997). To deal with secondary victim healing, two general perspectives will be brought together here, chaos theory and sociatry. First, however, primary victim healing process, secondary healing process and their interface will be overviewed briefly to provide a context.[1]

---

[1]   Terms from chaos and sociatry – applied sociometric theory – are mentioned parenthetically during this chapter to start to introduce the reader to them and their relationship to the healing processes.

Primary Survivors

To imply that one specific model can convey the healing of every trauma survivor is misleading. Most people understand that each survivor, being an individual, has a somewhat different healing process. Beyond the individual difference issue, the type of trauma from which the survivor is healing has an impact on the variations of the healing process (Whetsell 1990).

The Remer (Remer 1984; Worell and Remer 1992) model will be used here. Not only does this model share the majority of the salient aspects of the other models (Burgess and Holmstrom 1979a and 1979b; Figley 1985a; McCann, Sakheim and Abrahamson 1988; Scurfield 1985; Sutherland and Sherl 1970), but because of its unique initial stage, some of the differences seen as a result of type of trauma can also be anticipated and indicated without addressing each type of trauma specifically.

Remer (1984) recognizes the non-linearity and non-independence of the healing process. The adjacent stages are not mutually exclusive. (See Figure 17.1.) This distinction is important because complexity, and to some degree confusion, results. This caution is not a commentary on a weakness of the model. On the contrary, these 'overlaps' or 'mixings' allow the model to represent reality more accurately, from a chaos theory perspective. The hallmarks of both primary and secondary survivors' healing processes are chaotic patterns – complexity, non-linearity, non-independence – and consequent reactions.

Remer (1984) portrays the survivor's healing process in six stages: 1. pre-trauma, 2. trauma event, 3. crisis and disorientation, 4. outward adjustment, 5. reliving, and 6. integration and resolution. Her unique contribution to the understanding of the healing process is the pre-trauma stage. Note the recycling involved in the last four stages, which may occur simultaneously. Specific attention should be directed to the possible consequences of these overlaps. (See Remer 1990 and 1999a for details.)

Secondary survivors

The secondary survivor healing process, while intertwined with and in many ways parallel to that of primary victims (Ferguson 1993; Remer 1997; Remer and Ferguson 1995 and 1997), has unique aspects of its own. The model presented here benefits particularly from that developed by Remer (1984). Parallels are intentional and designed to capitalize on the strengths of Remer's model in order to provide as comprehensive and broad a view of

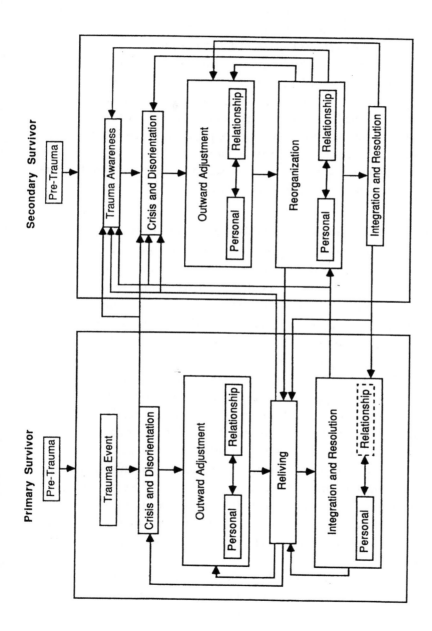

Figure 17.1: Interface between the models of primary and secondary survivors' healing processes. From Remer 1984.

the secondary victims' healing process as is possible and because the general adjustment in healing can be viewed similarly for both primary and secondary victims.

An example of non-independent/non-linear systems, the model is divided into six stages: 1. pre-trauma, 2. trauma awareness, 3. crisis and disorientation, 4. outward adjustment, 5. reorganization, and 6. integration and resolution. The first two stages happen in a linear fashion perforce. The final four can, and almost inevitably do, overlap and recycle. (See Figure 17.1.)

The right side of Figure 17.1 provides a schema of the healing process of secondary survivors; the left half of primary survivors. The interfaced flow charts presented in the figure indicate the complexities that can be expected in the secondary survivor recovery process; particular attention should be paid to interaction and non-linearity. A more comprehensive exposition, including examples of typical reactions of secondary survivors to illustrate each stage, is in Remer and Ferguson (1995 and 1997).

Perspective on interdependence/interconnectedness

A distinctive feature of the secondary survivor healing process is its dependence on information about and reaction to the healing process of the primary survivor. Unlike the primary survivor, the secondary victim awaits cues from the primary survivor to which to react. The complex interconnectedness of the two processes – the aspects of non-linear, non-independent systems contributing to chaos – can be most easily seen in Figure 17.1. Although the relationship aspect is important in the primary survivor healing process, predominantly because of the need for support and resources from the secondary survivors (support network), primary survivors nevertheless have to focus on their own personal/intrapsychic healing first. However, the explicit interaction between the personal and interpersonal aspects of adjustment is often under-emphasized for primary survivors.

Secondary survivors, on the other hand, must attend not only to their own personal adjustment but also to the vicissitudes of the primary victim healing and to the impact of those fluctuations on the relationship. Effective secondary survivors are keenly aware of the impact of the trauma on both the primary survivor and on the relationship. In fact, in many ways, they may be too attuned.

A relationship is not a relationship unless it is maintained by both those involved. While the secondary survivor healing process has been portrayed as reliant on and reactive to the healing process of the primary survivor, little has been said specifically about the ongoing role relationship dynamics in the overall healing (self-organization) process of the social support network involved.

In dealing with primary and secondary victims one of the main issues is how to mesh their healing processes. Familiarity with a number of perspectives on interconnected processes would be useful to both practitioners and victims. Most helpful are chaos (dynamical systems, non-linear/non-independent systems) theory, sociometric theory (including role, psychodramatic, sociometry, social atom, and spontaneity sub-theories) and the concept of interdependence (Remer 1990).

As presented elsewhere, particularly viewed from the perspective of the primary victim (Bass and Davis 1988), the conceptualizations of the healing processes do a disservice to the relationship importance. The relational considerations – the interplay, the give and take, the balance – are necessary not only for the resources to be available for healing of the primary survivor but also for the adjustment of all those impacted.

Primacy of the primary victim's healing

However one looks at the healing process, the primary victim is and must be the focal point of the healing process if the relationship is to survive. Without giving primacy to the healing of the primary victim, relationship healing will not occur, or at best will be difficult to achieve. But, exactly what does 'primacy' mean?

If by primacy we meant that the primary victim would have to heal entirely before the healing of any secondary victims could begin, the relationships would most likely break up before healing could occur. Therapeutic intervention is necessary to support the healing of the primary victim while at the same time supporting that of the secondary victims, to find a balance/interdependence between the requirements of the primary victim healing and the requirements of the secondary victims (and to prevent or eliminate, as much as possible, any tendencies toward co-dependency).

The 'dance of interconnectedness,' when it seems to take its perpetual lead from the process of the primary victim, almost appears as a form of co-dependency. At times when trauma awareness leads to crisis, the focus must be on the primary victim if that person is to survive to be part of the relationship. However, like a dance, the partnership(s) must develop a subtle communication that makes the flow, the movement, collaborative. Different partners develop different, even if very similar, patterns, and may dance very different dances. Co-dependent type actions may be part of the dance, but the overall pattern need not be co-dependency – enabling can have positive as well as negative connotations and effects. Learning the dance and changing the pattern over time, including the possibility of independent moves of each dancer and change of initiator, is not easy to accomplish but can be very gratifying to all involved when achieved.

Consequences of and approach to primary victim primacy: Possible interventions

After a severe trauma, the primary victim will be in great need of support. Even the most 'resourceful' person will be greatly stretched to cope without additional help from a functional social support network. At this point two things must occur. First, secondary victims must support and supply resources for the healing of the primary victim. Second, secondary victims must not attempt to draw on the resources of the primary victim. In the initial phases of healing, little if any reciprocity or balance can be expected in relationships. This situation may also be the case during other stages of healing, such as in particularly disturbing visits to the reliving stage.

When these difficulties are encountered, secondary victims must put some of their needs aside to support the primary victim in whatever way possible. In addition, when secondary victims experience needs, they will have to look elsewhere for the resources to meet those needs. However, meeting secondary victims' needs elsewhere may have to be delayed if, in the process of doing so, the healing of the primary victim, at least through the initial critical phases of the healing process, is disrupted. In the long run, however, a return to some semblance of an interdependent pattern must occur. Reliance of the primary victim on the secondary victims to channel the resources of all individuals involved in the support network to the primary victim cannot go on indefinitely. At some point the relationships will break down if some balance and reciprocity is not restored. The dissolution of any relationship may not be welcomed, but may be the only viable alternative available if optimal healing is to occur and the system is to self-organize. This alternative should not be denied when considered by those involved.

The restoration of the balance or the establishment of a new balance, a new pattern of interaction, may, and often does, necessitate therapeutic intervention. New methods of negotiating the give and take in the relationships may be necessary – learning how to encounter appropriately, for instance. In fact, given that the healing process of both primary and secondary victims will be ongoing for a long period, if not for a lifetime, an expectation that the original relationship patterns can be functionally re-established is unrealistic, unless they already include aspects of trauma patterns. Expectations should be that new patterns, hopefully as effective as or more effective than the old ones, will have to be implemented in their place.

The difficulties in establishing a balance between secondary and primary survivor demands increase exponentially as the number of people involved expand. In addition, many secondary victims are also primary victims in their own right, either by virtue of experiencing the traumatic events together (such as floods, wars) or because many primary victims gravitate to other primary victims (for example, abuse victims) to form relationships. The circularity (non-independence and mutual influence) of healing interactions escalates the complexity of co-ordinating multiple healing processes.

Often secondary victims, and their therapists, demand some indication of how long the healing process will take. Any normative estimates either of the amount of time required in any particular stage or of the healing process overall are nothing more than blind guesswork. No norms are possible since the whole process is non-linear and usually cyclical so that stages can be encountered more than once under varying conditions and the movement through the patterns is unpredictable. As Figley says: '(it) can last as little as a month or as long as a lifetime' (1993, p.2).

Because of the chaotic nature of change – the multitude of factors and their interaction involved in treating the secondary survivor and interfacing such treatment with those of the primary survivor and the relationship – some structure to facilitate co-ordination is helpful. Viewing intervention from two dimensions – treatment goals and therapeutic milieu – can be useful. Crossing three levels of goals (education, awareness and personal development, and skill acquisition) with three categories of milieu (individual, conjoint, and group therapy) produces a grid that better allows the balancing of efforts, proper timing of intervention, and the consideration of other confounding issues related to treatment (such as alcohol/drug abuse) (Remer and Ferguson 1995).

Trauma and chaos theory

Traumatic events wreak havoc in the lives of both primary and secondary victims. The impact of these events causes violent, severe disruptions in the patterns of these lives that must be addressed to return to some semblance of stability.

The impacts of traumatic events are often described as total chaos. The popular connotation of the term chaos is a completely disorganized, unpredictable, disjointed situation. From a more disciplined, scientific perspective this description is not accurate, at least not completely. Chaos, as opposed to havoc, not only has a pattern and type of predictability to it, but also possesses the property of self-organization (which is why the application of the term havoc when referring to the impact of trauma seems more appropriate). This distinction is essential to making meaning from the experience. Chaos Theory (ChT) is a perspective that promotes an understanding of patterns and how they are changed.

In some cases the impact of the trauma is so severe that the life pattern of the primary victim, if not the secondary victims, is not merely disrupted but rather destroyed. In most cases, however, the pattern remains intact to some degree, if only in that in the healing process the victim system – primary and secondary victims – and the other societal systems in which the victim system is embedded, attempts to reassert established patterns. However, people, both survivors and society at large, must be helped to understand and accept that the patterns have irrevocably altered, rather than deny the fact and fight the changes, which is usually to the detriment of the healing process.

Because these systems are dynamic, the patterns of interaction they produce even under the best of circumstances are chaotic in nature (Butz 1997; Butz, Chamberlain and McCown 1997). However, most people only rarely appreciate the chaotic nature of their lives, and certainly few understand the implications of this characterization in the scientific, non-colloquial sense. Such knowledge can be invaluable not only in furthering the healing process but also in coping with the vagaries of life in general.

ChT is a perspective on human dynamical systems that has its origins in the mathematical and physical study of non-linear/non-independent, dynamical systems (Gleick 1987) and fractal geometry (Falconer 1990). A detailed exposition of ChT is both impossible and unnecessary in the present context. An overview of the more relevant aspects will suffice here. In particular, a sense of the lessons ChT provides, if not a true grasp of both the constructs and their importance, will be more functional.

The main ChT concepts, if not the terms, of use in treating trauma victims are: strange attractors and their basins, self-affinity, fractalness, unpredictability and self-organization. Their utility is in the sense they can convey about the ebb and flow of life and human patterns of behaviour, thought, emotion, and interpersonal interaction.

Patterns are developed and maintained around focal points (strange attractors). These patterns are unpredictable in two ways: although patterns can be identified, small changes in initial position can lead to huge differences in later positions and, because of non-linearity and multiple influences, control is an impossibility. However, the patterns are contained within boundaries (their basins) and as the perspective on the patterns shifts from level to level (for example, individual to familial to support network to societal), both the patterns themselves and processes that produce them are similar (self-affine). When the pattern is disrupted, particularly to the point of becoming chaotic, a new pattern will be established incorporating the new influences, yet also resembling the previous pattern (the system evidences self-organization). Still, no matter what is done, the new pattern will never replicate the old exactly and where patterns meet, their boundaries are rarely, if ever, perfectly meshed (fractalness).

Traumatic events usually produce huge disruptions in life patterns at multiple levels – personal, familial, social (support network), and even societal. ChT provides a means for making some sense of the disruptions and changes in the patterns. Sociatry not only helps in understanding the impacts of these disruptions, but also can afford means for influencing the production of new more functional patterns.

Sociatry

Sociatry was conceived by Moreno (1951 and 1953/1993) as a science of normal human relationships. 'Sociatry is logically the healing of normal society...of inter-related individuals and of inter-related groups... Sociometry may just as often be applied sociatry as sociatry applied sociometry.' (Moreno 1953/1993, p.90)

Moreno's intention was to produce a system that promoted both understanding and useful applications/techniques for fostering and furthering functional interpersonal interactions. Traumas, affecting not simply individuals but rather producing rents in the fabric of the social network itself, demand a broader systemic approach than psychodrama (enactment theory) alone can supply. With the interconnectedness of primary and secondary healing processes, sociatry may be uniquely applicable to the present situation for the benefit not only of the relationships but also the individuals involved.

As with both ChT and trauma healing, only an overview of some aspects of sociatry/sociometric theory is possible here. Still, some basic common understanding is necessary to meet the goals of this chapter. A schematic representation of the components (sub-theories) of sociometric theory, similar to Hale's (1981), can be found in Figure 17.2. The general sense and some of the terms of psychodramatic, sociometry, social atom, role, and spontaneity theories will be briefly presented.

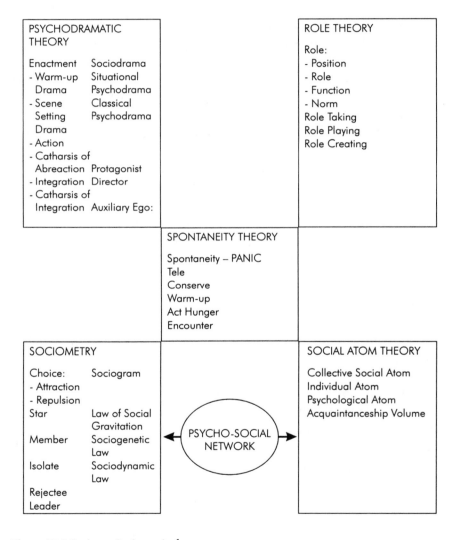

Figure 17.2 Sociatry: Sociometric theory components

Psychodramatic theory

Although psychodrama is usually considered only a therapeutic approach, even from this perspective it can be seen as taking enactments out of the flow of life for examination and remediation. Using this view, psychodramatic theory provides a guide to understanding the moment-to-moment actions and interactions of individuals. Life is viewed as the flow of enactments each with a lead-in (warm-up), an enactment proper, and a finish (closure) (Hollander 1969). People are the actors in these dramas, enacting a variety of roles. The outcomes of these enactments depend on the adequacy of the warm-ups of the actors, the interplay of the roles brought to the enactment, and the completeness of the closure. Adequate warm-ups lead to spontaneous actions and consequently to functional enactments and complete closures. Breakdowns at any time during the process can lead to dysfunctional outcomes (act-hunger – the need to re-engage in the process to a satisfactory completion). Besides the concepts and constructs to aid in characterizing interactions (such as protagonist, auxiliaries, stage), tools/interventions (such as role-reversal, mirroring, concretizing) are direct outgrowths of this and the other components – sociatry as a whole – for working on problematic aspects (for example, poor warm-ups, impulsive acts, inadequate role reper-toire). Isolating enactments – taking them out of the life flow, symbolically – to examine, replay, and rescript provides a vehicle for influencing and changing existing patterns of thinking, feeling, behaving and interacting.

Sociometry

Using constructs such as member, leader, star, isolate, and rejectee, socio-metry addresses the relatively transitory aspects of group interpersonal rela-tionship patterns, attractions and repulsions. The development and change in interpersonal connections (telic bonds) is the focus, as contextual factors (criteria of choice) vary. Methods to identify, investigate and influence the bonds (such as sociometric tests), and the patterns they produce, are logical extensions of principles of sociometry (these include sociogenetic law, law of social gravitation and the sociodynamic principle).

Social atom theory

Social atom theory can explain and guide the metamorphoses of long term relationships and the increases and decreases of the importance of others in our lives from mere acquaintances to central figures. Applying knowledge of collective, individual, and psychological social atoms and the theoretical implications of their connections particularly with other sociometric constructs, techniques from sociatry, and other modalities, can be used to influence social atom patterns.

Role theory

The concept of role is central to sociatry, a thread connecting all components. Roles are relatively stable patterns of thoughts, feelings, behaviours and interactions that are developed and modified throughout the lifetime by a process moving from role-taking, to role-playing, and, possibly finally, to role-creating. Role theory has been developed beyond the sociometric context, as focus of social psychology, to describe and explain human life patterns. Although terminology has been somewhat inconsistent, the organization of roles has been characterized by layers of complexity (Biddle 1979). Collections of roles are positions, major spheres of life endeavour (such as parent or spouse). Roles (for example, supporter and adviser) in turn are constellations of functions (such as listening, giving aid) that are implemented in accord with norms, expectations, and similar standards for judging acceptability. Roles are engaged and activated by the warm-up process to allow people to apply previously effective patterns in different situations.

Spontaneity theory

As represented in Figure 17.2, spontaneity theory is central to all aspects of sociatry. The ability to act spontaneously, as theoretically specified, not simply colloquially understood, is the goal of human development. Based on the canon of creativity (Moreno 1953/1993 and 1975) the relationship of spontaneity to conserves (for example, schemata) engaged in specific situations (warm-up) is used to explain and provide interventions to promote flexible, functional responses, thus avoiding act hunger (the need to rectify poor outcomes). In addition, because of the interpersonal focus of the theory, interactions (encounters), to be deemed spontaneous (that is, that meet the PANIC criteria – within Parameters, Adequate, Novel, Immediate, Creative), require the distinction of the authentic aspects (telic bonds) from the inauthentic ones (for example, transference) in order to engage appropriate warm-ups. Spontaneity theory guides such explorations, identifications, and training through vehicles such as spontaneity tests, spontaneity training, role tests, and role training.

Trauma, ChT and sociatry: theory and applications

Theories dealing with trauma, sociatry, and chaos address disruptions and fluctuations in patterns of life, in particular patterns of personal change and interpersonal interaction. When brought together they can support the understandings and interventions necessary to help victims become survivors.

In many ways trauma impacts life patterns no differently from such other influences as life transitions, although admittedly more obviously and dramatically. The impact of trauma on the patterns involved still leaves the patterns self-affine, that is, tending towards similar patterns and pressures, to some degree. This lesson is the one communicated by ChT. Some people cope better with the impact of trauma than do others, usually because they cope better with life's fluctuations generally. Precisely for this reason, sociatry and ChT can help guide the healing process for secondary, and primary, victims. By examining the healing process and its similarities to adapting to other life fluctuations, the information and interventions offered by ChT in conjunction with sociatry can not only help promote healing, but also these lessons can be applied to other life pattern changes inevitably faced. In other words, the challenge to healing and the central focus of the healing process is to foster spontaneity. The other aspects of sociatry are all brought to bear to further this end.

Case study: The Doe family and support network

Examining a specific case may help clarify the points being made. Below, the Doe family and the reactions and accommodations of their social support network members are examined. Each stage of the healing process is addressed with various sociatric and ChT constructs applied (though not comprehensively for each stage). Applications of theory are interspersed but set apart by italics.

Pre-trauma

If trauma and its effects could be foreseen, perhaps people would be motivated to prepare. By using the maps provided by sociatry and ChT they could examine the interpersonal patterns of role interactions to optimize spontaneity and, in doing so, be better able to cope with the disruptions of these patterns induced by trauma. Unfortunately most people are not moved to look at their social atom structures, roles, sociometric connections, warm-ups, and other factors that influence their day-to-day patterns of existence. They often trust (or hope for) consistency and predictability that ChT says they are unlikely either to attain or maintain.

Usually, only after trauma has occurred do secondary and primary victims become aware of the influences of their conserves – gender roles, culture, family rules. At that point, although these influences must be recognized, faced, and perhaps modified, other more immediate demands – such as personal safety – may draw on the resources available. In many instances, although these established patterns are intended to be facilitative, instead they add to the chaos.

A prime example is the disabling effect of stereotypical gender role messages. If males are restricted to operating instrumentally and females expressively, then should the primary victim be the female, no one may be available to offer emotional support to secondary victims in need or to the primary victim. Turning to the usual source of support, the primary victim, will interfere with the primary victim healing process. On the other hand, should the victim be the male, female secondary victims may lack the roles and functions to attend to the practical demands for action (for example, not know how to fix a leaky tap). Nor may the primary victim himself be capable of accepting emotional support from available sources (such as other males), because of gender role norms operating.

In the case cited above, most of these dynamics can be seen operating. Yvette, in her position as mother, has been ceded the family emotional support functions. When she does not receive the understanding and help from Sam she needs (as the result of his lack of role, function or norms appropriate to the situation), she feels betrayed. When she withdraws, Sam and the rest of the family are left ill-equipped to cope with the demands they face.

A proactive, preventive approach would be preferable. Attention to increasing role repertoires through attention to enactments, warm-ups, closures and the like using all the sociatric tools available could increase spontaneity, flexibility, and tolerance for chaotic processes. Better communication patterns might be fostered by understanding their both self-affine and fractal natures and teaching the skills of encounter – role reversal, doubling, mirroring – to address difficulties and capitalize on positive, telic aspects. If any preventive interventions have a chance of having an impact, action methods, such as psychodramatic simulation (Remer and Betts 1998), may impress people with the need to challenge their conserves, enhance their spontaneity, and increase their role repertoires.

Had Sam and Yvette not subscribed to stereotypical, societal, sex-role socialization messages they might have shared the family responsibilities more, their role repertoires could have been more extensive, and they would have had more resources available to address the problems that arose. The enactments in which they engaged could have been more productive — Sam could have heard Yvette in a more supportive manner. Even if Yvette had still needed to leave temporarily to get herself together, the family would have been able to concentrate on giving her the space she needed instead of falling into disarray. Would the trauma have been prevented by these proactive moves? No. But the impact could have been recognized and an attempt made to lessen it. Sociatric structures could have provided a perspective from which to develop the knowledge and skills to act more spontaneously in general and in response to the trauma specifically.

The ideal aside, the reality of most situations is that people only come for or are willing to accept help after the traumatic event. So we move to addressing the secondary victim healing process proper, still keeping in mind the pervasive influences of the pre-trauma stage.

Trauma awareness

For secondary victims, trauma awareness produces frustration because the process is completely out of their control. The best-intentioned attempts to help can have unpredictable repercussions throughout the psychosocial system, perhaps even retraumatizing the victim. Secondary victims need help in grasping the impact of the trauma on the lives of both primary victims and their own.

One example is using enactment theory to simulate aspects of the trauma awareness process. Secondary survivor healing will rely heavily on understanding the chaotic nature of remembering traumatic events and adjusting to them. Employing scene setting with secondary victims can give them a sense of experiencing what fragmentary recall and situation specific memory are like (olfactory triggers, such as a particular perfume, can bring aspects of a memory into focus that could not be recalled otherwise), aiding in understanding the process.

Sam could be helped to understand why Yvette had not remembered her own abuse until the new trauma triggered her memories. He could be taken through an enactment of his own to experience vagaries of memory, particularly those of unpleasant situations.

Using sociatric tools to maintain spontaneous response can also be key to coping. For example, secondary survivors can learn to recognize the primary victim's warm-ups as memory triggers and change their own warm-ups accordingly in order not to interfere with the awareness process (for example, not wearing a particular shirt that reminds a primary victim of the traumatic experience). They can leave psychological and physical space for the primary victim and attend to their own needs by adapting patterns and engaging different aspects of roles not often used, thus altering enactments. They also must understand that the awareness, while being self-affine, will not be predictably the same through each cycle. Conserving their responses will only work to the degree that the conserves are used to provide the basis for more flexible reactions. More to the point of secondary victim healing, secondary victims must learn to apply these same skills and knowledge to support each other in coping with their own reactions both to trauma realizations and responses of primary victims.

Spontaneity theory may help both secondary and primary victims have a structure from which to cope with the impact of trauma awareness. If family and friends understand the warming up process, they can detect Yvette's (and each other's) warm-up and allow for her (and others') needs and/or alter their own warm-ups accordingly to help each other and her. For example, friends, particularly female friends who also knew the murdered woman, could step in to support Yvette and give the family space to address each others' needs (perhaps from new roles that they will develop, such as taking turns preparing dinner). It is to be hoped that the need to be flexible and framing it as a challenge and an opportunity will decrease the resentment engendered by Yvette's tendency to withdraw. Then she may also withdraw less often, even sharing some of her memories and struggles with others more readily.

Crisis and disorientation

The most obviously chaotic stage is crisis and disorientation. The disorientation – cognitive, behavioural, relational, and emotional – is an indication of chaos and the need for re-organization (Remer 1998). Although many attempts to quell the chaos, some even partially successful, may manifest themselves in the application of old, previously functional roles and patterns (conserves), they often result in incomplete enactments and consequent act hunger. Setting the process, both psychodramatic and chaotic, of dynamical interaction and co-creative spontaneity in motion and trusting the self-organizing tendencies of chaotic systems may be all that can be done, again acting spontaneously. The need to be able to predict and control outcomes, however, may interfere. The ability just to be with someone by expressing a telic connection (using enactment techniques like doubling) can comfort and lend support while the system sorts itself out.

For secondary survivors in particular, knowledge and understanding of both social atom structure and sociometric choice may be essential to adapting. Family and friends usually relied upon in other contexts may not react as hoped for or needed. In fact, quite the contrary may occur (McFarlane and van der Kolk 1996). Others, not those with usual mutual or reciprocal warm-ups or those not chosen on many other criteria, may be found to support the healing process in surprising ways. Acquaintances and professional helpers not normally part of the social atom constellation may afford necessary role resources, if permitted to do so.

Focusing on enactment, Yvette, Sam and the children can be helped to recognize Yvette's warm-up to her trauma reactions. They can then collaborate either to help change that warm-up or, more likely, to change their own warm-ups in response. Perhaps Yvette can then find the physical and psychological space she needs in the home, obviating her need to withdraw and produce a more chaotic situation. Spontaneity and role theories can also play a part in examining the day-to-day interactions and deviations so that new roles (Sam as primary parent), functions (Marla doing grocery shopping), and norms (acceptance of more emotional expression by all family members) can be incorporated. Also important is using the structure to raise the awareness of all involved as to the unpredictability of the situation (Yvette cannot predict when she will be triggered), so everyone must be alert and forgiving of possible inconsistencies all around.

Yvette's family and friends can be helped to look at their social atom structures to see where resources not usually employed (aunts, uncles or cousins who can help with parenting responsibilities) might be found. Looking to collectives in the community (such as the Rape Crisis Centre) for people who might extend the support network would be a good strategy to entertain. Similarly, the sociometry of the social support network should be taken into account. If Yvette and the children are drawn more to Sam's family members, those family members should be approached first for support – the naturally existing affinities rather than the potential connections (Yvette's mother, perhaps) should be considered and approached realistically.

Outward adjustment

Of all the stages, sociatry – particularly spontaneity theory – may be the most important in helping secondary victims understand the paradoxical feature of outward adjustment. Everything seems the same, but nothing really is. Operating from conserves to try to re-establish and keep the old patterns in place will almost inevitably lead to their complete disruption. Secondary victims must be helped to see both the futility and utility of conserved

behaviour so that they can react spontaneously, being ever aware of the need
to modify conserves and adjust to situational demands (perhaps employing
the principles expressed in the canon of creativity). The period of outward
adjustment does offer a respite, a time to martial resources. Part of that preparation should be examining the aspects of sociatric theory for knowledge
and skills to lead to the next two stages of the healing process. Perhaps, for
example, social atom structure should be examined and extended by joining
support groups to increase the availability of interpersonal resources.

*The key construct to convey particularly to Sam and the children is act-hunger. They
need to understand that Yvette's need to address her abuse issues has not been met,
regardless of the seeming return to normality. They can also be helped to understand
their own act-hungers (wanting to help Mom and everyone else past the crisis). Again
enactment and spontaneity theories can promote acceptance of the variability of
reactions and what actions are spontaneous, functional rather than dysfunctional
depending on the situation. At times the kids may need to be disciplined stringently if they
are violating Sam's or Yvette's boundaries; at other times, when they have been putting
their own needs second to those of their parents, they should be allowed some latitude and
given the attention they desire.*

*While the lull exists, the time may be optimal for preparing the family for the next
onslaught. Understanding the act-hunger may motivate them to make necessary changes
while they can. Sam can learn to cook (expand his role repertoire), the children might
join support groups (extending their social atoms/support networks), empathy and
conflict resolution skills can be learned and implemented (learning more functional
modes of encounter), as well as other alterations suggested by sociatry and interventions.*

Reorganization

Successful reorganization brings all segments of sociatry together in a
dynamic balance or understanding. Roles, enactments, support network
sociometry and social atom configuration will all need to be modified
through encounter and spontaneous action relying on the telic qualities of
the relationships of those involved.

As an example, role repertoires may be increased (father may learn to
cook) influencing enactments (such as dinner interaction) with reverbera-
tions in family sociometry (the children may ask father to teach them to cook
certain dishes) and social atom structure (mother may go to work, increasing
her collectives).

*The sociometry of the immediate family, extended families and friendship networks
were upset by Yvette's traumatic reactions. Old friends may have fallen by the wayside*

because of the family's reactions and neediness or lack of belief in Yvette's memories of the abuse. Other family members and acquaintances have come forward to offer support. Role expectations have been challenged and changed, Sam, the kids and others finding they could operate well in ways (mundane roles and functions such as Frank's taking out the garbage and Selma's talking to Frank's friends about the new demands on him) they never would have imagined. The new organization, while having aspects of the former, is very different from the previous patterns of thinking, feeling and interacting. Or, Yvette and Sam could divorce because they are not able to recover from the impact of the trauma by remaining together. In which case another, still viable, reorganization will occur.

Successful or not, reorganization will not be static. Whether new demands of trauma healing or vagaries of life provide new challenges, the patterns will require adaptation again sooner or later. The knowledge – sociometric and ChT – and skills attained during the healing process can establish more functional patterns for future adaptation.

Integration and resolution

The essential differences between the integration and resolution stage and the previous one are awareness and acceptance. The chaotic nature of life, and certainly interpersonal dynamics, will need to be recognized and roles to live life more functionally assimilated into the role structures of those involved. Comfort with chaos and use of sociatric structures and interventions can support this ongoing process.

Perhaps family members will learn to share responsibilities previously assigned to specific individuals (such as driving the car). Or a 'tight' family unit may come to appreciate other collectives (for example, join in the Neighbourhood Watch).

Not only have Sam, Yvette, and the children learned to encounter more effectively, but also they now have the sociatric knowledge and tools to address the next cycle when it inevitably occurs. They, and, one hopes, friends and family members, are also more cognizant of the changes and challenges that all aspects of life offer, and better prepared to act and react spontaneously, not just to cope but rather to lead their lives more fully in both bad and good times.

Interdependence / interconnectedness

From both Figure 17.1 and the previous discussion, the interdependence of primary and secondary victim healing processes is evident. Two other facets of interdependence must also be kept in mind. The first is the interconnectedness of the components of the social support network – all the secondary victims – and the various levels of social organization patterns – individual, marital, familial, organizational, societal and cultural (deVries 1996). The second is the interconnectedness of the sociometric sub-theories, as illustrated in Figure 17.2.

By re-examining the Doe family case, this interplay is evident. Changes in role structures affect the social atom structure and impact the spontaneity/tele, realigning the sociometry, altering the enactments, co-creating and or re-creating the conserves. No wonder the results are unpredictable.

The implication of dealing with such dynamic systems is the necessity, and usually difficulty, of changing the thinking about such entities (that is, switching to a non-independent, non-linear, non-reductionistic view). If not the constructs themselves, at least the concepts represented by ChT are invaluable in implementing effective interventions to address these situations (not to mention a different perspective on research). This fact can be seen in the discourse examples. Suggesting an intervention from one sub-theory (for example, increasing role repertoires) cannot be separated from or discussed cogently without reference to others (such as addressing warm-ups). Any intervention will influence the patterns of interaction represented by the different levels (basins of strange attractors) mentioned and other aspects of sociatric characterizations.

Observations and conclusions

The complex nature of secondary survivor healing requires a perspective equipped to deal with the situation. Other approaches are possible, but sociatry has them all in one package and related to each other. With ChT to aid in characterizing the dynamical dimension encountered, enhancing the heuristic properties, sociatry can provide practical vehicles and theoretical guidance to professionals and lay individuals alike. The two combined meet the criteria required to produce a functional map, not only for dealing with trauma but for life demands as well (Remer 1996 and 1998).

Usually the question asked at this point – Where do we go from here? – is answered with 'More research is needed'. Although that answer cannot be disputed, research into trauma presents a tension between the objective scientific and the subjective therapeutic (McFarlane and van der Kolk 1996). That same tension has permeated the acceptance of both sociatric interventions and the sociometric research approach (participatory inclusion).

Sociatric interventions are known to be effective. However, the standard of proof for their efficacy has not been met adequately by the usually accepted standards. The problem, as recognized by many (Remer 1999b), is that these criteria are themselves inconsistent with the view of reality dictated by dynamic human systems. Does this discrepancy mean either abandoning hope of supporting the use of sociatric intervention or not requiring anything but anecdotal evidence of its usefulness? No.

Although continued efforts employing the present criteria (positivistic) will require resignation to a degree of frustration, they should not be abandoned. However, what must be accepted is that reductionistic/additive experiments are unlikely (at best) to yield their desired results – universally generalizable interventions and principles. On the other hand, the combination of sociometric theory and ChT suggests the use of another more holistic or interactive (and inclusive) paradigm (constructivist) relying on intersubjectivity and participant inclusion (like the one from which the descriptions provided here have been derived). While this approach will not, by definition, provide the universals desired it would provide both possibilities and an attitude towards adaptation and flexibility more consistent with the needs of therapeutic effectiveness – and life.

So, where from here? Forward, exploring both the old and new territories of traumatic experiences, using established maps to rechart and to develop better methods of mapping the way. What learning and development trauma work contributes can be applied to other areas as well, and vice versa. If violence – the 'V' central to HAVOC – can be supplanted by spontaneity – the transformative 'S' – people can be helped in knowing how to see their ways to the end of chaos.

References

Bass, E. and Davis, L. (1988) *The Courage to Heal: A Guide for Women Survivors of Child Sexual Abuse.* New York: Harper and Row.

Biddle, B.J. (1979) *Role Theory, Expectations, Identities, and Behaviors.* New York: Academic Press.

Briggs, J. and Peat, F.D. (1989) *Turbulent Mirror.* New York: Harper and Row Publishers.

Burgess, A.W. and Holmstrom, L.L. (1979a) 'Adaptive strategies and recovery from rape.' *American Journal of Psychiatry 136,* 1278–1282.

Burgess, A.W. and Holmstrom, L.L. (1979b) *Rape: Crisis and Recovery.* Bowie, MD: Robert J. Brady.

Butz, M.R. (1997) *Chaos and Complexity: Implications for Psychological Theory and Practice.* Washington, DC: Taylor and Francis.

Butz, M.R., Chamberlain, L.L. and McCown, W.G. (1997) *Strange Attractors: Chaos, Complexity, and the Art of Family Therapy.* New York: John Wiley and Sons.

Chard, K.M., Weaver, T.L. and Resick, P.A. (1997). 'Adapting cognitive processing therapy for child sexual abuse survivors.' *Cognitive and Behavioral Practice 4,* 31–52.

deVries, M.W. (1996) 'Trauma in cultural perspective.' In B.A. van der Kolk, A.C. McFarlane and L. Weisaeth (eds) *Traumatic Stress: The Effects of Overwhelming Experience on Mind, Body, and Society.* New York: Guilford Press.

Falconer, K. (1990) *Fractal Geometry: Mathematical Foundations and Applications.* New York: John Wiley and Sons.

Ferguson, R.A. (1993) 'Male partners of female survivors of childhood sexual abuse: an inquiry into the concept of secondary victimization.' Unpublished doctoral dissertation, University of Kentucky, Lexington.

Figley, C.R. (1985a) (ed) *Trauma and its Wake: The Study and Treatment of Post Traumatic Stress Disorder.* New York: Brunner/Mazel.

Figley, C.R. (1985b) (ed) *Trauma and its Wake. Volume 2: The Study and Treatment of Post Traumatic Stress Disorder.* New York: Brunner/Mazel.

Figley, C.R. (1989) *Helping Traumatized Families.* San Francisco: Jossey-Bass Publishers.

Figley, C.R. (1993) 'Compassion stress: Toward its measurement and management.' *Family Therapy News, 24,* 3–6.

Figley, C.R. (ed) (1997) *Burnout in Families: The Systemic Cost of Caring.* Delray Beach, FL: St Lucie Press.

Gleick, J. (1987) *Chaos: Making a New Science.* New York: Viking Penguin.

Hale, A.E. (1981) *Conducting Clinical Sociometric Explorations: A Manual for Psychodramatists and Sociometrists.* Roanoke, VA: Royal Publishing Co.

Hollander, C.E. (1969) *A Process for Psychodrama Training: The Hollander Psychodrama Curve.* Denver, CO: Snow Lion Press.

Kubler-Ross, E. (1969) *On Death and Dying.* New York: McMillan.

McCann, I.L., Sakheim, D.K. and Abrahamson, D.J. (1988) 'Trauma and victimization: a model of psychological adaptation.' *The Counseling Psychologist 16,* 531–595.

McFarlane, A.C. and van der Kolk, B.A. (1996) 'Trauma and its challenge to society.' In B.A. van der Kolk, A.C. McFarlane and L. Weisaeth (eds) *Traumatic Stress: The Effects of Overwhelming Experience on Mind, Body, and Society.* New York: Guilford Press.

Moreno, J.L. (1951) *Sociometry, Experimental Method and the Science of Society: An Approach to a New Political Orientation.* Ambler, PA: Beacon House/Horsham Foundation.

Moreno, J.L. (1953/1993) *Who Shall Survive? Foundations of Sociometry, Group Psychotherapy and Sociodrama* (student edition). Roanoke, VA: Royal.

Moreno, J.L. (1975) *Psychodrama, Volume 2: Foundations of Psychotherapy.* Beacon, NY: Beacon House.

Mounoud, P. (1976) 'The development of systems of representation and treatment in the child.' In B. Inhelder and H. Chipman (eds) *Piaget and his School.* New York: Springer-Verlag.

Piaget, J. and Inhelder, B. (1969) *The Psychology of the Child.* New York: Basic Books.

Remer, R. (1984) *Stages in Coping with Rape.* Unpublished manuscript. Lexington, KY: University of Kentucky.

Remer, R. (1990) *Secondary Victim/Secondary Survivor.* Unpublished manuscript. Lexington, KY: University of Kentucky.

Remer, R. (1996) 'Chaos theory and the canon of creativity.' *Journal Group Psychotherapy, Psychodrama and Sociometry 48*, 145–155.

Remer, R. (1997) 'The secondary survivors of sexual assault: a support group for men.' *The Division 51 Newsletter of the American Psychological Association.*

Remer, R. (1998) 'Chaos theory and the Hollander psychodrama curve: trusting the process.' *International Journal of Action Methods 50*, 51–70.

Remer, R. (1999a) *Sociatric Interventions with Secondary Victims of Trauma: Producing Secondary Survivors.* Unpublished manuscript. Lexington, KY: University of Kentucky.

Remer, R. (1999b) *Blinded by the Light.* Unpublished manuscript. Lexington, KY: University of Kentucky.

Remer, R. and Betts, G.R. (1998) 'The difference between strict analogue and interpersonal psychodramatic simulation methodology (IPS) in research on human dynamical systems.' *International Journal of Action Methods 51*, 3–23.

Remer, R. and Elliott, J.E. (1988a) 'Characteristics of secondary victims of sexual assault.' *International Journal of Family Psychiatry 9*, 4, 373–387.

Remer, R. and Elliott, J.E. (1988b) 'Management of secondary victims of sexual assault.' *International Journal of Family Psychiatry 9*, 4, 389–401.

Remer, R. and Ferguson, R. (1995) 'Becoming a secondary survivor of sexual assault.' *Journal of Counseling and Development 7*, 407–414.

Remer, R. and Ferguson, R. (1997) 'Treating traumatized partners: producing secondary survivors.' In C.R. Figley (ed) *Burnout in Families: The Systemic Cost of Caring.* Delray Beach, FL: St Lucie Press.

Scurfield, R. (1985) 'Post-trauma stress assessment and treatment: overview and formulations.' In C.R. Figley (ed) *Trauma and its Wake: The Study and Treatment of Post Traumatic Stress Disorder.* New York: Brunner/Mazel.

Sutherland, S. and Sherl, D.J. (1970) 'Patterns of response among victims of rape.' *American Journal of Orthopsychiatry 10*, 503–511.

van der Kolk, B.A., McFarlane, A.C. and Weisaeth, L. (eds) (1996) *Traumatic Stress: The Effects of Overwhelming Experience on Mind, Body, and Society.* New York: Guilford Press.

von Bertalanffy, L. (1968) *General System Theory.* New York: George Braziller.

Whetsell, M.S. (1990) *The Relationship of Abuse Factors and Revictimization to the Long-term Effects of Childhood Sexual Abuse in Women.* Unpublished doctoral dissertation. Lexington, KY: University of Kentucky.

Worell, J. and Remer, P. (1992) *Feminist Perspectives in Therapy: An Empowerment Model for Women.* New York: John Wiley and Sons.

The Contributors

Kerry Paul Altman, Ph.D., is a clinical psychologist in private practice in Fairfax, Virginia, USA. He is a certified trainer, educator, and practitioner in psychodrama, sociometry, and group psychotherapy and a former member of the training staff at St Elizabeths Hospital. Dr Altman has published articles dealing with the varied uses of psychodrama in clinical settings.

Clark Baim is an independent psychodramatist, trainer and consultant specializing in work with violent and sexually abusive offenders. Among his other work, Clark runs weekly psychodrama groups for sex offenders and violent offenders at HM Prison Grendon (a therapeutic community) in Buckinghamshire, UK, and co-runs groups for the West Midlands Probation Service Sex Offender Unit. A native of Chicago, Illinois, Clark was the founder and first director of Birmingham-based Geese Theatre UK, a company which continues to provide rehabilitative drama-based work with offenders in Britain and Ireland.

Anne Bannister is a psychodramatist, dramatherapist and play therapist. She has worked for 25 years with children who have been sexually abused, mostly for the National Society for the Prevention of Cruelty to Children, in Manchester, UK. She is a Research Fellow in the Centre for Applied Childhood Studies at the University of Huddersfield, where her doctoral research concerns the effect of creative therapies upon children who have been abused. She has published extensively on child protection and psychodrama.

José Antonio Espina Barrio, MD, is a psychiatrist, psychodramatist and family therapist and was president of the Spanish Association for Psychodrama. He wrote his doctoral thesis on 'Sociometric Evolution of Psychodrama's Groups: Therapeutics and Formations.' He was the second President of the Spanish Federation for Psychotherapists' Associations.

Adam Blatner, MD, is a certified trainer of psychodrama and a Fellow of the American Psychiatric Association, certified both in child and adult psychiatry, with over thirty-five years of clinical experience. He is also the author of some of the more widely-used books in psychodrama as well as many journal articles.

Marisol Filgueira Bouza, Ph.D., is a psychologist, psychodramatist and family therapist and has been president of the Spanish Association for Psychodrama. She wrote her doctoral thesis on 'The Burnout of Mental Health Caregivers'. She has published articles about grief and clinical and anthropological and sociological psychodrama.

Michael Burge is director of the Australian College of Trauma Treatment, and member of the College of Counselling Psychologists, the Australasian Society for Traumatic Stress Studies and the Australian and New Zealand Psychodrama Association. He is a former president of the Victoria branch of the EMDR Association and current chair of the Victoria branch of the Australian Psychological Society.

Jörg Burmeister is currently vice-director of a Swiss clinic for psychiatry and psychotherapy, having trained in psychodrama since 1985 with Dr G Leutz. Since 1993 he has directed long-term psychodrama groups in Bulgaria, Russia, Finland, Italy, Turkey, Spain, Portugal, Austria and Germany and has chaired the German Psychodrama Association. He is president of the German Association of Group Psychotherapy (DAGG), founding member of the Federation of Mediterranean and European Psychodrama Training Organizations, and an elected board member of the International Association of Group Psychotherapy. He has published widely on social constructivism, therapeutic application and psychodrama.

Tian Dayton, Ph.D., TEP holds a doctorate in clinical psychology and a masters in educational psychology. She is Director of Program Development and Staff Training at the Caron Foundation in Wernersville, Pennsylvania and New York City. She is a fellow and certified trainer of the American Society for Psychodrama, Sociometry and Group Psychotherapy and taught at New York University from 1992–1999. She is the author of ten books including *The Drama Within* and *Trauma and Addiction*.

M.K. Hudgins, Ph.D., TEP, is a licensed clinical psychologist and board certified trainer, educator and practitioner of psychodrama, sociometry, and group psychotherapy. She served on the American Board of Examiners as an elected member for nine years and was editor of the Psychodrama Network News for six years. She graduated from Virginia Commonwealth University in 1986 and did a post-graduate programme in psychodrama at St Elizabeths Hospital, Washington, DC. Dr. Hudgins is chair of the board of directors for the Therapeutic Spiral International Charity, created to fund psychodrama for trauma survivors in the global community. She provides ongoing training groups in Australia, England and the USA and builds action trauma teams in the local communities that use this model.

Matt W. Johnston was born into a typically dysfunctional Southern family on All Saints Day in Richmond, VA., 1952. Falling into art by accident during his senior year in high school, he wound up at Boston University for two years, dropped out to pursue painting and Boston's 'educating' night life for ten years, limped back to Richmond and wound up in a twelve-step recovery programme. He graduated from Virginia Commonwealth University in 1986 and eventually graduated to the Northern Neck, VA., where he lives quietly beside the Rappahanock River pursuing fishing and art.

Marcia Karp is co-director of the Hoewell International Psychodrama Centre, North Devon, UK. She is Honorary President of the British Psychodrama Association, a board member of the International Association of Group Psychodrama, a Fellow of the American Association of Group Psychotherapy and Psychodrama, on the Executive Council and a founding member of the Federation of Mediterranean and European Psychodrama Training Organizations.

Peter Felix Kellermann, Ph.D., is a clinical psychologist and international trainer of psychodrama, born in 1953 in Sweden. He is a Fellow of the American Society of Group Psychotherapy and Psychodrama, founding member of the Federation of European Psychodrama Training Organizations and elected chair of the Psychodrama section of the International Association of Group Psychotherapy. Holder of the Zerka T. Moreno Award, 1993, he is chief psychologist of AMCHA/Jerusalem, a psychosocial treatment centre for Holocaust survivors and the Second Generation.

Grete Anna Leutz, MD, is the Founder and Director of the Moreno Institute for Psychodrama, Sociometry and Group Psychotherapy at Überlingen on Lake Constance. She is a founding member of the Psychodrama Section of the German Association of Group Psychotherapy and Group Dynamics, and was President of the Section from 1973 to 1979. A fellow of the International Association of Group Psychotherapy, she was its President from 1986 to 1989 and is a fellow of the American Society of Group Psychotherapy and Psychodrama. She received the J.L. Moreno Award for Outstanding Lifelong Contributions to the Field of Psychodrama in 1992. Currently, she is teaching and supervising psychodrama at the Moreno Institute and at the University of Innsbruck/Austria.

John Raven Mosher, MA, is a Certified Mental Health Counselor and a trainer, educator and practitioner in psychodrama, sociometry, and group psychotherapy. A former Assistant Professor of English, John Mosher has been a therapist in private practice with Blue Sky Counselors in Seattle, Washington, since 1974. Mosher has presented his healing circle model internationally and is a recognized expert in the spirituality of psychotherapy.

Rory Remer, Ph.D., is Professor of Counseling Psychology in the Department of Educational and Counseling Psychology at the University of Kentucky (USA). He holds psychodrama certification as both CP and TEP and is a licensed psychologist. In his 25 years of teaching and clinical work, he has emphasized working with couples and families – most recently from a dynamical systems perspective (chaos theory). For the last ten years he has led and supervised students leading groups for secondary survivors of sexual assault trauma.

Marlyn Robson, B.D.S., was born in Scotland and trained orginally as a dental surgeon. She moved to Auckland, New Zealand, 25 years ago, and has now trained as a psychotherapist and is an advanced trainee in psychodrama. She works part-time in private practice and part-time at SAFE, an agency working with people who sexually offend.

Eva Røine, Ph.D., TEP is Director of the Norwegian Psychodrama Institute, Vice President of the Psychodrama Institute for Europe and a clinical psychologist. She is also a member of the Nordic Board of Examiners and author of *Psychodrama: Group Psychotherapy as Experimental Theatre*, published by Jessica Kingsley.

Anne Ancelin Schützenberger Ph.D., TEP, is Professor Emeritus of Psychology at the University of Nice and is co-founder and past vice-president of the International Association of Group Psychotherapy and a founding member of the Federation of European Psychodrama Training Organizations. She is an analyst and clinical psychologist and has written many books on psychodrama, sociometry and psychotherapy. She is also internationally renowned as a trainer in group psychotherapy and psychodrama.

Brigid Yukman, Ph.D., is a registered counsellor, in private practice with Blue Sky Counselors in Seattle, Washington. She also co-leads psychodrama groups and is a research assistant for the Children's Friendships and Families Study at the University of Washington. She was a Professor of Literature for 15 years before becoming a therapist and poet.

Subject Index

Author Index